The Phenomenological Movement

PHAENOMENOLOGICA
COLLECTION PUBLIÉE SOUS LE PATRONAGE DES CENTRES D'ARCHIVES-HUSSERL

6

HERBERT SPIEGELBERG

The Phenomenological Movement

A HISTORICAL INTRODUCTION

SECOND EDITION

Third impression

HERBERT SPIEGELBERG

The Phenomenological Movement

A HISTORICAL INTRODUCTION

SECOND EDITION

Third impression

VOLUME TWO

MARTINUS NIJHOFF / THE HAGUE / 1971

PRINTED IN THE NETHERLANDS

TABLE OF CONTENTS
VOLUME TWO

XII. CURRENT DEVELOPMENTS IN FRENCH PHENOMENOLOGY

Part Four | Phenomenology at Midcentury
XIII. THE WIDER SCENE

Part Five | Principles and Appraisals
XIV. THE ESSENTIALS OF THE PHENOMENOLOGICAL METHOD

PART THREE:

THE FRENCH PHASE OF THE MOVEMENT

There can be little question that since the early thirties the center of gravity of the Phenomenological Movement has moved to the French philosophical world; Belgium and the Netherlands may be considered as subsidiary strongholds. But how far is it justified to speak of phenomenology as a philosophical movement in France? Thus far the French-speaking world has certainly no such central figure as Husserl or any phenomenological circle comparable to those that sprang up under his influence, nor is there any such center of phenomenological publications as Husserl's yearbook had been. It is true that the magazine *Recherches philosophiques* in the years between 1931 and 1937 gave phenomenology preferential treatment. Also since 1947 *Les Études philosophiques* under the direction of Gaston Berger has devoted special attention to phenomenology. And even the old *Revue de métaphysique et de morale* has shown a strong phenomenological tinge of late. Even more important as a focus of phenomenological developments are the Husserl Archives at the University of Louvain under the directorship of Father H. L. Van Breda. For here is not only a center of historical research in phenomenology. Louvain has also organized meetings of phenomenologically interested thinkers, beginning with the international colloquium of 1951 in Brussels, and has just started to sponsor a series of original phenomenological studies (among which the present work is something of a maverick). But it is doubtful that any of the French attendants of these meetings who adopted phenomenology as their main philosophical tool would call themselves phenomenologists, or want to be counted as members of a movement. Even Van Breda, the editor of the Brussels colloquium, speaks only of a phenomenological "current." Presumably the French participants, as far as they would consent to labels at all, would prefer to be classed according to their major topics and conclusions rather than according to their methods, i.e., as existentialists (Sartre and Merleau-Ponty). Gabriel Marcel, who in repudiating the label "Christian existentialism" now calls himself a "Christian Socratic," thus stressing method again, avoids the phenomenological stamp altogether. However, it should be remembered that even existentialism has not become an organized movement. French philosophy simply does not lend itself to such gregariousness.

Nevertheless, those who in one way or another refer to phenomenology as their chief methodology form a sufficiently distinct group to justify their inclusion in a study of phenomenology as a movement. All of them acknowledge the inspiration of Husserl, or at least of Scheler or Heidegger. It remains to be seen how far a sense of solidarity will grow out of this common point of departure and common method, comparable to what could be found among the early German phenomenologists.

Are there any distinctive characteristics of this French phenomenological "current" as compared with its German predecessor? Some French interpreters see these chiefly in the new themes that French phenomenology has taken up, such as the significance of the body, the social world, or history. But some of these claims are based on insufficient acquaintance with the whole range of phenomenological studies during the German period – one of the characteristic handicaps and, in another sense, an asset of French phenomenologizing.

Much more characteristic are the different methods of French phenomenologists. But while a reading of their philosophical output reveals decided differences in approach, it would not be easy to put one's finger upon and distinguish differences in methods of research from differences in presentation. What is obvious is that they write in a much more literary vein, compared with the all too frequently plodding style of much German phenomenologizing. They do not press for terminological innovations, even though at times they have to take to neologisms. At times they adopt literary media not used before in phenomenological discourse, e.g., the diary, adopted directly and seriously by Gabriel Marcel, and indirectly and imaginatively by Sartre in his novel *La Nausée*. On the other hand a reader familiar with the German style of phenomenological writing will be struck by the relative absence of plain phenomenological description, even when announced in a title. Instead, the usual tenor of phenomenological writing is that of arguing a point discursively rather than of patiently reporting the findings of intuitive procedure.

The development of French phenomenology can be divided into two overlapping phases: a mainly receptive period, during which phenomenology remained almost completely an exotic affair, represented by German-trained scholars, of interest primarily to those concerned about philosophical international relations in philosophy; and a predominantly productive phase, when phenomenology became an active tool in the hands of native Frenchmen. The dividing line may be placed in 1936. The first landmark of the new period is the first independent phenomenological publication of Jean-Paul Sartre.

SELECTIVE BIBLIOGRAPHY

Hering, Jean, "'Phenomenology in France" in Farber, M., ed., *Philosophic Thought in France and the United States* (University of Buffalo, 1950), pp. 67-86

VIII

THE BEGINNINGS OF FRENCH PHENOMENOLOGY

1. The Soil

At first sight the advent of German phenomenology in France
and its growing success contain more than one paradox. Who
would have dared to predict that soon after the First World War
a philosophy with some of the worst earmarks of German style
would take root in France? And who would have believed that it
would become the dominant philosophy there in the wake of a
second World War which all but destroyed the political existence
of France? This is not the place to explain this cultural
paradox. The fact that the arrival of phenomenology coincided roughly with the period of the so-called Locarno spirit,
and that it established itself partly as a refugee from the Nazi
purge, is hardly enough to account for its sweeping success.
It is permissible to look upon this migration as one of the more
hopeful signs of a growing continental solidarity and of a
decline of philosophical nationalism.

For anyone not thoroughly familiar with the French philosophical scene during the first half of the century it would be
plainly presumptuous to attempt a full explanation of this
development.[1] I shall merely point out some of the factors which
seem to have favored its assimilation and which make it less
surprising.

α. Bergsonism was still the dominating philosophy in France
when phenomenology appeared on the scene. A certain similarity
between the two is obvious. Bergson and Husserl never met.

---

[1] In this connection it should be mentioned that as early as 1893 Maurice Blondel
used the expression "phenomenology" for an approximation to Hegel's phenomenology of the spirit. See Henry Duméry in Merleau-Ponty, Maurice, ed., *Les Philosophes célèbres* (1956), p. 301.

But when Alexandre Koyré brought word of Bergson's philosophy of intuition to the Göttingen Circle in 1911, Husserl exclaimed: "We are the true Bergsonians." [1] And it was Scheler who initiated the first translations of Bergson's works into German (see p. 236). The affinities between a philosophy which concentrated on the "immediate data of consciousness" and one whose prime concern was the faithful description of the given were obvious enough. There was even deeper common ground with regard to such parallel concerns as the inner consciousness of time in its unbroken flux. Such points of agreement were stressed and at times overstressed by the early advocates of phenomenology in France, e.g., Jean Hering, Bernard Groethuysen, and Eugène Minkowski.

However, phenomenology was both less and more than a German version of Bergsonian philosophy; less: for it was not committed to Bergson's metaphysical use of intuition nor, more specifically, to his metaphysics of creative evolution; more: for it did not share Bergson's anti-intellectualism and his hostility to the analytic approach including his strictures on mathematics in particular. Moreover, it allowed for a specific intuition of general essences that came very close to Platonism, which Bergson had always repudiated. Thus phenomenology could easily pass for a liberalized Bergsonism.

β. Léon Brunschvicg represented the opposite pole to Bergson's intuitionist metaphysics on the French philosophical stage of the twenties and thirties. Since his concept of consciousness was fundamentally Cartesian and his philosophy was oriented toward science, it was particularly fortunate that Husserl had associated Descartes' name with his conception of phenomenology, so much so that he even came to speak of it as Neo-Cartesianism. This, in combination with the program of philosophy as a rigorous science, was bound to appeal not only to Brunschvicg personally but to the classic French tradition in general. To Brunschvicg in particular Husserl's idealism meant an additional attraction.

γ. Catholic philosophy in France as elsewhere is chiefly Neo-Thomist. What recommended phenomenology to its followers

---

[1] See Jean Hering, "La Phénoménologie il y a trente ans" in *Revue internationale de philosophie* I (1939), 368.

from the very start was its stand against psychologism in logic, combined with its rehabilitation of general essences short of a "realistic'" Platonism. Husserl's idealism might easily have meant a stumbling block. But it could be played down, particularly in view of the fact that most of Husserl's students had not accepted it as a necessary implication of the phenomenological approach. Concepts like intentionality appeared, however mistakenly, as loans from scholastic philosophy. Phenomenology had perhaps an even stronger appeal for non-Thomist Catholics. Husserl himself in his Paris lectures had linked it up with St. Augustine. Scheler had stressed the Augustinian-Scotist character of phenomenology even more, a diagnosis with which an authority like Étienne Gilson concurred.

δ. Protestant philosophy of religion presented phenomenology with a particularly fruitful challenge and opportunity, actually its first in France after World War I. It had found itself caught between a psychologism based ultimately on Schleiermacher's reduction of religion to the subjectivity of feelings, and the Barthian anti-philosophical neo-orthodoxy. Phenomenology seemed to offer a conception of the religious consciousness which reached beyond mere feelings to their intentional referents. It thus gave access to a much wider range of religious phenomena and encouraged a less biased approach to the question of their validity.

ε. One of the remarkable things about French phenomenology is the ease with which it has penetrated such well established French studies as psychology, psychopathology, sociology, and the philosophy of history. While it would be particularly rash to generalize about the situation in these fields, a certain stagnation may well have been the background for the unusual interest in the new phenomenological approach. An additional incentive was the growing attraction of a Marxism for which the early Marx, with his humanistic leanings, supplied the main inspiration. This in turn promoted interest in one of Marx' chief sources, Hegel's *Phenomenology of the Spirit*, identified, however mistakenly, with Husserlian phenomenology. It also created the search for alternatives which could do justice to the legitimate core of Marx' social and historical theory without implying dialectical materialism.

Even more important than all these factors combined may well have been the mood and the needs of the new French generation in the late twenties. Its younger thinkers had grown increasingly dissatisfied with the French academic tradition symbolized by the idealistic rationalism of Léon Brunschvicg. Its problems seemed strangely irrelevant to a generation whose condition was expressed by the experiences of Kierkegaard, Kafka, Proust, and Gide, and by the much more sensitive medium of French non-philosophical writing. Apparently it was Gabriel Marcel who first succeeded in meeting these needs. His private seminar was actually a testing ground for new ideas, French and foreign. But his appeal was limited. For his approach and his conclusions remained far too unsystematic and mystifying to satisfy the demands of the more sophisticated philosophic youth. They were much more deeply and permanently struck by the elemental intensity of Heidegger's shorter essays. Here they found not only vital issues of existential import but also a treatment that had the semblance of structural clarity and rigor. But the search for rigor was also bound to send the reader back to what seemed to be Heidegger's main philosophical root, i.e., to Husserl's phenomenology. It was in this manner that phenomenology received its second and decisive hearing.

2. A Brief Outline of the Receptive Phase

There would be little point in presenting here in detail the story of the naturalization of phenomenology in the French world. The most telling and most concentrated way of supplying the main facts may be the chronological chart in Appendix II, supplemented by a few explanatory pointers.

α. The first public notice of Husserl's work outside Germany occurred interestingly enough in an article by Monsignor L. Noel – the second director of the Institut Supérieur de Philosophie at the Catholic University of Louvain, the present home of the Husserl Archives – which appeared in the Revue Néo-Scholastique in 1910. Here Husserl was welcomed primarily as an ally in the battle against psychologism, not yet as a phenomenologist. The same interest dominated the lecture given a year later by the historian Victor Delbos at the École des Hautes Études in Paris and published in 1911 in the Revue de métaphysique et de morale.

β. It was not until after World War I that phenomenology was recognized as the core of Husserl's enterprise. The transmitters of this new Husserl were for the most part either Alsatians brought up chiefly in the German tradition and after 1918 integrated into the French academic world, such as the Protestant theologians Jean Hering, a Göttingen student of Husserl, and Charles Hauter, who was also a student of Georg Simmel, or Russian and Polish scholars who had studied in Germany for some time and moved on to France, notably Alexandre Koyré, Georges Gurvitch, Eugène Minkowski, Alexandre Kojève, and Aron Gurwitsch. Lev Shestov and Nicolas Berdyaev, though antagonistic or less involved, nevertheless transmitted the impetus of phenomenology. Bernhard Groethuysen, originally a student of Wilhelm Dilthey, a friend of Max Scheler and an admirer of Heidegger, was the main native German source in the twenties, joined later by the Scheler student Paul-Ludwig Landsberg, who came to Paris as a refugee from Nazism.

γ. In the beginning, Husserl was by no means the center of French interest in phenomenology. For he was nearly eclipsed by Scheler and Heidegger. In fact, the history of the reception of phenomenology in France represents almost a reversal of the sequel in the German original history. Thus, of the first three book size introductions to the Phenomenological Movement which appeared between 1926 and 1930 only the lucid account by Jean Hering, aimed chiefly at Protestant philosophers of religion, had phenomenology represented by Husserl. Emmanuel Levinas, who also devoted some of his first studies to Husserl, felt actually much more attracted by Heidegger. Georges Gurvitch, in his highly influential book on the present tendencies in German philosophy, assigned its largest section (actually one third) to Max Scheler. Scheler was also the first of the leading German phenomenologists to visit France, first in 1924 when on invitation he addressed the annual gathering of French intellectuals at Pontigny; during a second visit of four weeks in 1926 he also seems to have had personal meetings with Meyerson, Lévy-Bruhl and Bergson,[1] leaving a vivid impression by his "agile

---

[1] I am indebted to Frau Maria Scheler (Munich) for these data. – About Scheler's impact on the Pontigny group see Ernst Robert Curtius, *Französischer Geist im neuen Europa* (Berlin, 1925), pp. 340 ff. and Peter Wust, *Unterwegs zur Heimat* (1956), p. 143 f.

restlessness, which made his personality so exciting" (Brunsch-vicg). Moreover, he was the first German phenomenologist to have his works, beginning with his phenomenology of sympathy, translated into French.

δ. Heidegger, though apparently never in France before 1955, was the second to be translated. His article from the *Festschrift* for Husserl appeared prominently in the first issue of the *Recherches philosophiques* in 1931. In the same year the lecture *Was ist Metaphysik?* came out in *Bifur* with a four-page intro-duction by Alexandre Koyré, who presented him as a star of the first magnitude, as the synthesis of Bergson and Husserl, and actually as the central figure of present-day German philosophy. In 1938 it was followed by a sizable volume of translations by Henri Corbin preceded by a special preface by Heidegger him-self, who also seems to have decided on the selections and the order of presentation under the aspect of "the fundamental question of the essence and truth of Being," as he saw it in 1937. This volume includes the entire essays on "What is Metaphy-sics?," "On the Essence of Being," two of the later chapters of the published parts of "Being and Time," one from the Kant book, and the essay on "Hölderlin and the Essence of Poetry." The term "phenomenology" hardly occurs in these texts. But this conscientious translation became particularly important as the source for some of the vocabulary of French phenomeno-logical existentialism. Thus it seems that not only such equi--valences as *Dasein* and *réalité humaine* were established by Cor-bin, but also that the expressions "authenticity" and "inauthen-ticity" go back to his rendering of Heidegger's *Eigentlichkeit* and *Uneigentlichkeit*.

ε. In Husserl's case it got to be 1950 before any of his major German works were published in translation. On the other hand there is the peculiar case of the *Méditations cartésiennes*, a not faultless translation of a text whose original Husserl never allowed to appear in German during his lifetime. Thus it could almost rank as an original publication. It was based on his Sorbonne lectures of 1929 given under the joint auspices of the German Department and the *Société française de philosophie*. Yet the personal impact of Husserl's visit was limited; the young Jean Cavaillès describes him on this occasion as "very much the small town university type, in a frock coat and bespectacled, but in his delivery the warmth and the simplicity of the true philosopher." [1]

Thus, Husserl appeared on the whole less as the central figure of the Phenomenological Movement than as its outdated founder. Apparently it was not until Sartre had turned to Husserl's original writings that the latter was studied for his own sake. Such careful studies as Gaston Berger's on Husserl's *cogito*, appearing in 1941 during the occupation, testify to this new and direct interest in Husserl on the part of native Frenchmen.

ζ. One of the most important events for the introduction of phenomenology into the French-speaking world was the study session of the Société Thomiste on Thomism and German contemporary phenomenology at Juvisy in September 1932. Jacques Maritain and Msgr. Noel presided. Father Daniel Feuling of the University of Salzburg gave an informed report on Husserl and Heidegger, and Father René Kremer of the University of Louvain compared the Thomist with the phenomenological position. In the momentous discussion not only Msgr. Noel and Étienne Gilson but also old phenomenologists like Alexandre Koyré and Edith Stein took a leading part, trying to play down the idealist character of phenomenology and to stress the differences between Husserl and Heidegger. The spirit of the discussion suggested the possibility of an assimilation of the phenomenological approach by Catholic philosophers without commitment to Husserl's or Heidegger's conclusions.

η. In the later twenties some of the most promising young Frenchmen began to study phenomenology in its native habitat, particularly in Freiburg. Emmanuel Levinas, co-translator of the *Méditations cartésiennes*, was a personal student of Husserl as well as of Heidegger. Jean Cavaillès, a brilliant logician, later a martyr of the Resistance Movement, came too late to study with Husserl himself but visited him; so did Gaston Berger. The most important guest was Jean-Paul Sartre, who spent the winter semester of 1933–34 in Freiburg, four years after Husserl's retirement.

Of even greater importance for the future of phenomenology was a visit to Freiburg by the Belgian Franciscan Herman L.

[1] Ferrières, Gabrielle, *Jean Cavaillès* (Paris, Presses Universitaires, 1950) p. 54.

Van Breda in 1938, four months after Husserl's death. His search for materials for his thesis on Husserl led in due course to the transfer of Husserl's entire manuscript remains and his library to Louvain, where the Husserl Archives soon became the center of all Husserl studies and editions.   [1]

θ. When did French phenomenology come of age? If Gabriel Marcel could be counted a genuine member of the Phenomenological Movement, his *Metaphysical Journal* of 1927 might be considered the first original achievement of French phenomenology. But Gabriel Marcel himself makes no such claims, and the term phenomenology does not occur prominently in the *Journal*. Only in retrospect can many sections of this book be interpreted as examples of what in the thirties Marcel himself liked to call phenomenological studies.

A much clearer case of original phenomenological contributions are the "phenomenological and psychopathological studies" of the psychiatrist-philosopher Eugène Minkowski dealing with "Lived Time" (*Le Temps vécu*, 1933) and the "phenomenological studies" united in his second book "Toward a Cosmology" (*Vers une Cosmologie*, 1936). However, apart from the fact that Minkowski, a native Pole, had not settled in France until after World War I, his major inspiration comes from Bergson. Husserl is mentioned only in passing. Otherwise he acknowledges only influences from Scheler, but, in spite of many parallels, not from Heidegger.

It would therefore seem that the main credit for having naturalized and activated phenomenology on Husserlian grounds has to go to Sartre, notably on the strength of his first essay in the *Recherches philosophiques* of 1936 and his book-size studies on the imagination and the emotions in the years between 1936 and 1940.

ι. Of particular importance during this phase was a new yearbook, the *Recherches philosophiques*, whose title, with its theme of "research," was slightly reminiscent of Husserl's yearbook, which had ceased to appear after 1930. Under the editorship of Koyré, H.-Ch. Puech, and A. Spaier it published six volumes between 1931 and 1936. The opening article of the first volume consisted of Jean Wahl's preface to his book *Vers le concret* (Toward Concreteness), a title which expressed the spirit of this period particularly well.[1] While the book itself studies as its prime examples of contemporary philosophers William James, A. N. Whitehead, and Gabriel Marcel, the Preface pays special tribute to Heidegger and Scheler, besides referring repeatedly to "the phenomenologists," among whom, to be sure, Husserl is not mentioned by name, but only referred to indirectly for his "principle of principles" and for the concept of intentionality. The first two volumes of the *Recherches* contained, in addition to original French contributions, translations of articles by Heidegger ("Vom Wesen des Grundes"), Hedwig Conrad-Martius, Oskar Becker, and Karl Löwith, but no specifically phenomenological topics. Beginning with the second volume, the yearbook carried a special section "Phenomenology" with critical reviews of new literature in the field. The third and later volumes included some of Minkowski's "phenomenological sketches." Gabriel Marcel contributed his "Phenomenology of Having" and his "Phenomenological Remarks about Being in a Situation." The final volume contained Sartre's first "phenomenological description" (*La Transcendence de l'égo*), which not only linked the new French phenomenology with Husserl's enterprise but at the same time marked the beginning of Sartre's independent career.

x. The beginning of the productive phase of French phenomenology did not mean that the study and assimilation of German phenomenology had come to an end. Some of the best interpretations of German phenomenology, such as Gaston Berger's of Husserl's *cogito*, appeared in the forties, Ricoeur's commentaries in the fifties. His monumental translation of Husserl's *Ideen*, with an important introduction and commentary, was published in 1950. More recently Jean Hyppolite's series "*Épiméthée*" has added important interpretative studies and some translations of Husserl's works by the American Quentin Lauer S.J. and Suzanne Bachelard.

Even so the absorption of German phenomenology in France is still far from completed. Its picture is not free from errors. In general, the French are inclined to find much more unity in German phenomenology than is warranted in the light of the

---

[1] See, e.g., Sartre's reference in "Questions de Méthode," *Les Temps modernes* XIII (1957), 350.

facts presented in the second part of this book. Thus the discrepancies between Husserl, Heidegger, and Scheler are usually overlooked. Husserl is mostly seen through his later works, which were much less effective in Germany, and his early phenomenological and pre-phenomenological writings are almost ignored, a circumstance which results in a perspective that is possibly much fairer to Husserl. It might even be argued that the very shortcomings of the French perspective provide some of its strengths. For they have left French phenomenologists free to attack phenomena and problems afresh without becoming involved in the discussion of earlier treatments. They also have made it possible to avoid divisive issues. Nevertheless, some of the best of early German phenomenology still remains to be reactivated in the light of the new French developments.

SELECTIVE BIBLIOGRAPHY

GURVITCH, GEORGES, *Les tendances actuelles de la philosophie allemande* (Paris, Vrin, 1930; second edition, 1949).

λ. This may be the most suitable place for recording the role and significance of the man who has given one of the best and most influential interpretations of Husserl's philosophy, but who also has shown considerable originality in demonstrating it: Gaston Berger (1896–1960). At the same time he should be mentioned for his organizing ability, which he has often put at the disposal of phenomenological enterprises (see, e.g., the space he assigned to phenomenology in the new *Encyclopédie française* vol. XIX). Finally, his official position as Director of French Higher Education, has given at least indirectly added prestige to phenomenological philosophy in France.

As an interpreter of Husserl's thought he has attempted to show the unity in Husserl's development, with the idea of the *cogito* as its center. But he has also stressed the connection between Husserl's thought and that of David Hume. In France Berger is perhaps the staunchest French defender of Husserl's authentic position. He insists on the indispensability of the transcendental reduction, a point on which only Raymond Polin seems to share his views. However, Berger's defense of Husserl does not prevent him from being critical of his conception of the ego. Also in his *Recherches sur les conditions de la connaissance* (1942) he presented a phenomenological epistemology of his own based on an intentional analysis in which, for instance, he denied precedence of one's own transcendental ego over that of others; the two are on a par. His more recent presentation of independent reflections about "Some phenomenological Aspects of Time" before the *Société française de philosophie* aroused an unusual amount of comment. Berger has also been active in the field of characterology. At the moment he sees the main task of phenomenology in the exploration of the possible contributions of a transcendental intellectualism to the present philosophical situation, and in the elucidation of the concept of constitution, particularly the constitution of "form" in the subject.

Main Writings with Phenomenological Import

"Husserl et Hume" in *Revue internationale de philosophie* I (1939), 342–353
Le Cogito dans la philosophie de Husserl (1941)
Recherches sur les conditions de la connaissance (1942)
"Quelques Aspects phénoménologiques du temps," *Bulletin de la Sociéte française de philosophie* XLIV (1950), 89–132
"L'Originalité de la phénoménologie," *Études Philosophiques* IX (1954), 249–59
"La Phénoménologie transcendentale," *Encyclopédie française* XIX
[1]   (1957), 19.10.6–8

3. Phenomenology and Existentialism

Perhaps the most characteristic feature of French phenomenology is its close association, if not coincidence, with existentialism, compared with their segregation and even antagonism in Germany, This would therefore seem to be the proper place for a brief clarification and discussion of the whole relationship between these two movements.

Even the terminology of existentialism calls for brief notice here. For it was not until 1944, i.e., one year after the appearance of Sartre's *L'Être et le néant*, that the label "existentialism" was officially accepted by him and by others of its present protagonists, as well as, though only temporarily, by Gabriel Marcel. Previously the word had turned up only sporadically since the late twenties in France, Germany, and Italy (earliest known occurrence), and was in use mostly among the opponents of the new way of thinking. It has been rejected consistently by both

Karl Jaspers and Martin Heidegger, supposedly its initiators; instead, Jaspers speaks only of *Existenzphilosophie*, Heidegger of *existenziale Analytik* or *Fundamentalontologie*.

But even under these different flags phenomenology and existential thinking did not mix in Germany. This is particularly true of Jaspers. His interest and share in phenomenology are restricted to his psychopathology, where he assigned a major role to the empathic description of pathological phenomena. But when it came to phenomenological philosophy, he drew the line sharply and irrevocably after the appearance of Husserl's article on "Philosophy as a Rigorous Science." For the idea of a scientific philosophy appeared to Jaspers as a contradiction in terms, which he considered revolting. So did a phenomenology that espoused this idea. Besides, Jaspers resented Husserl's early opposition to German speculative philosophy, especially to Schelling, as came out in a momentous conversation at Husserl's request in 1913, when Husserl may well have sought Jaspers' support for his new yearbook.[1]   [1]

Thus when Jaspers, who during the same year became acquainted with Kierkegaard's writings, began to develop his own philosophy of existence, he kept it strictly apart from phenomenology. This applies particularly to his method of elucidation of existence (*Existenzerhellung*), a method which, whatever its positive characteristics and merits may be, is certainly opposed to mere description and to the search for insights into essences. Instead, Jaspers made an appeal to his readers to step beyond (*transzendieren*) their mere empirical being by a Kierkegaardian leap in an attempt to "realize" existence. This objective shows at the same time that Jaspers uses the term "existence" for a possibility which is by no means always real in the concrete individual, and whose actual occurrence can never be proved objectively; in this he deviates from Kierkegaard's as well as from Heidegger's use of the elusive term.

As we have seen in an earlier chapter, Heidegger's philosophizing about existence concerns not only a different referent (*Dasein*), it also pursues a very different objective, namely that of

---

[1] See the account in Karl Jaspers, *Rechenschaft und Ausblick*. (München, Piper, 1951), p. 327. See also his more recent criticism of Heidegger's "scientific" phenomenological analysis of existence in Karl Jaspers and Rudolf Bultmann, *Myth and Christianity* (New York, Noonday Press, 1958), pp. 8–11.

determining the categories of existence (fundamental ontology) with a view to finding stepping stones for a universal ontology: Heidegger's concern is not to exist, but to know about a certain aspect of human being, i.e., its comprehension of Being. This does not exclude some overlapping in practice between existential analytics and elucidation of existence in Jaspers' sense. Heidegger, however, at least at the stage of *Sein und Zeit*, maintains that his existential analytics is phenomenology. He even claims that it constitutes a science in Husserl's sense, though hermeneutics implies a considerable modification of phenomenological science as Husserl understood it. But this remaining connection broke off when Husserl began to denounce Heidegger's enterprise along with other philosophies of existence, and when Heidegger himself ceased to talk phenomenology. From then on Phenomenology and Philosophy of Existence were two incompatible currents in Germany, and phenomenology was the loser in the contest between the two.

Considering these facts, how could it happen that in France the two movements became practically synonymous? A first reason may well have been that in the French perspective Husserl and Heidegger appeared as one team, especially after Heidegger's conspicuous succession to Husserl's chair in Freiburg, and in the absence of sufficient information about the seriousness of the subsequent break between them soon afterwards. Besides, Heidegger's *Sein und Zeit*, which contained only his ontological interpretation of human existence, had appeared under the flag of the phenomenological yearbook. The first translations of Heidegger's writings, introduced by an old-time phenomenologist like Koyré, made an impact mostly by their treatment of existential themes. Thus the view became almost inevitable that Heidegger's existential philosophy represented the logical development and fulfillment of the original Phenomenological Movement. The translation of Heidegger's *Dasein* as human reality (*réalité humaine*) gave to this existentialism definitely anthropological character.

This picture was confirmed, and created a new situation, when Sartre's original works began to appear. To be sure, Sartre himself became perhaps more aware of the difference between Husserl and Heidegger than most other French students of phenomenology. For he was possibly the first to see that Heidegger's ontology had not outdated Husserl's enterprise. However, especially at the stage of *L'Être et le néant*, it became manifest that it was Heidegger's problems in which Sartre was ultimately interested, although he attempted to tackle them primarily by the method of phenomenological description as he interpreted it. Thus Sartre's adoption of the term "existentialism" as the comprehensive title for his whole enterprise, soon after the appearance of his "essay in phenomenological ontology," meant the fusion of phenomenology and existentialism, at least as far as the most representative French phenomenologists were concerned. Yet there are signs that the wholesale condemnation of existentialism by the Encyclical "Humani generis," and Marcel's rejection of the label without a parallel denunciation of phenomenology, will lead to a new differentiation, especially since the interest in phenomenology among French Catholic circles seems to be undiminished.[1]

This is not the place for a discussion of the merits and defects of existentialism as a whole. In fact, the customary sweeping commendations and condemnations suffer from the fact that they presuppose the existence of an existentialist movement. But its existence is actually more doubtful than that of a phenomenological movement. Existentialists, acknowledged and unacknowledged, share hardly more than their common debt to Kierkegaard, who himself had no ambition to start a school or a movement. Otherwise their only link is the magic word "existence," whose meaning, on closer comparison of several "existentialists," turns out to be a nest of equivocations. This does not mean to deny the existence of a deeper common concern behind the misleading label. But its discovery is beyond our present task.[2]

In the present context the only question worth raising is this: What have the existentialist currents done to the cause of phenomenology? Had they meant nothing more than the addition of one or several themes to the range of its phenomena, this

[1] For an even more sympathetic appraisal of "existential phenomenology" as a badly needed supplement to Neo-Thomism see Albert Dondeyne, *Contemporary European Thought and Christian Faith* (Pittsburgh, Duquesne Studies, 1959).

[2] For a brief attempt at such a condensation see my paper on "Husserl's Phenomenology and Existentialism," *Journal of Philosophy* LVII (1960), 62–74.

could only have been welcomed. Moreover, some of the existential themes are certainly deeply significant for their own sake. But unfortunately these are stressed at the expense of "non-existential" phenomena, to an extent which arouses misgivings about the lopsidedness of a phenomenology preoccupied with "existence." The remarkable success of existentialism has however entailed for phenomenology, along with some dubious publicity, some more serious dangers. It has interfered particularly with the basic objective of Husserl's phenomenology to give philosophy greater scientific rigor. For the writings of too many phenomenological existentialists betray a more or less outspoken hostility to the idea of science as well as to its historical exemplifications. Sometimes, as in the case Merleau-Ponty, such anti-scientific statements are actually misleading, since they are only aimed at an objectivistic or mechanistic interpretation of science. The result is too often an atmosphere of elusiveness, ambiguity, and mystification. On the other hand, phenomenological existentialists often assume the role of prophetic awakeners, a pose which goes ill with the spirit of patient exploration which was the original ethos of phenomenology.

More specifically, the task of description is often taken rather lightly and superficially. Insufficient care is taken of the full range of significant phenomena. Such care would often throw a very different light on those few which are singled out too quickly as the basis for vast and precarious generalizations. Hermeneutic interpretations are introduced at once which show little consideration for possible alternative meanings of the phenomena. These interpretations are frequently linked to ambitious ontological and metaphysical schemes. The ease with which the transition from existential phenomena to interpretations of Being as a whole is carried out too often leaves the more careful reader baffled.

Pointing out such limitations before the introduction of concrete examples may sound like another set of precarious generalizations which do an injustice to the solid work and the potentialities of a genuinely phenomenological existentialism. This is not my intention. It is in part the disappointment caused by some of the most original work of this new phenomenology which makes me express these reservations and apprehensions, in the fond hope that eventually there will be no longer any reason for them.

One of the most moving things about Husserl was his insistence on the need for self-denying, patient, slow work on the foundations at the price of not yet being able to reach the really vital and urgent issues of life or, as he himself finally called it, "existence." For reasons which find ample excuse in the contemporary setting, phenomenology has too often rushed to attack such questions with insufficient preparation. Existentialist phenomenology provides one of the best examples of such a premature advance into areas full of promise but also of pitfalls. This does not mean that all its enterprises have been in vain. But it will demand a good deal of self-discipline to redeem both existentialism and its phenomenology and to detach them from their more precocious "engagements." There are fortunately enough indications that the old spirit of phenomenological thoroughness has not yet died out, and that French phenomenology will be able to improve on the score made by its pioneers. The following chapters are meant primarily as an attempt to present some of its more promising contributions.

SELECTIVE BIBLIOGRAPHY

RICOEUR, PAUL, "Phénoménologie existentielle," Encyclopédie Francaise XIX (1951) 9.10.8–12

DE WAELHENS, ALPHONSE, "De la phénoménologie à l'existentialisme," in Wahl, Jean, Le choix, le monde, l'existence (1948), pp. 37–82. – "Les constantes de l'existentialisme," Revue internationale de philosophie III (1949), 255–69

4. Phenomenology and Hegelianism

One of the surprising peculiarities of French phenomenology for anyone familiar with its German antecedents is the natural ease with which it takes it for granted that Husserl's phenomenology belongs with Hegel's Phenomenology of the Spirit and even originated from it.[1] Regardless of whether such a connection can be established,[2] there is certainly no adequate foundation for

---

[1] See, e.g., Maurice Merleau-Ponty, Sens et non-sens, p. 125; Francis Jeanson, La Phénoménologie, p. 117, and Jean-F. Lyotard, La Phénoménologie (Collection Que sais-je? 1954), pp. 42 ff. (helpful; very characteristic of the French perspective of phenomenology).

[2] For a recent interesting attempt to back up this belief see Alphonse de Waelhens, "Phénoménologie husserlienne et phénoménologie hégelienne" in Revue

believing in such a historical connection as far as the German phase of phenomenology is concerned. I have examined in the Introduction the facts and the justification, or rather the lack of it, for relating the two phenomenologies.

In view of this situation one may well wonder about the historical reasons for the French interpretation of the relationship between Hegel and Husserl, a relationship which incidentally is not yet asserted by Georges Gurvitch (1930), who refers to the anti-Hegelianism of phenomenology. On the surface these reasons seem to consist merely in a historical coincidence in combination with a piece of misinformation from a seemingly well-informed source. The coincidence was a long overdue spurt in Hegelian studies in France, beginning in the late twenties. Jean Wahl's examination of the role of the "unhappy consciousness" in Hegel's *Phenomenology of the Spirit* (*Le Malheur de la conscience dans la philosophie de Hegel*, 1929) aroused interest in the neglected early ideas of Hegel with their more romantic and less rigid conception of concrete human experience. The discussion of the master-slave dialectics proved of particular interest to the young Marxists. Finally, in 1939, the text of the Phenomenology was ably translated in full and later interpreted by Jean Hyppolite, one of Sartre's and Merleau-Ponty's fellow students at the *École Normale*, where he had first become interested in the text.[1] It was more than natural that this coincidence should suggest the search for deeper connections with the more recent version of German phenomenology.

The "misinformation," or at least misinterpretation, can be traced to Alexandre Kojève, a Russian Marxist, who had studied in Germany under Jaspers but apparently not under any of the phenomenologists. Taking over on a temporary basis Alexandre Koyré's course on Hegel at the *École des Hautes Études* he had interpreted Hegel's *Phenomenology of the Spirit* in lectures which were widely attended and later edited in book form as an introduction to Hegel. In these lectures he simply asserted that Hegel's phenomenology was "phenomenological description (in Husserl's sense of the word)" dealing with man

philosophique de Louvain, LII (1954), 234–250; also in *Existence et signification* (1958), pp. 7–30.
[1] Personal communication.

as an existential phenomenon like Heidegger's phenomenology. Such an interpretation became possible because to Kojève the Hegelian method, in contrast to the reality which it tried to explore, was "by no means dialectical; it is purely contemplative and descriptive, i.e., phenomenological in the Husserlian sense of the term." [1] Coming from one thoroughly familiar with both Hegel and German philosophy, such an interpretation was bound to find credence.

However, coincidence and misinterpretation alone would hardly be enough to account for the French fusion of the two phenomenologies. They both met the French need of the time for concreteness as well as for structure. Both Hegel's and Husserl's phenomenologies were interested in the problem of consciousness and its manifestations. Thus, by playing down the dialectical aspect of Hegel's philosophy the French were able not only to present a Husserlianized Hegel but even to Hegelianize Husserl. It is perhaps even more startling that Merleau-Ponty finally presented an existentialized Hegel.

How far have these mutual assimilations affected the spirit of French phenomenology? We shall have occasion to comment on this point in the following chapters. They certainly implied risks. At least Hegel's *Phaenomenologie* was flexible enough not to impose as rigid a logical framework on the phenomena as his *Logik* might have done.

5. Phenomenological Existentialism and Literature

One peculiarity of French phenomenology which is apt to puzzle newcomers used to the scholarly atmosphere of German phenomenology (except for Heidegger's later excursions into poetry) is its close linkage with literature. Sartre was writing short stories and novels from the very start, along with his philosophical work, and became even more of a literary success when he turned to the theatre and the screen after 1940. Marcel always combined the roles of playwright and philosopher. Jean Wahl has published poetry, some of it even under the same cover with philosophical pieces. There is, to be sure, no evidence

---

[1] *Introduction à la lecture de Hegel*, p. 38 f., 447. – See also Jean Wahl, "À propos de l'Introduction à la phénoménologie de Hegel par A. Kojève, " *Deucalion* 1955, 77–101.

of any literary activity in the case of Merleau-Ponty. But in one of his essays[1] he has made an impressive case for the essential connection between the novel and metaphysics, which was illustrated by Simone de Beauvoir's first novel *L'Invitée*.

To be sure, this close tie between philosophy and literature is nothing new in France. Long before existentialism had arrived, philosophical ideas had found effective expression in the novels of Balzac, Stendhal, Proust, Valéry, Bernanos, Julien Green, and especially of André Malraux, who was perhaps the strongest novelistic native influence upon the existentialists, matched by the contributions of the German Kafka, and Americans such as Hemingway, Dos Passos, and Faulkner. But never has the link between the "metaphysical novel" and the "theatre of ideas" on the one hand and philosophy on the other been as direct and personal as in the case of the phenomenological existentialists.

Does this mean that the scientific spirit of Husserl's phenomenology has been betrayed by that of irresponsible fiction, and that the earnest of Kierkegaard's existentialism has degenerated into mere estheticism after the model of his "Diary of a Seducer"? Part of the answer to this question can be derived from the essay of the non-writing Merleau-Ponty:

Phenomenological or existential philosophy assigns itself the task not of explaining the world or discovering the conditions of its possibility, but of formulating an experience of the world, a contact with the world which precedes all thought about the world. This also means that philosophy and metaphysics are omnipresent ... Hence the tasks of literature and of philosophy can no longer be separated (p. 54).

Simone de Beauvoir, who combines the two functions of novelist and philosopher in her own work, spells out the relationship even more fully:

The more vividly a philosopher underlines the role and the value of subjectivity, the more he will be led to describe the metaphysical experience under its singular and temporal form. ... Existentialist thought is an attempt to reconcile the objective and the subjective, the absolute and the relative, the non-temporal and the historical; it aspires to seize the essence at the heart of existence; and if the description of the essence stems from philosophy proper, the novel will permit us to evoke the original surge of existence in its complete, singular, and temporal truth.

Sens et non-sens, pp. 51–82.

The metaphysical novel in particular seems destined "to evoke in its living unity and its fundamental living ambiguity that destiny which is ours and which inscribes itself in time and eternity." [1]

While such interpretations from the inside throw a good deal of light on the connections between existentialist thought and fictional expression, the question remains whether the imaginary transformation of experience does not involve a substitution of an inauthentic phenomenon for the direct account of the existentialist's unexchangeable experience. The answer is that not only Aristotle's "poetry" but even fiction can be truer than history in the sense that it allows us to include more typical experiences, and also those extreme situations which existentialists, following Jaspers, are in the habit of calling limit situations (*Grenzsituationen*).

Phenomenology as the study of general essences may at first sight seem to have little to do with the interest in individuals and singular experiences that goes with fictional writing. However, it is well to remember that even in eidetic phenomenology the general essence is approached via individual examples as stepping stones for essential intuitions. Thus even the Older Phenomenological Movement was aware of the unique richness and perceptiveness of great poetry and of the imaginative novel, especially of the stream-of-consciousness variety, as a foundation for general phenomenological insights. Besides, Husserl had always stressed the significance of free variation in imagination as the basis for exploring essential relationships, and for such purposes even the superiority of fiction over mere empirical observation. Also, the esthetic modification of our consciousness is at least similar to the phenomenological reduction with its bracketing of our belief in existence.

Such features may explain the possibility of a sympathetic interest of phenomenologists in fictional writing. But it was only when the emphasis of phenomenological interest shifted from the general essence to human existence in its singularity that the potentialities of the literary approach became fully apparent. Thus a novelistic journal like Sartre's *La Nausée* not only

---

[1] "Littérature et métaphysique" in *L'Existentialisme et la sagesse des nations* Nagel, 1948), p. 118 ff.

opened up experiences not formerly explored in their weird poignancy, but also comprised general reflections and essential insights that sprang from the concreteness of the hero's unique situation.

This does not mean that literature as a philosophical tool is without its weaknesses and dangers, nor that philosophy always mixes well with literary media. There remains an atmosphere of ambiguity around most of this philosophical literature which often conceals its main objective. Some of the interpretations which view existentialism as a movement preoccupied with failure and with the seamier side of human existence may result from paying too much attention to its novels and plays and taking them at their face value as revelations of existence at its most authentic, which they rarely mean to be. Such writing does not make clear the meaning and place of its particular examples in the context of the author's over-all interpretation of life. Yet one cannot deny that it is at times this very ambiguity which fascinates the existentialists and which they want to express by means of their literary enterprises. Certainly, in order to understand the full meaning of French existentialist thinking one must pay attention to both its philosophical and its fictional output.

6. Phenomenological Existentialism and Marxism

A word might be in order about the ambivalent relations between phenomenological existentialism and the philosophy of communism.

On the one hand there can be no doubt about the uncompromising hostility, if not contempt, with which the Communists view existentialism as a form of subjective idealism and the ultimate in bourgeois decadence. There is also an element of annoyance in their attacks on this rival revolutionary movement with its strong appeal to the sympathies of French youth.[1]

The situation is not so clear from the other side. In general, with the conspicuous exception of Gabriel Marcel, the followers of phenomenological existentialism are politically on the "left."

[1] For a more serious criticism of Husserlian phenomenology, by a Vietminhese Communist educated in France, see Tran-Duc-Thao, *Phénoménologie et matérialisme dialectique* (Paris, 1951).

They are even in far-reaching agreement with the ultimate goals of the Communists as regards the final freedom to be reached once the State is supposed to have withered away. They also feel that in order to reach this goal some form of revolution may prove indispensable. But they are at the same time for democracy, an authentic democracy as opposed to the merely formal democracy of traditional liberalism. This explains a good many shifts in their political relations with the Communist Party. Sartre has moved from co-operation during the Resistance movement, through an abortive attempt at a left wing democratic movement without the communists, to a renewed tactical alliance, without ever becoming a Party member. The aftermath of the Hungarian revolt of 1956 led to a new violent break, which may well be irreparable. Merleau-Ponty, while in the beginning more sympathetic to the humanistic aspects of communism than Sartre, has lately turned away from the dialectical myths of communism toward renewed attempts at revitalizing the French left without the Communists, and has in the process parted company with Sartre completely.

But never has there or could there have been any compromise as far as the fundamental philosophy of communism, i.e., dialectical materialism, was concerned. Sartre has never hesitated to call this "objectivist" philosophy absurd. Moreover, he considers it incongruous for a revolutionary movement and has at some time gone to the extent of offering his existentialism of freedom and liberation as a much more adequate foundation for a revolutionary program than the wavering determinism of dialectical materialism.

Strange to say, this rejection of dialectical materialism does not imply a repudiation of Marx and of Marxism. In order to understand this distinction, one must take account of the peculiar French picture of Marx as a philosopher, which differs considerably from the picture in other countries based chiefly on the Marx of the *Communist Manifesto* and *Das Kapital*. The new French Marx stems from his early writings, made accessible in the first volume of his works edited by the Marx-Engels Institute and translated immediately into French in 1927 by Molitor in three little volumes that go by the name of his *Oeuvres philosophiques*. From some of these post-Hegelian writings Marx emerges as the philosopher for whom "man is the root of everything." It is this kind of Marxist humanism which obviously lends itself to an existentialist interpretation and assimilation, which can be found particularly in Merleau-Ponty's earlier writings. It even allows us to see in the class struggle an existential historical situation of man.

Are these sympathies of the French existentialists related to their existentialism and in particular to its phenomenological approach? In view of the non-political and often rightist sympathies of many existentialists outside France, this would seem questionable from the very start. In fact the remarkable thing about its French variety seems to be that here it enters the political arena for the first time, and that on the whole it takes its stand in the ranks of the non-communist left. This does not mean that its politics follows logically from this approach, but only that it is compatible with it. Nor do the political writings of the existentialists show many phenomenological ingredients. At best one might find in Sartre and Merleau-Ponty the rudiments of a phenomenology of class consciousness. Otherwise the connection between phenomenological existentialism and Marxism is merely incidental, explained by the concrete situation of the French intellectual.[1] It is paralleled by his interest in psychoanalysis.

BIBLIOGRAPHY

"French Political Writing," *Politics* IV (1947), 30–76

---

[1] "Those of my age know this very well: even more than the two world wars, the great issue of their lives was a constant confrontation with the laboring class and its ideology, which offered them an inescapable picture of the world and of themselves. For us Marxism is not only a philosophy. It is the climate of our ideas, the environment in which they feed, it is the true movement of what Hegel called the Objective Spirit. ... Since the death of bourgeois thought, Marxism alone is Culture itself; for it is the one principle which allows us to understand the people, their work, and the events." (J. P. Sartre, "Le Réformisme et les fétiches," *Les Temps modernes* XI (1956), 1158; see also XIII (1957), 348 ff.

18. Gabriel Marcel

IX

GABRIEL MARCEL (1889–   ) AS A PHENOMENOLOGIST

1. Marcel's Relations to the Phenomenological Movement

In his pioneering survey of Phenomenology in France Jean Hering concludes his two-page discussion of Gabriel Marcel as "an independent phenomenologist" with the following statement: "We believe we may affirm that, even if German phenomenology (to suppose the impossible) had remained unknown in France, nevertheless a phenomenology would have been constituted there; and this, to a large extent, would be due to the influence of Gabriel Marcel." Hering, an old-style phenomenologist and anything but an existentialist, supports this remarkable estimate by referring to Marcel's "concern for research" and for exploring the "essence" of things without separating them from the consciousness that presents them to us; to his sense of the "inanity" of *Weltanschauungsphilosophie*; and to his concrete studies of such phenomena as "having," which keep free from the "mania" of reducing the phenomena to "nothing but" something else.[1]

Against such an impressive estimate stands, however, the fact that Marcel himself has never claimed to be a phenomenologist. Nor do his publications contain any extensive discussion of phenomenology and of the Phenomenological Movement as such, favorable or adverse. Thus, Husserl's name hardly ever figures in Marcel's works. In *Being and Having* he pointedly refrains from using "the Husserlian terminology as well as that of the German phenomenologists" (*EA* 228), although in the Gifford Lectures he remarks twice with approval that Husserlian

---

[1] Marvin Farber, ed., *Philosophical Thought in France and the United States*, p. 75

phenomenology had developed the conception of consciousness as intentional, i.e., as referring to something other than itself.[1] But there is no evidence that apart from this particular doctrine Husserl had any important influence on Marcel's philosophy and phenomenology.[2]

For Marcel, the most important figure in the Phenomenological Movement is Max Scheler. There had even been personal contacts between them. But it is uncertain whether it was Scheler the phenomenologist or Scheler the human being and metaphysician that impressed Marcel more. Still, such concrete phenomenological studies as Scheler's essay on *"Ressentiment"* proved so important to Marcel that he prepared a special critical article on that essay.[3] After 1933 Marcel was in close contact with one of Scheler's main disciples, Paul-Ludwig Landsberg.

For Heidegger Marcel entertains a mixed admiration. Around 1950 he even visited him in Freiburg. In mentioning this fact he refers to him as "this difficult philosopher, without doubt the most profound of our time, but the least capable of formulating anything resembling clear directions which could orient effectively the youth that turns to him as a guide." [4] Marcel refers repeatedly to *Sein und Zeit*, of which he has made an intensive study. He also acknowledges the parallelism in Heidegger's and his own concerns. But this does not prevent him from protesting against the somberness of Heidegger's outlook and from making light of the pompousness of the Heideggerians. But again, in his comments on Heidegger the thinker of Being and existence, he does not pay any particular attention to Heidegger the phenomenologist.

Marcel's chief antagonist among the French "existentialists" is undoubtedly Sartre (who, however, hardly takes note of the much older Marcel). Yet in the beginning there were some friend-

---

[1] *Le Mystère de l'être* I, 60 f., 188; also, in *Les hommes contre l'humain*, p. 101,. where Brentano too is given credit for the idea of intentionality.

[2] In a memorable interview in 1953, Marcel told me that he had seen Husserl's *Ideen* in German not long after their appearance but without being impressed and wondering what it was all about. Husserl's Sorbonne lectures in 1929, which he had attended without meeting him personally, had left him with the impression of the typical German scholar. More recent information about Husserl's religious life had made him question this impression.

[3] Troisfontaines, Roger, *De l'Existence à l'être*, II, 424.

[4] *L'Homme problématique*, p. 147. See also "Autour de Heidegger" in *Dieu vivant* I (1945), 89–99.

ly contacts.[1] But after the appearance of *L'Être et le néant* in 1943 Marcel directed vigorous attacks on Sartre's ontology and social philosophy without denying Sartre's philosophical stature. However, Sartre's connection with phenomenology does not figure in these discussions. Sartre's relation to Husserl is not even mentioned, though Sartre's limited debt to Heidegger is stressed. On Merleau-Ponty Marcel does not seem to have expressed himself publicly thus far.

Clearly, then, Marcel has no intention of identifying himself with either the Phenomenological Movement as a whole or any of its main representatives. In fact he considers these mainly as individual thinkers, and pays little attention to their phenomenological orientation. On the other hand, Marcel has never taken as definite a stand against phenomenology as Jaspers has done. As far as his own view of the relation is concerned, he might be considered at best a well-wisher from the outside. But before discussing the relationship on more specific grounds, it will be necessary to determine the place of phenomenology in Marcel's actual work.

This might be done first by taking account of the role of the term "phenomenology" in Marcel's writings. None of these contains it in the main title. It occurs first in the second part of Marcel's *Journal métaphysique* (1927) in an entry dated October 27, 1920, i.e., at a time when phenomenology as a Movement was still practically unknown in France. In the passage in question, dealing with the "conditions of personal life," Marcel distinguishes between a phenomenological and an ontological point of view, the former being concerned with the conditions under which a being can appear to himself as a personality. But after making this distinction Marcel soon returns to the ontological or metaphysical viewpoint.

Phenomenology figures much more prominently in a sequel to this *Journal* which begins in 1929 and fills the better half of Marcel's second philosopical book, *Être et avoir* (1935). It shows Marcel fully aware of and acquainted with German

---

[1] Thus Marcel refers to a paper Sartre had read in his house ("Existence et liberté humaine" in *Les grands Appels de l'homme contemporain*, 1946); translated in *The Philosophy of Existence*, p. 36); in this connection Marcel tells that he had suggested to Sartre an analysis of the viscous.

phenomenology.[1] In 1933 the diary also discusses "Phenomenological Aspects of Death" (*EA* 179 ff.) and gives glimpses of a phenomenology of suicide; but they are matched immediately by references to "hyperphenomenology." These journal entries lead up to the "Sketch of a Phenomenology of Having" which Marcel presented to the Philosophical Society of Lyons in 1933 and published subsequently in *Recherches philosophiques* (1933/34) under that title. In the following years three more essays go by phenomenological titles.[2] In later works such as the Gifford Lectures (1950) and *Les Hommes contre l'humain* (1951) Marcel attaches the word "phenomenological" freely, but less conspicuously, to some of his own analyses.

[1]

These facts suggest that even within Marcel's own thinking phenomenology as such is no major factor. He used the term somewhat more frequently after German phenomenology had become an influence in France, notably between 1933 and 1945, though even then without referring to its German application, but with reference to the kind of topics which in the twenties he had first discussed in the *Metaphysical Journal*. It is on the basis of having taken up these topics in a new and peculiar manner, rather than of his making use of the label, that Marcel's title to being the first original French phenomenologist has to be examined.

However, even if this should reveal Marcel as the initiator of a peculiarly French phenomenology, it would still leave him in a rather marginal position with regard to the larger Movement. To be sure, one additional factor must be considered: Marcel's influence on some of the leading French phenomenologists. Among these is as solid a student of phenomenology as Paul Ricoeur. There are also strong indications that at one time Merleau-Ponty received considerable stimulation from Marcel, both in his selection of topics and in his approach.

Thus, Marcel's position is a peculiar one. A user of phenomenology to a limited extent, but certainly not a phenomenologist,

---

[1] See the entry of August 5, 1929, which is, incidentally, the year of Husserl's Sorbonne lectures (*EA* 49).

[2] "Aperçus phénoménologiques sur l'être en situation" (1937), first published in *Recherches philosophiques*, then in *Du Refus à l'invocation* (1940); the same volume contains an essay "Phénoménologie et dialectique de la tolérance." A "sketch," "Esquisse d'une phénoménologie et d'une métaphysique de l'espérance" (1942), forms the central chapter of *Homo viator* (1945).

he is nevertheless one of its main inspirers. His role could be remotely compared with that of a preparer of phenomenology in Germany like Franz Brentano. But here the comparison ends. For there is certainly little resemblance between the founder of a new scientific philosophy and psychology, Brentano, and the searcher for a new mystic of Being, Marcel.

Before discussing the nature and the place of Marcel's phenomenological research, I shall try to outline his major concern and the main phases of his development in their significance for his phenomenology.

2. Marcel's Concern

Few contemporary thinkers philosophize in as intensely personal a manner as Marcel. Hence there is no shortage of autobiographical statements nor of formulations in which he expresses his central themes (the musical term is particularly appropriate in view of Marcel's stake in music as well as in the drama). From these I shall choose as point of departure a particularly concise statement written in 1940 which runs as follows:

I am forced to state that my philosophical development has been dominated by two preoccupations which at first may seem contradictory ... the one is what I shall call the exigency of being (*l'exigence de l'être*), the other the haunting sense (*hantise*) of beings seized in their singularity and at the same time in the mysterious relations which connect them. (*RI* 192 f.).

"Exigency of being": this phrase means for Marcel more than the fascination by the "wonder of all wonders," i.e., that there is Being, a theme which we found in Heidegger. Exigency is something which Marcel seems to experience particularly in the face of the possibility that everything is merely appearance and illusion (*PA* 51). This is not merely a matter of contemplation but of a recognition of the stake we have in being. Behind the urge to give to experience its "ontological weight" (*poids ontologique*) of which empiricism had lost sight (*RI* 89), and to experience the "bite of reality" (*la morsure du réel*), lies also the urge to "participate" in being. Our involvement in Being: this is actually what Marcel expresses by the title of his most systematic work, the *Le Mystère de l'être*.

One might easily think that Marcel's emphasis on the mysteri-

ousness of Being amounts to a new mysticism, if not to a kind
of agnosticism. In fact Marcel himself, in the Introduction to the
publication of his *Journal métaphysique*, has spoken of a "pure
mysticism" (*mystique pure*) as one of his goals. It is therefore
important to realize that Marcel's use of the term "mystery" is a
highly personal one. It by no means converts Being into an
impenetrable secret. Marcel's distinction between problem and
mystery, elaborated only after the *Journal métaphysique*, has
nothing to do with the question of the possibility or impossibility
of a solution, a disjunction which applies only to problems.
For Marcel, the important difference between mystery and
problem is that the problem, as the Greek literal meaning suggests,
is "thrown" before us and can therefore be objectified, whereas
the mystery is "something in which I am myself involved
(*engagé*), and which consequently is not thinkable except as a
sphere in which the distinction of what is in me from what is
before me loses its meaning and its initial value" (*EA* 169).
In other words, Marcel sees the mystery of being as consisting
not in its mysteriousness, but in the fact, about which there is
nothing hidden or "mysterious," that we are involved in being,
participate in it. It might have been less misleading to describe
this "mystery" simply as a phenomenon which engulfs us,
concerns us, from which we cannot escape. It is on the mystery
of being in this sense that metaphysics in Marcel's sense is
focussed (*braquée*) (*EA*, 146).

The other "preoccupation" that "haunts" Marcel is no less
important, although he treats it more in his dramas than in his
philosophy: the concern with single individuals – which may
well remind us of Kierkegaard, although Marcel came to know
him relatively late – and with their intersubjective relations.
The first form of this problem seems to stand behind Marcel's
pervading question, "What am I?" He asks this question in a
spirit that is not so eager for an answer as for a deepening of the
experience behind the question. This spirit avoids the glib answer
which is implied in our usual reply by reference to our objective
functions, our professions, or our names. Any philosophy which
sidetracks (*escamoter*) these questions, as idealism seems to have
done for Marcel, is disqualified by that very fact. But there is
also the haunting sense of the concrete interpersonal relations

which philosophy has to confront in the "mystery" of our inescapable involvement with others. To do this requires an empiricism more concrete and more profound than what has traditionally gone under that name. It requires a new concept of experience.

It is therefore not only Being but beings in which we are involved, in whom we participate, and who are at the focus of Marcel's thought. The idea of participation is indeed fundamental for Marcel's conception of human existence. Existence is actually being-in-a-situation, and the fundamental situation is our participation in Being and in beings. In fact being-with-others is the very nature of selfhood. It is easy to see that such a conception of existence, once granted, has no difficulty in accounting for the connection of an isolated subject with its objects, with other subjects, and even with God.

One might expect that with such a key Marcel would be in a position to develop a complete system of philosophy. But it is one of the characteristic features of his thought that he has no such ambition. To some extent this may be explained by Marcel's conception of the primary function of his philosophy. For according to him philosophy is not to provide us with ready-made conclusions. Its real mission is to awaken, to sensitize, and to appeal, rather than to teach and to give transferable information. The sense of "research" can only be conveyed by making the reader participate in the search. A "concrete philosophy" such as Marcel envisages can be achieved only by concrete experience and by promoting concrete experiences in others.

But there is also reason to think that a metaphysical system is actually not within Marcel's philosophical range. As a thinker he is at his best when he uses the form of the diary. He will start from an insight which has come to him during a stroll in his familiar Luxembourg gardens or in the country, and which he puts down after returning to his desk. Even his essays lack the coherence of a sustained argument. It is mainly his personality, a conspicuous personality, which provides a certain unity. There is something strangely ambivalent in Marcel's attitude toward the idea of a philosophical system. On the one hand he seems to resent even the idea of a systematic organization of philosophical thought; apparently this sentiment had an important part in his

break with the idealist tradition. But at times he feels that he
cannot escape the "exigency" of unifying his own thought. In
his Gifford Lectúres he himself attempted a comprehensive
presentation of his major themes, with but limited success. Thus
we observe the unusual spectacle of Marcel asking his friend,
the Jesuit Roger Troisfontaines, to prepare a unified picture
of his thought after the latter had submitted to him a mere
outline of it as a stimulus for Marcel himself. (*De l'Existence à
l'être*. II, 376). Troisfontaines seems to have succeeded in this
to Marcel's satisfaction. His book, together with Paul Ricoeur's
comparative study of Marcel and Jaspers, also recommended by
Marcel, are of inestimable value for any serious student of
Marcel's thought. But even these works leave a number of
questions unanswered or only partially answered, particularly
those bearing on Marcel's relation to phenomenology. In trying
to find these answers for ourselves, we shall first have to understand the development of Marcel's thought in the light of his
basic motifs, and then to determine the role which phenomenology
acquired for him as his thought developed.

3. The Development of Marcel's Philosophy

Few French philosophers are as thoroughly steeped in Anglo-
American philosophy of the early century as Marcel. In a thinker
with his concerns it is not surprising to find an initial interest in
idealistic interpretations of the participation of man in the
mystery of Being. But what is unusual is the extent of his interest
in the Anglo-American development of idealism. His occupation
with German idealism found a first expression in a manuscript
dealing with Coleridge's metaphysical ideas in their relation to
Schelling. Neo-Hegelianism attracted him considerably, particularly in the version which Bradley had given it. Thus Bradley's
doctrine of internal relations made a lasting impression on him.
But this could not make up for the neglect of the individual
which Bradley's monism implied. This fact in itself accounts to a
considerable extent for Marcel's interest in the author of *The
World and the Individual*, Josiah Royce. To him he devoted his
first major study, which appeared in three articles in the *Revue
de Métaphysique et de Morale* (1917–18), republished in book form
as late as 1945 under the title of *"La Métaphysique de Royce,"*

a work which according to W. E. Hocking is "to this date, so far as I know, the best monograph on Royce's metaphysical thought." [1] Besides, Marcel saw in Royce's metaphysics "one of the boldest attempts to give the metaphysical problem a solution which goes beyond the too narrow confines of intellectualism; pragmatism, and the philosophy of intuition," and admired in him a philosopher who "recognizes an authentic and profound intellectual experience wherever he felt a direct contact with that experience in which we are suspended (*baigner*) and outside of which we are nothing" (Introduction). Moreover, in his Foreword to the English translation of 1956 Marcel gives Royce credit for having helped him in the "discovery" of the "thou" as the necessary correlate of the "I." Thus it would seem that Royce provided for Marcel something like a way-station on the road from absolute idealism to a philosophy of concrete personal existence. This did not prevent him from making in the "Conclusion" serious reservations as regards some of Royce's doctrines. Thus, without charging Royce with monism, Marcel maintained that Royce had not been able to avoid some of its pitfalls. To this end, Marcel recommends the use of the very "theory of participation in Being of which we have recognized important elements in Royce and which will become more precise in W. E. Hocking." Such a use will

direct us toward the definitive break with categories that are inadequate to the proper object of metaphysics, and toward a less systematic but more profound interpretation of the intellectual life: a philosophy of this type, which refrains from importuning the real for guarantees which inevitably tend to do violence to it (*contraintes*), and which tends to recognize explicitly an order of freedom and of love where the relations from being to being, far from consolidating into a single rational system, would remain the expression of solidaric and distinct individuals who participate in God to the degree in which they believe in him.

It is toward a concrete philosophy with these objectives that Marcel now turns his efforts. The steps of this emancipation can be traced in his next major works.

The *Journal métaphysique*, published in 1927, is in many ways Marcel's most characteristic work but by no means his easiest one: "characteristic," for it shows Marcel in the acute struggle with his ideas, and at the same time the strengths and the

[1] "Marcel and the Ground Issues of Metaphysics," *PPR* XIV (1954), 449.

limitations of his approach; "not easy," for too often Marcel's sinuous paths end in the thicket without clear results and without a later follow-up or summary.

The adjective "metaphysical" must not mislead one into expecting an attempt at a conventional metaphysics. True, there occur in the book such problems as the time-honored relation between soul and body. But for Marcel metaphysics is not simply a matter of curiosity about the transcendent (*curiosité transcendente*); it is an expression of a longing to be (*appétit d'être*). Hence, metaphysics is a matter of personal reorientation (*redressement*) and even of removal of tension (*détente*), resulting from the fact that man finds his customary position in the world fundamentally unacceptable (October 17, 1922). The *Journal métaphysique* may properly be described as the record of such a reorientation, in which its author emancipates himself from an idealistic metaphysics and develops a philosophy of existence wherein the mystery of being becomes the center of metaphysical thought. The double dedication to Henri Bergson and William Ernest Hocking is certainly not without significance. For they have been of major importance in this emancipation. To Hocking Marcel seems to be indebted chiefly for stimulation in his social and religious thinking.

[1]

The first part of the *Journal métaphysique*, written during the early months of 1914, contains chiefly Marcel's attempt to free himself from the burden of idealistic metaphysics in order to make room for a more immediate approach to Being; actually the tools of this liberation are, in Marcel's own view, still dialectical themselves. The second, larger part, extending from 1915 to 1923, is of a more constructive nature. It concentrates on phenomena neglected or sidetracked by rationalist thinking, such as sensation or the experience of the body in its relation to consciousness. It also deals with a topic in which Marcel had become intensely interested during the War on the basis of his own mediumistic experiences: psychic phenomena. The main outcome, as Marcel himself sees it, is that such reflections can "divest (*déstituer*) truth of a transcendent value which a certain rationalism automatically confers on it – and at the same time give to existence that metaphysical priority of which idealism had wanted to deprive it" (p. XI). Thus the *Journal* (JM) may well be considered the first expression of a French philosophy of existence.

In many ways the publication of this journal is a unique case. There have been plenty of philosophical journals before, to mention only Berkeley's *Commonplace Book* and Amiel's *Journal*. But these appeared posthumously. As a matter of fact, even Marcel had originally not thought of publishing these records of his reflections, the major part of which is apparently still unpublished. It was only four years after the last entry of the second part that the *Journal* appeared, when Marcel had come to the conclusion that he was unable to condense his results in a systematic work. By that time he had decided that he might as well make a virtue of this impossibility.

However, before the *Journal* appeared Marcel published his main positive conclusion, "the primacy of existence over objectivity" (i.e., the objective approach by science and scientific philosophies), in an article in the *Revue de métaphysique et de morale* of 1925. While this article establishes Marcel's priority as an independent philosopher of existence, unaware at that time even of Kierkegaard, it should be realized that existence in Marcel's sense did not mean primarily the existence of the single individual, but comprised all being. In asserting the primacy of existence or of the "existential index," Marcel asserts chiefly the indubitability of the existence of the world, distinguished from its objective characteristics (*objectivité*) as mere objects of our thought. The mind finds itself supplied with an indubitable assurance that refers not to the existence of any particular thing which it knows, nor to existence in general, but to the existing universe.

Thus far there is no mention of phenomenology as a method. But one notices that the problem of a proper method becomes more and more urgent for Marcel. Thus one can find occasional references to a reflection designed to restore the continuity of existence which an imprudent analysis had destroyed. (*JM* 324).

During the later twenties Marcel transferred his main energies to playwriting and the theater. Yet this was more than a sideline for him, since his plays have considerable significance for the development of his philosophical ideas. This is expressed, for instance, in the fact that his next important philosophical statement is attached to one of these plays (*Le Monde cassé*). It should also be mentioned that 1929 was the year of his conversion from a non-committed religion to Catholicism, not as a result of any particular crisis but of the realization, precipitated by a letter from his friend François Mauriac, that he had already reached the Catholic position. This has never prevented him from strongly opposing Scholastic philosophy.

The title of the play just mentioned (*The Broken World*) is meant to suggest that the watchspring of the modern world has stopped functioning because it has lost the sense of what Marcel calls "the ontological mystery." The philosophical Appendix to this play, compared by Étienne Gilson with Bergson's *Introduction à la métaphysique*, undertakes not only to clarify the meaning of this mystery but also to consider the proper method of restoring it. The title, "Formulation (*position*) and Concrete Approaches to the Ontological Mystery," emphasizes the need of a "concrete" method. This is in line with Marcel's demand for a "concrete philosophy" as the need of the hour. In order to supply such a new approach, the essay distinguishes between two types of reflection, a First and a Second Reflection. The First Reflection is nothing but the analysis practiced by science and also by an idealistic philosophy. The Second Reflection, or reflection raised to the second power, has as its main function to break up the rigid division between that which is *before* us as an objective problem and that which is *within* us as a "mystery." He does so by showing the way in which we are "implicated" in a genuine mystery. The Second Reflection is also characterized as a movement of conversion reflecting on the First Reflection. In speaking of it as an act of recovery (*recueillement*) Marcel refers to the English phrase "to recollect oneself." Yet it would seem that at this stage Marcel had not yet succeeded in clarifying his "concrete approach" sufficiently. It is hardly without significance that around this time Marcel began to publish the essays with the phenomenological titles which we mentioned in the first section of this chapter. The word "phenomenological" also occurs frequently in a sequel to the first *Metaphysical Journal*, later incorporated in Marcel's second philosophical book, *Être et avoir*, which consists otherwise of essays grouped around a "phenomenological sketch." In this little volume the phenomenology of having proves to be the primary means for showing the difference between problem and mystery.

Marcel's third book, again a collection of essays, appeared in 1940. It is entitled *Du Refus à l'invocation* (*From Rejection to Invocation*). The rejection still aims at idealist philosophy, especially in the professedly agnostic form of Léon Brunschvicg. The "invocation" as conceived by Marcel comprises not only the religious invocation of prayer but any type of appeal to oneself or to the other which leads us closer to the ontological mystery. The mystery of man's incarnated being serves as the focal point (*repère*) of "metaphysical reflection." But other topics such as being-in-a-situation (as man's essence) and tolerance provide further subjects for Marcel's phenomenology as "concrete philosophy."

Homo viator (Man the Wayfarer), published in 1945, follows the same pattern. Marcel himself calls it apologetically a labyrinth. It centers in the idea of a metaphysical anthropology which shows man as essentially a transcendent being, destined for a beyond (*au delà*). The revealing subtitle is "Prolegomena to a Metaphysics of Hope," and the central essay is in fact a "Sketch of a Phenomenology and Metaphysics of Hope." Hope forms the opening wedge for a transcendence which, however, never frees us from our incarnated situation, for which the German poet Rilke is invoked as a main witness. While phenomenology thus serves as an approach, it clearly is not considered adequate without additional steps of a more metaphysical nature.

During the brief period between *Homo Viator* and the Gifford Lectures, i.e., from 1946–1948, Marcel accepted the label of "Christian existentialism" for his philosophy. It occurs chiefly as the title of a collection of interpretative essays which had been assembled by Étienne Gilson for his sixtieth birthday, to which Marcel himself added an illuminating autobiographical sketch. But as early as 1948 Marcel began to regret his "weakness," and finally he denounced it, most solemnly in the French Preface to the Gifford Lectures of 1951, shortly after the wholesale condemnation of all existentialism in the Encyclical "Humani generis." Instead of the "horrible word existentialism"

(*l'affreux vocable*) Marcel now suggests as a possible substitute
"Christian Socratism" or "Neo-Socratism," in order to express
"the attitude of interrogation that is constant with me and
appears perhaps even more clearly in my stage plays." One
might suspect that, at least for a brief period, Marcel hoped that
the word "Christian existentialism" could take the wind out
of the sails of the "atheistic" existentialists, only to discover
that it exposed his own cause to even worse misunderstandings.
The use of the symbol "Socrates" indicates how much importance
Marcel still attaches to the problem of finding the proper
approach, for which the Socratic dialogue seemed to him a
particularly effective solution.

The Gifford Lectures on *Le Mystère de l'Être* (*The Mystery of
Being*), published first in English, show a different structure from
that of Marcel's preceding works. They constitute Marcel's
supreme effort to give systematic form to his ideas. Each lecture
returns to one of his favorite themes but without a strict systematic sequence. Among these phenomenology does not figure
as such. But in several places, in trying to explain his method
of metaphysical reflection, Marcel refers to it without noticeable
reservations.

The situation is similar in his latest small volumes (*Les
Hommes contre l'humain*) (1951) and *L'Homme problématique*
(1955), in which certain aspects of social and existential anthropology are Marcel's main concern. The former contains chiefly a
critique of the spirit of abstraction as responsible for fanaticism:
it includes a phenomenological analysis of the fanaticized consciousness, which refers specifically to the model of Brentano's
and Husserl's analyses. "Problematic Man" gives chiefly a
critical discussion of the existentialism of anxiety without
explicit references to phenomenology.

4. Marcel's Conception of Phenomenology

The preceding survey of Marcel's development makes it clear
that his stake in phenomenology is merely of a subordinate
nature. It represents an episode in his search for a concrete
philosophy and for concrete approaches to it and to the ontological mystery. After his rejection of dialectical idealism Marcel
had fundamentally two choices left, Bergsonism and Neo-

Scholasticism, which might have recommended itself to him particularly after his conversion to Catholicism. But Marcel has been uncompromising in his opposition to Scholastic philosophy with its appeal to rationalism and its belief in logical demonstration. Bergsonism offered a much stronger attraction. Indeed Bergson's influence on Marcel has been considerable. The co-dedication of the *Metaphysical Journal* to him and to Hocking had its deep reasons: "Without the Bergsonian adventure and the admirable courage which it attested I would probably never have had the strength or even simply the courage to engage in my own research." [1] But while Marcel saw in Bergson a liberator from dialectical idealism, he could not adopt Bergson's metaphysical intuition and the implied metaphysics of creative evolution. In fact, now he considers the very term "intuition" too dangerous and too loaded to call his metaphysical reflection "reflective intuition," as he once contemplated doing. (*EA* 141 f., October 8, 1931)

Hence Marcel had to develop his own method and a minimum of theory about it. He called it "reflection." For it involved a certain retreat from the immediacy of acting and living. But it meant at the same time a return to the immediacy of lived experience, though on a higher level. Reflection in its first form as objectivating analysis actually threatens the immediacy of this experience. It is only a second reflection which Marcel credits with the power of recovering the lost concreteness of immediate experience and the sense of the ontological mystery. Marcel's interest in phenomenology has to be seen in the light of his efforts to develop his conception of this second or restorative reflection. It was at the time when German phenomenology entered the French scene that he felt this need most keenly. It is therefore not surprising that he tried to assimilate some of it for his more definite objectives.

However it is important to realize that Marcel never identified phenomenology with his second reflection, which is essentially a metaphysical or ontological approach. In fact, his very earliest reference to the "phenomenological viewpoint" contrasts it immediately with the metaphysical or ontological perspective (JM 249), which does not confine itself to appearances but raises

[1] Troisfontaines, *De l'Existence à l'être*, I, 204.

the question of reality. In *Being and Having* he distinguishes even more explicitly the phenomenological question from a hyperphenomenological one, for which the phenomenological approach is supposed to pave the way (*EA* 206, March 31, 1933; *RI*, 106 f.). A phenomenology of suicide, for instance, will show this act only as an attempt to get rid of oneself; yet hyperphenomenology questions and presumably refutes this perspective, in which my existence appears as too isolated. There is however no further development of this hyperphenomenological approach. The context and other passages and titles show that Marcel means by it what is elsewhere called metaphysics or dialectics. But even then it is by no means made clear how such a hyperphenomenology would proceed in order to solve the question of the validity of the appearances. Presumably it is this fact, in combination with the fuller development of Marcel's phenomenological analyses, which has given rise to the impression that Marcel's method is phenomenological in character.

What does Marcel mean by phenomenology? Nowhere in his published writings is there anything like an explicit discussion of this question. All the evidence so far available consists of incidental remarks that occur in connection with concrete analyses labeled at the time or in retrospect as phenomenological. Marcel does not often refer to other philosophers' writings as suitable models. Thus his interpretation of phenomenology must be derived indirectly from a study of his own writings, chiefly at the stage of *Être et avoir* and *Du Refus à l'invocation*.

Marcel contrasts phenomenological analysis with psychological analysis. The former deals with the "implicit content of thought," the latter with states (of mind?) [1]. The phenomenology of having is a case in point. "Having," as Marcel sees it, must be interpreted not as a state but as a content. It is the task of phenomenological analysis to detach (*dégager*) what is implied in experience (*ME* 1, 109; translation I, 94), without introducing oversimplifying reductions.

Thus far Marcel's phenomenology would seem to be at least compatible with the initial phase of Husserl's version. But one

---

[1] *EA* 229 (translation p. 158,; *RI*, p. 269. Actually, Marcel expresses the view that the whole conception of psychological states, comparable to states of things, is erroneous (*ME* I, 59 f.).

important difference has to be considered from the very start: Marcel's opposition to Descartes, to his principle of doubt, and to his reconstruction of philosophy on the basis of the indubitable *cogito*. To Marcel it is not doubt which represents the fundamental attitude, but wonder, amazement, in fact, admiration. Doubt is a degradation of it. Likewise the conception of a disembodied *cogito* is based on an artificial separation; for the cogitating ego is essentially an incarnated being, inserted and participating in Being (*EA* 11; November 22, 1928). Finally, what is undubitable to Marcel is not the "I think," nor even the "I exist," but ultimately the "we are." A phenomenology with such a non-Cartesian axis is bound to differ basically from any phenomenology in the Husserlian sense. It is obvious that it will also reject Husserl's phenomenological reduction and his transcendental idealism.

To what extent, then, is Marcel's conception of phenomenology a parallel to that of the Phenomenological Movement? Insofar as its objective is an analytic description of the contents of experience, it certainly coincides with the basic phenomenological approach. There is to be sure no talk about essences and essential structures and relations in Marcel's accounts, but one might apply these categories without much violence to what Marcel's analyses actually yield. Reflection too is a typical feature of the phenomenological approach, although Marcel's Second Reflection cannot be simply identified with a phenomenological reflection upon the phenomena and especially upon the intentional acts. Yet the assignment of the questions of validity and reality to a "hyperphenomenology" may again fit in with the initial idea of suspending belief as the entrance gate to phenomenology.

But this must not make one overlook the deep differences, both in structure and in function, between Marcel's phenomenology and that of the Movement. These are perhaps most pronounced when it comes to the function of phenomenology. For to Marcel it serves merely as a useful introduction to a renewed analysis of Being (*EA* 219; October 13, 1933). Hence it is hardly the only valid basis of philosophy and human knowledge, but merely an ally of a concrete philosophy, a handmaiden of metaphysics in its quest for the mystery of Being.

5. Marcel's Phenomenology in Action

Marcel is certainly not a theorist of phenomenology. Is he at least a good practitioner of it? Before selecting suitable examples of his phenomenological analyses, one has to decide what parts of his work should be considered phenomenological. Should his own labelling be followed? In that case only some of the essays of his middle period would qualify, with the addition of an essay like the one on "Self and Others" (*Moi et autrui*) in *Homo Viator*, which in retrospect he has called phenomenological (*ME* I, 191; II, 175). There is, however, not much difference in character between Marcel's labelled analyses and most of his unlabelled ones.

The most important case in point is the *Journal métaphysique*, Marcel's major and probably most original work. If it can be considered phenomenological, then indeed Marcel can be called the first original French phenomenologist. Now it certainly differs in style from all previous phenomenological works and gives at best the impression of a phenomenological workshop. To follow Marcel on the meandering and disconnected trails of his *Journal* can be an experience both exciting and frustrating. Seemingly casual observations, often triggered by observations of certain phrases in French or some other language, very often English, give rise to chains of suggestive reflections. But too often these reflections peter out or are set aside for further "research," which does not always follow or, if undertaken, oftentimes cancels out previous results. The *Journal* is certainly revealing about the way in which Marcel's mind operates. It shows him at his best when he records his fresh amazement in front of a new phenomenon never touched by other philosophers before him, poses new questions, is struck by new perspectives, or stopped by difficulties, which he never minimizes. For his chief concern at this level is not to suppress phenomena. In all these respects the *Journal* shows the features of genuine phenomenology at its best: the zest for finding new and neglected phenomena, the effort to make them stand out, and the ability to find new angles in, and new approaches to, the perennial issues. Nevertheless, Marcel's descriptions often lack the spirit of patient and many-sided analysis and the determination to penetrate to the essential structure and the essential laws. Too many of his descriptions read like preludes or improvisations, which remain at the impressionistic stage. "To be deepened" is a typical instruction which Marcel addresses to himself at the end of ever so many reflections,

However, in fairness to Marcel it should be remembered that his first and last ambition in the *Journal* is metaphysical: he wants to discover ultimate reality, not only phenomena regardless of their validity. Whatever phenomenological insights he gains in the process are steps on the road of this larger enterprise. It is another question how far he has been successful in this quest. He certainly did not succeed in giving his new metaphysics systematic form. It may be that it is precisely this unfinished character of his metaphysics which is responsible for the fact that most of his research remains on the phenomenological level. And it was this aspect of his enterprise which attracted the attention of those whose primary interest was phenomenology. Here were examples of a new undogmatic approach to new phenomena, carried out with caution and humility, yet always animated by the concern for human existence as participating in a wider pattern of being.

At this point it may be best simply to list some of these phenomena, without following through Marcel's accounts of them:

α. The body (*corps*) as a content of experience: in its centrality for the very conception of existence this theme had never been considered before so explicitly. Incarnation in a body actually appears to Marcel as the core of human existence. But existence does not coincide with it, and the ambivalent relations between existence and body are one of the most intriguing subjects in Marcel's reflections.

β. "Having" as distinguished from "Being"; I shall present Marcel's phenomenology of "having" more fully below.

γ. Commitment (*engagement*); Marcel may well have been the first to introduce this central category into the philosophy of existence.

δ. Participation, as opposed to mere spectatorship: this is actually one of the pillars in Marcel's conception of existence. Sensation is to him the most elementary form of participation in Being, rather than a mere receiving of messages from outside.

ε. Witnessing (*témoignage*), as distinguished from mere experiencing.

ζ. Availability (*disponibilité*) and unavailability of the existing individual.

η. Belonging (*appartenance*), with particular emphasis on the way in which persons can belong to each other.

θ. Creative fidelity: this conception is to replace Bergson's creative élan by stressing the complementary values of stability, as expressed in a promise.

ι. Encounter (*rencontre*), as distinguished from mere meeting and as related to the phenomenon of thou-ness.

κ. The "mystery of the family": this gives Marcel occasion to reflect on such relationships as sonship, marriage, motherhood, fatherhood, and brotherhood.

Among phenomena in the field of religious philosophy Marcel dwells chiefly on such more familiar topics as hope and faith, but sees them in a new light. Invocation, not only in the form of prayer, provides a new focus for these topics.

This catalog is not meant to be exhaustive. Sometimes Marcel will drop merely casual hints based on the observation of a linguistic peculiarity or on a preposition like the French "chez" (living with) and meditate on what it implies. Most of these phenomena are illustrations of "mysteries" in Marcel's sense, i.e., forms of existential participation.

6. *The Phenomenology of Having*

In most of the cases surveyed above Marcel does not go much beyond drawing our attention to the phenomena. Then he leaves it to us to contemplate them on the basis of suggestive examples, often supplied by his own plays. The closest he comes to an analysis for essential characteristics is in the case of the phenomenon of "having," which we shall therefore single out for a fuller account. Marcel's special stake in this topic can be explained by his interest in the most ambivalent case of such "having," the having of our own body in which we are incarnated. Here is the place where the transition between a problem, a question before us, and a mystery, a situation in which we are involved, becomes particularly striking. This may explain why the phenomenology of "having" follows immediately on the attempt to clarify the "concrete approaches to the ontological mystery." To be sure, Marcel had reflected on this subject for a long time, particularly in his *Journal*, before he attempted to condense his insights in the form of a lecture. And even the lecture as published in *Être et avoir* is far from comprehensive and well organized. Nor is it Marcel's final word on the subject. A full picture of Marcel's phenomenology of having would thus have to be based on several texts.

After eliminating such cases as "having" a headache, or "having" a need, which he considers irrelevant, Marcel distinguishes two main types of having: "possessive having" (*avoir possession*) and "implicative having" (*avoir implication*), the latter referring to the way a thing "has" a property. His primary interest however is only in possessive having.

All possessive having includes a "who," i.e., a personal possessor, and a "what," i.e., a possession, set apart from him (*"transcendent"*). The main characteristics of the relationship between these two poles are: (1) the possessor has a "claim" on the possession which is centered in him and excludes others, who conceivably might be in his place and to whom it could be transferred. For possession can always be alienated. To the extent that it can, it is apt to be socially divisive. (2) Possession requires some care or maintenance. Hence it involves a constant risk of loss and destruction, which is apt to produce fear and jealous watchfulness for it. (3) Possession implies power over the possessed, either in the form of obedience (as when a pet obeys) or of control over it. But the very concern for such control has a tendency to enslave the master, especially when the master of the possession does not coincide with its creator, who is in active contact with it.

One may think that some of these characteristics of possession had already been found in the legal doctrine of possession as developed by Roman jurisprudence. But quite apart from Marcel's extension to such non-legal cases as the having of a secret or the having of ideas, his main concern is the significance of the external characteristics for the possessor, the recoil action of possession, as it were. For there is a peculiar dialectics and dynamism in the whole relationship between persons and things.

Even more important is the fact that the relation between

possessor and possession is never the same. There is a difference between having a bicycle and having one's ideas on something. The external relation of possession can actually be internalized, so much so that the possession becomes part of my being. Certain qualities of the possession with which I have "identified" myself (a term not used by Marcel) simply cannot be transmitted.

The model case of such a possession half-way between having and being is that of my body. It is not a clear case of external possession; nor is it one of complete identity, as a crude materialism asserts. The body of my experience is in a border zone between having and being. Its status is ambivalent. Depending on the way I "live it," it "belongs" to me, or I "belong" to my body. In fact, as Marcel sees it, I become the body's slave by "having it" in a merely possessive way, its master by "being it" in loving participation.

Our relationship to our body constitutes for Marcel at the same time one of the prime cases of the ontological mystery. For inasmuch as we are our body, are incarnated in it, and do not merely possess it, we participate in being in a unique intimacy. This relationship can never be fully objectified. It can only be lived and recaught in reflection. The body is thus a privileged avenue to the mystery of being in a manner which may remind one of Schopenhauer's metaphysics of the body, with which Marcel is clearly familiar. The obvious incompleteness and some of the defects of this pioneer study have to be seen in the light of such an ultimate objective of Marcel's enterprise.

7. Concluding Observations

I shall not attempt to appraise Marcel's phenomenological work explicitly beyond what was already implied in its presentation. By now it should be clear that Marcel's phenomenology is to him only a step in his metaphysical reflection – and not even an essential one – a useful introduction to his metaphysical concern.

Phenomenology in the narrower sense has no right to take any credit for Marcel's analyses, nor has it any responsibility for any of their shortcomings. Some of his phenomenological studies show the earmarks of the best phenomenological work: its freshness, its perceptiveness, and its tentativeness. In this respect it might well reach the level of some of Scheler's writing. But beyond that Marcel has little interest in phenomenology as such, in its essences and essential relations and especially its studies of phenomenological constitution. And he would have little patience with any attempt to make phenomenology a rigorous and objective science, as Husserl attempted to do.

Marcel is the pacemaker of French phenomenology, and to a considerable degree one of its allies. He is not one of its protagonists.

SELECTIVE BIBLIOGRAPHY

Major Works

Journal métaphysique (1927; written in 1914 and 1915–1923) (*JM*)
 Translations: English (1952) by Bernard Wall – good
La Métaphysique de Royce (1943; written 1917–18)
 Translation: English (1956) by V. and R. Ringer; with special preface by Marcel
Être et avoir (1935) (*E.A.*)
 Translation: English (1951) by K. Farrer – good, some errors
Du Refus à l'invocation (1940) (*R.I.*)   [1]
Homo viator, Prolégomènes à une métaphysique de l'espérance (1945) (*H.V*)
 Translation: English (1951) by Emma Craufurd – readable, at times unnecessarily free
Positions et approches du mystère ontologique (1949); first published in 1933 as an appendix to *Le monde cassé*. (*PA*)
 Translation: English (1949) by M. Harari in *The Philosophy of Existence* – not always accurate
Le Mystère de l'être (1951) Gifford lectures. 2 vols. (*ME*)
 Translation: English (1951) by G. S. Fraser; there are considerable differences between the English version and the French, which appeared a year later. The translation is apparently quite free.
Les Hommes contre l'humain (1952)
 Translation: English (1950) by G. S. Fraser
L'Homme problématique (1955)   [2]

Monographs

GILSON, ÉTIENNE, ed., *Existentialisme chrétien: Gabriel Marcel* (1947)
 Contains four analytical essays, followed by an autobiographical essay, translated in *The Philosophy of Existence.*
PRINI, PIETRO, *Gabriel Marcel e la Metodologia dell' Inverificabile*
 With interesting preface by Marcel; translated into French.
RICOEUR, PAUL, *Gabriel Marcel et Karl Jaspers* (1947)
 Analytical confrontation.
SOTTIAUX, EDGARD, *Gabriel Marcel, philosophe et dramaturge* (1956)
TROISFONTAINES, ROGER, S. J., *De l'Existence à l'être. La philosophie de Gabriel Marcel.* 2 vols. (1952). With preface by Marcel.   [3]

Articles in English

HOCKING, W. E., *"Marcel and the Ground Issues of Metaphysics,"* PPR XIV, 439–69

JARRETT-KERR M., "Gabriel Marcel on Faith and Unbelief," *Hibbert Journal* XLV (1947), 321–26

OSTERMANN, ROBERT, "G. Marcel (I) The Discovery of Being (II) The Recovery of Being, (III) Existence and the Idea of Being," *The Modern Schoolman* XXXI (1953), 99–116, 289–305, XXXII (1954), 19–33

Ph. D. Theses

[1]   GALLAGHER, KENNETH T., *The Philosophical Method of Gabriel Marcel.* Fordham University, 1958

Most Complete Recent Bibliographies

[2]   For Marcel's own writings, see Troisfontaines, II, 381–425; for studies about Marcel, see Collins, James, *The Existentialists* (Chicago, 1952), pp. 258 f.

19. Jean-Paul Sartre

X

THE PHENOMENOLOGY OF JEAN-PAUL SARTRE (1905–   )

1. On Understanding Sartre

The attempt to present and discuss Sartre's phenomenology without including the whole of his philosophical thought has to face more than the usual amount of difficulties presented by such a selective enterprise. They begin with the fact that a man of Sartre's versatility and vigor defies all conventional classifications. Thus, in studying Sartre the philosopher and phenomenologist, one must consider not only Sartre the novelist, the critic, the playwright, and the editor, but also the political figure. For since the war Sartre has become so involved in political action and in the theatre that one might well wonder whether he has not turned away from philosophy for good, were it not for the persistent announcements of a major philosophical work to appear in the near future. One might conceive of dividing up the task by concentrating on either the philosopher, the dramatist, or the novelist Sartre, as some of the more successful studies published thus far have approached him.[1] But Sartre's work is more than the sum of the output of his separate talents. There is a common source for all his multifarious activities. At their center is a unique philosophic concern. Some attempt to determine this core is therefore indispensable for any attempt to understand Sartre.

There are other peculiar obstacles to an understanding of Sartre's phenomenology caused by the general character of his work. A major one lies in its incompleteness. This incompleteness means more than the lack of some parts in a puzzle. One of

---

[1] See, e.g., Iris Murdoch (*Sartre. Romantic Rationalist*) for the novelist, and Francis Jeanson (*Sartre par lui-même*) for the dramatist Sartre.

Sartre's most original doctrines is that the future creates the meaning of the past, and that hence the meaning of our past must remain in suspense until death has deprived us of all future. This applies in an exceptional and tantalizing sense to Sartre's own philosophical production. As long as Sartre's work on the moral perspectives of his ontology, *L'Homme* – announced for at least ten years but obviously delayed and apparently growing into a whole series of books – has not appeared, much of the meaning of his published work must remain ambiguous. This is all the more true since even Sartre's earlier works, such as his first phenomenological studies, have received new and often surprising meanings in the light of his subsequent ontology. The same seems to hold for *L'Être et le néant*, especially for its social philosophy, much of which is unreconciled and not easily reconcilable with the pronouncements of Sartre's subsequent "existentialism." [1] Nevertheless, even such reinterpretations will have to incorporate Sartre's past, while giving it new and partially unpredictable meanings.

The difficulty of determining the meaning of Sartre's writings within the framework of his total production is intensified by the fact that thus far he has offered very few explicit clues to the connections between his works in their surprising and often puzzling sequence, and to their place within his wider plans. Any interpretation an outsider can give must therefore remain a conjecture. This is particularly true of the present attempt, since, in spite of repeated efforts, I have been unable to secure better material from the only qualified source. In the meantime there is hope that an announced autobiography will verify or falsify the following interpretation, which is based almost completely on sources which are generally accessible.

A word should be added about the real and the alleged difficulties in understanding Sartre's philosophical writings. Some of these difficulties persist throughout his production, such as the inordinate length of his paragraphs, which he shares with many recent French philosophical writers. What seems to be more peculiar to Sartre is the frequent failure to state his ultimate, and often even his immediate, objective in tackling a

---

[1] See "French Existentialism: Its Social Philosophies," *Kenyon Review* XVI (1954), 446–62.

particular subject. Sartre shows a tendency, creditable in many respects for the artist in Sartre and even for the original phenomenologist, to plunge his reader into a concrete analysis from which his real purposes emerge only gradually; the beginnings of *L'Imagination*, of *L'Imaginaire*, and even of *L'Être et le néant* are cases in point. One often has to wait for the none too frequent summaries to see his work in proper perspective. At least as far as organization and structure are concerned, Heidegger's writing is generally far superior, especially to Sartre's philosophical magnum opus. On the other hand, Sartre's French can be understood much more easily than Heidegger's German, which yields only too readily to the violence of his "hermeneutics." Sartre has not tampered with his native language in any comparable degree. The number of his neologisms is relatively small, though they grate badly enough on the sensitive ears of the French reader. In fact, up to the time of *L'Être et le néant* Sartre wrote completely within the framework of the current French philosophical idiom. Sartre's philosophical style of thinking and writing changed, however, considerably with this work. The influence of Heidegger's *Sein und Zeit* in this regard can hardly be doubted. But beginning with *L'Être et le néant* his writing shows also the impact of Hegel, as did that of many other French philosophers of his generation. Thus Sartre's fondness for the verbal paradox shows how deeply Hegel's dialectics has affected his way of thinking, even though he does not try for the final glory of Hegel's synthesis. There are also times when I cannot suppress the feeling that Sartre enjoys the shock and bewilderment that he can evoke in his more conventional readers. In fact he may even enjoy surprising himself.[1]

One particularly serious difficulty, especially for French and other non-German readers, is that in *L'Être et le néant* Sartre simply presupposes their familiarity with German phenomenology, and in particular their knowledge of Husserl's and Heidegger's major works. While this may have stimulated the interest in Husserl's work, it has made the access to some parts of Sartre's own writings forbidding for the average philosophical

---

[1] See the somewhat chatty but highly perceptive and informed profile by Simone de Beauvoir in *Harper's Bazaar*, 1946 (pp. 113, 158, 160), about the boy Sartre: "He was particularly happy when he could not understand what he was writing."

reader. Here nothing but a commentary can help; introductions like the present one can only hope to shorten the labor.

In the public eye Sartre's philosophy and, almost more, his non-philosophical work passes for a philosophy of despair and futility – an expression of the decadence of French and European thinking. There is enough fuel for such an interpretation, if one considers only his novels and a good many of his plays in isolation. Besides, the conclusion of *L'Être et le néant* (1943) is certainly anything but reassuring, particularly considering the end of the last part on the note: "Man is a useless passion." Compared with these texts, the boldly optimistic protestations of Sartre's partly disowned lecture, *L'Existentialisme est un humanisme*, seem rather forced and unconvincing. One way to account for this contradiction is to assume a development in Sartre: we shall see that his earliest (pre-phenomenological) statements long before the War were his bleakest, whereas, especially since the Liberation, the tone becomes at least more activistic, if not belligerent. The main difficulty may be that for the reader of isolated works, especially the merely literary ones, it is almost impossible to appraise their place in the pattern of Sartre's total enterprise. This applies especially to the incomplete tetralogy *Les Chemins de la liberté* (The Ways of Freedom), ways which prove to lead anywhere but into the open and could much more aptly be called blind alleys. Perhaps only Sartre's Goetz in the last act of *Le Diable et le bon Dieu* is a significant exception to this rule. It is thus a fatal though understandable mistake to see in the Antoine Rocquentin of *La Nausée* or in Matthieu Delarue of the *Chemins de la liberté* valid instances of Sartre's program. Only a comprehensive survey of his work allows a proper appraisal of the significance of these characters.

In view of such handicaps one may indeed wonder how Sartre's thought and particularly his philosophy could have such an impact. Part of the explanation is that Sartre's literary success preceded that of Sartre the philosopher. This success began with *La Nausée* (1938), a diary in fiction form, with some of Sartre's most striking characterizations of philosophic experiences, to which, according to his biographer Marc Beigbedder, he gave the subtitle of "novel" in order to improve its sales. It was in the wake of the spectacular success of this work, followed by his short stories, by critical writings, mostly in the literary field, and by such topical and gripping plays as *Les Mouches* and *Huis Clos*, that his first major philosophical work *L'Être et le néant* made its entrance into the French philosophical scene and established Sartre at once as one of the foremost *"philosophes"* in more than the merely academic sense.

However, such explanations of the phenomenon Sartre have little to do with the weight of his ideas. What he has to say would certainly be important enough to warrant the extra effort that some of his texts demand. What is needed in order to achieve maximum understanding of his work is to lay hold of its fundamental motivation. It is from this angle that I shall try to approach him, as soon as I shall have determined his relation to the Phenomenological Movement.

2. Sartre's Place in the Phenomenological Movement

How far is Sartre a phenomenologist? There is no clear and authentic answer to this question. It may even differ in Sartre's own perspective (*pour soi*) and in that of the public (*pour autrui*). As far as the public is concerned, there can be little question that even as an exponent of phenomenology Sartre still outranks any other French thinker, at least in historical importance. For it was Sartre who first demonstrated the possibilities and the vitality of the phenomenological approach at a time when in Germany it seemed to have become a matter of the past, to be left to the historians of philosophy.

Yet Sartre himself, to my knowledge, has never referred to himself as a phenomenologist. He has only accepted, though after initial reluctance, the label "existentialist" pinned on him by outsiders and notably only *after* the appearance of his magnum opus *L'Être et le néant*, where it never occurs. There is even a passage in this work (*EN* 12; transl. XLVIII) where he refers to *"la Phénoménologie"* of Husserl and of Heidegger in quotes, as if he considered them a merely German school, with which he does not want to be identified. Presumably he looks upon his own phenomenology merely as the basic tool for his ontological existentialism, and a development as such of what the German phenomenologists had started, and prefers to think of his philosophy as characterized primarily by its content.

It is of course true that Sartre's philosophical thinking spills over the dams of any school or movement, as does that of the great seminal minds of past centuries. The whole question is probably a matter of indifference to Sartre himself, especially since his resignation as a teacher of philosophy at the Lycée Condorcet in Paris (1944). Thus he never had the chance to establish anything like a school. Since then all his teaching has been through his books and through occasional lectures and discussions.

Any serious attempt to place Sartre within the Phenomenological Movement must therefore consider carefully his position in relation to its major figures. In doing so one must take account, however, of Sartre's peculiar perspective on it. For in Sartre's eyes to all intents and purposes the Phenomenological Movement consists merely of Husserl and Heidegger. Not even Nicolai Hartmann, whom Sartre must have met during his stay in Berlin, is ever mentioned in his writings. Scheler's name, to be sure, does figure in several places, especially in *L'Être et le néant*, in connection with phenomenological psychology, for his insights into the intentional structure of the emotional life, his theory of *"ressentiment,"* and his essay on suffering. Sartre even gives qualified assent to Scheler's intuition of values, although he interprets their ontological structure quite differently. But there is no indication that Scheler's conception of phenomenology meant for Sartre an original and equivalent variety of it. Sartre's acquaintance with German phenomenological literature was as limited as that as of most other French phenomenologists.

Hence Sartre defines his position within phenomenology exclusively in terms of his relation to Husserl and to Heidegger. Indications are that immediately after his return from Germany in 1935 he felt himself even closer to Husserl than to Heidegger, despite, and perhaps even because of, the fact that it was Heidegger and not Husserl whom he had met in person. Thus in his first philosophical work on *L'Imagination* he refers exclusively to Husserl, crediting him with having opened up the path for his own studies of the subject and adding that no such study must "neglect the rich observations he gives us: we know today that we must start again from zero and disregard the whole pre-phenomenological literature." (pp. 139, 158). Also, in a remarkable brief article in the literary *Nouvelle Revue Française* of 1939, "Une Idée fondamentale de la phénoménologie de Husserl: L'intentionalité," republished in *Situations* I, 31–35 (which was based on the strange interpretation of intentionality as making the intentional object independent of consciousness), he claims for Husserl that

he has reinstated horror and charm in the objects (*choses*). He has restored to us the world of the artists and of the prophets: terrifying, hostile, dangerous, with its harbors of grace and of love. Here we are liberated from Proust and liberated at the same time from the "inward life".[1]

However, even at this period Sartre was by no means uncritical of Husserl. Thus in his important article in the *Recherches philosophiques* of 1936 on "La Transcendance de l'égo" he takes issue with Husserl's conception of the pure ego, yet with the purpose of thus improving on Husserl's fundamental conception of phenomenology and freeing it from unnecessary encumbrances.

Sartre's tone became even more critical as he developed his ontology far beyond anything that Husserl had ever attempted. *L'Être et le néant* (EN) makes clear the degree of this emancipation. While Husserl and Heidegger are the two philosophers to whom Sartre refers most frequently, there is hardly any explicit praise for Husserl's concrete work. Instead, Sartre charges Husserl twice with "infidelity" to his original conception of phenomenology (by his Berkeleyan idealism in interpreting Being and the transcendent objects of intentional consciousness as non-real; *EN* 24, 28; transl. LVIII, LXIII); with the guilt of "pure immanentism" (*EN* 719; tr. 625); for not having escaped the "thing-illusion" (*illusion chosiste* — by introducing a passive *hyle* and the doctrine of sensation into the picture of consciousness; *EN* 26, 63, 389; tr. LXI, 27, 315); with "remaining timidly (*craintivement*)" on the level of purely "functional description" which encases him in a mere account of appearances as such and makes him unable to move on to "existential dialectics"; with being "in spite of all his denials a phenomenalist rather than a phenomenologist" (*EN* 115; tr. 73); with giving us a mere caricature of genuine transcendence, which should pass

---

[1] It is probably this liberation to which Sartre refers when he credits Husserl with having given him the means to "evacuate" all things from consciousness (F. Jeanson, *Sartre par lui-même*, p. 187 note).

beyond consciousness into a world and beyond the immediate present into a past and future (*EN* 152, 165, 543; tr. 109, 120, 415); with being unable to escape solipsism any more than Kant, particularly by the introduction of the "useless and fateful (*néfaste*) hypothesis of a transcendental subject" (*EN* 291; tr. 235); with not taking sufficient account of the obstructiveness (*coefficient d'adversité*) in our immediaté experience (*EN* 389; tr. 325); and with mistakenly thinking that an eidetic phenomenology of essences can lay hold of freedom, which Sartre identifies with consciousness and with an existence that is at the root of all human essence (*EN* 514; tr. 430 f.) – the last, in the light of Sartre's final existentialism, perhaps the most serious charge of all.

To these far-reaching criticisms must be added those which he expressed in a paper read to the *Société Française de philosophie* (Séance du 2 juin 1947), on "Conscience de soi et connaissance de soi": "We have in Husserl . . . a gradual elucidation and a remarkable description of the essential structures of consciousness" (*un pointillisme d'essences*) "but never the posing of the . . . ontological problem, namely that of the being of consciousness" ....[1] In the same manner the problem of the being of the world remains in suspense. . . . We never return from the phenomenological *epoché* to the world" (p. 55). This spells the final disqualification of eidetic phenomenology as the adequate foundation for the task that Sartre had set his own philosophy. It does not eliminate the fact that Husserl was for Sartre the most important philosophical stimulus. But precisely because Husserl was to Sartre chiefly a liberator it would not do to see in Sartre a mere disciple of Husserl.

Next we shall have to determine what is Sartre's attitude toward Heidegger, whose philosophy would seem to be so much more germane to his own enterprise in *L'Être et le néant*. Sartre appears to be familiar with Heidegger's major writings from *Sein und Zeit* to the first Hölderlin lecture (*EN*, 440; tr. 373). Notwithstanding this fact, he lists him as an existentialist – and as an atheistic existentialist, to boot – in his lecture on "Existentialism is a Humanism."

It is not unlikely that in the thirties Sartre was not fully aware

[1] Here Sartre echoes one of Heidegger's basic criticisms of Husserl. See p. 300 f.

of the gulf between Husserl's and Heidegger's phenomenology. The earliest explicit reference to Heidegger appears in his *Esquisse d'une théorie des émotions* (1939), where, in the introductory characterization of phenomenology, Sartre adds Heidegger's ideas to those of Husserl within the same paragraph without implying any essential difference between the two (p. 8). The same seems to be true of *L'Imaginaire*, his book on the world of the imagination (1940), where Heidegger's conception of being-in-the-world is utilized in describing the structure of the imaginary world, and where the *Conclusion* makes reference to Heidegger's conception of the Nothing, apparently without serious reservations.

The situation is very different in *L'Être et le néant*, whose theme brings Sartre into immediate rivalry with Heidegger's incomplete central work. To be sure, nowhere does Sartre criticize the work of his predecessor as a whole. Nor does he extend much explicit credit to it beyond the fact that he usually acknowledges Heidegger's solutions as superior to Husserl's and to Hegel's. On the other hand, Sartre goes so far as to apply to Heidegger twice his favorite charge of "bad faith," once in connection with his interpretation of transcendence (where Heidegger, while claiming to go beyond idealism, is said to end in a pseudo-idealism; *EN* 307; tr. 249), the other time in mentioning Heidegger's discussion of the fact that no one can die another person's death (which, according to Sartre, would hold equally of any other conscious act (*EN* 616; tr. 532). In referring to Heidegger's way of discussing social existence (*Mitsein*), Sartre speaks about his "brusk and slightly barbaric method," which cuts the Gordian knot rather than disentangles it (*EN* 304; tr. 244). As to more important and substantial disagreements, he objects to Heidegger's elimination of Descartes' and Husserl's consciousness from his *Dasein* (a conception which he otherwise adopts under the name of *réalité humaine*); to Heidegger's attempt at grounding "the phenomenological concept of the nothing" on the experience of anxiety (rather than on the negative element in human spontaneity (*EN* 25 ff.; tr. 16 ff.); to the "insufficiency of his hermeneutic descriptions" in passing over in silence the fact that man is not only an ontological being with a certain comprehension of being, but also one whose projects bring ontic modifications into the world (*EN* 503; tr. 430); and to his preoccupation with death as man's only authentic project. There are also specific criticisms of Heidegger for his over-emphasis on the future dimension in his analysis of temporality, and for his making human existence not only body-less but sex-less. (*EN* 451; tr. 383)

But in spite of such more or less outspoken dissents, it seems plain enough that Sartre's ontological enterprise leads him closer to Heidegger than to any other philosopher before him. Yet the differences and the originality of Sartre's philosophizing, combined with his unwillingness to abandon Husserl's phenome-nology of consciousness, make it impossible to see in Sartre nothing but a French Heidegger.[1]

Sartre himself in his paper before the *Société française de philo-sophie* of 1947 proposed "a synthesis of Husserl's contemplative and non-dialectical consciousness, which leads us to the contem-plation of essences, with the activity of the dialectical, but non-conscious, and hence unfounded project that we find in Heideg-ger, where we discover that the primary element is transcen-dence." (p. 76) Obviously, this formula is far from self-expla-natory. It is not even free from misinterpretations, for instance in ascribing to Heidegger a dialectical conception of existence. This alone makes it plain that Sartre's final conception of phenomenology does not consist in a mere combination of the phenomenology of Husserl's *Ideen* and Heidegger's hermeneutics of human being, as developed in *Sein und Zeit*. Sartre's own contribution and the final relationship of the two main ingre-dients within his total conception will be discussed below.

Sartre may never have called himself a phenomenologist. But phenomenology is certainly a decisive part of his philosophical method. Besides, Husserl and Heidegger supply him with the main points of departure for his philosophizing. They are

---

[1] Heidegger's own reaction to Sartre's philosophy is not without interest. The occasion was Jean Beaufret's attempt to establish common ground after Sartre's lecture on "Existentialism." In declining this proposal, Heidegger contrasted Sartre's humanistic existentialism, as a philosophy for which there are "merely men," with his own thought that there is "principally Being" (thus not excluding a second-ary interest in man; *Brief über den Humanismus* p. 79 f.). Heidegger sees in Sartre's philosophy mainly a philosophical anthropology culminating in his existential psychoanalysis. He has, however, not commented publicly on Sartre's ontology nor on his phenomenology. One might anticipate that his criticisms would renew his objections to Husserl and to Descartes as subjectivists.

philosophically much nearer to him than is any contemporary French philosopher. There is only one French thinker to whom he may feel fundamentally even closer: Descartes. Sartre's persistent though qualified Cartesianism is also the basis for his greater methodological affinity to Husserl than to Heidegger. It also foreshadows the basic difference between his phenomenology and that of his closest rival, the anti-Cartesian Maurice Merleau-Ponty.

3. Sartre's Central Theme: Freedom versus Being

Sartre's most authentic statement of his fundamental objective thus far is contained in the closing paragraph of his latest book, *Saint Genet*: "To reconcile the object and the subject." [1] Such a phrase raises the obvious question: Why do the two need any reconciliation? Whence this strange warfare? The answer can perhaps best be given by reference to two fundamental experiences which Sartre describes in terms that leave little doubt about his personal involvement: the experience of freedom and the experience of "the Thing."

Introducing Descartes [2] as one of the Classics of Human Freedom, Sartre addresses to the philosophical defenders of freedom the question: "In connection with what privileged situation have you experienced your freedom?" If we return this question to Sartre himself, the answer must be culled chiefly from his literary production. Here some of his formulations are so striking and poignant that they clearly mirror Sartre's own experience.

A characteristic situation occurs, for instance, in Sartre's first philosophical novel, *La Nausée*. Here, after having made his decision to leave the small town world of Bouville (Sartre's Le Havre) and looking out over the sea, the hero reflects:

Is this what freedom is? ... I am free; there remains for me no reason to live. ... Alone and free. But this freedom slightly resembles death. (p. 220 f.)

---

[1] *Saint Genet*, p. 550. That this formula contains the clue to Sartre's enterprise is confirmed by Francis Jeanson's interpretation in *Sartre par lui-même*, p. 186.

[2] This little volume (*Descartes. Introduction et choix par J. P. Sartre*. Éditions des trois collines, 1946) contains a very revealing selection of texts from Descartes' writings and letters, in addition to Sartre's *Introduction*, which is republished in *Situations* I under the title "La liberté cartésienne" and translated in *Literary and Philosophical Essays*.

This rather uneasy and diffident experience of freedom soon gives way to a much more spectacular and positive expression, voiced by Orestes, the hero of *Les Mouches*, in his challenge to Zeus:

Suddenly freedom swooped down on me and penetrated me. Nature leaped back . . . And I have felt all alone in the midst of our little benign world, like someone who has lost his shadow. (*Théatre*, p. 101)

Then there is an even more personal and at the same time more social expression of the experience of freedom in a little essay on "*La République du silence.*" It was actually the Nazi occupation which elicited from Sartre the almost paradoxical statement:

Never have we been freer than under the German occupation. . . . The very question of freedom was posed, and we were at the verge of the most profound knowledge which man can have about himself. . . . This total responsibility in total solitude, wasn't this the revelation of our freedom? (*Situations* III, 11–14)

Closely related with this experience of freedom is for Sartre that of his own consciousness. It is by no means a very happy and reassuring one at the start. Sartre refers to it in his Baudelaire study in the following revealing sentence:

Each one of us has been able to observe in his childhood the unannounced and shattering appearance of the consciousness of his own self. (p. 217)

He illustrates this further by references to several French and English novels.

Clearly, Sartre's own experience of his consciousness and his freedom was never an easy and smug one. His freedom was at best embattled and threatened. What is the threat?

La Nausée shows its hero in the clutches of a peculiar metaphysical experience which he calls "nausea," but which has clearly very little to do with the common physiological variety of it. Circumstantial evidence indicates that Sartre himself underwent this experience, particularly during his period in Le Havre (the "Bouville" of the novel) as a teacher at the Lycée, the major part of which (1931–33) antedates his contact with German phenomenology. Nausea in this sense attacks its victim seemingly without a cause, for instance on picking up a slightly moist pebble on the beach. It reaches its climax at the sight of the sprawling root of the chestnut tree in a public park, and later grips him

even as he looks at the flesh (*chair*) of his own estranged body. Its
source is "the Thing" (*la Chose* with a capital C) [1] and its "existence" [2]. Massive, opaque, and sprawling, the Thing is to Sartre
essentially senseless, "absurd," "without *raison d'être*," and thus
"in excess" (*de trop*). But it is not merely a harmless nuisance.
It has an insidious aggressiveness. In fact, it "swoops down" on
man in his freedom (Sartre uses here the same verb "*fondre*"
which described Orestes' experience of freedom). It constitutes a
constant threat to freedom. *La Nausée* contains the record of
"the Thing's" attempt to engulf Antoine Roquentin and finally
convert him into thing-like "existence" and its final failure.
Later on Sartre finds this threat of "the Thing" most vividly
expressed in certain qualities of matter such as its viscosity;
particularly in his "existential psychoanalysis" of matter he
describes in considerable detail the way in which the soft
stickiness of the viscous tries to ensnare human freedom.

This second experience may at first sight sound like a ration-
alization of a personal idiosyncrasy, if not of a paranoid perse-
cution idea. But one may well wonder whether Bishop Berkeley's
phobia of matter or Fichte's battle with the Non-ego are not
expressions of a similar experience and attitude. Even to the
ordinary person the mere fact of inertia in matter may appear
as indifference, if not obstructiveness, to human purpose. Saying
this does not deny that some of Sartre's pseudo-anthropo-
morphisms include extravagances of expression which endanger
the defensible core of his experience.

I do not mean to imply that the experiences of freedom and
of the Thing can account for the whole range of Sartre's
thought and philosophy; for instance, the experience of the
human gaze seems to have been of similar intensity. But these
two seem to have been the ones at the root of Sartre's dualism –
the antagonism between the subjective and the objective, or, as
he calls it in *L'Être et le néant*, of the *pour-soi* and the *en-soi* which
calls for a reconciliation. Apparently these experiences precede
even Sartre's contacts with phenomenology. Our first task will

---

[1] *La Nausée*, p. 141; tr. p. 134. – According to both Sartre and Merleau-Ponty
"chosisme," perhaps rendered best as thing-thinking, is one of the major sins of most
scientific philosophy.

[2] At this stage Sartre still uses the term "existence" primarily for the being of
non-human objects, not for man's own being.

be to examine how this contact affected the struggle between the two poles of his universe.

Are there any deeper roots for Sartre's basic dualism? Francis Jeanson's recent semi-authentic presentation of Sartre, based in part on personal information he had received from the biographee, gives at least some clues for such a search. Thus Jeanson emphasizes the theme of bastardy, especially in Sartre's recent works. Even more significantly, he reports that Sartre himself, growing up as a half-orphan, suspected (contrary to all evidence) that he was illegitimate ("I was the false bastard") (p. 117). What is philosophically significant about this experience is that the bastard, more than anyone else, feels his existence in the world as "illegitimate," unjustified, unwanted, in need of [1] justification. Somehow this experience may have impressed Sartre as symbolic of the human condition in an alien and hostile world. It is perhaps characteristic that Sartre renders Heidegger's term "thrownness" (*Geworfenheit*) by "abandonment" (*délaisse-ment*). The essential bastardy of man, his uncertainty about his origins, may well have intensified his feeling about the basic antagonism between free man and "the Things."

Finally Jeanson reports (p. 187) this self-interpretation of Sartre: "The heart of the matter is: pride (*orgueil*): the choice to be someone, no matter who, and not to be a thing (*rien*). (Pride in this sense is not meant as a "sentiment which involves any idea of superiority over others, but on the contrary that of recognition, of the assurance that the same is true of them too"). It is in this context that Jeanson mentions Sartre's lasting debt to Husserl for having freed him by enabling him to eject (*évacuer*) the "things" from his consciousness. This suggests that it was "pride" in the first place which was responsible for the experience of the things as intruders into our freedom. Sartre's battle is the climax of the spirit of Promethean revolt against the universe which has been building up especially since the Romantic age. But it is more than blind revolt. It is at the same time the revolt of Cartesian reason whose light is needed to conquer the opaqueness of unconscious being. It also breathes something of the spirit of Kantian autonomy in its final ambition to bring about a kingdom of ends in which each freedom wants the freedom of the other.

4. The Role of Phenomenology in the Development of Sartre's Thought

There is clearly no easy solution to Sartre's problem of a reconciliation between subjective freedom and objective Being. Sartre did not arrive at his best known solution, that of *L'Être et le néant*, without a number of trials and failures. The scarcity of biographical material would make it unwise at this time to attempt a detailed reconstruction of his philosophical development. But enough is accessible to allow a sketch of the main phases of his thought with a view to determining the role of phenomenology in each of them. So I shall try to obtain an idea of what Sartre's thought was like before he came in intensive contact with phenomenology, what it looked like during the period characterized by his work in phenomenological psychology, what it became at the stage of the phenomenological ontology of *L'Être et le néant*, and finally how it has since then been modified under the name of existentialism.

a. SARTRE'S PRE-PHENOMENOLOGICAL PERIOD – Information about Sartre's first period is still very sketchy, indirect, and hardly reliable. Most authentic and illuminating would seem to me the reflection of the brief period between 1928 and 29 in the *Mémoires d'une fille rangée* by Simone de Beauvoir (pp. 272 to end). Only three minor pieces of his appeared during this phase. Two short stories were published in a short-lived little magazine, the *Revue sans titre* of 1923, when Sartre was still a student at the Lycee.[1] A semi-philosophical essay under the title "Légende de la verité" was published eight years later in *Bifur* (1931), which featured in the same issue Corbin's translation of Heidegger's "What is Metaphysics?". It is sufficiently attested, however, that during the interval, which includes his four years at the *École Normale*, his *agrégation*, and his military service in Tours, he wrote prolifically. Thus Beigbeder (p. 16) mentions an "important novel" under the significant title "*Défaite*," which was turned down by the publishers, and a collection of lost *Essais*, of which the article in *Bifur* is the only survivor. *Bifur* introduced Sartre on this occasion as "a young philosopher who is preparing a volume of destructive philosophy."

[1] See *Le Figaro Littéraire*, July 5, 1958.

The first short story of 1923, *"L'ange du morbide,"* deals with a young university professor who is fascinated by the phenomenon of "morbidity," which he pursues in an adventure with a tubercular girl, but who is promptly scared back into bourgeois mediocrity by the full truth of this ailment. It sounds like the defeat of the intellectual libertine in his attempt to conquer Being in one of its more nauseating aspects. "The Legend of Truth" presents in highly symbolic language a genealogy of truth based on the view that truth is nothing but a transition stage in human history, corresponding to the age of commerce, but due to be replaced by the standard of the "probable."

One other document from this period, a letter which Sartre sent to *Les Nouvelles littéraires* of February 2, 1929 in answer to an inquiry among French students of the time,[1] is perhaps even more revealing of Sartre's state of mind during this decade, particularly since it mentions explicitly some of the themes which he took up in his later philosophy. The letter contains, for instance, the following rather enigmatic and incoherent pronouncements:

It is the paradox of the human spirit ... that man, whose job it is to create the necessary, cannot raise himself to the level of being. ... It is for this reason that I see at the root of both man and nature sadness and boredom. This does not mean that man does not think of himself as something which is (*un être*). On the contrary, he puts all his efforts into it. Hence the Good and Evil, ideas of man working upon man. Vain ideas. A vain idea is also that determinism which tempts us strangely to produce the synthesis of existence (*existence*) and being (*être*). We are as free as you please, but powerless. ... Everything is too weak: all things tend to die. ...

"We are more unhappy but we inspire more sympathy" in comparison with the preceeding generation, Sartre is quoted as saying in an editorial of the same issue.

Insofar as such evidence permits one to draw any conclusion about Sartre's thinking and philosophizing, it certainly indicates a mood of utter perplexity and disillusionment: the human spirit unrelated to being, free but powerless to achieve a synthesis, truth and knowledge at best a myth.

Jeanson informs us that Sartre himself refers to this early

---

[1] It has since been republished in Simone de Beauvoir's *Mémoires d'une fille rangée* (Paris, Gallimard, 1958), pp. 341–2.

period as dominated by his "theological" attitude, i.e., by a need for the Transcendent (p. 175). This does not mean that he considered himself still a theist, since we are told that he abandoned belief in a God for good at the age of 11 (p. 173). What it does mean is that Sartre "wants to see in the seizure of each phenomenon a certain contact with Being itself, the presence of the Absolute in the relative, and that he believes that one does not become man unless one escapes from the relative condition of humanity." (p. 175) This desire for the Absolute seems to have persisted until the period of *La Nausée* (1938).

Up to this point, then, the urge for the Absolute ended in total failure, leaving freedom and Being unrelated and unreconciled. Apparently the French philosophy with which Sartre had come in contact in the course of his studies had failed to alter this metaphysical defeatism and pessimism. Why this failure? The answer may seem comparatively obvious in the case of French academic philosophy, especially of Brunschvicg's version of idealism. Its attitude toward the problem of Being must have seemed to Sartre nothing short of a shallow optimism. It is less obvious why Bergson's philosophy, which in so many ways anticipated German phenomenology, left him dissatisfied. Sartre's critique of Bergson is therefore of particular interest, although we know it only from the time after his decisive contact with Husserl, notably from *L'Imagination* (1936).

Here Bergson's theory of the imagination offers Sartre at first sight a promising alternative to Taine's associationist conception. However, his theory of creative synthesis, as examined in fourteen pages, still incurs Sartre's stricture for having nothing to offer but a syncretism of consciousness and thinghood, which also results in "perpetual ambiguity and perpetual shifting from one sphere to another without good faith." (p. 51) Sartre's general charge is that the state of mind created by Bergsonism is "a superficial optimism without good faith, which believes it has solved a problem when it has dissolved its terms in an amorphous continuity" (p. 68). What Sartre charges specifically is that Bergson's theory of the imagination leaves the image an inert thing, a "curdled" element; this too is a form of materialism or *chosisme*. Consciousness, to be sure, is represented in Bergson's creative intuition. But Bergson's consciousness, according to Sartre, is nothing separate from the things: it constitutes something like a substantial form for them. This leads to a confusion between the world and consciousness. It took Husserl to find the "liberating" distinction between the two. *L'Être et le néant* contains further strictures, though less violent ones. Among these are Sartre's criticisms of Bergson's inadequate concept of freedom, which remains an opaque *en-soi*, a mere passive "given." Likewise his duration (*durée*) is in Sartre's eyes merely a passive item, a substantialization of consciousness.

What all this adds up to is that Bergson's attempt to mediate between consciousness and the thing by way of an appeal to a vital principle at the root of both is not only precarious but blurs the issues. Besides, it introduces a passivism that Sartre cannot accept: freedom is saved only at the price of metaphysical adulteration. Bergson has not overcome *chosisme*, but actually strengthened its hold by assimilating consciousness to thinghood, as it persists even in a non-mechanistic metaphysics of life.

[1]   b. PHENOMENOLOGICAL PSYCHOLOGY – Thus far there is no way of telling how early Sartre came in contact with German phenomenology. There is of course every probability that during his philosophic studies at the *École normale* (1924–28) he became aware of the existence of such a movement, as the first accounts of it began to appear. Jean Wahl's reference to Bernard Groethuysen as having "launched the career of Sartre" [1] suggests that he may have had something to do with Sartre's first acquaintance with Husserl, Scheler, and Heidegger during the late twenties. [2] But there is not yet any explanation for the fact that the young agrégé of philosophy and professor at the Lycée of Le Havre became interested in a fellowship of the *Institut Français* in Germany, which lasted for two years (October 1932 to 1934). Sartre spent the first year chiefly in Berlin, studying particularly the works of Husserl, Scheler, Heidegger, Jaspers, and the psychoanalysts on his own and making only few important personal contacts, conceivably because his German was some-

---

[1] "The Present Situation and the Present Future of French Philosophy" in Farber, Marvin, ed., *Philosophic Thought in France and the United States*, p. 38.
[2] Did Sartre attend Husserl's Sorbonne lectures in February 1929 around the time of his *agrégation*? At least it is not unlikely that he saw the printed *Sommaire* now published in *Husserliana* I, 194–201.

what limited at the time. During the second year he went for the winter semester 1933–34 to Freiburg.[1] This was clearly not a particularly auspicious time for pursuing the study of phenomenology at its former center. Husserl had been working in retirement for four years, and there is no evidence for the clearly impossible story, found for instance in the accounts of Beigbeder and Lauer, that Sartre studied under Husserl, or even that he made his personal acquaintance. Heidegger was still *Rektor* of the University, and issued some of his strongest Nazi appeals during this very semester. He had announced a lecture course, "Fundamental Questions of Philosophy: Of Truth," presumably an expanded version of his momentous lecture of 1930 in which he had undertaken a new approach to Being no longer based on the hermeneutic phenomenology of *Sein und Zeit*, and a seminar on Nature, History, and the State. It seems that there were some contacts between the young French visitor and Heidegger, though of little consequence beyond the immediate academic situation.[2]

Thus far Sartre has not made more than casual references to his German experiences before the War and to their significance for him. Indications are that the permanent effect was based more on his private studies than on his contacts and exchanges with German phenomenologists. In any event he returned with the conviction that Husserl's *Ideen* was the most important book he had come across. Otherwise all we have to go on is the record of his publications after his return. These begin two years later with his critical discussion of the psychology of the imagination for a series called *"Nouvelle Encyclopédie philosophique,"* where

[1] I am indebted for these data to the then Director of the *Institut Français de Berlin*, M. Henri Jourdan.

[2] Heidegger does not seem to have retained a ready memory of such contacts prior to Sartre's Freiburg lecture of 1953. The following story, which I owe to Professor Louis Sauzin of the Université de Rennes, in charge of cultural affairs in the French zone of Germany during the early Occupation, reveals the nature of these contacts. When asked soon after the War about his early acquaintance with Sartre, Heidegger did not first remember him by name; then he identified him as "the Frenchman who had always confused him with Husserl." Sartre's primary interest at the time was clearly in Husserl. It was not until the period of *L'Être et le néant* that he became more keenly interested in Heidegger's own philosophy. His reaction to Heidegger personally was apparently negative. Thus, in commenting on Heidegger's political role, he stated publicly: "Heidegger n'a pas de caractère. Voilà la vérité." (*Action*, December 27, 1944; *Lettres*, Genève, I (1945) p. 83). Nevertheless, Sartre was one of the first to intercede for Heidegger after the French occupation of Freiburg to the extent of wanting him to be invited to Paris.

the climactic chapter on Husserl hails the appearance of the first volume of his yearbook (which also contained contributions by Pfänder, Scheler, and Geiger) as "certainly the great event of pre-(First World)-war philosophy." About the same time Sartre published his essay *"La Transcendance de l'égo,"* subtitled "Outline of a Phenomenological Description," in which he tried to push the phenomenological reduction even beyond Husserl's range by "reducing" the concept of the transcendental ego. The following years yielded not only several literary works, among them his first major success, *La Nausée,* but also two studies in phenomenological psychology, the *Esquisse d'une théorie des émotions* and *L'Imaginaire* in 1939 and 1940 respectively. Then followed another pause, explained by the War, by Sartre's nine months' captivity, by the German Occupation, by Sartre's activity in the Resistance Movement (group "Socialisme et Liberté)," and also by the preparation of his amazing production immediately after the Liberation. *L'Être et le néant,* his next major publication, marks his transition to "phenomenological ontology." It seems therefore legitimate to set off the preceding period as that of Sartre's phenomenological psychology. During this period Husserl is for him the outstanding exponent of phenomenology.

Comparing Sartre's literary output during this second period with that of the pre-phenomenological stage, one is struck by the complete difference in approach, which is not only scholarly and concrete, but free from scepticism and vague *Weltschmerz.* There seems to be no doubt in Sartre's mind that phenomenology can give us more than "legend" and probability. The probable, for instance in *L'Imaginaire,* is simply the fringe of empirical knowledge around the core of what phenomenology can determine as certain. At the same time phenomenology enables Sartre to make a fresh start, unhampered by traditional philosophy and psychology.

How far did this new approach help Sartre in solving his central problem, the relation between freedom and Being? At first sight, a novel like *La Nausée* may suggest that it did not. But it would be a mistake to see in the diary of Antoine Roquentin simply the record of his defeat before the nauseating "Thing." The end of the novel shows the sufferer from this metaphysical disease at least on the way to a cure after he has made it fully conscious. The "salvation" begins with the experience of the "rigor" he discovers in a jazz recording and with the plan to create something "beautiful ... durable like steel which will make people ashamed of their existence." In a similar vein the Conclusion of *L'Imaginaire* speaks of beauty as a realm beyond the reality of nauseating and unjustifiable existence, in which we can find a refuge. Husserl's phenomenology of essences would seem to be congenial to such a liberation. To this we may add Sartre's tribute to Husserl in his article in the *Nouvelle Revue Française*, where his idea of the intentionality of consciousness is invoked as being able to purge consciousness of the encroachment of the world. This does not yet suggest a "reconciliation" of Freedom and "the Thing," but it can at least serve as a protection and an escape into another dimension.

Superficially it is not easy to see the connection between this general motif and the topics of Sartre's first phenomenological publications.[1] Most prominent among these is the world of the imagination, to which Sartre devoted three separate publications between 1936 and 1939. Not only his own work as a fiction writer but his interest in freedom as embodied in the imagination can account for this particular interest.

Less obvious is Sartre's stake in the problem of the ego. The essay on the "Transcendence of the Ego," is actually an attempt to radicalize Husserl's phenomenology by showing that his transcendental or absolute ego was not the immanent identical pole of all our conscious acts, but the transcendent result of constitutive acts of consciousness.

Why does Sartre object to this central tenet of Husserl's phenomenology? I shall discuss his phenomenological reasons later. Apart from these he makes it clear that, compared to consciousness in its lightness and lucidity, the ego is something so opaque that he actually calls it "the death of consciousness" (p. 90; tr. 40). Removing the ego from the transcendental field thus means to

---

[1] A certain clue to the motivation for Sartre's selection may be found in the fact that Georges Gurvitch's critical observations on Husserl's philosophy in his *Les Tendances actuelles de la philosophie allemande* (pp. 57 ff.) deal both with the inadequacy of Husserl's distinction between perception and imagination and the difficulties raised by his conception of the pure ego, as if these represented the unfinished business of Husserlian phenomenology.

Sartre a final liberation from the thingness in favor of pure, free spontaneity (p. 117; tr. 93). This implies that transcendental consciousness is in itself impersonal and that "every moment of our conscious life reveals to us a creation out of nothing." Thus Sartre's concern for freedom actually goes so far as to dissolve even its owner, converting him into a string of products of acts. In fact spontaneity is something over which the self has no longer any control. No wonder Sartre sees something frightening (*angoissant*) in this pattern of a ceaseless impersonal creation of which we are not the creators (p. 119; tr. 98). However, Sartre hopes that such a conception will help in laying the spectre of solipsism; for it implies that one's own self no longer enjoys any priority over the selves of others, who are constituted likewise by the impersonal stream of consciousness. He also believes that this view can undermine a philosophy of inwardness like Brunschvicg's, which appears to him to be unsuited for realistic political action – a new concern which begins to take shape in Sartre's thinking.

Sartre's interest in a phenomenology of the emotions may at first sight seem equally surprising. No clue is given beyond the one that his "outline" can serve as an example of phenomenological psychology. What Sartre undertakes to show in this relatively brief study is that, contrary to the classical doctrine, illustrated by the James-Lange theory, and to the new psychoanalytic theories with their mechanisms, the emotions have meanings in the sense that they constitute purposive behavior. In particular, they are not simply passive states but "spontaneous degradations of consciousness"; as such they are basically insincere and "in bad faith." By way of emotions consciousness tries to reach its objective "magically" in running away from reality. The liberation from such an attitude presupposes a "purifying reflection," which is related to the phenomenological reduction and which will reveal the bad faith of the emotions. It stands to reason that Sartre's interest in the emotions is related to his concern for freedom, in opposition to the theories which make man a slave of his emotions and acquit him of all responsibility for them.

This same interest becomes even more explicit in the concluding part of *L'Imaginaire*, where the imagination in its essential detachment from the world of causal reality is used as a proof of freedom against determinism. Specifically, it is the negative or "irrealizing" function of the imagination in setting off the imagined world against the real world, which serves as the basis for the view that the imagination cannot be reduced to the world of positive causal forces. In this emphasis on the negative function of the imagination we can find anticipations of *L'Être et le néant*.

The method by which Sartre pursues these goals is meant to be strictly phenomenological in Husserl's sense, i.e., it is to consist of the application of both the eidetic and the transcendental reduction as Sartre interprets them. In his own eyes it has enabled him to reach certain knowledge in psychology and philosophy. Specifically, it has shown him that the ego is constituted by the acts of free consciousness, that the imagination is irreducible to any kind of perception which might enmesh it in the world of causality, and that the "magic" of the emotions is not a fatal threat to our freedom, but actually our own doing, for which we are fully responsible. It has also offered us a refuge in the esthetic world of imaginative creation outside the world of perceived reality.

But while all this established and vindicated the realm of freedom, it still left undetermined its relationship to the world of non-conscious Being. Its clarification will be the major task of Sartre's phenomenological ontology.

c. PHENOMENOLOGICAL ONTOLOGY – *L'Être et le néant*, published in 1943 while France was still under German occupation, contains Sartre's most ambitious and comprehensive attempt thus far to state his philosophical position. According to his own statement [1] it had been in the making since 1930, i.e., for thirteen years. Its 722 closely printed pages are thus clearly the final version of the volume of "destructive philosophy" on which Sartre had been working even before he had gone to Germany and come in contact with phenomenology.

The sub-title, "Outline of a *Phenomenological Ontology*," indicates the changed objective, compared with the studies in phenomenological psychology of his preceding period. Sartre

[1] See his "Questions de méthode," *Les Temps modernes* XIII (1957), 363.

now is ready to attack the problem of Being, the counterpart of free consciousness, and to relate the two. Phenomenology is considered capable of accomplishing this task.

Both the title and the subtitle invite immediate comparison with Heidegger's *Sein und Zeit*. There can be little question that Heidegger's book was very much on Sartre's mind in this enterprise, although he does not include a full-scale discussion of the work of his predecessor. Most of the incidental references [1] are highly critical. Also, for the first time Sartre brings out fundamental differences between Heidegger and Husserl.

A comparison of the two rival titles can show a good deal about both the similarities and the differences between Sartre's and Heidegger's respective ontologies. Taken superficially, the first words of the two titles have identical meanings, even though Sartre's *être* is usually not as rigidly opposed to the things-in-being (*existents*) as is Heidegger's *Sein:* often it stands for the whole of the world outside consciousness. The second and divergent parts of the two titles, "Time" and "Nothing," suggest a much more definite difference. But even the function of the two companions of Being is by no means the same in both works. Time in Heidegger's torso was meant to constitute the main property of Being, not anything opposed to it. "Nothing" in Sartre's larger and completed work is certainly not meant as a property of Being but as its great antagonist. The first paragraph of *L'Être et le néant* makes it plain that this dualism constitutes the fundamental problem of Sartre's ontology, not the attempt to understand Being through the Nothing, as Heidegger attempted to some extent to do in *Was ist Metaphysik?* The Nothing, which turns out to be none other than free consciousness, is actually the great challenger of Being and certainly more than the "horizon" for it, as is Heidegger's Time. Sartre's ultimate problem is to determine the remaining unity between Being and Nothingness.

It would be next to impossible to convey here an adequate idea of how Sartre develops this theme. At first sight it may appear like the queerest combination of the most forbidding ontology spiced with such weird attractions – never treated before in philosophical treatises – as the gaze, the anomalies of sex, nausea, and a new type of psychoanalysis applicable even to matter.

Such a collection outdoes even Heidegger's injection of themes like everyday-ness (*Alltäglichkeit*) or concern (*Sorge*), which, incidentally, hardly occur in Sartre's discussions. Suffice it to point out the general plot. The momentous Introduction, entitled "In Search of Being" – an obvious allusion to Marcel Proust's great novel – plunges the reader immediately into the struggle between consciousness, in Sartre's enlarged sense, which is only "for itself" (*pour soi*), and Being-in-itself (*en soi*), to which it refers by virtue of its intentionality. Significantly, the explicit discussion of Being-in-itself, which Sartre characterizes as intrinsically opaque and massive (as, incidentally, William James had already done in his essay on "The Sentiment of Rationality"), is restricted to a few pages of this introduction. The balance of the four following parts is devoted to "the Nothing," i.e., primarily to consciousness and its modifications.

The first part is concerned with the relation between "nothing" and the structure of consciousness: Consciousness as such, beginning with its questioning behavior, not only the imaginative consciousness, proves to be the opening wedge for the "nothing"; without it there would be no place for the "nothing" in the universe of Being. In fact, since consciousness sets itself off against Being by a fundamental act of negation, Sartre soon identifies the source of such negation, by way of a characteristic overstatement, with the nothing.

A second part deals more fully with the structure of this consciousness, first with its "immediate structures," such as its "facticity," then with its temporality, and with its "transcendence," i.e., its passing beyond itself, toward Being. Here, in spite of minor differences in emphasis, Sartre is probably closest to Heidegger, although he deliberately ascribes these characteristics to consciousness, rather than to *Dasein*.

The third part takes up in great detail a new subject, relatively neglected even by Heidegger: the relationship of one's own consciousness to that of others. Here a new type of being, being for others (*pour autrui*), makes its appearance. It is given when one's gaze (*regard*) looks into the other's gaze. The role of the body in the experience of one's own self and in the experience of the other's is explored. Finally, the drama of the relationships between consciousness and consciousness is interpreted as a fundamental conflict among incompatible freedoms, for which at the time Sartre did not seem to see any clear constructive solution.

The last part looks almost like a new beginning based on the active and free nature of consciousness. Here, in supposed contrast to Heidegger, Sartre stresses the activistic features of human existence. Absolute freedom and responsibility provide the foundation, and man's being is derived from his doing. It is based on an original choice, to be explored by a new existential psychoanalysis on phenomenological grounds.

The "Conclusion" of the book formulates the final relationship between consciousness and Being, as it emerges from the preceding "ontology," and states some of its "metaphysical" and moral implications.

What is Sartre's new solution of his fundamental problem, the dual conflict between free consciousness and "the Thing"? At first sight there could hardly be any more irreconcilable opposition than that between Being and Nothing. However, Sartre believes that his interpretation of consciousness as a negation of Being allows him to achieve a new and genuine synthesis. For the lucidity of consciousness, its lack of massive opaqueness, also implies a privation or lack of Being. Like Hegel, he calls it metaphorically a hole in the midst of Being, a decompression of its fullness. Moreover consciousness, which feeds on Being, is at the same time its disintegrator. This strange negative symbiosis may well suggest the analogy of a cancer: consciousness could not exist without Being as its soil, yet it preys on it. By contrast, Being could very well exist without consciousness and has in this sense ontological priority. All this sounds like a weird if original Neo-Platonism turned upside down, with "matter" as the starting point and the spirit as the negative derivation from it. Thus the new unity is bought at the price of the primacy of Being over consciousness. Yet the fact remains that in all its negativity consciousness still has the positive freedom of introducing meaning into the meaningless universe of Being. Specifically, consciousness provides not only an opening for nothingness, but also for possibility and for the past and future dimensions of temporality, which could not exist without the soil of consciousness. Moreover, consciousness proves to be the counterpart of Sartre's conception of a "world" (*monde*), in which the two form a system of mutual reference. Here, then, in the circuit between consciousness and its world ("*circuit d'ipseité*") we find indeed something like a reconciliation of the subjective and the objective, based upon the active project by which consciousness cuts a clearing through the jungle of Being. The "world" in contrast to Being is indeed dependent upon consciousness and its choice; in this sense and to this extent even a phenomenological idealism would be defensible. However, in spite of such relative achievements, the fundamental choice of consciousness in Sartre's interpretation condemns it not only to freedom but also to the impossible project of being absolute, i.e., of combining consciousness (or nothingness) in its essential lucidity with being-in-itself in its essential opaqueness. The self-contradictoriness of such a conception in Sartre's terms entails not only his notorious atheism (which is really an "ontological" disproof based on the definition of God as the for-itself-in-itself, i.e., the conscious Absolute), but, much more seriously, the essential futility of the human enterprise as the attempt to become God, which Sartre calls a "useless passion" (*passion inutile*).

Thus the active freedom of consciousness can achieve at best a Pyrrhic victory over Being. The reconciliation of the subjective and the objective is ultimately secured at the expense of the subject. Only in a few minor places, e.g., in discussing the social and moral perspectives of his ontology, does Sartre hint at the possibility of a less disheartening alternative. (See, e.g., the footnotes to *EN* 111; tr. 70, *EN* 484; tr. 413, and the last pages of the book.)

Where, in this grandiose and at times highly speculative panorama, does phenomenology come in? How far is it to be credited for it, how far discredited by it? Much, particularly the derivation of consciousness from Being in its dogmatic assertiveness, sounds more like a mythological phantasmagoria than like phenomenology. There is in the whole work no explicit discussion of phenomenology as such, as it can be found in most of Sartre's preceding writings. A few subsections, notably those on the conception of the nothing and on the three temporal dimensions, are labelled as phenomenological and are seemingly contrasted to the adjacent "dialectical" or "ontological" discussions. But, especially in view of the subtitle of the whole work, there can be little doubt that Sartre did not mean to restrict phenomenology to these portions but considered it as basic to his entire ontology. Besides, analyses like those of negativity or of the gaze are certainly phenomenological in the sense of his earlier analyses, although they are not labelled so explicitly. Nevertheless, the role of the phenomenology implied in different sections of the book varies, and even his phenomenological "descriptions" differ considerably in character in different parts of the book. In general Sartre is apt to begin with descriptive analyses but to push them soon in the direction of hermeneutic interpretations far beyond what immediate inspection would seem to warrant. A particularly interesting development of hermeneutics is Sartre's existential psychoanalysis, an attempt to replace the speculative constructions of psychoanalysis by the "deciphering" of a person's conscious though pre-reflexive choices.

One feature of Sartre's style in *L'Être et le néant* calls for special comment, his new fondness for paradoxical and baffling formulations, which at times suggest even plays on words. Among the latter there is for instance the description of consciousness as "that which is what it is not, and is not what it is," a formulation which is meant to express that man in his freedom is essentially a projection of what he is not yet and has to be, and that he is at the same time the being which escapes from his essence as expressed in his past and which he hence no longer is (*EN*, p. 515; tr. 439). Even further goes the identification of consciousness with nothingness on the basis of its negative function (*néantisation*), an obvious but by now characteristic overstatement.

Formulations of this type suggest an increased tendency toward Hegelian dialectics which does not appear in Sartre's earlier writings. One might suspect this even more in the case of Sartre's concepts of the In-itself, (*en-soi*), the For-itself (*pour-soi*), and the In-itself-for-itself (*en-soi-pour-soi*), which may seem to be taken immediately from Hegel's system. But the meanings of these terms in Sartre are not identical with those in Hegel and the Hegelians (see *EN* 138 note; tr. 94). The same is true of Sartre's additional category, the For-others (*pour autrui*), which can be traced before him to Alfred Fouillée. Nevertheless, it is true that in *L'Être et le néant* references to Hegel are almost as numerous as those to Husserl or Heidegger. In this respect Sartre's book reflects the vogue of Hegel's phenomenology in the France of the middle thirties. However, in Sartre's case it affects more his formulations than his substantial conclusions, much as Hegelian motifs can be spotted for instance in his social philosophy of the period (e.g., in his thesis that "each consciousness wants the death of other consciousnesses").

d. Phenomenological existentialism – The name "existentialism," which is conspicuous by its complete absence from *L'Être et le néant*, seems to have been espoused by Sartre only after initial protest. It occurs first in print in his concise "clarification" (*Mise au point*) in reply to communist attacks in *Action* of December 20, 1944.[1] But Sartre's existentialism became best known in the form which he gave it in his lecture "Existentialism is a Humanism" of 1946. Actually this formulation is largely an apologia of existentialism in reply to both communist and Catholic attacks combined with a rather dogmatic statement of his new ethics of "authenticity" which he had hinted at in the last pages of *L'Être et le néant*, and which has been promised repeatedly as part of a work to bear the significant title *L'Homme*. In the absence of real substantiation and development of its theses Sartre himself seems to have considered its publication a mistake,[2] although he did not interfere with its continued wide circulation.

What is much more important than the new label is of course the question whether it signifies a new stage in the development of Sartre's thought and a new solution of his basic problem. That it does so is suggested immediately by the espousal of the word "humanism," which had been a target of derision in Sartre's earlier literary work. Now existentialist humanism is presented as a new and different form of humanism, whose main contention is that there is nothing but a human universe, which results from man's self-transcending projects and is constituted by human

[1] Republished in *Lettres*, Genève, I (1945), 82–88. See also Maurice Merleau-Ponty, *Sens et non-sens*, p. 96, and Francis Jeanson, *Le Problème moral et la pensée de Sartre*, p. 344.

[2] See, e.g., F. Jeanson, *op. cit* p. 46.

subjectivity. This humanism is advocated even more explicitly and belligerently in the play *Le Diable et le bon Dieu* (*Lucifer and the Lord*) of 1951. Its emphasis is both atheistic and social ("There are only men"). In fact, Sartre declares that the simultaneous existence of both God and man is incompatible: "If God exists, man is nothing; if man exists. . . ." One may well wonder whether this arresting formulation, in which existence is opposed to nothingness, does not imply a rejection of the ontology of *L'Être et le néant*, especially since the thesis that "man is nothing" is now assigned to Goetz-Sartre's main antagonist, the theist Heinrich. More significant in this sense may be the fact that Sartre's recent writings, though not directly concerned with ontology, move away from the negativistic interpretation of existence which dominates *L'Être et le néant* and take on a much more positive tenor. No longer does Sartre describe the human enterprise in terms of a "useless passion." Instead he professes an "extreme but hard optimism" in the name of man's total freedom and total responsibility for his world.

Even more striking is the change in Sartre's social philosophy. Instead of the previous stress on the basic and deadly conflict of freedoms in the social field, he now tells us that in choosing our own freedom we choose freedom for all our fellow-beings, and that there can be such a thing as a pact of freedoms as exemplified by the relation between the writer and his readers. This is the period when Sartre becomes "engaged" in political action, and when existentialism acts as the philosophy of political commitment (*engagement*). The occasion for this new turn was the experience of the Resistance Movement, in which Sartre had taken an active part, followed by the era of liberation and painful reconstruction. In this new situation Sartre's liberation of human existence, instead of taking the form of escape into the world of beauty and artistic creation, finds its prime expression in the social struggle and, more specifically, in the commitment to the cause of social revolution in the interest of the least free members of society, the proletariat. But while Sartre thus accepts the Marxist diagnosis of the class struggle, he rejects all the more strongly the metaphysics of the dialectical materialism that underlies it. Nor is Sartre's political commitment absolute and total. Politics is the realm of the relative, and his temporary tactical alliances with the Communists were just as conditional as was his abortive attempt in 1949 to bring about a non-communist "Revolutionary Democratic Rally."

But Sartre's political activity does not mean that he has abandoned his vaster enterprises. One recent proof of his continuing philosophical interests is his second-largest prose work, a 550-page biographical essay introducing an edition of the complete works of Jean Genet, the author of the scandalous best-seller, the *Journal d'un voleur*. In more than one sense this work represents a puzzler. Ostensibly its aim is

to show the limits of psychoanalytic interpretation and of Marxist explanation and demonstrate the idea that freedom alone can account for a personality in his totality; to exhibit this freedom at grips with destiny, at first crushed by its fateful blows, then turning against them in order to digest them gradually; to prove that genius is not a gift, but the way out a person invents in desperate cases; to rediscover the choice which a writer makes of himself, his life, and the meaning of the universe down to the formal characteristics of his style and of his composition, reaching into the structure of his imagery and the peculiarity of his tastes; in short to retrace in detail the history of a liberation. (p. 536)

Such a demonstration of Sartre's existential psychoanalysis on an unprecedented scale is of course apt to bring in some of the basic questions of his philosophy, especially his unfinished ethics, and to throw light on its growth. Whether of not it will stand out eventually as "the capital work of contemporary philosophy" (Jeanson) can remain undecided for the time being, particularly in view of the much more modest claims of its author.

What does this work contribute to the solution of Sartre's fundamental problem? According to his own intentions it represents an attempt to push to the extreme the analysis of the subjective side in man's being. As such, so Sartre suggests, it has to be matched by the objective approach of Marxism. For, as he now sees it, the reconciliation of the object and the subject by a "last effort" can take place only "if we have the courage to go to the limit of ourselves in both directions simultaneously" (p. 550). While the need of these two enterprises makes sense for any project to understand man and his world, one wonders why such a move, i.e., to ride off in opposite directions should offer any special hope for a reconciliation. In the meantime, this program would seem to imply that Sartre, while defending the rights of the subjective approach against its objectivist opponents, wants to reserve a place for the more objective methods of the social sciences as being of equal significance.

Phenomenology as such is mentioned only once explicitly. The context is Sartre's attempt to trace Genet's original choice of becoming a thief, of which he tries to give what he now calls a "phenomenological description" (p. 57). However, this passage leaves little doubt that the whole enterprise of interpreting Genet's development – and particularly his "metamorphoses" from orphan to thief, esthete, writer, and man – constitutes for Sartre a case study in existential psychoanalysis, hence a phenomenological enterprise, although it represents applied phenomenology rather than phenomenology as a generalized study. It should be noted, however, that this phenomenology is applied to the subjectivity of another person, in that sense to an objective fact. – It seems that Sartre's project of a detailed autobiography will put his method to an even more direct test.

Thus phenomenology continues to be an integral part of Sartre's philosophizing, even in its latest existentialist phase. Its foundation is the fact that existence is to Sartre primarily a subjective phenomenon based on Cartesian consciousness. As such it calls for a special approach, that of phenomenological description and interpretation. It is this insistence on the essential subjectivity of existence which provides the ultimate reason for Sartre's combination of phenomenology and existentialism. The priority of consciousness and of phenomenology is at the same time the reason why Sartre's existentialism is incompatible with any type of orthodox dialectial materialism.[1]

[1]

5. Sartre's Conception of Phenomenology

Is there anything distinctive about Sartre's version of phenomenology? More than in other cases it will be important to distinguish between Sartre's theory of phenomenology and his

---

[1] At the time this manuscript went to print, Sartre's book, *Questions de méthode*, announced for early publication in 1958 had not yet appeared. Judging from the "fragments" printed in two installments of *Les Temps modernes* (1957), this very illuminating restatement of existentialism in its relation to Marxism will not add a great deal to Sartre's general methodology; its "dialectics" attempts to do equal justice to the objective elements of the situation stressed by orthodox Marxism and to the subjective "projects," which are the major factor in individual "existence."

actual practice of it. His interest in the theory of phenomenology is in fact only incidental. None of his works carries the word "phenomenology" in its main title. Also, his explicit discussions of the phenomenological method date chiefly from the period when he was most under the influence of Husserl and to a lesser degree of Heidegger. Thus his *Esquisse d'une théorie des émotions* of 1939 contains a ten-page introduction dealing with the relationship between psychology, phenomenology, and phenomenological psychology, in which the main emphasis is on the connection between empirical psychology and phenomenological psychology. Phenomenological psychology is introduced as the basis for empirical study; but it is never suggested that it should take its place. Accordingly, in what furnishes probably the purest example of such a phenomenological psychology, his *L'Imaginaire* (1940), Sartre separates strictly the phenomenologically certain from the merely empirically probable, drawing freely on the hypotheses and experimental evidence of traditional psychology. It is, however, noteworthy that in his theoretical discussion Sartre charges phenomenology with the additional task of finding "synthetic unity" within the phenomena analyzed by empirical science, and with determining their significance as goal-directed ways of behavior (*conduites*); the chief instance of such a hermeneutic interpretation is that of the emotions. While phenomenological psychology is thus characterized as an eidetic description of essential relationships of behavior, it is at the same time presented as hermeneutics in Heidegger's sense.

No parallel discussion can be found at the stage of *L'Être et le néant*, particularly not concerning the relationship between phenomenology and ontology, nor has such a discussion appeared thus far at the stage of Existentialism. This leaves us with the task of trying to determine Sartre's general conception of phenomenology from the theory implicit in his phenomenological studies. I shall approach it by determining first the ground which Sartre's phenomenology and that of his German predecessors has in common and by subsequently bringing out some of his most characteristic innovations.

a. THE COMMON GROUND – At first sight Sartre's conception of phenomenology might seem to fit easily into the general framework of Husserl's phenomenology. His phenomenological studies are always introduced as descriptive and contrasted to explanatory hypotheses. Intuition is more or less explicitly invoked as the final test of all phenomenological claims. Reflection is its supposed basis. Eidetic insight into essences is stressed, particularly at the stage of the phenomenological psychology, and certainly never rejected on principle, even though Sartre later criticizes Husserl's *"pointillism of essences."* Also, at least before Sartre published *L'Être et le néant*, the appeal to phenomenological reduction or *epoché* is for him almost a matter of course, even though its actual application does not become manifest in the form of a step-by-step procedure, but rather as a fairly summary bracketing (*mise-en-parenthèses*). In its "purifying function" it is, for instance, credited with being able to show the "magic" function of the emotions in our relationship to the world (*Esquisse*, p. 49). The phenomenological reduction is however not very prominent in *L'Être et le néant*. In fact, in discussing our consciousness of the other, Sartre expresses serious doubts that such a method can give us any help, since an element of falsifying abstraction is involved (*EN* 330; tr. 271). Eventually, in his paper before the *Société française de philosophie* (1947) he stated: "(In Husserl) we begin with the world of our knowledge, we leave it by the phenomenological *epoché*, and we never return to the world ·from the *epoché*." And he goes on to complain about philosophers dragged from Plato's cave who refuse to re-enter it, while in fact it is in the cave that one has to think and to act (p. 55). He leaves plenty of scope, however, for Husserl's conception of phenomenological constitution. For Sartre attributes to consciousness the function of constituting the world of our experience, at least as far as its meanings are concerned. However, just as in Husserl's case, it is not always easy to make out what constitution in Sartre's sense involves.

This adoption of Husserl's main methodological terminology and of what it stands for does not prevent Sartre from assimilating a considerable number of concepts from Heidegger's hermeneutic phenomenology. Thus he takes over unquestioningly the latter's conception of the phenomenon as "what reveals itself." He espouses Heidegger's project of a hermeneutics as a legitimate enterprise, in fact even within the framework of a descriptive phenomenology. And he shares Heidegger's criticism of Husserl's enterprise as ignoring the problem of Being as far as consciousness is concerned in favor of its mere essence. But there remains one momentous difference: Heidegger's phenomenology was pointedly a phenomenology of *Dasein*, of human Being, as contrasted to Husserl's consciousness. In contrast to Heidegger, Sartre conceives of this *Dasein* (*réalité humaine*) again as consciousness. In this sense even his ontology of consciousness remains closer to Husserl than to Heidegger. In fact, Sartre's conception of consciousness, like Husserl's, sails under the traditional French flag of the *cogito*, which Heidegger repudiates. Thus Sartrianism is ultimately a form of Cartesianism, although it rejects most of Descartes' metaphysics. Its motto is: "One must start from the *cogito*" (*EN* 115 f.; tr. 74).

b. DISTINGUISHING CHARACTERISTICS – However, Sartre's return to consciousness as the basic theme of phenomenology by no means implies that Sartre conceives of it in the same way as Husserl or Descartes does. We shall select the most important differences before formulating the basic originality of Sartre's position.

(*I*) *The Elimination of the Transcendental Ego and Its Final Significance: Phenomenology of Human Existence.* Sartre's very first attempt at "phenomenological description," his article on "The Transcendence of the Ego," for all its admiration of Husserl and even its acceptance of Husserl's phenomenological reduction and constitution, is based on a momentous dissent from Husserl, the rejection of his concept of the transcendental ego. Beginning with his *Ideen*, Husserl had not only admitted the phenomenon of an ego as part of the indubitable field of consciousness, but had also developed a whole doctrine which, under the formidable name of "egology," was to account for the constitution of the transcendental field. In an authorized and much discussed article by his then assistant and collaborator Eugen Fink, this ego had actually proliferated into a trinity of egos. Sartre's article was the first full-scale challenge to this new egology. However, it did not go as far as to deny the ego, after the manner of David Hume. Nevertheless, to Sartre the ego was "transcendent," no longer "transcendental"; in non-technical language: the ego is not part of the original structure of consciousness but something that grows out of its constantly renewed stream by constituting acts. These acts support and relate all objects, whether external or internal, to which consciousness refers.

What are Sartre's reasons for this apparent retreat from an insight which Husserl himself had accepted only slowly in the years after the appearance of the *Logische Untersuchungen*? Some seem to be direct. While Sartre admits that whenever we reflect upon an experience we always find it associated with an experiencing "I," he claims that in the unreflected experience, for instance that of reading a book, all that is given is the book and its characters but without the reading "I" (p. 86; tr. 46 f.). Implicitly (*athétiquement*) we are also conscious of the act of reading. But the reading "I" is only a modification added by the reflection which constitutes it. However, Sartre's main reason for denying the "I" transcendental status is that he finds it to be unnecessary and hence useless, a reason which sounds more like the logic of Occam's razor than like phenomenology. An additional and, to Sartre himself, possibly more weighty reason is that to him an identical ego in the flux of consciousness would mean a threat to the unity of consciousness, a divisive principle like an "opaque blade," which would result in the "death of consciousness" (p. 90; tr. 40). Only an impersonal consciousness is completely transparent in Sartre's sense.

There is no need to evaluate this reasoning here.[1] It is more important to appraise its significance for Sartre's conception of phenomenology. To be sure, it leaves the transcendental sphere as such intact: the now "impersonal" stream of consciousness without an "I" is the constituting foundation for the Ego, as it is for the other phenomena of the world. Consequently the ego now "makes its appearance at the level of humanity." In other words, what was previously the hinge of phenomenology has now been transferred into the world of human existence; the self is a phenomenon among others in the human world. Sartre actually

---

[1] See my paper on "Husserl's Phenomenology and Existentialism," *Journal of Philosophy* LVII (1960), 71 ff.

takes special pride in the fact that his new conception puts phenomenology back into the thick of human reality rather than making it withdraw from reality into the refuge of transcendentalism – a motif, to be sure, which differs strangely from the escapism of *L'Imaginaire*.

This still leaves to impersonal transcendental consciousness the role of the ultimate root of all phenomena. Sartre has never explicitly repudiated the doctrine of a transcendental realm. It merely seems to be withering away in the further development of his own phenomenology, first psychological and later ontological. For in his actual analyses Sartre deals only with the consciousness which appears on the level of man, the constituted ego, his imagination, his emotions, and his relationship to the human world. In other words, Sartre's actual phenomenology establishes itself completely on the level of human existence. It is this tacit dropping out of the transcendental dimension and the implied humanization or "mundanization" of consciousness which constitute the most significant change in Sartre's version of Husserlian phenomenology. This is the turning point at which phenomenology becomes a phenomenology of human existence concerned with the phenomena as they occur in the context of concrete human existence, including the concrete world of the individual writer or worker.

Except for its interpretation of existence as a form of consciousness, then, Sartre's phenomenology coincides with a philosophy of existence in Heidegger's sense (*existentielle Philosophie*) – a philosophy which Heidegger himself specifically disclaimed – though not with his analytics of existence, which deals only with the ontological categories of existence. But there remains a more important difference between Sartre's and Heidegger's conceptions of existence. It can be derived from Sartre's much quoted though rather baffling formula "Existence precedes essence." This means that to Sartre the "essence," i.e., the character of man, is the outcome of his free acts. Hence he uses "existence" as the title for the concrete consciousness of man in its free creativity. By contrast, Heidegger's "existence" is usually nothing but the possibility of authentic or inauthentic being, which supposedly forms the essence or at least one of the major constituents of the essence of man. Hence for Heidegger

existence is certainly not the "preceding" source of the essence
of man, as it is for Sartre.

Related to this property of Sartre's "existence" is the fact
that, contrary to all customary usage, he uses the verb "to exist"
at times transitively, speaking, e.g., of "existing one's body."
What is involved is that our consciousness may or may not
assume and maintain our body in the way by which we live in
and through it. In other words, Sartre is not only concerned with
existence as a particular mode of Being. Existence is to him the
concrete behavior of a human being in his conscious situation
within an experienced world and responding to it. This almost
sounds like the program of a philosophical anthropology. While
the vagueness of this oversold term makes such a classification
a rather moot issue, Sartre would presumably claim that his
enterprise is even more basic than the philosophical anthropology of Max Scheler, its best known rival in this field.

(2) *Pre-Reflective Consciousness. Reflection and Phenomenology.* For Sartre, existence does not simply coincide with
human consciousness in the world. One of his most important
additions to earlier phenomenology is his enlarged conception
of consciousness. There is for Sartre such a thing as a "non-
conscious" consciousness under the name of pre-reflective
consciousness. Even for Husserl, though possibly not for Descartes, not all consciousness is reflexive. He knows a naive
consciousness, directed straight ahead (*geradeaus*) toward objects
of our daily or scientific concerns, which differs essentially from
its reflective modification, in which this naive consciousness
becomes thematic. Phenomenology consists largely in a further
stage in the development of this reflective consciousness.

Sartre, however, does not stop with a reflective consciousness
in which our own acts are the explicit theme of our reflection.
He raises the question of how we know about our own reflective
acts. If we say "by a further act of reflection," this involves us
in an infinite regress. If we assert that reflective acts are themselves not in need of further reflection ("To know is to know
that one knows," as (E. Chartier-) Alain used to say, following
the tradition of Spinoza), we fly in the face of the phenomena.
For even in clear knowing, as in any other form of consciousness,

in which we are absorbed in the objects known straight ahead of us, we are by no means always explicitly aware of our knowing. Sartre's solution consists in directing us to a peculiar awareness of our acts other than thematic consciousness by explicit re-flection. This "non-thetic" consciousness (*conscience*) constitutes a phenomenon different in kind from explicit knowledge (*con-naissance*). He calls it "pre-reflective consciousness" or the "pre-reflective *cogito*." It accompanies all our direct consciousness of objects as well as our acts of reflexion. It is in this pre-reflective quality that he also sees the mode of being of our consciousness. He illustrates it by the consciousness we have of counting numbers without reflecting upon this activity of ours.

In pre-reflective consciousness our reflecting actually coincides with that upon which we reflect. Thus to Sartre it makes no sense to distinguish between pleasure and our (pre-reflective) consciousness of pleasure: pleasure is essentially conscious. In fact he suggests that it is really misleading to speak of a con-sciousness of pleasure. At least the preposition "of" (*de* ...) should here be put between parentheses: "consciousness (of) pleasure."

The significance of the introduction of such a new type of consciousness – which may not be as new among phenome-ologists as Sartre believes, and can be traced not only in Husserl's *Ideen* (§ 77), but in the writings of Pfänder and Geiger – goes considerably beyond the mere addition of another phenomenon. Pre-reflective consciousness is to Sartre the means to extend the Cartesian *cogito* far enough to embrace all of human existence; and it allows us to see in consciousness its basic factor. In a way this is the triumph of Cartesianism, though at the price of a further decrease in its clearness and distinctness; yet it makes it possible for reflection to bring about eventual clarification and distinctness. It reveals at the same time what are the tasks and the chances of a phenomenology of such an expanded consciousness.

Even according to Sartre phenomenological description proper is based on explicit acts of reflection. But here Sartre makes further distinctions: reflection can be pure or impure ("*ac-complice*") reflection. This distinction, however, occurs in the context of a rather involved discussion of the temporal structure

of consciousness, and is not fully developed. Moralizing connotations intrude, especially in connection with the idea of a
purifying reflection. Thus it is hinted that purifying reflection
can break the vicious cycle which condemns to utter failure our
relations with others. Impure reflection is also characterized as
the one which "constitutes" the ego with its psychological states
and qualities (EN 206 ff; tr. 159 ff.). It stands to reason that pure
reflection must have something to do with the recovery of the
pristine innocence of a consciousness which does not lose itself
in as futile an enterprise as the attempt to achieve absolute being.
But no definite text would authorize an interpretation according
to which the phenomenological method coincides with such a
purifying reflection. There are indications, however, that Sartre
will assign to phenomenological reflection an important role in
his ethics.

(3) *The Negative Character of Consciousness.* Probably the most
original feature in Sartre's conception of consciousness is his
insistence on its essential negativity; neither Husserl nor Heidegger gives the negative function such a central place.

As early as in Sartre's studies in phenomenological psychology,
especially those on the imagination, one can observe a somewhat
unusual emphasis on the negative element: imagination poses
its object as a nothing, i.e., as non-existing, absent, existing
elsewhere. In *L'Être et le néant* we start with a sober analysis of
interrogation as called for by the ontological problem, not unlike
the discussion with which Heidegger introduced the question
of Being in *Sein und Zeit*. But in Sartre the main emphasis is on
the implied possibility of an answer by "yes" or "no," and, by
implication, upon the readiness to be faced by the non-existence
of the situation inquired about. The question thus reveals that
"nothings" (*néants*) are constant possibilities of our experience.
In fact consciousness is shot through with "nothings": it appears
not only as the foil to Being, as in Heidegger, but it is immanent at
at the heart of Being, "like a worm" (EN 57; tr. 21). Hence
Heidegger's merely positive characterization of *Dasein* is misleading.

But what does Sartre mean by "nothing"? Its primary
manifestations are such phenomena as absences, gaps, missing

parts in the total field of Being. For these ontic phenomena Sartre coined the term *"negatités"* (negativities). This does not mean that he hypostatizes nothingness into an entity on a level with Being – a view which can be ascribed to some extent to Heidegger, who conceives of the Nothing as the permanent background of Being. To Sartre, Being in its fullness has no room for such negativities as absences. Absences are something which "comes into the world" and is actualized only by the expectations of a conscious being. In this sense it would also be legitimate to speak of the Nothing as constituted by consciousness or, more precisely, as relative to its questions and expectations.

Soon, however, Sartre makes the much bolder assertion that "the being through which the nothing comes into the world must be its own nothing," an assertion which allows him to characterize consciousness itself as a nothing. This characteristic overstatement does not mean that consciousness does not exist. What it does seem to mean is that the negative function is the most characteristic feature in consciousness, compared with non-conscious beings. Other formulations suggest that consciousness consists of a peculiar dialectical mixture of being and non-being, which need not be considered here in detail.

(4) *Freedom.* For Sartre, the negative aspect of consciousness is closely connected with another basic feature, its freedom; in fact, he uses the terms at times synonymously. The connection of freedom with the structure of consciousness is not entirely new in phenomenology. Husserl had often stressed the free consciousness of "I can" as an important part of our consciousness of the world and its objects, e.g., in *Ideen* II, 60. For Heidegger, freedom was linked particularly with the "essence of truth" as its "foundation" in a sense that need not concern us here. But nowhere among phenomenologists has freedom been so completely identified with the very structure of consciousness as in Sartre's thought.

Sartre's insistence on freedom may at first appear not only extreme but dogmatic, reminding one at times of Fichte. But that does not mean that he has never tried to demonstrate the existence of such freedom by direct methods rather than by attempts to discredit his deterministic opponents. There are, for instance, his phenomenological studies of the imagination, in which he tries to show that imaginative consciousness presupposes the capacity of standing off from the world of causal associations in a way which emancipates consciousness from them. But soon Sartre decides that this capacity is the condition of every kind of consciousness in which we take cognizance of the world. It presupposes an emancipation and even a negation of the world of causal order, from which consciousness has to unhinge itself, as it were, in order to be itself.

No matter how convincing these "arguments" may be, Sartre's primary evidence is clearly the direct consciousness of his freedom in determining the meaning and direction of his own existence. This freedom appears to him so unlimited that he does not hesitate to call it absolute. It should not be overlooked, however, that in describing it he always shows it as imbedded in a given situation. It never is credited with the power of doing away with the situation as such but only with that of changing its meaning within the framework of freely chosen projects. Besides, freedom has to cope with "factors of adversity." Nevertheless, consciousness is permeated by the sense of its absolute freedom to choose its projects and thus to define the meaning of the situations with which it finds itself confronted.

(5) *Anguish* constitutes almost the most notorious, if not actually ridiculed, category of existentialism. This does not mean that it stands everywhere for the same thing. In the present context it is of particular importance to realize the difference between Sartre's and Heidegger's conception of it. Heidegger's anxiety (*Angst*) is the privileged access to the phenomenon of the Nothing, and as such related to our consciousness of Being as a whole. Sartre's anguish (*angoisse*) has a much more limited and practical concern, notably our own freedom. For freedom sets consciousness apart from man's own essence as sedimented in his past:

I emerge alone and in anguish in the face of the unique and prime project which constitutes my being; all the barriers and hand-rails give way, annihilated by the consciousness of my freedom. I do not have, nor can I have, any recourse to any value to protect me from the fact that it is I who keep all values in existence; nothing can give me assurance against myself, cut off as I am from the world and from my essence by the nothing that I am. I have to realize the sense of the world and of my essence: I decide about it alone, without possible justifications and excuses." (*EN* 77; tr. 39)

A passage like this, which is typical of Sartre at his persuasive best and his overstating worst, should make it clear that Sartre's anguish has nothing to do with cowardly timidity in the face of real or imaginary dangers. It expresses man's response to his assumed responsibilities, which in Sartre's case are particularly overwhelming since they embrace no less than the meaning of his world as a whole. On the other hand, this passage includes in its sweep such phenomenologically surprising assertions as the dependence of all values upon our freedom, which Sartre asserts in a number of other places, but without attempting any real demonstration. Suffice it to say that in cases like these Sartre seems to be starting from original and significant observations, only to be carried away to paradoxical formulations bordering on the nonsensical.

(6) *Bad Faith.* Anxiety as an essential attribute of free consciousness leads to another rather surprising characteristic of it: its "bad faith." Even anxiety is in most cases conspicuous by its apparent absence. But Sartre tries to explain this very fact by the phenomenon of bad faith. It consists in the flight from the fundamental anxiety which is essential to freedom. If we seem to hide this anxiety from ourselves, it is because of our bad faith. While Sartre wants to sterilize this expression from its moralistic implications, these nevertheless prove irrepressible in the further course of his philosophizing, especially in his existentialist ethics. The most important example of bad faith in Sartre's sense is provided by psychological determinism. For it is to him merely the expression of excuses for not assuming one's responsibility (*EN* 78; tr. 40). However, such "bad faith" is far from the conscious bad faith of a lie. It occurs on that pre-reflective level which for Sartre forms the equivalent of the psychoanalytic unconscious. It is only natural that under these circumstances good faith or sincerity becomes an impossibility and the attempts to achieve it even a form of bad faith (*EN* 102 f.; tr. 62). The possibility of an escape from this dilemma by a conversion to

authenticity is promised in a final footnote (*EN* 111; tr. 70), whose development is still missing.

(7) *Intentionality and Transphenomenality.* For Sartre as well as for Husserl, intentionality is the most essential feature of consciousness. But that does not mean that they interpret it in the same manner. Apparently Sartre believed he did when he wrote his enthusiastic article for the *Nouvelle Revue Française* on "A Fundamental Idea of Husserl's Phenomenology: *Intentionality.*" Here he had credited Husserl's intentionality with having destroyed the idea of immanence, since consciousness-of referred essentially to something beyond, thus "expelling" the things (*choses*) from consciousness and "liberating" it. Sartre did not mention the fact that according to Husserl the intended object is constituted by consciousness and certainly not independent of it. Only *L'Être et le néant* refers to this aspect of Husserl's conception and consequently denounces it as a corruption and a caricature of his original idea (*EN* 28, 152; tr. LXIII, 109).

For Sartre a consciousness-of means in the first place a reference from the intending act to the intended object beyond as a distinct entity, in a sense not dissimilar to Brentano's original conception. But the preposition "of" has to him an even stronger meaning. It establishes "ontological proof" (in a sense which is only superficially related to its ancestor, the Anselmian proof of God) that the referent of intention is independent of consciousness. Consciousness is congenitally oriented toward (*naît portée sur*) being other than itself (*EN* 28; LXIII),[1] which is not constituted but revealed by it. What it reveals in this manner is primarily the "transphenomenal" existence of the intended. It almost sounds as if the preposition "*de*" in the French phrase "*conscience de* . . ." is to be understood in the sense of the Latin *de*, i.e., as expressing its origin from its referent. In any event, Sartre's intentionality is the expression of the strict separation and the existential independence of its referent, not of its linkage with and dependence upon conscience, as especially in Husserl's later writings. Sartre makes no detailed attempt to

---

[1] Hazel E. Barnes renders this phrase erroneously as "supported by."

demonstrate this relationship phenomenologically, however, beyond the simple assertion of his "ontological proof."

Sartre's interpretation of intentionality and of its ontological implications raises the question as to his stand in the controversy over idealism and realism. Like many other phenomenologists, Sartre gives the impression of rejecting both positions. There can be no question about the fact that he repudiates an idealism according to which there is nothing but phenomena dependent upon consciousness. For this reason he rejects both the phenomenalism of Berkeley and that of Husserl. Sartre's equal rejection of realism must be understood in the light of his interpretation of realism as asserting a causal influence from the known upon the knower in the sense of a crude naturalism. There is however no reason to think that a wider interpretation of realism, not committed to a particular theory about the causal genesis of knowledge and concentrating upon the status of the known as independent of the knower, would be unable to assimilate Sartre's account of the relationship between Being and consciousness, as expressed in his interpretation of intentionality and the "ontological proof."

Certainly Sartre's phenomenology is anti-phenomenalistic. One of its main concerns is to make room for what he calls the transphenomenal or, more generally, the ontological. The term "transphenomenal" may easily lead to the misconception that Sartre advocated a thing-in-itself beyond the phenomena, all the more since he uses for it the Kantian label "in-itself" (*an-sich*). However, his protests against such a dualism leave no doubt about his opposition to the Kantian solution. Perhaps the most appropriate way of characterizing Sartre's position would be to call it a combination of a phenomenalism of essences with a realism of existence. He feels no hesitation to admit that phenomena are all there is, and that the old dualism between appearance and reality is without foundation. Like any British phenomenalist he is thus ready to define objects in terms of series of phenomena. Where he differs from Berkeley is in the assertion that both the perceived and the perceiving have a characteristic kind of being over and above their essence which cannot be fully described in terms of perceiving (*percipere*). Sartre calls the being of the two poles of this relationship "transphenomenal." What is involved is that on the one hand consciousness in its being is independent of appearing to itself and especially to reflection, and that on the other hand what we are conscious of is autonomous in its being and not merely constituted by consciousness. We never reach out beyond consciousness, nor do we have a right to do so. But the phenomena that appear within this range are transphenomenal in the sense that they are more than mere phenomena and have a being of their own.

But if Sartre would thus seem to be a realist concerning the being of the phenomena or the Being-in-itself, this does not commit him to the belief that all phenomena are independent of our consciousness. While Sartre does not make the difference sufficiently explicit, we have to distinguish between the concept of the absolute In-itself and the concept of the world, i.e., our meaningful environment. This world with its meanings is actually the correlate of our conscious projects and free choices. Sartre even speaks of a circuit between self and world. Whether this would justify us in saying that our concrete world is a matter of constitution in the sense of an idealistic interpretation may be debated in view of the fact that all these projects have to cope with objective factors, for which Sartre borrows from Gaston Bachelard the term "coefficient of adversity." Nevertheless, our world would seem to be determined by an interaction of the two factors in a way which amounts to a peculiar combination of idealism and realism in the area of our concrete experience.

(8) *Facticity and "Engagement."* "Facticity" is one of the peculiar characteristics of Sartre's consciousness which actually makes its first appearance in Heidegger's account of *Dasein*. Its peculiarity in Sartre's case is that it now attaches to consciousness. Primarily, "facticity" signifies the contingency of a particular fact which, for all we know, might just as well not have been. In applying it to the plight of man Heidegger had also used the striking neologism "thrownness" (*Geworfenheit*), translated by Sartre as "abandonment" (*délaissement*) in a situation, bringing in the connotation of cosmic loneliness or even of condemnation. To apply such characterizations to Husserl's transcendental consciousness in its eidetic purity would have been completely out of place. Here again it becomes

apparent that the axis of Sartre's phenomenology has shifted into the area of concrete human experience – something which from Husserl's standpoint can only be called "anthropologism." This shift links Sartre's phenomenology all the more firmly to the philosophy of existence. It also explains how Sartre, particularly in his analysis of Jean Genet, can work out phenomenologies of particular individuals and their worlds. —Phenomenology now descends from the level of a priori essences into the thick of the concrete experiences of the Kierkegaardian individual. Consciousness becomes essentially "engaged" consciousness.

The meaning of the term "engagement" remains, as a matter of fact, always somewhat ambiguous. It means involvement by virtue of our actual situation even prior to any explicit choice as well as commitment by a special decision. But the common core is that consciousness in Sartre's sense is primarily not a detached consciousness, to be studied in its pure forms as distilled by various reductions. For Sartre this would mean a falsification. Consciousness is essentially "engaged" in a concrete world, and phenomenology must study it in this world.

(9) *Transcendence*. We shall bypass Sartre's extended discussion of the temporality of consciousness as one of its essential dimensions. While it is true that there are differences in his interpretation of this aspect both from Husserl (whom he charges, with doubtful right, with a merely instantaneous conception of consciousness) and from Heidegger (who, though credited with an "ek-static" interpretation of conscious temporality according to its three main dimensions, is criticized for his excessive emphasis on the dimension of the future), these differences are partly based on misunderstandings; in the present context these are not worth pursuing.

The differences are much more pronounced, however, in the area of another concept, "transcendence." This too had previously made its appearance in the phenomenology of both Husserl and Heidegger. But each of them uses the term in his own way. Consequently it is one of the main troublemakers in the interpretation of phenomenology. No wonder that this term provides one of the best targets for phenomenology's critics.

Thus in Husserl it characterizes chiefly the intentional object, for instance a cube constituted by the intentional interpretations of immanent content, i.e., the hyletic sense data. Transcendent objects are the chief field for the application of the transcendental reduction. On the whole, Husserl distinguishes strictly between the transcendental and the transcendent, though at least in one case he uses the expression "transcendence in immanence" for the absolute existence of transcendental consciousness. By contrast, Heidegger applied the term to his human Being. Its function is to designate the fundamental property of *Dasein* which underlies our intentional acts and makes it possible to refer to intentional objects beyond our acts. Heidegger's transcendence is therefore not the static property of these objects beyond an immanent sphere. It is unrelated to the distinction between immanent and transcendent. "Transcendent" stands here for the present participle of the verb "to transcend" and characterizes any act which steps across, primarily from human being, into the world and ultimately, in the context of Heidegger's ontology, from the things-in-being to Being itself.

It is not easy to determine the exact meaning of the term for Sartre. Its chief carrier is again consciousness (*pour soi*). The term is to bring out the fact that consciousness refers essentially to something beyond itself which it lacks (*manque*). But this transcendence also has the meaning of a flight or escape beyond consciousness as exemplified by "bad faith," a flight toward other dimensions of time away from the present, but also toward other persons. Thus Sartre's transcendence often reminds one of Heidegger's existential category of falling into inauthentic being (*Verfall*). In any case, for Sartre "transcendence" is the expression of the incompleteness of consciousness in its lack of ontological self-sufficiency. Consciousness transcends because it is never satisfied with itself and passes beyond its present, which it thus negates (*dépassement*).

(*10*) *Phenomenological Method and Existential Psychoanalysis.* Thus far the chief distinguishing characteristic of Sartre's phenomenology appears to be his changed conception of its subject matter, i.e., consciousness, which is no longer conceived as "transcendental" but as concrete human existence situated in a human world, as pre-reflective, as absolutely free – though haunted by an anxiety of this freedom and by bad faith – as contingent, and as transcending itself. How far does this altered conception require for its exploration a change in the phenomenological method?

Sartre himself does not suggest this explicitly, especially since in his later writings he avoids methodological discussions almost completely. However, he introduces at this point one original development of the phenomenological method under the rather surprising title of "existential psychoanalysis" which is at least partially the result of the new interpretation of consciousness. I shall first attempt to present this new method and then try to determine how far it throws light on Sartre's general conception of the phenomenological method.

At first blush, Sartre's existential psychoanalysis may appear as a rather extraneous sideline of his philosophy, even though he himself seems to take considerable pride in having launched at least the idea of it. What has psychoanalysis to do with ontology? The connection may seem a little less strange if we remember that even in Sartre's ontology the focus is man, so much so that now *L'Homme* seems to be the central concern and the unfinished business of his philosophic enterprise. Not in vain does Jeanson's semi-official biography of Sartre carry the motto from his *Jean Genet:* "I have the passion to understand men (*les hommes*)." But there is this additional incentive for Sartre's interest in methods like psychoanalysis: consciousness as conceived by Husserl (at least in Sartre's interpretation) is something to which we have always full access by reflection. Sartre's pre-reflective consciousness is no longer presented with equal directness. Particularly is this true of man's motivations, his loves and aversions, his likes and dislikes, his cravings and rejections. Sartre's ambition to penetrate and to elucidate even these opaquer aspects of man well explains his interest in what he claims to be the most advanced method of such understanding.

There is evidence that, during his stay in Germany, Sartre studied extensively the writings of Freud, Adler, and other psychoanalysts like Wilhelm Stekel at the same time that he immersed himself in German phenomenology. Yet it would seem that he was less interested in the therapeutic aspects of psychoanalysis than in its theoretical views, its assumptions, and its implications. Even his own existential psychoanalysis has thus far not made any therapeutic claims.

It would exceed the scope of the present account to include a detailed discussion of Sartre's reaction to Freudian and other types of psychoanalysis. Suffice it to say that he finds himself in agreement with their general objective of penetrating below the surface of our manifest behavior and our first superficial self-interpretations. Besides, he shares their belief that this behavior is filled with symbolic meanings which, properly interpreted, reveal deeper purposive forces at work than are accessible without "analysis." But he differs from the original psychoanalysts by rejecting their set of gratuitous explanatory concepts. In particular, he objects to their conception of the unconscious as something essentially opaque and impenetrable to consciousness, and to their introduction of such constructions as the Id and the Superego, and such subconscious mechanisms as repression and sublimation. Also, he takes them to task for not going beyond such ultimately unexplained and unintelligible entities as libido and the will-to-power. He is most adamantly opposed to their assumption of a universal mechanistic determinism. Finally and most significantly, he insists that the interpretative hypotheses of psychoanalysis can and must be verified directly rather than indirectly.

By contrast, Sartre himself undertakes to account for the same phenomena by factors that can at least in principle be reached by consciousness. First among these is the concept of a fundamental choice which is supposed to explain our theoretical, practical, and emotional surface behavior. This fundamental choice consists in the adoption of a certain mode or style of being-in-the-world. Sartre illustrates such choices well enough in some of his literary portraits, for instance in his book essays on Baudelaire and his own contemporary, Jean Genet. In analyzing their lives he shows in detail how they choose their roles in response to given situations in which they find themselves placed in a way which gives meaning to all their concrete behavior. If one asks, however, what ultimate sense there is to such a role as being a failure, a martyr, or a saint, Sartre refers us back to his ontology and to the general project of man which, at least according to the pattern of *L'Être et le néant*, consists in wanting to be God. Thus in Sartre's version of existential psychoanalysis the claim to ultimate intelligibility depends in the last resort upon the validity and convincingness of this ontology. Besides, one may also wonder whether this uniform fundamental choice can actually account for the full variety of projects which Sartre wants to explain, and for which differentiating material can apparently come only from the differences in the accidental situations.

In a similar manner, for Freud's subconscious mechanisms like censure, repression, or sublimation Sartre finds a substitute in the shape of the phenomena of bad faith: it is our own pre-reflective consciousness which engineers these measures of evasion and is normally successful in concealing our better knowledge from ourselves. Thus existential psychoanalysis claims to be able to dispense with the whole apparatus of more or less hypothetical entities of classic psychoanalysis and to replace them by such phenomena as choice and faith, which are certainly within the range of our possible experience. In this way psychoanalysis becomes accessible to phenomenological treatment. Cartesianism, by liberalizing its concept of consciousness, bids fair to assimilate facts which had been considered previously as beyond its ken. The extension is reminiscent in many ways of Leibniz' widening of the concept of perception by the addition of his "small perceptions."

However, most important in the present context is a consideration of the method by which Sartre believes he can penetrate from the surface behavior to the fundamental choices of human existence. On this point the pertinent sections of *L'Être et le néant* contain at least some programmatic clarifications. Like "empirical" psychoanalysis, its existential counterpart must start with immediately accessible behavior, as observed not only by introspective but also by "objective" methods. Yet after this merely descriptive phase psychoanalysis is to pass on to a "deciphering" of the meanings of this behavior. The basic assumption underlying this method is that man is a whole, not an aggregate; that consequently every single part of his behavior down to his gestures and tastes has meaning and is related to his fundamental choices; and that each part is therefore "revealing" as to his choice, once this behavior is properly deciphered.

Sartre does not provide us with any definite code for such deciphering; in fact he takes issue with the rigid symbolism on which so many psychoanalytic interpretations are based. Instead, he suggests that we make use of our implicit or "a priori" understanding of human personality, which he, using a Heideggerian term, calls pre-ontological (*EN* 656; tr. 568). Deciphering in this sense is to be followed by what Sartre calls "fixation" and "conceptualization," of which, to be sure, he does not give any explicit demonstration.

But what is the final test for such a deciphering? Here Sartre again parts company with the classic psychoanalysts, with the exception of one of its heretics, Wilhelm Stekel. For he believes that the ultimate choices behind our conscious behavior can be made fully conscious by "analytic" procedure. Classic psychoanalysis gives the patient at best an abstract knowledge of his own subconscious motivations. Existential psychoanalysis expects to provide him with final intuitive insight into them. Here is the foundation for Sartre's claim that existential psychoanalysis is a phenomenological method which can vindicate the best insights of its classic predecessors.

How far has existential psychoanalysis made good on this claim? Sartre himself admits that it is still waiting for its Freud. However, he himself has given a number of impressive illustrations of this new method, not only by interpreting the personalities of specific artists but even by analyzing such social types as the anti-Semite. But however persuasive and brilliant such interpretations may be, Sartre presents them almost always with a finality which makes one wonder about their methodical soundness. Sometimes, as in the case of Baudelaire, one feels that to Sartre the worst explanation of his behavior is the best, whereas in that of Sartre's contemporary Jean Genet he reads into him, with his likely approval, only the most favorable motivations possible. More serious is the fact that Sartre almost always starts out by stating his conclusions, and, as far as he lets us see his evidence, he never seems to have considered alternative interpretations. It may be unfair to subject Sartre's critical essays to the requirements of a scientific case study. Nor does his analytic dogmatism invalidate the correctness of his diagnoses. But it certainly gives rise to the wish for a more methodical discussion of his evidence. Besides, it cannot be overlooked that Sartre's use of the concept of fundamental choice as the ultimate explanation of human conduct, in combination with his passionate rejection of psychological determinism, is conducive to a complacent moralizing of which his verdict on Baudelaire may give an example:

We look in vain for a circumstance for which he is not fully and lucidly responsible. ... The free choice that a man makes of himself is absolutely identical with what one calls his destiny.

How far does Sartre's original extension of phenomenology throw light on his general phenomenological approach? In the absence of any fuller statements on his part, the answer to this question must be tentative. Sartre's phenomenology is certainly no longer restricted to a mere description of the immediate phenomena. It undertakes to decipher them, i.e., to explore them "analytically" as purposive manifestations of more fundamental phenomena from which they flow. Never, however, are we allowed to step completely beyond intuitive verification. In this sense we still remain within the range of a "phenomenological description." Thus the ideal of Sartre's phenomenological method would seem to be the reflective elucidation of the pre-reflective consciousness according to its structures and meanings with the intent to intuit and to describe the fundamental phenomena based on a deciphering of their more immediately accessible manifestations. This certainly represents an extension of Husserl's program. Nevertheless, even Sartre intends, at least in principle, to submit his findings to the ultimate test of Husserl's original criterion, intuitive evidence.

6. Sartre's Phenomenology in Action

It is not easy to select illustrations of Sartre's phenomenology. For the subtitles of his major philosophical works indicate that he considers them all as phenomenological. Besides, some of his most original phenomenological observations occur outside his philosophical writing, for instance in *La Nausée*, to which he refers as evidence even in *L'Être et le néant*, and in plays like *Huis clos*. Also, such critical essays as the ones on Baudelaire and Jean Genet are clearly meant as examples of the new phenomenological method of existential psychoanalysis.

The items chosen below may not be the most important ones in the light of Sartre's ultimate objectives. The main reason for their selection is that they represent original contributions, however preliminary, to the general store of phenomenological insights. They are also clear cases, fairly easy to demonstrate and not dependent on previous understanding and acceptance of Sartre's ontological scheme. At the same time they show some of the characteristic defects of Sartre's phenomenologizing, especially in his shift from psychological to existentialist preoccupations.

a. IMAGINATION – Imagination constitutes by no means a new topic for phenomenological investigation. Husserl refers to it repeatedly in the context of his published work. In fact, a diary entry of 1906 reveals that in connection with his Göttingen lectures he had prepared "a very comprehensive work on perception, imagination, and time." [1] Besides, there is Eugen Fink's important though incomplete dissertation on "Presentation and Image" (*Vergegenwärtigung und Bild*), published in Husserl's *yearbook* XI (1930), which attacks the problems from the angle of Husserl's advanced transcendental phenomenology, of which Sartre seems to be strangely unaware.

Compared with these scattered beginnings, Sartre's two books constitute by far the most detailed and concrete phenomenological studies of the imagination we have. They are, on the whole, specimens of eidetic description in Husserl's earlier style. The first book, *"L'Imagination,"* consists largely of a critical survey of the preceding philosophical and psychological theories of the imagination, showing their shortcomings and pleading the superiority of Husserl's new approach in the *Ideen*, while pointing out its incompleteness. Sartre gives him credit chiefly for the radical distinction between perception and imagination, neither of which can be reduced to the other, and for the insight into the intentional structure of the imagination, according to which we have to distinguish sharply between the immanent imagining act and the transcendent imagined object, a distinction

---

[1] See his "Persönliche Aufzeichnungen," edited by Walter Biemel in *PPR* XVI (1956), 299.

overlooked by the "immanentism" of the traditional theories.

Sartre's own positive phenomenology of the imagination is contained in his "phenomenological psychology of the imagination," which appeared under the main title *L'Imaginaire*, perhaps rendered best as *"The World of Imagination."* It would be impossible to render here in detail the contents of this phenomenologically richest work of Sartre, although only part of it, dealing with what is "certain" about imagination, claims to be phenomenological in the strict sense, leaving the "probable" to empirical psychology. The only function of the present account is to select some particularly representative and suggestive features of this study. I shall therefore concentrate on the description of the imagination according to its four basic characteristics, leaving aside the perhaps even more colorful collection of related phenomena which Sartre calls its "family," and which includes portraits, caricatures, imitations, rock formations, and day-dream images.

Under the heading "The image is a consciousness" Sartre at once challenges the belief that there is such a thing as an image within our imagination; he calls this the "immanentist illusion" of Humean psychology. The first difference between perception and imagination is not the presence or absence of an image but a different way of referring to the intentional objects of our consciousness. There is no essential difference between the imagined object and the perceived object in character or location, nor is there in the case of the imagination any duplication of image and imagined object. The real difference is on the side of the imagining act.

A second difference between imagination and perception concerns the way in which we look at their objects. In the case of perception we depend on observation. What corresponds to it in the case of imagination is a peculiar *quasi-observation*. While in the case of perception continued observation can bring up constantly new items, no such enrichment can result from the corresponding observation of the imagined object. It remains as rich or poor as our original imagination was. Quasi-observation is essentially sterile and hence to no avail, once the original imagination has done its work.

Thirdly, the imagination presents its object with a negative

character or, as Sartre himself puts it, revealing some of his
ulterior objectives, as a nothing. His point is that the imagined
object is characterized either as non-existent, as absent, as
existing elsewhere, or as merely neutral (when no particular form
of existence is indicated). This adds a negative element to the
positive ones mentioned thus far. That the imaginative act lacks
something compared with the perceptive act is certainly correct.
Yet one may wonder whether this is the result of a specific
negative factor rather than the mere obverse of the fact that the
positive imaginative act is constitutionally unfit to supply the
positive characteristic of existence.

The final essential characteristic of Sartre's imagining consciousness is spontaneity. It is described, though much too
briefly, as productive of and supporting the imagined object,
in contrast to the non-creative and passive character of perception.

All this is original and adds considerably to a phenomenological understanding of the imagination. But it is hardly the
last word on the subject. Thus, Jean Hering[1] has pointed out
some of the limitations of these analyses, which do not seem
to take sufficient account of the difference between the genuine
consciousness of an image and an imageless consciousness of an
imagined object. Also one may wonder whether there are not
more and more central positive characteristics of the genuinely
creative imagination. But this does not diminish the merits of
this earliest French first-hand study in phenomenology. With
its direct attack on a relatively new field, carried out with an
abundance of examples and with a highly developed consciousness of the eidetic method, it represents phenomenological description at its freshest and richest.

b. THE MAGIC OF THE EMOTIONS – Sartre's *Esquisse d'une
théorie des émotions*, prepared probably simultaneously with his
studies of the imagination, presents a different type of phenomenological psychology. For it is less concerned with the
essence of the emotions than with their signification. Here
Sartre's primary concern is: What is the function of the emotions
in human existence? This question presupposes that emotions

---

[1] "Concerning Image, Idea, and Dream " in *PPR* VIII (1948), 188–205.

have a teleological structure and are not simply meaningless by-products or, worse, interruptions of our normal rational life. Put differently, emotion must be a behavior in the sense of a form of conduct (*conduite*). Sartre tries to establish this as a fact, beginning with a critique of the "classical theories" of the emotions according to which they are nothing but mechanical projections of physiological events into consciousness. By contrast, Sartre sees in them an organized system of means toward an end. On this point he agrees with some of the gestaltists, who had interpreted the emotions as "brusque solutions of conflicts, a manner of cutting the Gordian knot." The psycho-analysts deserve the credit for having introduced openly the idea of purposiveness into the interpretation of the emotions. However, in subscribing to the conception of the subconscious they continued to combine it with mechanistic conceptions which Sartre considers incompatible with the idea of functional purpose. Sartre's ambition is to go the whole way. Armed with his conception of the pre-reflective consciousness, he tries to remodel the hypothesis of the unconscious in such a way that he can account even for the irrationality of our emotional life.

Sartre was clearly not the first to apply the phenomenological approach to the world of the emotions. Scheler in particular, whom Sartre strangely ignores in this context, had initiated a vast study of the laws of meaning (*Sinngesetze*) of the emotional life, and Husserl's yearbook contains other significant contri-butions to the field, for instance by Moritz Geiger (vol. VI) and Aurel Kolnai (vol. X), which are apparently unknown to Sartre. His main originality consists in the type of meaning which he assigns to the emotions as compared with other types of behavior. For Sartre sees in the emotions forms of conduct which refer to our position in the world as a whole. In fact he interprets them as attempts to transform the world, attempts resulting from frustrations in our immediate dealings with it. Not being able to change it effectively by direct methods, we try to modify it by conferring upon it qualities of a type very different from those we normally encounter. These qualities, to be sure, have less reality than those we meet in the real world: they are parts of a new "magic" world. The chief method by which we can build such a magic environment in line with our desires is to change the relationship of our body to the world. Fainting or flight are devices to this end. The emotions with their psychological accompaniments belong in the same context. Perhaps the best illustration of this process that one might find is the way in which in English anger and hostility are expressed by the phrase "being mad," i.e., changing over into the world of a madman.

The emotions are not the only place where Sartre introduces the term "magic." Thus he attributes magic function to the imagination and to our social acts. But he never gives any detailed phenomenological account of the magical act and its significance. What is involved is apparently a kind of make-believe, supported by a pre-reflective bad faith which allows us to change if not the world itself at least its meanings for us by some kind of incantation, verbal or non-verbal. Such make-believe, however, is at times also backed up by a real change in the condition of our body as the mediator between consciousness and the world. Sartre illustrates the situation by the story of the fox and the sour grapes, which he interprets as the "little comedy" in which we try to confer the quality "too green" on the grapes. Once the situation becomes more urgent and we try to use a more serious kind of incantation, we reach the stage of emotion. The accompanying change in the condition of our body allows us to carry through the implied make-believe more effectively.

Perhaps the most significant implication of Sartre's hermeneutics of the emotions is the view that they are the results of frustration and constitute a "degraded form of consciousness," an act of bad faith that tries to tamper with the world beyond our reach – part of an escapist scheme. This strikingly low estimate of the place and right of the emotions in the human economy would seem to suggest that an authentic existence which faces up to the world would not only have to purify but to eliminate the emotions completely, as the Stoics would have us do. Sartre does not suggest this explicitly. But this is one of the occasions where his underlying Cartesianism comes to the fore. Certainly, Sartre is anything but on emotive irrationalist.

It is another question how far such an account of the emotions can pass as an adequate interpretation of the significance and the role of the emotions in general. In discussing the case of joy Sartre himself points out a difference between joy as a "sentiment" and joy as an emotion, thus implying that his sense of the term "emotion" is much narrower than the customary one. The best way of vindicating Sartre's admittedly sketchy study may be to interpret the term "emotion" as strictly as his examples suggest. Within such a limited scope his "theory" may well serve as a working hypothesis, provided it does not block our way to alternative hypotheses. A less rationalistic and moralistic approach might well consider whether emotions do not have such alternative functions as preparation for active change rather than for futile escape from reality.

> The notion of non-entity may be called the parent of philosophic craving in its subtilest and profoundest sense.
>
> William James, *The Sentiment of Rationality*.

c. ABSENCE AND NOTHINGNESS – The extraordinary role given to the Nothing in Sartre's scheme and the paradoxical statements he often makes about it easily cause us to overlook the fact that some of his observations about it are not without independent phenomenological merit. An example is the way in which he introduces and describes concretely the primary experiences that confront us with the phenomenon of the negative (*négatité*).

The philosophers of nothingness have often been charged with faulty semantics in overlooking the fact that negative terms have no independent meaning but are merely "syncategorematic." There is no good reason to think that the advocates of "meontology," as Jean Wahl has called Sartre, are not aware of this. But even the semanticists do not want us to do away with negative terms and expressions. Why not? There must be something in the world of designata which makes the use of the negative expression more "convenient" or more "economical." Could it not be that our direct experience is confronted with peculiar phenomena that call for such negative expressions? Sartre's first endeavor is to establish the occurrence of such phenomena. Only then does he use them as spring boards for his more ambitious – and precarious – interpretations.

As a matter of fact, Sartre was not the first to take up the phenomenology of the negative. Even Husserl had devoted to it some highly suggestive pages in the studies which Ludwig Landgrebe edited and published in 1939, but which were hardly known to Sartre at the time. Here he suggested, for instance, that the negative judgment has its foundation in certain pre-predicative experiences such as the disappointment of prior anticipations.[1] Much better known at the time was Heidegger's attempt to show that the Nothing has a status independent of negations, on a par with Being, even though he did not credit it with the same type of existence but with a peculiar mode of being which he called "naughting" (*nichten*). For Heidegger it is primarily the experience of anxiety in extreme situations through which the Nothing is manifested. This is definitely not the case in Sartre, for whom anxiety has its root in the vertiginous experience of freedom, not in the Nothing.

Sartre's account, which is much closer to Husserl's, is more direct and concrete. It takes its start from such phenomena as absence or destruction in the midst of our daily experience. Absence is exemplified in the episode of the futile search for a friend in a café where we had reason to expect him. In itself such a locality is a completely positive phenomenon without anything negative attached to it. But as we experience it while looking for our friend it constitutes itself as "ground" for the "figure" of the missing friend, as the gestaltists, to whom Sartre often refers, might put it. Under these circumstances every face we pass appears as "not my friend." This slipping away (*glissement*) Sartre calls a first *néantisation* or constitution of a nothing. A second and actually somewhat different experience is the one when we finally abandon hope of finding our friend and he "vanishes." Here the phenomenon of absence constitutes itself for good. In a similar way Sartre tries to show us that in itself nature does not contain any such events as destructions. All that occurs, even in a catastrophe such as a hurricane, is a positive transformation or rearrangement; the quality of being remains the same. The negativity of destruction manifests itself only in man, with his expectations and plans. It is thus essentially a human phenomenon.

[1] *Erfahrung und Urteil*, p. 94 ff.

Actually this seems to leave the phenomenon of the negative in a strange twilight. For on the one hand we are told that the negative is not merely a matter of human negation and negative judgment, but that it has a status of its own, in fact that it "haunts" being, which is surrounded by the nothing. (This would seem to be pretty much in line with Heidegger's view of the matter. On the other hand we learn that the nothing differs essentially from "things." For to Sartre it depends on man for its manifestation. This sounds almost like a subjectivistic account of nothingness and certainly reduces it ontologically to a secondary status, far below the one that Heidegger had bestowed on it.) The solution would seem to be that, while Sartre credits man with being the actualizer of the nothing, he nevertheless thinks that it has its potential root in Being. In other words, the phenomenon of the nothing is at this stage a typically hybrid affair, an outcome of the encounter of man and the things, and yet not simply the product of his judgmental activities. It is a case of what Husserl called passive constitution by consciousness.

Of course this is just the beginning of Sartre's phenomenology of the nothing. For it leads him at an accelerated pace to the interpretation of consciousness itself as nothingness. However, these much more problematic developments of his ontological theory do not affect the valid core in his initial phenomenological descriptions of negative phenomena.

d. THE GAZE (*Regard*) – One of the most remarkable and original [1] phenomenological descriptions in Sartre's ontological phase occurs in the context of his social philosophy: that of the human gaze.

Along with all other French phenomenologists, Sartre never took the problem of solipsism, even of Husserl's transcendental solipsism, seriously. His rejection of the latter's "egology" and subsequently of the whole transcendental approach allowed him to ignore this stumbling block. But this did not mean that Sartre overlooked the phenomenological problem of how other people and their existence are given and constituted in our

[1] A striking anticipation can, however, be found in as unexpected a place as W. E. Hocking's *The Meaning of God in Human Experience* (1912), pp. 271-2.

consciousness. It is with this problem in mind that he advanced his description of the human gaze, one of his most concrete and methodical phenomenological demonstrations in *L'Être et le néant*. This is a subject which had not been taken up explicitly by earlier phenomenology, although Husserl and Pfänder, when they discussed perceptual consciousness, referred not infrequently to the glance (*Blick*) or even, somewhat metaphorically, to its beam (*Blickstrahl*).

Sartre introduces the subject by considering the case of our glancing at a passing stranger and varying, in approved phenomenological fashion, the situation gradually. At first we may look at the stranger merely as if he were an inanimate object, a chair, or a puppet, in external juxtaposition with other such objects. The pattern changes fundamentally when we see him and recognize him as a human being. For now we see him as a being with a gaze looking at the same objects we ourselves see. This means that these cease to be merely our private objects. He too is now a potential focus for them. To this extent they "escape" me, as through a leakage. Yet even with such a new focus the other is still an object of my gaze. The decisive moment when he becomes a subject for me arrives when his gaze turns from our common world to me, and I experience the shock of being looked at, as it occurs especially in the shame that goes with the situation of being surprised in an embarrassing situation. This is the experience which establishes the existence of the other as definite, in fact as indubitable.

Without giving a detailed description of the gaze and especially of the other's gaze, Sartre brings out some of its more striking characteristics. Thus seeing his gaze as resting on us is something entirely different from seeing his eyes. Perceiving his eye and perceiving his gaze are actually two mutually exclusive experiences.[1] Also, we can have the experience of being gazed at (which may be mistaken) without seeing the other's face or eyes.

One of the most characteristic features of this gaze is that it has a definite effect upon the consciousness which experiences itself as gazed at. Comparable to the stare of the mythical Medusa, this gaze "petrifies" or "curdles" (*figer*) its object

---

[1] This is particularly well described in a little known independent study *Visages* (Paris, Seghers, 1948).

(EN 502; tr. 420). In fact, it even "enslaves" it (EN 326; tr. 267). One might easily think of the fascinating effect of the gaze of the hypnotist, whom Sartre, however, concerned only with everyday situations, never mentions. Some of Sartre's plays like *Huis clos* give striking illustrations of this phenomenon.

For Sartre the main significance of this "magic" function of the gaze is that it provides him with the basis for interpreting the social fabric as one of fundamental conflict. It is also the foundation for Sartre's subsequent interpretation of the social drama as a series of futile attempts to settle this conflict at the expense of one or the other consciousness.

This is not the place to submit Sartre's description and interpretation to a full-scale examination. Even without it, one might suggest that while he throws penetrating light on some of the more disturbing characteristics of the gaze, which a merely "scientific" account is apt to brush aside, he does so at the price of omitting some of its more reassuring and constructive properties and potentialities. Also, the fact that social relationships are approached exclusively from the experience of being gazed at creates a more sinister picture than a fuller phenomenology of social relationships such as Merleau-Ponty's would justify.

e. THE BODY – One of the frequent claims for the originality of the French phenomenologists is their interest in a phenomenology of the human body. The claim is only partially justified and should be judged in the light of their incomplete awareness of the work of their German predecessors. Only now has it become generally known that Husserl, especially in *Ideen* II, had devoted very important studies to the constitution of the body-consciousness. Scheler, beginning with his ethics, had discussed the phenomenon of the *Leib* extensively in the less read sections of his *Formalismus*. The main reason for the French perspective is presumably the conspicuous absence of any discussion of the body-consciousness from Heidegger's writings.

This does not preclude the recognition of the fact that the French phenomenologists have found new and significant angles in the exploration of a topic which is of considerable importance even beyond mere philosophy. This is true particularly of Sartre's approach to the problem. Its originality appears from the very

fact that he introduces the subject in connection with his phenomenology of social existence. For to Sartre the most important
function of the body is its role as a link in social contact. It will
be impossible to convey here an adequate idea of Sartre's phenomenology of the body. Partly because it is imbedded in his
social ontology, it defies separate and simplifying presentation.
It will suffice if the following paragraphs can suggest some of
its originality and some of its potentialities.

It almost goes without saying that Sartre is not interested in
the body as a scientific object studied by anatomy and physiology, i.e., as a mere thing side by side with other things. His concern is a description of the body as consciously experienced
and functioning in our relations with others, in which, for
example, we never know of our brain or our endocrine glands.
This is of course nothing new. But the following more original
features deserve special mention:

α. Our body-consciousness has three "dimensions" or, as one
might better call them, three "facets": one for its owner, a
second one for others, and a third for the owner as being conscious
of the other's facet of his own body. (Except for the reduced
interest of additional reflections, which might however still be
of interest for instance to the psychiatrist, there would seem to
be no reason to stop with this third "dimension.")

β. As to the first dimension, Sartre's most important observation is that on the pre-reflective level we "exist" or "live"
our body, that our consciousness is automatically "engaged"
in the body and even identifies itself with it. Only in reflection
do we dissociate ourselves to some extent from it. The main
function of the body is to serve as an observation point in our
relationship to the world. Thanks to it we can vary our perspectives of the world, while no such variation is possible in our
relation to our own body. Besides, our own body is given us as
the primary instrument presupposed by all secondary instruments which we may use. In general, we "transcend" the body
in our relations with the world and "pass it over in silence."
Yet it forms part of our pre-reflective consciousness. There is
also a peculiar element of contingency in our experience of our
body, of which we are aware in a peculiar "nausea." To be sure,
Sartre does not elaborate on this point sufficiently to avoid the

suspicion that he reports here merely private and idiosyncratic reactions. While this whole section contains highly suggestive phenomenological descriptions of the way in which we concretely experience, for instance, bodily pain, no attempt is made to give a comprehensive picture of the body image, as first described by Paul Schilder.

γ. The body as it appears to others presents actually a much richer phenomenon. As a complex whole of flesh and blood it must not be confused with the scientific picture of the body. The possibility of changing our point of observation with regard to the other's body can further enrich this social aspect of the body – one more reason for Sartre to insert the phenomenology of the body in his discussion of social existence.

δ. Bodily embarrassment and timidity are characteristic expressions of our consciousness of and concern with others' consciousness of our body. It represents in a sense a second layer of our consciousness of our own body. And since its sources are so much fuller than our direct body consciousness, Sartre can go so far as to state that we need the other to know who we are, not only to see ourselves as others see us. "We are resigned to see ourselves through the eyes of the other."

7. Toward an Appraisal of Sartre's Phenomenology

No matter how much one might care to qualify one's recommendation of Sartre as a descriptive phenomenologist, he remains undeniably the first French philosopher to reactivate phenomenology after a period of mere assimilation and interpretative study. And no matter how incomplete and one-sided his picture of Husserl may be, Sartre is the one who, after a period when Husserl was in the shadow of Heidegger, revived the interest in the founder of phenomenology and particularly in his subjective approach, which Heidegger had rejected. Occasionally he may have overestimated the common ground between Husserl and Heidegger and stripped Husserl's phenomenology of some of its main emphases, such as its transcendental radicalism. But he succeeded all the more in making it relevant to the French situation.

It is also due to Sartre's work that French phenomenology became fused with existentialism, not only, as in Heidegger's case, with a "fundamental ontology" of existence. How far has phenomenology been distorted in this process? The mere fact that phenomenology is now directed toward the phenomena of human existence can hardly be considered as a betrayal of the idea of phenomenology, especially as long as human existence is still studied and explored as a fundamentally conscious phenomenon, and as long as its givenness is not simply asserted dogmatically.

The danger to phenomenology comes chiefly from the peculiar methods preached and practiced by some of the existentialists. Sartre maintains at least the principle of a descriptive method based on intuition. However, in trying to incorporate in it a hermeneutic method of deciphering, he not only introduces interpretations of the sense of the phenomena which run far beyond the direct evidence but are even apt to interfere with the unbiased description of the directly accessible phenomena.

Some of Sartre's "descriptions" are striking not only for their originality but for their penetration in depth. But there usually comes a point where a less committed reader will wonder why Sartre has not considered a neighboring or parallel phenomenon of a very different character, and why, to take one example, he selects as typical the gaze in its most aggressive form of "fixating" the other, rather than in its function of meeting and recognizing him, as in a friendly smile, or why he interprets the emotions as attempts to magically transform the world, rather than as accepting and confirming it, as in responsive joy. On such occasions one receives the impression that Sartre plunges into the phenomena under the fascination of some of their more sinister aspects before looking at them in perspective. At times it is even hard to escape the impression that Sartre's picture is affected by idiosyncrasies such as the one against the property of the viscous, an idiosyncrasy which, while still understandable, seems to a less oversensitive observer to be out of all proportion. Such occasions seem to call for an existential psychoanalysis of Sartre himself. This is clearly not our task, all the less since he may be undertaking it in his autobiography. But there are other aspects of his approach which need discussion, since they affect the validity of his phenomenological findings.

There is in Sartre's thinking an activism which expresses

itself in a kind of revolt not only against the "Thing" but against the given as such. Like Fichte, he sees the given as a challenge, as a task, if not even as a threat. Jeanson reports a characteristic statement of his to this effect: "I believe that in every occasion there is something to be done." One wonders whether this attitude is the best possible qualification for the phenomenologist. For it is apt to lead to the immediate conversion of the given into the conducive or the obstructive in the light of the existential· project which springs from Sartre's "fundamental choice."

Sartre's phenomenology is certainly not free from preconceptions. And he shows little if any patience with those of his readers who are not willing to share them with him sight unseen. I referred at the outset to the difficulties Sartre's presentation creates for the average reader and even more for the critical one. Some of these may be the result of Sartre's tendency to revolutionize the world while also wanting to describe it. Even his reader is at the outset his opponent. The "pact of freedom" which he offers him in *Qu'est-ce que la littérature?* (1947) is a pact on Sartre's own terms.

Nevertheless, it was Sartre who naturalized phenomenology in France. He also emancipated and remodelled it in essential points. But he did not reconstruct it methodically and systematically. For the explicit and deliberate constitution of French phenomenology we have to turn to his associates, beginning with Maurice Merleau-Ponty.

8. Sartre's Following

Sartre's influence in present-day philosophy is not based upon academic position. It is comparable to the position of the great philosophers of the earlier Modern Age, whose relations to the academic world were at best peripheral, or of the *"philosophes"* in France. He has no school, but he has a following clustered around his magazine *Les Temps modernes*, whose central concern is, however, less philosophy and phenomenology in the technical sense than "engaged literature." His philosophical influence is less tangible and is perhaps stronger by provocation than by transmission. Nevertheless, even as the target of more or less violent reactions and during a period of relative philosophical silence on his part, his name dominates the French philosophical scene, second only to that of Heidegger.

There are, however, relatively few writers and thinkers who reflect and carry on his philosophical line in his own sense. (SIMONE DE BEAUVOIR (1908–   ) may be said to express his general philosophical ideas most directly and unconditionally, particularly in the field of ethics. But the phenomenological component in her writing is comparatively slight and rarely explicit. Nevertheless, she once stated the character and objective of French phenomenology in connection with a review of Merleau-Ponty's *Phénoménologie de la Perception* so well that it bears quoting:

> One of the immense merits of phenomenology consists in having restored to man the right to an authentic existence by abolishing the opposition between subject and object. It is impossible to define an object while cutting it off from the subject by which and for which it is object. And the subject reveals itself only through the objects in which it engages itself. Such an affirmation merely makes explicit the content of our naive experience. But it is rich in consequences. Only by making it one's foundation will one succeed in building an ethics to which man can totally and sincerely adhere. Hence it is of extreme importance to establish solidly and to restore to man that child-like audacity of which his years of verbal docility have deprived him: the audacity to say: "Here I am" (*je suis là*).[1]

Writings by S. de Beauvoir particularly relevant to phenomenology

Pyrrhus et Cinéas (1944)
Pour une Morale de l'ambiguité (1947)
    Translation: English (1948) by B. Frechtman – good.
L'Existentialisme et la sagesse des nations (1948)

FRANCIS JEANSON (1922–   ), known chiefly as an authoritative interpreter of Sartre, has also given a rather original and unorthodox presentation of phenomenology, in which he characterizes it chiefly as a practical and "purifying" technique based on a special effort of human existence.[2] He has also published a perceptive and suggestive study of the meaning of laughter,[3] which shows him as an independent and well informed phenomenologist in his own right.

---

[1] *Les Temps modernes* I (1946), 363.
[2] *La phénoménologie* (1951).
[3] *La signification humaine du rire* (1950).

SELECTIVE BIBLIOGRAPHY

Major Works

L'Imagination (1936)

"La Transcendance de l'égo," *Recherches philosophiques* VI (1936), 85–123
    Translation: English (1957) by Forest Williams and Robert Kirk-
    patrick – carefully done, with introduction and helpful notes.   [1]

La Nausée (1938)
    Translation: English (1949) by Lloyd Alexander – good.

Esquisse d'une théorie des émotions (1939)
    Translation: English (1948) under the title *The Emotions: Outline of
    Theory*, by B. Frechtman – fair.

L'Imaginaire: Psychologie phénoménologique de l'imagination (1940)
    Translation: English (1948) under the title *Psychology of Imagination*,
    anonymous – fair, but not without misleading mistakes.

Les Mouches. A play (1943)
    Translation: English (1947) by Stuart Gilbert – quite free.

Huis clos. A play (1943)
    Translation: English (1947) under the title *No Exit*, by Stuart Gilbert
    – quite free.

L'Être et le néant. Essai d'ontologie phénoménologique (1943) (EN)
    Translation: English (1956) by Hazel E. Barnes – on the whole good,
    but not free from serious errors. Adds an introduction, a helpful index
    of names, and a key to special terminology of limited value, but no
    index of subjects.

L'Existentialisme est un humanisme (1946)
    Translation: English (1947) under the title *Existentialism* by B.
    Frechtman – adequate, but not free from glaring mistakes.

Situations. 3 vols. (1947, '48, '49)
    Translations: English (Part of volumes I and III in *Literary and
    Philosophical Essays* (1955) by Anette Michelson; Part of vol. II in
    What is literature? (1949) by B. Frechtman – good.

Réflexions sur la question juive (1946)
    Translation: (1948) under the title "Anti-Semite and Jew," by George
    J. Becker.

Visages, précédé de *Portraits officiels* (1948)

Le Diable et le bon Dieu. A Play. (1951)
    Translation: English (1952) under the title "Lucifer and the Lord,"
    by Kitty Black – quite free.

Saint Genet, comédien et martyre. (1952)   [2]

"Questions de méthode," *Les Temps Modernes* XIII (1957), 338–417,
    658–97   [3]

Monographs

BEIGBEDER, MARC, *L'Homme Sartre* (1947)
    Not always reliable.

CAMPBELL, ROBERT, *Jean-Paul Sartre ou une littérature philosophique* (1945)
    Helpful study of the connections between Sartre's philosophical and
    literary works.

JEANSON, FRANCIS, *Sartre par lui-même*. Images et textes presentées par
    J.F. (1955)
    Emphasizes Sartre's plays; contains much new material.

JEANSON, FRANCIS, *Le problème moral et la pensée de Sartre* (1947)
Preface by Sartre.
VARET, GILBERT, *L'Ontologie de Sartre* (1948)
Penetrating analysis; chiefly an attempt to show Sartre's ontology
as a necessary consequence of Husserl's phenomenological method,
based on insufficient acquaintance with the German sources.

Studies in English

DEMPSEY, J. R. PETER, *The Psychology of Sartre* (1950)
The expository part is well organized, although the grasp of the German
background of Sartre's thought is inadequate. Criticism from the
Thomist position.
DESAN, WILFRED, *The Tragic Finale* (1954)
Most complete study in English, based largely on Varet and equally
inadequate on the German background. Ph. D. Thesis, Harvard Uni-
versity.
MURDOCH, IRIS, *Sartre, Romantic Rationalist* (1953)
Perceptive and sympathetic study, based largely on Sartre's novels.
NATANSON, MAURICE, *A Critique of Jean-Paul Sartre's Ontology* (1951)
Tries in addition to a condensed presentation to derive the defects of
Sartre's ontology from his failure to apply Husserl's phenomenological
reduction. Ph. D. Thesis, University of Nebraska.
STERN, ALFRED, *Sartre. His Philosophy and Psychoanalysis* (1953)
Unsympathetic and in some places quite superficial.

Articles in English

AYER, A. J., "Novelist-Philosophers: J. P. Sartre," *Horizon* XII (1945),
12–26, 101–10
BROWN, Jr., STUART M., "The Atheistic Existentialism of Jean-Paul
Sartre," *Philosophical Review* LVII (1948), 158–66
GURWITSCH, ARON, "A Non-Egological Conception of Consciousness,"
[1] *PPR* I (1941), 325–38
MARCUSE, HERBERT, "Existentialism: Remarks on J. P. Sartre's *L'Être
et le néant*," *PPR* VIII (1948), 309–36
McGILL, V. J., "Sartre's Doctrine of Freedom," *Revue internationale de
[2] philosophie* IX (1949), 329–59
NATANSON, MAURICE, "Jean-Paul Sartre's Philosophy of Freedom,"
Social Research XIX (1952) 362–80
OLSON, ROBERT G., "The Three Theories of Motivation in the Philosophy
of J. P. Sartre," *Ethics* LXVI, 176–87
——, "Authenticity, Metaphysics, and Moral Responsibility," *Philosophy*
[3] XXXIV (1959), 99–110
RAU, CATHERINE, "The Ethical Theory of J. P. Sartre," *Journal of
Philosophy* XLVI (1949) 536–45
SCHUETZ, ALFRED, "Sartre's Theory of the Alter Ego," *PPR* IX (1948),
181–99
SPIEGELBERG, HERBERT, "French Existentialism: Its Social Philosophies,
Kenyon Review XVI (1954), 446–62

STERN, GUENTHER ANDERS, "Emotion and Reality (in Connection with Sartre's *The Emotions*)," *PPR* X (1951), 553–62)

Most complete Bibliography of the Sartre Literature up to 1950

DOUGLAS, KENNETH, *A Critical Bibliography of Existentialism* (The Paris School) *Yale French Studies.* Special Monograph, No. 1 (1950), items 301–442

For Sartre's more important writings since 1950, see Jeanson, Francis, *Sartre par lui-même*, pp. 190–91

XI

THE PHENOMENOLOGICAL PHILOSOPHY OF
MAURICE MERLEAU-PONTY (1908–1961)

[1]

1. Merleau-Ponty's Position in the Phenomenological Movement

Maurice Merleau-Ponty is the author of the first French systematic work which displays the word *"phénoménologie"* in its main title, the *Phénoménologie de la perception*. This fact in itself establishes for him an important place in the annals of the Phenomenological Movement. But even apart from that, he has gone further than most other French philosophers, including Sartre, by identifying phenomenology with philosophy as such. This fact would seem to require the inclusion of his entire philosophy in the present account of the French phase. The only circumstance which can free me from such a vast assignment is the relative and, to some extent, intrinsic incompleteness and fluidity of his philosophy at this time.

His key position in the pattern of French philosophy is sufficiently attested by his unprecedentedly early accession in 1952 to the chair at the Collège de France once held by Henri Bergson. But what is more important in the present context is his place in the Phenomenological Movement, especially in relation to its other major figures like Husserl, Scheler, Heidegger, and Sartre. This relation has to be described almost completely in terms of Merleau-Ponty's own appraisal of his major partners. For of his contemporaries even Heidegger seems to be thus far largely unfamiliar with his work. And Sartre, who has not published any systematic philosophical treatise dealing with phenomenology since Merleau-Ponty's "Phenomenology of Perception" appeared, has mentioned him only incidentally, chiefly as a supplementary witness to some of his political views. There is thus far no reason to believe that, in connection with the recent "friendly secession"

[2]

20. Maurice Merleau-Ponty

(Sartre's words), he would dispute Merleau-Ponty's place as a phenomenologist. Nevertheless, the divergences that have now come out into the open are basic enough to affect eventually even their conceptions of phenomenology.

To Merleau-Ponty himself, the key figure for his interpretation of phenomenology is and remains the man whom he considers its founder, Edmund Husserl. Yet Merleau-Ponty's Husserl is by no means the conventional Husserl or, for that matter, Sartre's Husserl. For Merleau-Ponty the most significant phase in Husserl's thought is the very last one. But quite apart [1] from this rather unusual perspective on Husserl, Merleau-Ponty is certainly not his uncritical admirer. It is true that Merleau-Ponty's criticisms are never as explicit and blunt as Sartre's. But even before touching here on more specific matters we might point out that Merleau-Ponty, in attacking Descartes' *cogito*, also opposes the Husserl of the *Cartesian Meditations* and his conspicuous tribute to Augustinian subjectivity. Likewise, his rejection of all idealism includes even Husserl's phenomenological version of it. In short, what Merleau-Ponty attempts is to go beyond Husserl by consciously extrapolating certain lines, mostly from unpublished texts as far as he knows them, and by playing down others in the published writings. Nevertheless, in doing so he seems to consider himself the executor of the ultimate and best inspirations of the master.[1]

References to Scheler are comparatively rare in Merleau-Ponty's writings[2]; he appeals to him chiefly as a witness for

[1] Merleau-Ponty's references to Husserl's unpublished MSS usually do not allow identifications in the texts as they have appeared since in the *Husserliana* edition. Not all of these references should be taken at face value. Thus, the repeated quotation of a Husserl statement to the effect that "transcendental subjectivity is an intersubjectivity" (*PP* VII; *Problèmes actuels de la phénoménologie*, p. 108 and elsewhere), supposedly contained in the unpublished sections of Husserl's *Krisis* articles, cannot be traced in this form in the text of Walter Biemel's recent edition in *Husserliana* VI, and the passages that come closest to it (p. 175) clearly indicate the prerogative of transcendental subjectivity over transcendental intersubjectivity. This case is most revealing of the changed perspective of French phenomenology. – A similar instance is Merleau-Ponty's recurring reference to Husserl's view that our reflections form an influx into the world ("*sich einströmen*" is the German phrase, as quoted in *PP* IX and elsewhere). This particular expression seems to occur only in Fink's article on "*Die phänomenologische Philosophie Edmund Husserls in der gegenwärtigen Kritik*," which, to be sure, had been ratified by Husserl in a special preface: but even Fink refers only to our naive apperception of the world ("*Weltgläubigkeit als die universal einströmende Weltapperzeption*") rather than to our reflective acts.

[2] Only after this book had gone to the printer did I become aware of an early article by Merleau-Ponty, "Christianisme et Ressentiment" in *La Vie intellectuelle* VII

specific psychological and sociological points rather than as a leading interpreter of phenomenology. Where, as in his Sorbonne course of 1951, he compares him with Husserl he finds him uncritical and lacking in rigor. Specifically he sees a curious incongruity in Scheler's juxtaposition of a philosophy of the "alogical essences" and his claim to absolute knowledge as essential to philosophy.

His relation to Heidegger is not quite so clear. On the one hand, in Merleau-Ponty's writings references to Heidegger are far outnumbered by those to Husserl. But Merleau-Ponty does not seem to feel that there are any basic differences between them. Thus in the *Phénoménologie de la perception* he presents Husserl's phenomenological reduction, to be sure in his own reinterpretation, as the indispensable foundation for Heidegger's conception of being-in-the-world, and implies that Heidegger's *"philosophie existentielle"* is a legitimate prolongation of Husserl's phenomenology. Besides, the climactic chapter on "Temporality" in the *Phenomenology of Perception* is preceded by a motto from *Sein und Zeit* and leans heavily on Heidegger's text. However, in the Sorbonne lectures on Husserl of 1951 he ranks Heidegger's phenomenology behind Husserl's. Here he sees a basic inconsistency between Heidegger's conception of *Dasein* as inherent in the world and his claims to absolute access to, and knowledge of, Being in itself. Also Merleau-Ponty, especially in his more recent statements, displays a much higher regard for the sciences than Heidegger, and at the same time a much more modest estimate of the capacity of philosophy, even of a phenomenological philosophy, to reach anything like absolute truth.

It is much more difficult, but also more important, to place Merleau-Ponty in relation to Sartre's phenomenology. It is still customary, especially outside France, to see in Merleau-Ponty simply a disciple and close associate of Sartre, and philosophically merely a more academic version of him. It is high time that this picture, which was always one of limited validity, should be corrected. Until recently, in his book on *Les Aventures de la*

_____

(1935), 278–306 based on Scheler's essay on *Ressentiment*. It reveals not only his intense interest in Scheler at the time, but also gives important information on his critical attitude toward French philosophy and his expectations for phenomenology.

dialectique (1955), Merleau-Ponty had never stated his dissents from Sartre fully and explicitly. Up to that time he had referred particularly to Sartre's studies on the imagination and his treatise on the emotions as outstanding examples of phenomenological psychology in the sense of Husserl's middle period.[1] The phenomenological ontology of *L'Être et néant* was mentioned much less frequently.

Some of this restraint has to be seen against the background of the history of their personal relationship, which is not without poignancy. It dates back to Sartre's intervention for Merleau-Ponty on the occasion of a riot of their classmates at the *École normale* in the middle twenties. Since then they were connected by a personal friendship, which seems to have lasted until the "friendly secession" caused by the Korean War in 1953. In its early stages one finds Merleau-Ponty reviewing Sartre's thesis on the imagination, not without charging him for taking over Husserl's views too uncritically, and defending him in a review of *Les Mouches* (*Confluences* 1943), in essays like "La Querelle de l'existentialisme" (1945) and "Jean-Paul Sartre, un auteur scandaleux" (1948), against Marxists like Georges Lukacs and Catholics like Gabriel Marcel. Also, up to at least 1950, Merleau-Ponty collaborated closely with Sartre's magazine *Les Temps modernes*, signing as coeditor with him for an affiliated series of books and for a *Bibliothèque de Philosophie*, which comprised mostly translations of German phenomenological classics and related texts.

Nevertheless, differences between the positions of Sartre and Merleau-Ponty were always noticeable, and at times Merleau-Ponty stated them explicitly in connection with concrete issues. But never before had he subjected Sartre's philosophy to such a wholesale criticism as in the chapter on "Sartre's Ultra-bolshevism" in his book on the adventures of dialectics (1955). It is certainly strange to watch him now taking Sartre's philosophy apart as if there had never been any personal ties between them, and to an extent which goes far beyond the immediate political issue of Sartre's pro-communism, from which Merleau-Ponty dissociated himself unequivocally at this time. The

---

[1] See especially *Les Sciences de l'homme et la phénoménologie.* – For recent criticisms of *L'Imaginaire* see *AD* 189.

disappearance of Merleau-Ponty's name from their joint publications, and Simone de Beauvoir's bitter counter-attack in *Les Temps modernes* under the title "*Merleau Ponty et le Pseudo-Sartrisme*" [1] leave little doubt about the degree of estrangement between the two former comrades.

[1]

But it is not this personal and political story which is pertinent to the present context. How far does it involve philosophical issues? How far does it reveal differences in their conceptions of phenomenology? Perhaps the best way to bring out these deeper differences in a preliminary fashion is to quote two brief formulas from Merleau-Ponty's earlier writings which can hardly have been written without Sartre's parallel statements in mind. The first occurs in the Preface of the *Phenomenology of Perception*, where Merleau-Ponty declares: "We are condemned to meaning." [2] This passage is reminiscent at once of Sartre's counterpart: "We are condemned to freedom." The difference does not mean that Merleau-Ponty denies Sartre's doctrine of freedom, although even then Merleau-Ponty contested Sartre's assertion of absolute freedom. But more important is the fact that to Merleau-Ponty our existence is essentially imbued with sense. Thus he rejects by implication the doctrine of a meaningless opaque Being-in-itself in a world whose meaning depends entirely on human freedom. Meaning is not merely a matter of choice.

A similar clue may be found by contrasting the almost notorious line from Sartre's play *Huis clos* "Hell is other people" with a formula used by Merleau-Ponty in the presentation of his philosophy before the *Société Française de philosophie* ("Le Primat de la perception"): "History is other people." By thus equating history, instead of hell, with social existence, or "coexistence," as he also often says, Merleau-Ponty implicitly challenges Sartre's dismal diagnosis of the social world as one of diabolic conflict between hostile gazers. History, the new center of social existence, which played only a minor role in Sartre's

---

[1] X (1955), 2072–2122; republished in *Privilèges* (1955), pp. 203–72. The main point of this article is that Merleau-Ponty's picture of Sartre applies only to an earlier phase, which the latter has since transcended. Whether or not Merleau-Ponty has misinterpreted Sartre, the very fact that such a question could arise is significant for their entire relationship. Also Merleau-Ponty's possible misinterpretations are certainly illuminating for his own different perspective.

[2] p. XIV; a later passage reads: "We are condemned always to express something" (p. 516).

L'Être et le néant, is for Merleau-Ponty the field not only of conflict but of the realization of meaning.

But it is only in *Les Aventures de la dialectique* that Merleau-Ponty spells out the basic differences between Sartre's outlook and his own, which is "as personal and as general as possible: it is philosophical" (*AD* 253). Its basis, as Merleau-Ponty now identifies it, is Sartre's dualism between man and "the things" (*les choses*) or, more specifically, between the free *cogito* (Merleau-Ponty even speaks of Sartre's "folly" of the *cogito*) and Being-in-itself (the *en-soi*). Behind this and behind the difficulties Sartre encounters in his social and political philosophy Merleau-Ponty sees Sartre's refusal to recognize his historical and practical relation to the world with which he finds himself confronted. The result is that Sartre's commitment takes the form of a negation of the tie between us and the world, or of a "protest of indignation" (*AD* 260). In terms of Merleau-Ponty's main topic: Sartre's phenomenology suppresses the world of perception in its unity, on which Merleau-Ponty is going to found his interpretation of existence and coexistence: "Neither in our private nor in our public history is the formula for the relation (between the self and the other) that of 'either he or I,' the alternative of solipsism or self-denial (*abnégation*). For their relations are no longer those of head-on collisions between two consciousnesses (*pour-soi*) but the dovetailing into one another of two experiences which, without ever coinciding, stem from one and the same world." [1]

The basic difference between Sartre and Merleau-Ponty comes out most sharply in their different conception of dialectics and its role in philosophy. As early as 1946, in an article on "Existentialism in Hegel" (*Sens et Non-Sens,* p. 137 f.), Merleau-Ponty had expressed the view that, whereas Hegel converts death into higher life and passes from the individual to history, for Sartre the contradictions between the self and others are beyond remedy, and hence his dialectics is "truncated" (*tronquée*). It stops with the antithesis but does not know the acme of the

---

[1] AD 269. – Merleau-Ponty uses here the French *"engrenage,"* which characterizes the interlocking of two cogwheels. In Sartre this word occurs significantly as the title of one of his movie scripts, whose hero is the victim of the merciless operation of historical forces which work havoc with his best intentions and convert him into a ruthless dictator.

climactic synthesis and remains caught in the dualism between a Cartesian subjectivity, which Merleau-Ponty abhors, and the opacity of a meaningless objectivity. By contrast Merleau-Ponty undertakes to reunite the subjective and the objective in the primary phenomenon of the world, as given in our lived experience. Perhaps the most striking confrontation of these two conceptions can be obtained if we remember that to Sartre the synthesis of Consciousness (the For-itself) and Being (the In-itself) – a synthesis which he identifies with the meaning of God – constitutes a contradiction in terms. To Merleau-Ponty such a synthesis is not only conceivable, he finds it realized "every moment under our very eyes in the phenomenon, i.e., in our being-within-the-world" (*être-au-monde*) (PP 519).[1] Merleau-Ponty's universe is one of potential unity in which finite sense confronts the contingent, the ambiguous, and the risky, but where man has a fighting chance to enlarge the area of meaning. Yet there is no essential and hopeless struggle between existence [1] and Being as in Sartre.

This fundamental difference in outlook between Sartre and Merleau-Ponty was bound to have consequences even for their conceptions and their uses of phenomenology. Merleau-Ponty, in criticizing Sartre for not doing justice to the "mediations" between subject and object and to the synthesis of history, clearly implies that Sartre's activism blinds him to a whole range of phenomena, notably those of unity prior to our constituting acts (AD 190). This intolerance toward the given is to Merleau-Ponty clearly the result of a preconception on Sartre's part. One might think that this involves not more than Sartre's inconsistent use of the phenomenological method. But more is at stake. For Merleau-Ponty challenges the point of departure

[1] The rendition of "*être-au-monde*" by "being-within-the-world" or "presence-at-the-world" calls for explanation. French usage has two expressions, *être-dans-le monde*, i.e., being in the world, which carries a more spatial meaning, and *être-au-monde*, i.e., literally, being upon the world, with the customary connotation of "being alive." In philosophy "*être-au-monde*" is utilized not only in order to get away from the merely spatial conception but to bring out a lived contact with the world. Gabriel Marcel seems to have been the first to use the phrase in this sense, i.e., of "having business with the world" (*avoir affaire au monde*), while expressing his reservations to Heidegger's too "spatializing" conception of *être-dans-le-monde* (*in der Welt sein*). "Autour de Heidegger"; see *Dieu vivant* I (1945), 91. Merleau-Ponty spells out this difference only in his Sorbonne lectures of 1951 (*SP* 55), where he stresses the "inherence of the philosopher in the world" as something which Heidegger's phrase "*in-der-Welt-sein*" does not sufficiently express.

of Sartre's phenomenology: the Cartesian *cogito* in its subjectivistic interpretation, which Husserl had so conspicuously
adopted before him. It is this anti-Cartesianism and the related
attempt to find a new center for the phenomenological enterprise
which characterizes the fundamental originality of Merleau-
Ponty's phenomenology. Even his attempt to identify his
enterprise with the deeper intentions of Husserl in his late
phase depends on the possibility of purging phenomenology of
its Cartesianism. In a sense this is precisely what Heidegger had
tried, but only at the price of sacrificing transcendental phenomenology itself in the process. It is Merleau-Ponty's ambition to
develop a non-Cartesian phenomenology which tries to preserve
the basic intentions of Husserl's transcendental phenomenology.

Little need be added here about the proper approach to Merleau-Ponty's works. Even his philosophical writings reveal the
mentality of a man grown up in the tradition and style of
scientific writing. Thus in most of them the atmosphere differs
considerably from that of Sartre's philosophical texts, even his
earlier ones. But the more academic character of Merleau-
Ponty's work does not always make for easier reading. His sense
of the essential ambiguity of the phenomena is reflected even in
his style of thinking and writing. At times he rises to a type of
inspirational appeal which is common among existentialist
writers. But these features do not set him apart from the traditional style of French philosophical writing.

A comprehensive account of Merleau-Ponty's philosophy is
still impossible. Alphonse de Waelhens' book on Merleau-Ponty
provides considerable help as a systematic introduction. It is
also remarkable because its introduction has been sanctioned by
its subject to the extent that he prefixed it to the second edition
of his first work, *La Structure du comportement*. But he does not
want this fact to be interpreted as proof of his acceptance of the
main title of the book ("*A Philosophy of Ambiguity*") as the
proper label for his philosophy. However, de Waelhens' book
shows comparatively little interest in the phenomenological
aspects of Merleau-Ponty's philosophy and in his method in
comparison with that of other phenomenologists, since his
major interest is in Merleau-Ponty's conclusions. The present
chapter is meant to narrow the remaining gap.

A major handicap for the Anglo-American reader is the almost complete absence of translations. This is all the more regrettable since on closer inspection Merleau-Ponty's philosophizing reveals perhaps more parallels and possible points of contact with important doctrines of Anglo-American philosophy than the thought of any other phenomenologist. Whitehead's theory of prehensions, John Dewey's conception of experience and his criticism of the reflex arc, G. H. Mead's "Philosophy of the Present," and Lovejoy's temporalism all have striking counterparts in the philosophy of Merleau-Ponty, who himself seems to be little aware of them. This does not detract from his originality and independence but only corroborates it. What remains as the indisputably novel part of his philosophy is his attempt to anchor these doctrines in a new conception of phenomenology.

> "His position is, in principle, just that which I should take even if, *by chance*, we might have different preferences."
>
> George Santayana on Merleau-Ponty in *The Letters of G.S.* (New York, Scribner's Sons, 1955), p. 367, referring to the Preface of *Humanisme et Terreur*.

2. Guiding Themes in the Philosophy of Merleau-Ponty

Usually the writings of Merleau-Ponty avoid the first person singular. This is hardly accident. The focus of his thought is not on the ego, but on the phenomenon ahead, the *Sache*. It is therefore not surprising that Merleau-Ponty has not yet given any autobiographical statement nor has any formulation of his comprehensive plans or guiding motifs appeared. Hence at this stage any attempt to determine the central core of his philosophizing has to remain hypothetical.

Perhaps the most revealing among the titles of Merleau-Ponty's books to appear thus far is that of the collection of his essays, *Sens et non-sens*.[1] The French *"non-sens"* in this connection had best be rendered in English by "absence (or 'lack') of sense," not by "utter absurdity" or "counter-sense," for which it would stand with those existentialists who, like Sartre or Camus, see the world as the battlefield between two deadly

---

[1] For this combination see also *PP* 490.

antagonists. To Merleau-Ponty, meaning and lack of meaning are matters of transition and degree, not of either-or.

One cannot say that everything has sense or that nothing has sense, but only that there is sense. ... A truth against the background of absurdity, an absurdity which the teleology of consciousness presumes to be able to convert into truth, this is the primary phenomenon (*PP* 342).

This passage reveals at the same time that Merleau-Ponty, in this respect not different from Sartre, by no means takes the side of irrationalism, as existentialists are so often supposed to do, in the struggle between reason and life. Nor does he advocate a simple return to Cartesian reason. His answer is "a new idea of reason, which does not forget the experience of unreason" (*déraison*) (SN 8). For this idea of an enlarged reason he refers to Hegel, without however subscribing to the latter's sublime confidence in the inevitable victory of reason. To Merleau-Ponty what is real is only part rational, and what is rational is only part real. Furthermore, Merleau-Ponty's reason is not that of the Hegelian logic, which is intelligible through and through and self-sufficient. In one characteristic passage Merleau-Ponty even speaks of a "mystery of Reason" (PP XVI). In his world contingency must be considered just as fundamental as necessity, "adversity" as essential as meaning. Thus in one of his striking metaphors he characterizes the universe as composed of "radiating centers" (*noyaux rayonnants*) separated by panels (*pans*) of night (*SN* 9). This is the world half wild and half tame of William James's pluralism with its melioristic clearings in the jungle. The contingency of existence and the factor of adversity are at the same time the reason why Merleau-Ponty refuses the answer of theism. In fact, though only under pressure and without fanfare, he admits being an atheist. His philosophy excludes the thought of an "infinitely Infinite," i.e., Absolute Being, since it "sees the world in its strangeness," i.e., essential contingency (*RI* 251). Clearly this is a type of atheism very different from Sartre's belligerent version, which was based on a supposed ontological contradiction in the conception of God. In fact, Merleau-Ponty's outlook allows him to find meaning in the idea of Christ's incarnation and death, which he sees reflected in Nietzsche's idea of God's death (*PPCP* 135; *RI* 74).

Merleau-Ponty's thought has been called a "Philosophy of

Ambiguity." This label, designed in 1947 by one of his best critics, Ferdinand Alquié, was taken up by Alphonse de Waelhens in a positive sense. However, the term "ambiguity" has a much more pejorative meaning in English than in French, and thus overemphasizes the negative aspect of this philosophy. Merleau-Ponty never uses it himself and has on occasion even discouraged it as misleading (*RI* 221). Even the word "ambiguous" appears by no means as conspicuously as is often assumed. In fact, in his inaugural lecture at the Collège de France he characterized the true philosopher by his equal taste for clarity (*évidence*) and ambiguity (*EP* 10 f.). Here he also distinguishes a positive sense of ambiguity, i.e., the repudiation of absolute knowledge, from the bad sense of mere equivocation. Merleau-Ponty's philosophy is not one of twilight but of chiaroscuro.

It is true, however, that to Merleau-Ponty, philosophy does not know final answers. For philosophy is essentially interrogation, an interrogation which is omnipresent in history (*PC* 12). This may well account for his recent interest in editing a composite history of the great philosophers including the oriental ones, from the early beginnings down to Sartre. Actually in this perspective the "concrete philosophy" of our time is even in a particularly precarious position: dominated by the themes of existence and dialectics, it is not a "happy philosophy" like those of the great classics: it has forfeited its claims to the a priori, the system, and a construction which can go beyond experience (*PC* 290).

Merleau-Ponty is an avowed existentialist. It is customary to present this philosophy as "engaged," i.e., as involved in or committed to action, particularly to social action. And it is true that Merleau-Ponty himself emphasizes the fact that not only consciousness but even philosophy is "engaged" in the world, and that it cannot and must not detach itself from its essential "incarnation" in it. But this is not to be understood in the sense that the philosopher should rush head-long into all kinds of ill-considered enterprises. His problem is that of the proper balance between involvement and detachment, of philosophizing in the world, without becoming engulfed by it. In this context the figure of Socrates acquires a new symbolic value for Merleau-Ponty as that of the philosopher who is both citizen and philosopher, neither a revolutionary nor a conformist, obeying and disobeying at the same time. This delicate balance characterizes also the ambiguity of Merleau-Ponty's "a-communism" in its ambivalent position between Marxist action and Hegelian contemplation.

However, the motif of a new existentialized rationalism is not sufficient to account for the content of Merleau-Ponty's philosophy. Merleau-Ponty is not only a brilliant academic teacher but also thoroughly at home in the sciences of man, and particularly in psychology. Hence the relation between science, especially the anthropological sciences, and philosophy provides one of the pervading themes for Merleau-Ponty's thought. His point of departure is what he calls "a crisis of philosophy, a crisis of the sciences of man, and a crisis of science as such, from which we have not yet emerged" (*SP* 1 f.). He turns to Husserl as the philosopher who

understood that these different disciplines have entered a stage of permanent crisis and will not emerge from it unless, by a new elucidation of their relations and their ways of knowing, we succeed in making each one possible in itself, and also their coexistence. We have to show that science is possible, that the science of man is possible, and that all the same philosophy is possible. It is necessary in particular to end the rift (*divergence*) between systematic philosophy and progressive knowledge or science.

What this means concretely in the case of Merleau-Ponty is the attempt to find a new unity between the objectivism of the traditional sciences and the subjectivism which is characteristic of a philosophy centered too narrowly in the Cartesian tradition.

The foundation for the necessary reconciliation and reorganization is indicated by the title of Merleau-Ponty's exposition of the centerpiece of his philosophy before the *Société Française de philosophie* in 1947, "The Primacy of Perception." For perception is to him the matrix for science as well as for philosophy. The world as perceived or experienced, with all its subjective and objective features, is the common ground for both. To make sure of this ground is the first task of the new phenomenology.

However, this primacy of perception does not mean that either philosophy or science are to remain at the level of perception. Philosophy in particular is to move on from here to the higher levels of cultural phenomena and particularly to those of predicative or judgmental truths, to history, language, and art. Thus far Merleau-Ponty has attacked such subjects only in brief essays. The systematic treatment of these more complex phenomena is his main unfinished business.

How are these basic themes related to phenomenology and to Merleau-Ponty's particular version of it? Before we try to answer this question, we will have to trace briefly the development of Merleau-Ponty's phenomenology.

3. The Development of Merleau-Ponty's Phenomenology

Judging from the record of his publications, Merleau-Ponty matured much more slowly than Sartre, his senior by only two years. His first book, *La Structure du comportement*, did not appear until 1942, though it seems to have been completed before the War in 1938, when he was 31. Apparently only two book reviews, one of Sartre's *L'Imagination*, the other of Gabriel Marcel's *Être et avoir*, preceded it in 1936.[1] But while his ideas seem to have been slower in growing, they have undergone much less change than Sartre's. There is therefore in his case no need to distinguish several periods in his development.

[1]

Little is known thus far about Merleau-Ponty's philosophical evolution. Among the accessible data the following ones seem pertinent to a better understanding of his phenomenology. A native Catholic from Normandy (La Rochelle), he received his main philosophical education at the *École Normale*, where he became the friend of Sartre and Jean Hyppolite, among others. The incident which led to his friendship with Sartre, as he reports it in *"Un Auteur scandaleux"* (*Sens et non-sens*), may well be characteristic of his early ways: he and a friend hissing at certain traditional songs of the school "too crude for our tastes" (*trop grossières à notre gré*) and thus incurring the rage of their classmates.

A first indication of Merleau-Ponty's dominating interest at the stage of his philosophical emancipation may be found in the opening sentence of his Introduction to *La Structure du comportement:* "Our goal is to understand the relations between consciousness and nature." The implication is that for Merleau-

---

[1] About an earlier review article (1935) see p. 517 footnote (2)

Ponty the present sciences, particularly biology and psychology, were unable to account for these relations. But he is equally dissatisfied with such philosophical solutions as the idealistic or "critical" philosophy of Brunschvicg or its opponent, "naturalism." Thus his first concern is to find a mediation and synthesis between the two uncorrelated disciplines. Psychology was the field where he looked for the solution first. It became his specialty to the extent that when he joined the Sorbonne in 1950 his main assignment was child psychology, a fact not without significance in view of his continued interest in the study of phenomena in the making (*à l'état naissant*). Gestalt psychology was coming to France during this period, especially through such able interpreters as Paul Guillaume. In the early thirties it found an even more authorized interpreter from Germany in Aron Gurwitsch, who was at the same time fully at home in Husserl's phenomenology and in Scheler's work, and who also brought to France the organismic biology of Kurt Goldstein. Moreover, during this period Alfred Schuetz, coming from Vienna, introduced the phenomenology of the social world, based on ideas of Husserl, Scheler, and Max Weber. Merleau-Ponty absorbed all these new ideas in personal contacts with their German interpreters. (Gurwitsch even acknowledges his assistance in the edition of one of his articles on gestalt psychology.[1]) But according to what Merleau-Ponty told the present writer in 1953, it was Sartre who, after his return from Germany in 1934, first acquainted him with Husserl's writings when he showed him the *Ideen* as the work which he would have to study. While the first section of this book, dealing with "Essence and Fact," appealed little to Merleau-Ponty, he was all the more impressed by the subsequent section on the problem of the natural world and on the phenomenological reductions, and by the concrete phenomenological analyses that followed. The *Logische Untersuchungen*, taken up next, held less interest for him. Then he turned to the study of the *Méditations cartésiennes* and the *Formale und transzendentale Logik*. Perhaps most important for Merleau-Ponty was the publication of the first two parts of Husserl's last incomplete work on "The Crisis of the European

---

[1] "Quelques aspects et quelques développements de la psychologie de la Forme." *Journal de psychologie normale et pathologique* XXXIII (1936) 413–71.

Sciences and Transcendental Phenomenology" in the new international magazine *Philosophia* (Belgrad) in 1936. For its problem coincided with one of Merleau-Ponty's major concerns. It also gave for the first time an idea of Husserl's concept of the life world (*Lebenswelt*) as the foundation for both science and a renewed philosophy in the form of "transcendental phenomenology." It was thus clearly the later and the last phases of Husserl's phenomenology which aroused Merleau-Ponty's chief interest and won him over to the new movement. However he never met Husserl and did not study in Germany. But as early as 1939 he spent one week in Louvain as one of the first users of the new Husserl Archives. It seems that his interest turned exclusively to Husserl's later unpublished manuscripts, to which he refers extensively in his second work, the *Phénoménologie de la perception*. He repeated his visit in 1947.

[1]

It is much more difficult to determine Gabriel Marcel's significance for Merleau-Ponty's development. His detailed review of *Être et avoir* (1936) clearly shows his initial strong interest in Marcel. One can also easily observe striking agreements in terminology, in topics, and in some conclusions, although their final outlook differs fundamentally. Cases in point are terms like incarnation, *être-au-monde*, first and second reflection, *mystère*, or topics like sensation, on which their views are strikingly parallel, as are those on the phenomenology of the body (in spite of opposite terminology; see *PP* 203 note) and on the inadequacies of the Cartesian *cogito*. At least some kind of osmosis from Marcel to Merleau-Ponty seems a plausible hypothesis.

During the thirties Merleau-Ponty was also under the spell of Hegel, apparently much more than Sartre was. Thus he not only attended Kojève's course on Hegel, but there were also close personal contacts between the two.[1]

Merleau-Ponty was one of the few Frenchmen of his generation who escaped captivity or an even more violent fate during the War. But the experience of the war left indelible traces on his thinking. Thus the motif of history as the medium of our essential

---

[1] See Rudolf W. Meyer, "Merleau-Ponty und das Schicksal des französischen Existentialismus," *Philosophische Rundschau* III (1955), 138.

incarnation, and that of existence as essentially coexistence now assume major roles in his philosophy.[1] However, during these years Merleau-Ponty was also able to prepare his largest work, the *Phenomenology of Perception*, which appeared in 1945. It was followed by a considerable number of important essays, dealing with a remarkable variety of topics, from the esthetics of painting and the cinema to politics; most of them appeared in Sartre's new magazine, *Les Temps modernes*, and were later united, though with omissions, in volumes like *Humanisme et Terreur* (1947) and *Sens et Non-sens* (1948). The central subject here is man, the social problems raised by Marxism, the reality of communism, and the sciences of man. Phenomenology as such does not figure prominently. Nor does it in the new book which Merleau-Ponty devoted in 1955 to social and political philosophy under the title *Les Aventures de la dialectique*. [1]

However, in smaller but largely preliminary studies he pursues his phenomenological work more explicitly. Among these his presentation before the *Société Française de philosophie*, "Le Primat de la perception et ses conséquences philosophiques," and his lectures at the Sorbonne on "Les Sciences de l'homme et la phénoménologie" are of considerable importance for interpreting his conception of phenomenology. Other publications show him attempting to work out a phenomenology of language and of history. They point in the direction of a systematic treatment of these phenomena as a highler level above the primary phenomena of perception, and promise a phenomenology of human culture in which the results of the sciences of man will be assimilated by phenomenology. [2]

4. Merleau-Ponty's Conception of Phenomenology

"In a sense phenomenology is everything or nothing." With this statement, which occurs in the context of a paper read at the first international Symposium for Phenomenology (PA, 105), Merleau-Ponty goes deliberately even beyond Husserl, for whom pure phenomenology and the phenomenological philosophy based upon it were still two different things. According to Merleau-Ponty, phenomenology already commits us to a certain

[1] See especially the impressive essay "There Has Been a War" (*La guerre a eu lieu*) in SN 281–309.

conception of being and to an entire philosophy. It is not merely a preparatory discipline for it; it "envelops" it. This does not mean that Merleau-Ponty displays the blessed word on every page or, for that matter, in all of his publications. But this is due to the omnipresence of the thing meant rather than to its absence.[1] What is this all-embracing phenomenology?

It is interesting to note that in one of his first reviews, that of Marcel's *Être et avoir* (1936), Merleau-Ponty shows particular interest in the role phenomenology plays in this book and considers the possibility of its application to the totality of human existence. But it is also significant that he expresses uneasiness because of the difficulty for Marcel to distinguish between genuine and pseudo-intuition whose appeals to existence in the manner of Jaspers are merely subjective.

In Merleau-Ponty's first major book, *La Structure du comportement*, phenomenology and particularly the term "phenomenology" do not yet occupy a very conspicuous place. Phenomenology is not mentioned explicitly until the last chapter, which deals with the "relations between soul and body" as they are involved particularly in the problem of knowledge. Nevertheless, there can be no doubt that Merleau-Ponty's methodical and circumspect approach is meant to introduce phenomenology as the solution for the problems of behavior which even Gestalt psychology had not been able to solve. When phenomenology is finally mentioned, it is presented as a

---

[1] An interesting illustration of this fact occurred in the discussion of Merleau-Ponty's lecture on "Man and Adversity," which never mentioned the word "phenomenology." But when in the discussion Father Daniélou introduced the distinction between phenomenological description and philosophical system, Merleau-Ponty protested: "I have never thought that phenomenology was nothing but an introduction to philosophy, I believe that it *is* philosophy" (R.I., 1951, p. 246). The use of phenomenology (which, incidentally, he identifies here with existentialism) as a mere "vestibule," in the way in which the Christian existentialists attempt it, is for Merleau-Ponty the denial of philosophy and of phenomenology. On the other hand, Merleau-Ponty denies to philosophy the right to go beyond phenomenological description to "explanations": "To my mind this is the philosophical attitude. Philosophy is amazement (*thaumazein*), the consciousness of strangeness (*étrangeté*). It means to suppress 'philosophical' explanations by systems." And in answer to the question, "Do you leave the people in a situation which you yourself call vertiginous?" he replied, "Philosophy is no hospital. If people feel dizzy and want to take drugs against dizziness, I do not stop them, but I say: These are drugs." Here Merleau-Ponty rejoins the ascetic position of the essay "Science as a Vocation" by Max Weber, with whom Merleau-Ponty has lately identified himself in his social philosophy to a remarkable extent. It is thus hardly an accident that he even refers to the "phenomenology" of Max Weber (AD 35).

philosophy of "criticist," i.e., largely idealist, inspiration. Husserl is mentioned as its exclusive fountainhead. To the term "phenomenon" Merleau-Ponty assigns the function of expressing "the intimate relation between the objects and the subject and the presence of solid structures in both which distinguish phenomena from mere appearances"; yet the term "essence" is almost conspicuous by its absence. A philosophy devoted to the study of these phenomena becomes a "phenomenology," i.e., an "inventory of consciousness as a 'milieu'" (i.e., a medium for the appearance) "of the world" (SC 215). While these are not strictly Husserlian formulations there is no indication that Merleau-Ponty intended to deviate from Husserl. Even the phenomenological reduction, interpreted in the sense of Husserl's last philosophy, is mentioned as the necessary procedure for reaching the level of our primary perceptual experience in which the world constitutes itself (*SC* 236).

Merleau-Ponty's most explicit and most significant statement about the meaning of phenomenology is his *Préface* to the *Phénoménologie de la perception*. It combines a unique reaffirmation with a reinterpretation of Husserl's phenomenology, of which I shall try to outline at least the major aspects. It begins with the frank admission that no commonly agreed definition of phenomenology exists and that phenomenology has practically become all things to all people. But this does not prevent his asserting that "phenomenology can be practiced and recognized as a mode of thought (*manière*) or as a style; it exists as a movement before having arrived at a full philosophical consciousness. ... It is in ourselves that we shall find the unity and the true sense of phenomenology. ... Phenomenology is accessible only to a phenomenological method." Such pronouncements make it clear that Merleau-Ponty claims for himself the right to interpret phenomenology in the light of his own needs and insights. Yet he begins by discussing each one of the major features of phenomenology as developed by Husserl. I shall review this discussion briefly.

α. *Phenomenological description*, originally an attempt to go to the "things" themselves and to give a scientifically rigorous account of them, means to Merleau-Ponty primarily a protest against science, understood in the sense of an objective study of

the things and of their external causal relations, in favor of a
return to the *Lebenswelt*, the world as met in lived experience in
the sense of the later Husserl. Yet by implication Merleau-Ponty
refuses to follow Husserl in his reflective analysis designed to
trace back this life world to its roots in the subject. "The return
to the things themselves ... differs absolutely from the idealistic
return to consciousness (PP III). The world is here (*là*) before
any analysis I can make of it. The real must be described,
not constructed or constituted" (PP IV). Thereupon, with
obvious allusion to Husserl's climactic quotation from St.
Augustine at the end of the Paris lectures and the *Cartesian
Meditations* ("Turn into yourself: truth dwells in the inner man"),
Merleau-Ponty declares: "Truth does not dwell only in the inner
man, or rather, there is no such thing as an inner man: man is
within the world (*au monde*); it is in the world that he recognizes
himself." What I find in myself is "a subject vowed (*voué*) to
the world."

β. *Phenomenological reduction*, with its bracketing of belief
in the reality of the natural world, for Husserl the lever for his
phenomenological idealism, becomes for Merleau-Ponty the
device which permits us to discover the spontaneous surge of
the life world. It does so by loosening our habitual ties with the
world. Merleau-Ponty refers for this interpretation to Eugen
Fink's discussion of the phenomenological reduction in an article
which, to be sure, had Husserl's summary ratification, and in
which Fink had referred to the "awakening of an immense
amazement at the mysteriousness of the belief in the world"
as the foundation for the operation of suspending it. Merleau-
Ponty sees in this account of the fundamental amazement (an
amazement which is never to be overcome) the "best formula
of the reduction" itself. Hence "the great lesson of reduction
is the impossibility of complete reduction." Thus, oddly enough,
in Merleau-Ponty's hands the phenomenological reduction
becomes the means of refuting constitutive or phenomenological idealism.

γ. Similarly the *eidetic reduction*, for Husserl the way from existence to essence, becomes in Merleau-Ponty's frame a "means"
rather than an "end," a "net" designed to catch "like fish
and palpitating algae" the living relations of experience. Phe-

nomenology, as Merleau-Ponty sees it, attempts to catch the facts in their uniqueness prior to all linguistic formulations. Eidetic reduction helps us indirectly in this attempt by letting the world stand out against the background of the essences. It embodies the "resolution to make the world appear as it is before reducing it to subjective states or thoughts." This reversal of the phenomenology of essences in a way which makes phenomenology actually subservient to the study of existent fact is clearly in line with the shift of the existentialists from essence to existence. In Merleau-Ponty's opinion even Husserl himself in his latest work had abandoned the belief in essences.

δ. *Intentionality*, according to Husserl the fundamental structure of consciousness, its main theme and clue to the theory of constitution, also assumes a new role in Merleau-Ponty's pattern. Its main function now is to reveal the world as ready-made and already "there" (*déjà là*), very much in the way Sartre had used it in his "ontological proof" of transphenomenal being. Ultimately Merleau-Ponty aims at an "enlarged" conception of intentionality, which applies not only to our conscious acts but underlies our entire relation to the world and our "comportment" toward others.

ε. "The most important attainment of phenomenology is without doubt to have combined extreme subjectivism and extreme objectivism in the idea of the *world* or of *rationality*" (*PP* XV). This final claim for phenomenology contains again a momentous reinterpretation of Husserl's conception. Husserl's clear objective had been to find the ultimate foundation for all knowledge in pure subjectivity. Merleau-Ponty's interpretation shifts decisively the center of gravity in phenomenology. It denounces by implication the appeal to subjectivity and attempts to combine the subjective with the objective approach through something which might be called "bipolar phenomenology." There is also a significant difference in the interpretation of the role of Merleau-Ponty's unifying conception "world." For Husserl's philosophy is certainly not world-*centered*, even though it became increasingly world-*based* when he decided on the fresh start from the description of the *Lebenswelt*.

What is, however, quite congenial to Husserl in Merleau-

Ponty's formula is the emphasis on rationality. But even this rationality differs in tone from that of Husserl. For phenomenology is now declared as engaged in the task of revealing the "mystery of the world and the mystery of reason." It is at times even called an *"engagement,"* a "violent act" which justifies itself by its performance (PP XVI).

How far can this reinterpretation of phenomenology be considered legitimate? For anyone familiar with the texts there can be no doubt – and Merleau-Ponty does not deny it – that he has extrapolated far beyond Husserl's own declarations. The only question in this respect can be whether these extrapolations are justifiable in the light of Husserl's expressed intentions. The present incompleteness of the Louvain edition of Husserl's works makes any discussion of this point premature. In the meantime there is every reason to examine Merleau-Ponty's conception of phenomenology on its own merits. This is anyhow the only decisive test for a philosophy whose final criterion is the verdict of the "things themselves." This test has to be conducted primarily on the basis of the demonstration of Merleau-Ponty's method in the *Phénoménologie de la perception* itself. Actually, this work contains no attempt to apply explicitly and methodically the procedures described in the independent *Préface.* The Introduction of the book leads from a detailed critique of the "classical prejudices" about the nature of perception to the demonstration of the necessity of a "return to the phenomena." Of the three main parts the first two, dealing respectively with the body as the vantage point of perception and the world as perceived, are applications of what Merleau-Ponty calls a "first reflection" which begins with, but is not restricted to, psychology. Its function is to describe the "phenomenal field" as perceived or lived. But on closer inspection it turns out that this phenomenal field is not self-sufficient and self-explanatory. Features such as gestalt and meaning are more than merely accidental data. They lead to the question of the way in which they constitute or establish themselves in our consciousness. In the light of this new question the phenomenal field, considered as the field in which the world of perceptions appears, becomes the transcendental field. Here a second "more radical reflection" is needed to explore the "phenomenon of the

phenomenon" (*PP* 77, 419). Transcendental phenomenology
so conceived will focus on the reexamination of the phenomenological *cogito* as the transcendental ground upon which the
primary phenomena constitute themselves, with a view to finding
a more fundamental stratum or "*Logos*" than the *cogito*, notably
"existence." The third and last part, actually the shortest, is
devoted to this enterprise under the title of "Being-for-oneself
(*être-pour-soi*) and Being-present-within-the-world (*être-au-
monde*)," which will be considered in a special section below.

Apart from this reinterpretation of the transcendental fields
as not based on pure consciousness in the Cartesian sense, it is
noteworthy that Merleau-Ponty's transcendental existence is by
no means an impersonal or super-individual subject. He makes a
special point of stressing this as a difference between the traditional idealistic transcendentalism and transcendental phenomenology. For the transcendental subject is no longer a separate
entity located everywhere and nowhere; its center is our individual existence (PP 75 f.). To be sure, Merleau-Ponty's accounts of the second phase of his phenomenological method
are not very explicit. Apparently no special technique is involved,
merely a change in the direction of our reflection, notably from
the phenomenal field to our consciousness *of* it and specifically
to its temporal structure. In due course this is to reveal the
foundation for perception and for its possibility. It will demonstrate the fundamental fact that the "engaged consciousness"
is "within the world" or present to a world. In the characterization of the two reflections, however, there is no clear
reference to Husserl's reductions nor any attempt to parallel any
of Husserl's specific descriptions. Merleau-Ponty's technique
seems to have been developed without special consideration of
Husserl's methods, but simply in an attempt to do justice to
the phenomena at hand.

By way of a preliminary summary I might state that the
first phenomenological reflection in Merleau-Ponty's sense
consists of an attempt to view and to describe the world as
experienced, free from scientific interpretations, additions, and
subtractions, and free from philosophic preconceptions; or, more
briefly, it consists in the study of the *Lebenswelt* in Husserl's
sense. The second phenomenological reflection is an attempt to

account for our contact with the phenomena by turning this reflection toward the relation between the world and the subject to which it appears, or, specifically, to the perceiver.

There is one later semi-official text, which can be used for a fuller understanding of Merleau-Ponty's conception of phenomenology, the mimeographed transcript of his Sorbonne course on *The Sciences of Man and Phenomenology* of 1950/51. Unfortunately only the Introduction and the First Part of this text, dealing with Husserl's conception of the sciences of man and adding brief comments on Scheler and Heidegger, have been published. Thus it can at best serve as a critical picture of Husserl's phenomenology seen under the aspect of the problems of the sciences of man, i.e., psychology, sociology, history, and linguistics. Its chief value is that it allows us to appraise more fully Merleau-Ponty's perspective on Husserl, with whom he usually sides against Scheler and Heidegger, especially in view of their much more dogmatic claims to having attained absolute knowledge. But even in this text Merleau-Ponty often pushes on beyond Husserl. Thus, in place of Husserl's view about the essential parallelism between phenomenology and descriptive psychology he puts the thesis of their actual homogeneity (p. 32). He even claims that scientific induction and phenomenological intuition (*Wesensschau*) are essentially the same thing. Nor is there for him any sharp break between the certainty of our knowledge of essences and the mere probability of our knowledge of facts, as even Sartre had maintained. Phenomenology and the sciences of man converge. The main evidence that Merleau-Ponty presents for this new interpretation comes from the Husserl of the last decade. But he promises further evidence from an examination of the sciences of man. An article on "The Philosopher and Sociology" (1951) provides some of it.

Merleau-Ponty's new emphasis on the essential unity of phenomenology and science may at first sight come as a surprise. And it may well be that it indicates a certain shift. For in the *Phenomenology of Perception*, especially in its Preface, we find repeated expressions of opposition to science which could make one wonder how Merleau-Ponty's version of phenomenology jibes at all with Husserl's ideal of philosophy as a rigorous science. Thus he declares that "going back to the things means to start with a repudiation (*désaveu*) of science" (*PP* II), a formulation which, read in isolation, certainly sounds like the expression of an extreme anti-scientific attitude. Yet a closer examination of this and similar passages reveals that they have to be interpreted in the light of a peculiarly French conception of science, according to which science coincides with an "objective" approach for which there are only "things" (*choses*) in their external juxtaposition (*partes extra partes*) and in their causal interactions, and which ignores the concreteness of lived experience and of the meanings it carries with it. In short, this is the abstract science of Whitehead's *Science and the Modern World*. In Merleau-Ponty's view the objectivism of abstract science breaks down in the human sciences, which cannot dispense with a consideration of subjectively lived experiences and meanings. It is therefore not surprising to find Merleau-Ponty now asserting the convergence of precisely the sciences of man and phenomenology.

It is another question whether Merleau-Ponty would go so far as to subscribe to Husserl's ideal of phenomenology as a rigorous science. Certainly Merleau-Ponty has much more the sense of the ambiguous, the relative, and the tentative than especially the earlier Husserl professed. It was only as a result of his growing sense of the scope and difficulties of his task that Husserl had arrived at an increasingly more modest estimate of the chances of phenomenology to reach absolute and final insight; what could at best be hoped for were approximations to an infinite goal. Such statements of epistemological humility and even resignation obviously fit in much better with Merleau-Ponty's conception of truth as in the making and as essentially historical than did Husserl's earlier battle for absolute knowledge against the attacks of historicism and other relativisms. It would clearly go too far to say that for Merleau-Ponty phenomenology is a science. But it would still make sense to call it the foundation of all science insofar as it describes reflectively the phenomena of lived experience, from which all science, "objective" as well as human, takes its start. As an attempt to investigate and to describe the phenomena of the life world as faithfully as possible, it has certainly a claim to be considered as research, just as any human enterprise which explores our world.

5. Some Key Chapters from Merleau-Ponty's Phenomenology

The fact that Merleau-Ponty himself has made phenomenology coterminous with philosophy would make his entire philosophy eligible as an illustration of his conception of phenomenology. Considerations of space and balance prohibit such aspirations. The compromise aimed at in the following pages is a combination of a bird's-eye view of Merleau-Ponty's philosophy with a more detailed introduction to some of its parts which can show his phenomenological method in operation. I shall begin with a characterization of Merleau-Ponty's two major books on behavior and perception as the two focal topics for his conception of the basic phenomenological stratum, and concentrate on some of the most characteristic descriptions in these areas. In the later sections I shall also try to give samples of his unfinished work on phenomena above the level of the immediate life world (*Lebenswelt*), notably in the range of such social and cultural phenomena as speech and language.

a. THE STRUCTURE OF BEHAVIOR AND THE PHE-NOMENOLOGY OF 'GESTALT' – What is perhaps most characteristic of the early Merleau-Ponty is the concrete and painstaking manner in which he uses science as his point of departure and works his way methodically to the place where only a new philosophical solution can do justice to the problem posed by it. This is particularly true of his first work, in which he leads the reader from an objectivist behaviorism via gestalt psychology to a new phenomenology of gestalt.

Merleau-Ponty is far from brushing aside behaviorism after the manner of quite a few psychologists and philosophers, who regards it simply as "silly" (C. D. Broad). He tries to meet it on its own grounds and to show not only the inadequacy of the merely physiological interpretation of behavior but the full implications of a concept which he considers quite legitimate in its proper place, and which, fully thought through, can be a most valuable link in a psychology and philosophy which is neither anti-mentalistic nor mentalistic. What is wrong in behaviorism is not its concept of behavior. But behavior fully understood is more than merely objective movements. The new phenomenological and existential approach can redeem this much richer sense of the term.[1] Taken as a whole "it is not a material reality and not a psychical one either, but a structure, which does not properly belong to the external world or to the internal life" (SC 197).

Merleau-Ponty begins with an examination of the "reflexology" of the Watsonian physiologists. The most significant result of this examination is that it is impossible to predict responses from the objective nature of the stimuli alone. It is actually the organism which determines the stimuli that can affect it. In fact the whole reflex chain forms an equilibrated gestalt pattern which controls the mutual relationship of stimulus and response. John Dewey's criticism of *"The Reflex Arc Concept in Psychology"* (1896) may be said to have anticipated a good deal of this critical revision.

In similar fashion Merleau-Ponty studies the higher types of behavior, beginning with Pavlov's conditioned reflexes. Certain revealing gaps of this theory, particularly those brought to light by Gelb and Goldstein's studies on brain lesions and their compensations, show again that only a gestaltist interpretation of the total behavior can account for the phenomena. "Behavior is a gestalt," as Merleau-Ponty puts it finally.

But Merleau-Ponty does not stop with gestalt theory, much as he believes in its superiority and indispensability for an interpretation of behavior. His principal criticism of the gestalt theory, especially in the form given it by Wolfgang Köhler, is that it does not go far enough, that it is still a "naturalist" theory which accepts the superiority and causal control of the physical phenomena over the psychical phenomena. To Merleau-Ponty this attempt to make the gestalt phenomena dependent on physical causes is a remnant of an unphilosophical realism.[2] A consistent phenomenology of gestalt has to base its account on a study of the phenomena as given in direct experience, without

[1] Merleau-Ponty believes that John Watson himself wavers between a materialistic interpretation of behavior in terms of physiology and an "environmental" one which sees in it a relation between man and his world, "the vision of man as a debate and a constant coming to terms (*explication*) with a physical and a social world." (SC 3, note).

[2] For Merleau-Ponty's perspective of gestalt psychology, which at times overestimates the historical connections with phenomenology, see also *PP 62* note, and *SN* 166–176.

resorting to hypotheses about their causal origins. But that does not mean reducing behavior to a mere phenomenon of consciousness. At this point Merleau-Ponty introduces the term "existence" as an expression of the insight that behavior is neither merely physical nor completely psychical. It is a "manner of existing": "The world, inasmuch as it contains living beings, is no longer matter filled with parts next to each other but 'hollows' itself (*se creuser*) at the place where behavior appears" (*SC* 136). What this metaphor means is apparently that behavior is less of a break in the texture of the universe than full consciousness, which, according to Hegel and more recently to Sartre, is not only a hollow (*creux*) but a hole (*trou*) in the framework of being. Behavior indicates a decompression in the compact fabric of being which allows it to become centered in focal points. Thus existence, as Merleau-Ponty understands it, expresses a pre-conscious type of behavior, a transition between the massive In-itself and the perfectly transparent For-itself (consciousness). Existence is thus by no means restricted to human beings. All living beings have some kind of existence, although different from its human form.

Of particular interest is Merleau-Ponty's attempt to describe three forms of behavior which he calls respectively syncretic forms, removable forms, and symbolic forms. Briefly and incompletely described, *syncretic forms (formes syncrétiques)* occur where stimulus and response are "grown together," i.e., are tied so closely to their setting that any change in the stimulus will prevent the response. This pattern is characteristic for the level of lower organisms. *Removable forms (formes amovibles)* occur in behavior patterns where it is no longer the identical stimulus but its gestalt in relation to the total situation (for instance relative brightness in relation to other stimuli which have possibly the same absolute hue), which is the determining factor. Even animals at the level of intelligence of Köhler's chimpanzees seem to depend on the chance discovery of such forms in the relation between stimuli and behavior. *Symbolic forms* are characteristic of behavior in which stimulus and response are related by virtue of systematic principles established by special acts. They are known only at the level of human beings, who can shift their frames of reference on their own initiative.

On the basis of such a gestaltist interpretation of forms of behavior, Merleau-Ponty undertakes next to compare different orders of nature. The result is a philosophy of nature which determines the levels of the physical, the biological or vital, and the human in terms of their different configurations. None of them requires new substantial principles, but merely a restructuring of behavior. Thus the physical order is determined by an equilibrium of external factors. A vital organism can be defined as an equilibrium maintained by circular or "dialectical" processes among its factors in a manner for whose interpretation Merleau-Ponty is indebted to Kurt Goldstein. There is no need to appeal to vitalistic principles or to such an indefensible metaphysical hypothesis as Bergson's *élan vital*. On the human level this equilibrium of forms becomes dependent on man's intentions as expressed in the cultural world; it is based on his power to choose and to vary his points of view and his objectives, since he has the capacity to orient himself according to possibilities and to transcend (*dépasser*) given and even chosen meanings.

This section, which is in effect full-fledged metaphysics, leads to a relatively brief last chapter in which Merleau-Ponty considers the systematic significance of his findings for his original problem, that of the relations between consciousness and nature. What he is aiming at here is a position between a naive realism, with its causal account of behavior, and a criticist or idealist solution which derives behavior exclusively from consciousness. The answer as Merleau-Ponty envisages it is to be found by means of a systematic phenomenology of perception in which the new concepts of form, structure, and meaning have their primary foundation. However, this last chapter of *La Structure du comportement* cannot do more than set the stage for such an enterprise and give first indications of its direction.

As a whole the book does not present the characteristics of an explicitly phenomenological treatise, nor does it pretend to be one. It is based very largely on material derived from science, particularly from psychology including animal psychology with its less directly given materials. *La Structure du comportement* should therefore be considered chiefly as prolegomena to a phenomenology by way of a demonstration of the need for a new start, based on the inadequacies of mechanical behaviorism and, to a lesser degree, of gestalt psychology. Implicitly, however, even Merleau-Ponty's first book contains a considerable number of results which fit into a phenomenological framework. What he has to say about behavior as a structure and about the main types of behavior may well be claimed as phenomenological insights into the essence of behavior and into its relationships with its context.

b. PERCEPTION – The "primacy" of perception is Merleau-Ponty's most cherished thesis, and the phenomenology of perception the central part of his philosophy. It is important, however, to realize that "primacy" in this case does not mean the exclusive right of perception or even its prerogative in case of indecisive evidence, as in the case of the primacy of Kant's practical reason. It simply means that perception constitutes the ground level for all knowledge, and that its study has to precede that of all other strata such as those of the cultural world and specifically that of science.

It is even more important to be fully aware of the objective of Merleau-Ponty's phenomenology of perception as compared with the usual studies of perception, and particularly with the philosophical studies of perception in the Anglo-American world, of which the penetrating book by H. H. Price, apparently unknown to Merleau-Ponty at the time, may serve as an example.[1] It would not be hard and would be extremely worth while to establish points of contact. For Price is just as critical of the accounts of perception by "objective science" and particularly of its "causal theory"; and his modified defense of common-sense realism is not without parallel to Merleau-Ponty's return to the phenomena. But where a study like Merleau-Ponty's begins to differ from Price's is by the absence of any discussion of the central topic of sense-data, sensa, or sensibilia, their existence and non-existence. This absence is by no means accidental. For one of Merleau-Ponty's main points is the denial of such meaningless items as "red patches of a round and somewhat bulgy shape standing out from a background of other color-patches, and having a certain visual depth," which is Price's description of the sense-datum of a tomato (*Perception*, p. 3).

[1] Price, H. H., *Perception*, 1933.

For Merleau-Ponty there is no such thing as Price's meaningless data.

This does not mean that Merleau-Ponty's approach to perception simply coincides with the standard phenomenological pattern established by Husserl. Actually we hardly find any mention of Husserl's characterization of perception as the act in which an object is bodily given (*leibhafte Selbstgegebenheit*). Nor is there much reference to perception as an act of fulfillment for previous anticipations ("empty intentions"), and very little to Husserl's celebrated perspective shadings (*Abschattungen*), the modifications of perception, the various ways in which perceptual objects can be presented, and the acts of perceiving them. For Merleau-Ponty's book is not a study of perception by itself and simply for its own sake. In spite of its comprehensive title, this is not the final phenomenological monograph on perception. It contains less and more. Less: for it omits any number of phenomena of interest in their own right; more: for it includes the core of a philosophy which exceeds by far the phenomenon of perception in the traditional sense. Merleau-Ponty's phenomenology of perception is primarily an attempt to explore the basic stratum in our experience of the world as it is given prior to all scientific interpretation. Perception is simply our privileged access to this stratum. Hence the primary task is to see and to describe how the world presents itself to perception as concretely as possible, without omitting its meanings and absences of meaning, its clarities and its ambiguities. The *Phénoménologie de la perception* is actually a phenomenology of the world as perceived rather than of the perceiving act.

A quick survey of the main topics of the book will be the best way to make this apparent. After the Preface, which contains Merleau-Ponty's general conception of phenomenology and which was discussed in the preceding section, the Introduction undertakes to prepare for the way back to the phenomena of the perceived life world (*Lebenswelt*). This "return" is blocked by two types of "classical prejudices," empiricism" and "intellectualism." Both have their root in what Merleau-Ponty calls the "prejudice of the world," i.e., the assumption of a pre-given objective world consisting of meaningless sense data, which either associate passively to form the phenomena of perception or are put together by such acts as attention or judgment. This "prejudice" is based on what psychology has called the "principle of constancy," according to which each objective stimulus is connected with a sensation in a one-to-one relationship. Merleau-Ponty's point of departure is the defeat of this principle at the hand of the gestaltists: primarily sensations do not depend on external stimuli, but on the context of figure-ground in which they belong and which determines their "sense," a term which for Merleau-Ponty has an unusually wide meaning that includes "form" (*Gestalt*) and even essence, in fact any kind of reference beyond its carrier. To see the elements that go into perception in such a context brings out two features overlooked in the traditional theory of sensation: that these elements are intrinsically "meaningful," not "silent," and that they are open, indeterminate, and ambiguous at the margin, not closed, determinate, and unambiguous like so many little separate blocks. Only when a phenomenological account has eliminated this distorting start can it return to the field of the phenomena as presented to a *"first"* or *"psychological"* reflection.

The exploration of the phenomenal field carried out by this reflection as the first stage of Merleau-Ponty's phenomenological method takes up the first two of the three parts of the book and considerably more than two thirds of its pages. The first part deals with the body seen as man's characteristic access to the world. Beginning with the demonstration that a merely mechanistic physiology of the nervous system simply cannot account for the experience of our own body – a demonstration which considers especially such "pathological experiences" as the "phantom limb" of the mutilated – Merleau-Ponty tries to show that the experience of our own body has its basis in our "existence," i.e., in our mode of "existing our body." Utilizing materials from recent psychopathology, his existential analysis deals first with the spatial and motor patterns of the body. Next the body is studied as a sexual being; the basis for these studies is again certain psychopathological variations, which are to show how sexuality too, as an essential part of our body experience, is a function or expression of our existence, a fact which is distorted in the Freudian interpretation of sex as the underlying causal factor of all human behavior. Finally Merleau-Ponty explores the body as a being expressing itself in gestures and in speech and language, of which again the body is experienced as an integral component.

The second part explores the world as perceived (*le monde perçu*), to which our body gives us access. Sensation is considered first. In the new perspective, data such as colors turn out to be intimately included in the "circuit" of our existence: our glance (*regard*) and the datum belong together. We are involved (*engagés*) in sensation. The same existential involvement can be found in our experience of space. Characteristics such as up and down, depth and relative motion, and our whole space of living are related to our mode of existence and to its organ, the body. It also turns out that "the thing" (*la chose*), being the objective pole for all its varying appearances to us, is related in its constancy to the constancy of our own body (*PP* 366), in fact that it is a "correlative of our body and of our life" (*PP* 372). Our momentary perception of such a "thing" is transcendent since it refers to other perceptual perspectives. Likewise any particular thing contains open references to a "natural world" as its horizon (*PP* 384). Finally other people and the human or cultural world are integrated into the picture of the natural world and of our perception. For the "other" is actually a part of the pattern of possible perspectives that belong to each thing. Coexistence represents an essential prolongation of the natural world of our individual existence.

The relatively brief third part is the one which goes beyond the mere "psychological" reflection on the phenomena of our "*Lebenswelt*" with their transcendences, ambiguities, and even contradictions. Here Merleau-Ponty wants to show how the world of phenomena constitutes itself in us and how it is "possible." Under the title "Being-for-itself" (*L'Être-pour-soi*) and "Being-within-the-world" (*L'Être-au-monde*) he undertakes to replace the Cartesian *cogito* (consciousness) by the "true *cogito*" of our "presence within the world." Since this part no longer deals with perception in itself, but with its possibility, we shall consider this most original feature of Merleau-Ponty's phenomenology in a special section.

What can be considered as fundamentally new in Merleau-Ponty's treatment of perception thus far? At first sight it might seem that little of it would have to be added to the stock of phenomenological insights into the structure of perception. Its most noteworthy aspect is the concrete study of the objects perceived and its sweep over most areas of the perceptual world, far beyond the usual preoccupation with the perception of immediate sense objects. But there are much more original features. The best way to bring these out is to list some of Merleau-Ponty's most succinct formulae for the nature of perception.

"Perceiving is to see an immanent sense surging (*jaillir*) from a constellation of data" (*PP* 30), or "to seize an immanent sense in a sensible form prior to any judgment" (*PP* 44). From such accounts perception emerges as the act designed to trace elementary meaning as actually already present in the world prior to our interpretations. This emphasis on meaning as discovered, not bestowed by investing acts, is certainly new, even though it is not an absolute innovation.

No less important is the characterization of perception as "a human act which at one stroke breaks through (*traverser*) all possible doubts in order to install itself in the full truth" (*PP* 50). This may at first sight sound like the rather extravagant claim that perception is essentially veridical. That this is not Merleau-Ponty's contention can be gathered from a later formulation like the following: "Perceiving is committing (*engager*) at one stroke a whole future of experiences in a present which does not strictly guarantee it: it is believing in a world" (*PP* 344). Perceiving is therefore by no means illusion-proof, but always involves a risk, as far as any particular perception is concerned. Like John Dewey, Merleau-Ponty rejects the extravagance of the absolutist quest for certainty.

But the main implication of these additional formulae for perception is that it now appears as an existential act, an act in which we are not only passively involved but also commit ourselves in a world which is only partly given, since it is always partly ambiguous, and only partly of our own making, since we depend on our "incarnation" in a pre-given world. It is neither a merely receptive nor a merely creative act. It expresses our fundamentally ambiguous relation to the world. This existential role of perception constitutes clearly the most original, if debatable, feature of Merleau-Ponty's theory of perception.

But this does not exclude other contributions of his book which do not depend on the acceptance of the existentialist framework. They often occur inconspicuously in connection with familiar topics, and are not always marked off as particularly new. The phenomenology of the perceptual field is perhaps the most noteworthy among these more specific phenomenological insights. Other valuable contributions that can be found in the course of Merleau-Ponty's argument include descriptions of the more ambiguous parts of the field, and of what is only indirectly and incompletely given. But most significant is clearly the unusually comprehensive phenomenology of the body, which, while being far from exhaustive, goes considerably beyond what Sartre had included in the pertinent sections of *L'Être et le néant*, where the main emphasis had been on the social function of the body experience, or what Gabriel Marcel had more intimated than actually described.

c. THE NEW *'Cogito'*: BEING-WITHIN-THE-WORLD ('ÊTRE-AU-MONDE') – One of the chief obstacles to an unbiased hearing for phenomenology, particularly in America, has been its supposed Cartesianism. It cannot be denied that Husserl himself after the publication of the *Logische Untersuchungen* saw in Descartes the chief forerunner of phenomenology, although he never followed him into his dualistic metaphysics. It is also true that Sartre, though not for the same reasons, considers himself to be in the Cartesian succession, inasmuch as Descartes' *cogito*, however enlarged, is for him closely related to his doctrine of freedom. It is all the more important to realize that phenomenology also includes an anti-Cartesian strain. Scheler, in his critique of the idols of self-knowledge, was anything but a Cartesian. And Heidegger, who now sees in Descartes the main root of modern subjectivism and ultimately of nihilism, is the chief German voice of anti-Cartesianism. Even more surprising in a way is Merleau-Ponty's criticism of the Cartesian *cogito*, since the critic is a phenomenologist who otherwise claims to be carrying out Husserl's fundamental and final intentions. Merleau-Ponty's reinterpretation of the Cartesian *cogito* is indeed his most distinctive, if not his most convincing, change in the pattern of phenomenology.

The best way to describe Merleau-Ponty's position on this point may be to begin with his criticisms of the "old" *cogito*. Merleau-Ponty contests the indubitability of consciousness and its various modes, such as perceiving and even doubting. Thus it is simply an illusion to believe that, while the existence of the perceived is always open to doubt, that of our perceiving is not. Once the perceived turns out to be a hallucination, we have to admit that we have not truly perceived. For perceiving and the perceived are inseparable. Nor is my supposed doubt always genuine doubt. There is therefore no good reason to attach to the immanent acts of the *cogito* any greater certainty than to the transcendent cogitata. "Consciousness is transcendence through and through" (*de part en part*). However, this does not mean that Merleau-Ponty abandons the doctrine of the *cogito* completely. For there is a "true *cogito*" (*cogito véritable*), which can be expressed in impersonal formulations like: "there is consciousness, something shows itself, there is a phenomenon" (*PP* 342). It reveals the "deep movement which constitutes my very being, the simultaneous contact with my being and with the being of the world" (*PP* 432). Or, to use Merleau-Ponty's new and pointed expression, the new *cogito* is my being-present-within-the-world (*être-au-monde*). It would be misleading to think of this new *cogito* as illusion-proof. The only way to pass beyond the range of possible doubt is by "throwing oneself with closed eyes into action" (*PP* 438), i.e., by an act of commitment, be it love, hate, or even effective doubt. The only indubitable consciousness is committed consciousness. In fact, for Merleau-Ponty committed consciousness (*conscience engagée*) constitutes the very meaning of the term "existence."

But *engagement* has not only the implication of a freely chosen commitment. Even such a commitment presupposes that consciousness is already involved by previous commitment and ultimately by its birth and "incarnation" in a certain body in space, and, equally important, in history, as manifested particularly in the form of our native language. I can never step completely outside being, not even by the most radical form of doubt.

Subjectivity thus assumes the form of "inherence in the world" (*PP* 464). In fact, the world is nothing but the field of our experience, and we are nothing but a certain perspective of it. In other words, the internal and the external, the subjective and the objective are inseparable. "The world is all in us, and I am all outside myself" (*PP* 467). We are "presence within the world" (*au monde*), not only inside the world (*dans le monde*), as Heidegger had put it. It is deeply significant that the end of the *Phenomenology of Perception* consists of a quotation from Antoine de Saint-Exupéry's *Pilote de Guerre* with the concluding sentence: "Man is nothing but a knot of relations; the relations alone count for man" (*PP* 529).

Such a reinterpretation of the *cogito* is meant as a deliberate challenge to subjectivism in both the Cartesian and the Husserlian sense. It does of course not mean the denial of the subjective as such. But it implies that the subjective is merely an inseparable facet of an embracing structure.

How far has Merleau-Ponty been successful in liberating phenomenology from Cartesianism? How far is this goal even legitimate? To begin with the second question, one might well wonder whether the justified suspicion of Descartes the metaphysician, with his interest in the immortal substance "soul," has not made Merleau-Ponty, as it had so many others, overly suspicious of Descartes the phenomenologist, who insisted on the inescapable phenomenon expressed by the first person singular in its unmistakable though fluid difference from the body. True, even the experience of the self is not illusion-proof. But this does not prevent the phenomenon of the ego from presenting itself as clearly and distinctly as other phenomena. Besides, no matter how far we retreat in declaring any particular form of the *cogito* to be not beyond possible doubt, there is at least the consciousness of the doubt of our doubt, and so on. At least one of these consciousnesses must be indubitable for the others to be dubitable by them.

"Presence within the world" may at first sight appear to be a rather ingenious way of replacing the *ego cogito* by a neutral datum which finally bridges the gap between the subject and the object that epistemology had not been able to fill. But does it really do so? In what sense can we really assert that we are in contact with the world? Isn't the price of such an assertion, if we do not want to be dogmatic, a grading down of our concept

of the world from something which exists, whether or not we are
in contact with it, to something which is nothing apart from
our being inserted in it? As such the world becomes what
Merleau-Ponty himself has called at times an "interworld"
(*intermonde*).

But what if this world should really be the only world we have
a right to talk about, what if the *en-soi* of the realist has really
to be abandoned just like the subject of the idealist? Then we
still have to answer the question of what will be left of "the
world" once we disrupt our contact with it. Simply to assert our
presence within the world seems to be an attempt to cut the
Gordian knot instead of untangling it. Is Merleau-Ponty's sword
even strong enough to do it?

d. SUBJECTIVITY AND TEMPORALITY – However, the
full reinterpretation and recasting of the concept of subjectivity
is the result of Merleau-Ponty's analysis of time and temporality.
The climactic chapter on "Temporality" in the *Phénoménologie
de la perception* is actually an attempt to combine Husserl's
phenomenology of time with that of Heidegger, from whose
Sein und Zeit Merleau-Ponty suddenly quotes extensively,
beginning with a motto that follows one from Paul Claudel,
both to the effect that temporality is the meaning of existence.

Time, according to Merleau-Ponty, is not part of the objective
world. Past and future, in particular, "withdraw" (*se retirer*)
from being and can be found only as dimensions of our own
subjectivity (*PP* 471). As such they appear in the field of our
present. This emphasis on the primacy of the present may
remind American readers of G. H. Mead's *Philosophy of the
Present*, which Merleau-Ponty's philosophizing parallels remarkably at times. But Merleau-Ponty describes the relation of
past and future to the present much more concretely by showing
their inbeddedness in our present-time consciousness. This he does
by means of a diagram (taken over with some modifications
from Husserl's lectures on the inner time consciousness) which
indicates the sinking off of present time to deeper and deeper
levels, as we move on. There is also one other difference: past
and future cannot be supported simply by an objective present.
They can occur only in a subject that is a temporal being.

A subject is characterized in this respect by the fact that it breaks up the "fullness of being" and introduces into it the phenomenon of perspective and, in Merleau-Ponty's view, of non-being (*PP* 481). It thus can reach out beyond the present into past and future. Merleau-Ponty calls this property of the subject "ecstatic," using a term which had been applied before by Hegel, Heidegger, and Sartre for similar purposes. The ecstatic character of temporality and that of the temporal subject are so intimately related that Merleau-Ponty finally characterizes "time as the subject and the subject as time." By this he means that the subject is not simply *in* time, for it assumes and lives time (*PP* 483) and is involved (*engagé*) in time: it is permeated with time.

This ecstatic outreaching of temporality makes possible not only subjectivity but also "sense" and "reason," as they imply the open movement toward referents other than themselves. It thus constitutes an "operative intentionality" that underlies the "intentionality of the (conscious) act" (*PP* 490). The foundation for such acts can only be a being oriented or polarized toward something which it is not, which transcends itself toward a world. Thus the world is again inseparable from the subject, but the subject is also inseparable from the world (*PP* 491). This interdependence is at the same time Merleau-Ponty's settlement of the perennial controversy over idealism and realism, which thus far even phenomenology had been unable to achieve. The recognition of the mutual dependence of subject and object allows us to pass beyond this stale and hopeless controversy; it seems almost too obvious to refer here to the pattern of the Hegelian synthesis, which Merleau-Ponty himself does not mention on this occasion. Instead, Merleau-Ponty calls subject and object two abstract elements of one single structure called "presence" (*présence*), in which the subject is essentially presence at the world (*être-au-monde*), and the world is "subjective" (*PP* 491 f.). The ecstatic transcendence laid out in the temporality of the subject provides the ultimate bond of this interconnectedness.

e. CONDITIONED FREEDOM – Merleau-Ponty's doctrine of incarnated consciousness, where subject and world determine each other reciprocally, finds its concluding expression in the

reformulation of the existentialist doctrine of freedom. Sartre
had stated this doctrine with his characteristic extremism:
Freedom is either total or non-existent. Yet in actual practice
even his freedom was only a freedom within a given situation
which served as the raw material for the free choices of new
meanings. For Merleau-Ponty the given situation stands for
considerably more. It is part of the essential involvement of man
as a being within the world. Even before any choice is made
this situation has meanings which we may be able to change but
not ignore. We never start from zero. Consequently the idea of a
first or fundamental choice is to Merleau-Ponty an illusion. We
must exist in a certain incarnation, hence have a certain "essence"
along with our existence. Sartre's celebrated and over-publicized
formula "existence precedes essence" would therefore not hold
for Merleau-Ponty. It is not only we who choose the world. It is
just as much the world which chooses us (PP 518). Freedom
stands out against a field of "sedimented" meanings, as Merleau-
Ponty puts it, using a characteristic metaphor from Husserl.
History forms the background for every free act. Between an
objectivist determinism and the absolute freedom of idealist
reflection the phenomena themselves reveal existence as conditioned freedom within a given style of life. From a perception
of such involvement arises the possibility of new existential
projects by way of a polarization of the situation.

As a phenomenological illustration of such a conditioned free
choice Merleau-Ponty offers a description of the rise of class
consciousness and the ensuing revolutionary decision. According
to Marxist objectivism this is a matter of strict determination,
according to Sartre a completely free project. According to
Merleau-Ponty, the rise of class consciousness emerges from a
realization of the situation by existing individuals who see
themselves as working men in typical communication with the
world around them; no choice is involved at this stage, but
simply the experience of a certain style of being and of being-
within-the-world. The transition from here to class consciousness
takes place on the basis of the workers' perception of a solidarity
between themselves and other workers in similar situations as
revealed in witnessing a strike. Now "the social space begins to
polarize itself, one sees a field of the exploited group taking

shape" (*PP* 508). This situation is lived in the perception of a common obstacle to everybody's life. Closer and less close projects begin to connect. But "the revolutionary project is not the result of a deliberate judgment, the explicit setting of a goal" (*PP* 508 f.). The decision "ripens in the coexistence before erupting in words and relating itself to objective goals." Instead of the intellectual project we have to consider the existential project, the "polarization of a life against a determined-undetermined goal of which it has no explicit idea and which it does not recognize until the moment when it achieves it. . . . . It is not a matter of the indicative but of the interrogative, the subjunctive, the vow and the wait. Projects are lived in ambiguity" (*PP* 508). "It is I who give a meaning and a future to my life, but this does not mean that this meaning and that future are conceptual (*conçus*); they surge from my present and from my past, and in particular from my present and past coexistence." (*PP* 510)

Thus there are two limitations to Merleau-Ponty's freedom: (1) it starts from a "situation which I exist" and over which I have no control; (2) my choice is really not a conscious but a preconscious or existential one. The fact that freedom does not start from nothing does not mean, however, that I am unable to interrupt my existential project at any time. But even that freedom means only freedom to begin something else (*autre chose*): we never remain suspended in the nothing (as Sartre often seems to be saying, at least to Merleau-Ponty). "We are always in the full, in being, like a face, which even at rest, even in death, is always condemned to express something" (PP 516). "One must not say that I choose myself constantly, under the pretext that I could constantly refuse to be what I am. Not to refuse is not the same thing as to choose. We could not equate non-interfering (*laisser faire*) and doing (*faire*) short of depriving what is (merely) implicit of all phenomenal value. . . ." (*PP* 516).

True, it is never possible to distinguish clearly the part of the situation and the part of freedom. "We are mingled with the world and with other prople in an inextricable intermixture" (*confusion*) (*PP* 518). But this does not abolish the fact that there is the "*engagement*" of history together with the disengaging freedom of our acts. A phenomenological account allows us to see distinctly at least the ambiguity of this situation and its components.

f. THE SOCIAL WORLD – SPEECH AND LANGUAGE:
Sartre had based his phenomenology of the social world on the
experience of the gaze, or, more specifically, on the experience
of being gazed at. Merleau-Ponty knows this phenomenon too.
But to him it is much too narrow a basis for a social phenomenology. In particular, the gaze has to be seen in the context
of a total social situation, of communication and its patholo-
gy. This context includes also the cultural phenomena, beginning
with speech and language. It is to these phenomena that Merleau-
Ponty has given increasing phenomenological attention.

Merleau-Ponty's first approach to the social world is by the
phenomenology of perception, beginning with the perception of
our own body. This body, as Merleau-Ponty interprets it, is
primarily a focus of varying perspectives of the world. But each
perspective refers to other possible perspectives. And these
perspectives dovetail with the perspectives of other human beings
of which we are aware in seeing their bodies. "It is precisely my
body which perceives the other's body and finds there something
like a miraculous prolongation of our own intentions ...
Henceforth, just as the parts of my body jointly form a system,
the other's body and mine are a single whole, the face and the
reverse of one sole phenomenon..." (*PP* 406).

But cultural phenomena are at least as important bridges as
the body. Most important among these is language. Merleau-
Ponty has given increasing attention to its phenomena based on
the work of such linguists as Saussure. Seen from the social angle
(which is by no means the only significant one for Merleau-
Ponty) language occurs primarily in the form of the dialogue.
Here my thought and that of the other "insert" each other into
a common ground

in a common operation of which neither of us is the creator. There is a
being-at-two, and the other is here no longer for me a mere behavior in
my transcendental field, nor am I in his; we are both mutually collaborators in a perfect reciprocity, our perspectives slide (*glisser*) into each other,
we coexist across a same world. In the present immediate dialogue I
am liberated from myself; the thoughts of the other are really his own,
it is not I who form them, although I grasp them as soon as born or
anticipate them, and even the objection which my partner makes to me
elicits from me thoughts which I did not know I had, so that if (it is true
that) I lend him thoughts, he makes me think in turn. It is only afterwards, when I return from the dialogue and recall it, that I can reintegrate

it into my life, make of it an episode of my history, and that the other returns to his absence or, inasmuch as he remains present to me, is felt as a menace (*PP* 407).

Or, as Merleau-Ponty expresses it in his paper "On the Phenomenology of Language" (1951):

When I speak or when I understand, I experience the presence of others in myself and of myself in others, a presence which is the cornerstone of the theory of intersubjectivity ... and I finally understand the enigmatic saying of Husserl: "The transcendental subjectivity is intersubjectivity." [1] To the extent that what I say makes sense, I am for myself when I am speaking a different "other" (*un autre "autre"*), and to the extent that I understand I no longer know who is speaking and who is listening (*PA* 108).

This second passage, which clearly needs further development, is significant also as an indication of how Merleau-Ponty sees in the coexistence of interrelated subjectivities a bridge between mere subjectivism and objectivism and a possible foundation for a non-subjectivist phenomenology through intersubjectivity.

Coexistence, however, does not prevent the fact of solitude, and not even the relative "truth of solipsism." But solitude and communication are the two aspects of one and the same phenomenon. In fact they are so interdependent that "I would not even talk of solitude, and I could not even pronounce others as inaccessible if I had not the experience of others" (*PP* 412/3).

Perception is thus again the wedge which allows us to break through our immediate data into a phenomenal field into which they are inserted. It shows how our own world passes over unnoticeably into a wider world of coexistence toward which it is open on several sides, not only in our own body but also in the world of cultural expressions.

6. *Toward an Appraisal of Merleau-Ponty's Phenomenology*

The frame of this book and the amount of the information supplied thus far obviously do not require or allow a critical evaluation of Merleau-Ponty's philosophy as a whole. Nor would it be possible here to do justice to Merleau-Ponty's existentialist views, which differ so significantly from those of other contemporary existential philosophers, from Jaspers to Sartre.

[1] Concerning this seeming quotation see p. 517 note (1).

Were this my assignment, I would have had to put much more emphasis on his concrete picture of human existence. Such an account would give me a much needed chance to appraise the virtues of an existentialism which, while thoroughly humanistic in approach, expresses a much more sober and balanced estimate of the human situation than the more extreme and at times sensationalist forms of this movement. At least an existentialism for which human existence is neither absurd nor saved without remnant, which is dialectical without getting bogged down in antinomies, has a right to an independent hearing.

Our responsibility in the present context is more limited – and more exacting: to prepare an estimate of Merleau-Ponty's philosophy qua phenomenology and a comparison with the phenomenologies of other and particularly of French phenomenologists. The following paragraphs will mention at least some of the points which such an estimate would have to consider.

Before touching on more specific points a word should be said about the general significance of Merleau-Ponty's work for French phenomenology. It is probably safe to say that without Merleau-Ponty, and particularly without his *Phénoménologie de la perception*, phenomenology would have longer remained a mere tool of existentialism, as it has increasingly become in the hands of Sartre. On a more tangible level, without Merleau-Ponty and without his academic presence phenomenology would hardly have achieved so early the prestige which he has secured for it by his own spectacular career.

But Merleau-Ponty's stature as a phenomenologist will have to rest on more intrinsic merits than his personal success and the formal qualities of his presentation, outstanding though these may be. In the following paragraphs I shall raise certain questions pertaining first to more general matters and to his method and then to some specific items concerning his phenomenological achievements.

The first impression one receives in surveying Merleau-Ponty's writings may easily be that of a systematic spirit whose main interest is in taking up major traditional themes and fitting them into a new synthesis. There is in him little of that pioneering approach of the early phenomenologists or even of Sartre who preferred exploring the frontier to cultivating charted territory.

Nor do his writings carry the provocative impact of Sartre's so much more debatable analyses. The significance of his contributions is based precisely on the fact that he resumes the more conventional themes, considers carefully the traditional solutions and particularly the scientific evidence, before attacking them directly, and integrates them into a systematic new frame based on phenomenological principles.

How far can Merleau-Ponty's writings be considered to be demonstrations of the phenomenological method? This is not an easy question to answer. Few if any of his texts read like protocols of phenomenological research. The reason is not only that he usually starts out from a critical discussion of the traditional views. Most of the presentation of his own position takes the form of simple assertions of findings that he seems to have made long before. Rarely does he carry out the analysis before our very eyes or invite us to look with him at the phenomena by a methodical and painstaking investigation. Instead, he gives us his results ready-made, leaving it to us to do our own verifying. These results are usually imbedded in the context of a discursive argument without being identified as new and original intuitions. Hence, if one wants to isolate his most original phenomenological insights, it is necessary to extricate them from the context, which is not made any easier by the often inordinately long paragraphs of his texts. This is clearly no accident. Merleau-Ponty is not interested in advertising phenomenology for its own sake or in exploring phenomena in all their variety without any further purpose. He wants to practice phenomenology within the philosophical field and to demonstrate its value in concrete application.

There would be little point in discussing here the question how far Merleau-Ponty's phenomenology carries out the last, if not the ultimate, intentions of Husserl's program. His version has a right to be examined on its own merits. Now one of the most characteristic things about Merleau-Ponty's phenomenology is his attempt to bring it down from the level of pure consciousness into the world of concrete life, in fact to incarnate it in individual and social human existence. To be sure, even Sartre had emphasized the role of the human body, particularly in connection with his social phenomenology. But no one before had gone so far in identifying human existence with the body in which it finds itself "incarnated." Thus introducing phenomenology into the concrete rough-and-tumble of life and research is certainly apt to make it much more relevant. But it may be asked whether the identification of existence and body does not at times come dangerously close to selling the birthright of phenomenology for the dubious chance of participating in all sorts of enterprises which may or may not be congruous. More seriously, how far does the *engagement* in the body and in history still allow phenomenology to look upon itself from the necessary distance? How is phenomenology still possible when it no longer can detach itself from the *"engagement"* in the phenomena? Merleau-Ponty's reaffirmation of the need of the phenomenological reduction in his Preface to the *Phénoménologie de la perception* indicates that he is at least aware of this problem. – Similar questions may be asked with regard to the volatilization of man into a mere bundle of relations to the world.

I called it an overstatement to characterize Merleau-Ponty's thought as a philosophy of ambiguity. But it is nevertheless true that there is in his phenomenology a tendency to leave the phenomena in an atmosphere of indefiniteness which results in blurring the issues and the decisions. Thus the attempt to fuse the difference between consciousness and the non-conscious by the introduction of a term like "existence," which is never explicitly clarified, is apt to bring about a confused mixture instead of a synthesis. "Dialectical" formulations may help to keep us from premature decisions but they cannot save us from facing the phenomena directly, however hard it may be to pin them down.

It is one of Merleau-Ponty's fondest claims that his phenomenology can break the deadlock between realism and idealism and between empiricism and rationalism by making use of the best insights of gestalt psychology in a manner which the gestaltists themselves had not been able to do. This raises the question of the legitimacy of his critique of the gestaltist theory as still enmeshed in an outdated conception of science. Specifically, does not Merleau-Ponty himself take some points for granted which the gestaltists cannot be expected to accept without fuller demonstration? Thus, he seems to consider it as axiomatic that causation from the physical world to that of consciousness is inconceivable. He does this often in terms which suggest that the very category of causation has no status in phenomenology. Now the study of causation is indeed one of the more difficult and unfinished tasks of phenomenology, and causal relationships between physical and conscious entities may be particularly obscure. But that does not imply that all belief in causation is illegitimate "causalism" from the very start. Not even Husserl had abandoned it to that extent.

But it is not my intention to subject Merleau-Ponty's phenomenology to a point-by-point critical review. Suffice it to say that the scholarly sobriety of Merleau-Ponty's structures does not dispense us from a critical check on his general and specific claims. Merleau-Ponty himself would be the last to claim finality for all of his findings. For even the phenomenologist is subject to the essential limitations of an incarnated existent being to whom the world always remains partly transcendent. Merleau-Ponty's phenomenology is human phenomenology: it is the phenomenology of man's unfinishable business.

7. Merleau-Ponty's Following

It would be premature to speak of Merleau-Ponty's influence in terms of an academic following. Reasons for this may be his relatively recent emergence, the rapid shift of his academic location up till 1952, and the rather impersonal atmosphere of the Collège de France since then.

Nevertheless, his impact must not be minimized. Besides, in ALPHONSE DE WAELHENS (1911–   ) he has found not only a remarkable interpreter but also a thinker in his own right who seems to feel closer to him than to any of the phenomenologists or philosophers of existence from Husserl to Heidegger – which does not prevent him from expressing dissent when theological questions are involved. His latest collection of essays, Existence et signification (1958) states explicitly his program for a phenomenological "return to the things" in a way which implies a dialectical consideration of subjective existence and objective signification; a systematic justification of this program is promised for the future.

SELECTIVE BIBLIOGRAPHY

Major Works

[1]   *La Structure du comportement* (1942) (SC)
       Phénoménologie de la perception (1945) (PP)
       Translation: English (Preface only) in *Crosscurrents* VI (1956), 59–70,
[2]   by John F. Bannan – fair, not free from serious mistakes.
       Humanisme et terreur (1947) (HT)
       "Le Primat de la perception et ses conséquences philosophiques," *Bulletin
       de la Société Française de Philosophie*, Oct-Dec. 1947 (PPCP)
[3]   *Sens et non-sens* (1948) (SN)
       "Le Philosophe et la sociologie," *Cahiers Internationaux de Sociologie* X
       (1951) 55–69
       Les Sciences de l'homme et la phénoménologie. Cours de Sorbonne. Intro-
       duction et première partie. 1951–2 (SP)
       "L'Homme et l'adversité," *Rencontres internationales de Genève* (1952)
       51–75 (RI)
       "Sur la Phénoménologie du langage" *Problèmes actuels de la phénoménolo-
[4]   gie* (1952) (PA), 91–109
[5]   *Éloge de la philosophie* (1953) (EP)
       Les Aventures de la dialectique (1955) (AD)
[6]   *Les Philosophes célèbres* (1956) (PC)

Studies on Merleau-Ponty

ALQUIÉ, F., "Une Philosophie de l'ambiguité: L'existentialisme de Maurice
[7]   Merleau-Ponty," *Fontaine* no. 59 (1947), 47–70
       DE WAELHENS, ALPHONSE, *Une philosophie de l'ambiguité: L'Existentia-
       lisme de Maurice Merleau-Ponty* (1951)

[8]   Articles in English

BANNAN, JOHN F., "Philosophical Reflection and the Phenomenology of
Merleau-Ponty," *Review of Metaphysics* VIII (1954), 418–42.
BAYER, RAYMOND, "Merleau-Ponty's Existentialism," *The University of
[9]   Buffalo Studies* 19 (1953), 95–104.
SCHUETZ, ALFRED, "Language, Language Disturbances, and the Texture
of Consciousness," *Social Research* XVII (1950), 380–2.
SPIEGELBERG, HERBERT, "French Existentialism: Its Social Philosophies,"
Kenyon Review XVI (1954), 454–62.

Most Complete Bibliography up to 1950

DOUGLAS, KENNETH, *A Critical Bibliography of Existentialism* (The Paris
School) *Yale French Studies*. Special Monograph no. 1 (1950), items
[10]   201–229. (Some omissions)

XII

CURRENT DEVELOPMENTS IN FRENCH PHENOMENOLOGY

Phenomenology is anything but a closed chapter in the history of French philosophy. In fact, it is stirring to such a degree that it would be premature to attempt a complete survey or even to collect titles in a more than provisional spirit. Much will depend on how the men whose names have appeared above the horizon continue their work on the phenomenological basis from which they have started.

As of the time of this survey Paul Ricoeur, Mikel Dufrenne, and Raymond Polin seem to deserve special attention and at least a preliminary characterization of their work. In the following three sections I shall attempt to give mostly an intensive analysis of the phenomenological work of these three, arranged according to the approximate importance of their contributions.

A. PAUL RICOEUR (1913–

There is considerable agreement that among the younger philosophers listed above the outstanding contribution to phenomenology, both in size and originality, has been made by Paul Ricoeur. This contribution consists not only of his own phenomenological studies, especially in the field of the practical and emotional phenomena; Ricoeur is also the best informed French historian of phenomenology. As translator of and at the same time commentator on Husserl's *Ideen* he has created a unique instrument for future Husserl studies. His critical analyses of Husserl's posthumous works in the Louvain edition are also considerable aids in the assimilation of these often problematical texts. Being in charge of the – so far unique – deposit of the

transcripts of the Louvain Archives in France, Ricoeur had made
Strasbourg a center of Husserl studies on a level with Cologne
and Freiburg; since his transfer to the Sorbonne this center
has been moved to Paris.

It would be one-sided, however, to present Ricoeur simply as
the French phenomenologist best informed about German phenomenology. For on the one hand Ricoeur's interests and commitments outreach by far his stake in phenomenology. On the
other hand his adherence to phenomenology is not unqualified,
and the problem of the limits and limitations of phenomenology
is one of his constant concerns. It is also not without significance
that his major work, the *Philosophy of the Will*, of which only
the first phenomenological volume has appeared thus far, does
not carry the word "phenomenological" in its title, although its
method is distinctly phenomenological; nor does the word
appear often in his important essays.

1. Ricoeur's Place in the Phenomenological Movement

Ricoeur's position in the pattern of the present Phenomenological Movement has to be determined largely on the basis of his own
more or less incidental statements about his position. To Ricoeur
too Husserl is the "knot" (*noeud*) of the Phenomenological
Movement. But he does not identify the Movement with its
Husserlian version. Nevertheless he thinks that phenomenology
can be described as "the sum of the variations of Husserl's
work and the heresies which have sprung from Husserl." (*HPA*
185; *SLP* 836). He also sees the stages in Husserl's development.[1] And in contrast to such French phenomenologists as
Merleau-Ponty, he insists that especially the Husserl of the *Ideen*
cannot be played down in favor of the Husserl of the very
last period (*PA* 115).

But this plea for a fuller study of the earlier stages of Husserl's
phenomenology does not mean that Ricoeur accepts his answers
at any particular stage as adequate. Specifically, he makes it

---

[1] An exception to his remarkable grasp of this development seems to me his view
that in his last phase, that of the *Krisis* publication, Husserl had abandoned the
extreme idealism of the *Cartesian Meditations* of 1929. (*HPA* 195 ff.; *PE* 19. 10. 9).
Passages in the recent *Husserliana* edition of this text, notably in VI 266, 271 ff.,
415 ff., show that there has been no such change, except possibly in emphasis.

plain that in his own *Philosophy of the Will* "everything sets us apart from the celebrated (*fameuse*) and obscure transcendental reduction to which, according to us, a true comprehension of one's own body sets a checkmate" (*PV* 7). But this did not keep Ricoeur from admitting in 1954 that the "reduction is the straight and narrow gate to phenomenology" (KH 45), whose function he sees in "reducing" the things to their way of appearing. But while accepting this "methodological conversion" he objects to Husserl's "metaphysical decision" which slides (*glisser*) from mere suspension of our ontological beliefs to their negation and thus "deontologizes" phenomenology to the extent of ending with a phenomenology devoid of ontology (*KH* 57). This also means that Ricoeur is not prepared to adopt Husserl's transcendental idealism beyond a mere "methodological idealism" (which makes reality its theme only insofar as it is given, without deciding whether reality is exhausted by its givenness) in contrast to a "dogmatic idealism," which he repudiates (*SLP* 838, *KH* 64). In fact, Ricoeur believes that this *Philosophie de la volonté* can refute the idealistic interpretation of Husserl's "constitution" as a creative rather than as a "transmitting" (*donnant*) act (*PA* 133). Moreover, Ricoeur objects to Husserl's "logicist prejudice," which gives the theoretical acts of consciousness priority over the affective and volitional acts as merely "founded" on theoretical acts (*PA* 124). Also, while making out a good case for Husserl's growing sense of history, he believes that his final view of history, according to which it represents the history of human reason, is too unaware of the powers stressed, though overstressed, by the Marxists, that it does not do justice to the unpredictable element in history ("historicity"), and that it does not reconcile its view of an objective spirit with its transcendental subjectivism. Thus Ricoeur, who is clearly the best French interpreter of Husserl, is anything but Husserl's most orthodox French disciple.

Ricoeur is also one of the few Frenchmen who are aware of the Older Phenomenological Movement. The extent of this awareness can best be seen from the Appendix which he added to Émile Bréhier's *Histoire de la philosophie allemande*, in which he deals with "Some Figures of Contemporary German Philosophy," i.e., specifically, with Husserl, Scheler, Hartmann, Jaspers, and

Heidegger, thus putting the main emphasis on phenomenology and on the philosophy of existence. But he is also acquainted to a considerable extent with the Munich Circle and
refers particularly and with distinct appreciation to Pfänder's
phenomenological psychology and to von Hildebrand's ethical
studies.

Ricoeur's unusually penetrating and objective analysis of the
major figures is obviously not supposed to reflect his own reaction
to them. But in combination with occasional remarks in his more
systematic studies this analysis gives a fairly clear idea of his
own position in relation to them. Thus when he states that it
was Scheler's "fundamental contribution (*apport*) to phenomenology to have taken it away (*soustraire*) from the narrowly
rationalist frame of the 'objectivating,' i.e., theoretical acts in
which Husserl remained confined" (*HPA* 199), it is pretty clear
that he approves of such an extension. But he also sees, largely
influenced by Paul-Ludwig Landsberg, that phenomenology
was actually only a tool and ultimately a phase in Scheler's
development, as it is clearly not for Ricoeur himself. Ricoeur
accepts Scheler's general view of the nature of values and of
their "emotional" givenness. But he also believes that a loyal
devotion to them in Royce's sense, as expressed in historical
action, is a condition for their presentation (*PV* 69). Thus he
tries to combine the idea of existential commitment with the
phenomenology of a priori values. (Scheler's own ideas about
the function of love in value cognition actually coincide with
Ricoeur's much more than the latter seems to realize in this
context.)

In the case of Heidegger, of whose philosophical development
Ricoeur shows an unusually good grasp, Ricoeur recognizes very
well that phenomenology was to him largely a phase, which was
being transcended as early as in *Sein und Zeit* (HPA 245): even
in this work the Husserlian line is matched by a Kierkegaardian
strand, and the phenomenological descriptions are subordinated
to the ontological objective. Nor is Ricoeur prepared to accept
uncritically Heidegger's phenomenological descriptions in *Sein
und Zeit*. True, in some of his systematic works he expresses
implicit approval of such Heideggerian conceptions as that
of the "world" in an enlarged sense, or of the affective disposition

(*Befindlichkeit*). But otherwise Ricoeur's sympathy with Heidegger's general outlook and with his conception of phenomenology is clearly limited.

There is much less information about Ricoeur's precise place within French phenomenology. I shall have to say more about the decisive importance of Gabriel Marcel for Ricoeur's philosophizing presently. But Marcel the phenomenologist plays only a very subordinate place in this context, and Ricoeur makes no attempt to present Marcel as one of the exponents of phenomenology. In this regard he is much closer to Sartre and Merleau-Ponty, from whom he differs however fundamentally in his metaphysical and especially in his religious outlook. The fact that Ricoeur's translation of Husserl's *Ideen* appeared as the first work in Merleau-Ponty's and Sartre's new *Bibliothèque de Philosophie* is certainly indicative of their common concerns. But in a number of places Ricoeur unmistakably expresses implicit criticisms of his French fellow phenomenologists. Thus it stands to reason that when he deplores the inflation which expressions like "project," "motive," "action," and "situation" have undergone in recent phenomenological literature, he has in mind, if not Sartre himself, at least some of his uncritical imitators (*PA* 116). And when he insists on the indispensability of eidetic description prior to a study of significations, he seems to be hinting at Merleau-Ponty as well as at a general French tendency to make phenomenology exclusively a study of existential significations (*PA* 116). Yet he refers not infrequently to both Sartre and Merleau-Ponty for illustration and comparison, and adopts, for instance, Sartre's views of intentionality, the imagination, and, though with more reservations, the magic of the emotions (*PV* 257 ff.). At first sight Ricoeur's enterprise in his *Philosophy of the Will* may look like a deliberate counterpart to and complement of Merleau-Ponty's *Phenomenology of Perception*. But while relations between the two fellow phenomenologists have been friendly, their styles of approach differ vastly. Besides, Ricoeur feels that Merleau-Ponty interprets Husserl too exclusively from his last phase (*PA* 115; *Idées directrices*, p. XXXVIII note). He also implies that he neglects "intentional analysis" according to act and content as practiced in Husserl's *Ideen*. And he questions how a philosophy without any absolute, in which man is identified with his insertion into the perceptual field, remains possible. (*PE* 19.10.11)

Thus Ricoeur clearly advocates a phenomenology of his own, though one related to that of his predecessors. Its positive aspects will have to be considered as soon as we have discussed the main motifs that have shaped and affected the development of his philosophy.

2. *Ricoeur's Guiding Interests*

In what is perhaps Ricoeur's most revealing self-interpretation thus far, the Introduction to a collection of essays on *Histoire et Vérité* (1955), he mentions as his main roles those of a university teacher, a teacher of the history of philosophy, a member of the team (*équipe*) *Esprit* (the leading left-wing Christian Monthly started by the founder of a new Christian personalism, Emmanuel Mounier), and a listener to the Christian message. One wonders why neither systematic philosophy nor phenomenology are mentioned in this connection. It would probably be a mistake to infer from this that these are none of his major concerns. But they are apparently subsidiary to his major interests, which seem to converge on the philosophical buttressing of a Christian synthesis with a concrete program of social and international action in a spirit of conciliation.

The following lines contain perhaps the most outspoken statement of this objective:

> The philosophical faith which inspires us is the will to restore on a higher plane of lucidity and happiness that unity of being which negation has killed more radically than reflection. For us philosophy is the meditation on the "yes" and by no means the quarrelsome dwelling (*renchérissement hargneux*) on the "no." Freedom does not want to be a leper but the very accomplishment of nature, as far as that is possible in this world, where we pass through as wayfarers. This is why we meditate on the negation only with the ardent hope of going beyond it (*surpasser*) (*PV* 419).

The context makes it clear that what Ricoeur protests against is the Sartrian philosophy of freedom as essentially negation. Ricoeur's existentialism (he does not call it so himself) is essentially one of affirmation.

In this philosophy of regained unity the central motif is that of reconciliation, a reconciliation of man with himself, his body, and the world. And behind it appears the even vaster scheme of a reconciliation in ontology. Such a program raises the question of why a conciliation is needed. The answer can only be found in what is clearly Ricoeur's fundamental philosophical experience, that of man as a broken unity (*unité brisée*). The crack, or, as Ricoeur also puts it in geological language, the fault, manifests itself in the human passions as exemplified particularly in ambition and hatred. Only in the dimension of Transcendence can the final reunification be hoped for.

The foundation for such a philosophy of restoration has to be a comprehensive philosophy of human nature. But human nature cannot be understood from one angle alone. The phenomenology of the *cogito* in its theoretical and practical aspects constitutes one such angle. Yet in order to do justice to man, the incarnated being, it has to be supplemented by a philosophy of existence that transcends consciousness. But even this new angle can only be reached by passing through the phenomenological approach.

Thus Ricoeur's goal is a philosophy which combines clarity of understanding with the sense of mystery. Phenomenology is "the crestline (*ligne de crête*) which divides romantic effusion and an intellectualism without depth" (*PV* 20).

3. Ricoeur's Development

Certain facts of Ricoeur's development, for some of which I am indebted to him personally, are relevant to an understanding of his stake in phenomenology. Born of Protestant stock in the Provence, Ricoeur was first exposed to Barthian theology, which repelled him (as it did the phenomenologists of the *Nouvelle École de Strasbourg*). But as the "decisive philosophical shock" he singles out his encounter with the thought of Gabriel Marcel (*MJ* 13). Even in his systematic *Philosophie de la volonté*, which he dedicated to Marcel, he stated that "meditation on the work of Gabriel Marcel is in fact at the root of the analyses in this work." Nevertheless, Ricoeur wanted to put Marcel's thought "to the test of the precise problems posed by classical psychology." Thus his project was "to put himself at the intersection of two exigencies: that of a thought nurtured (like Marcel's) by the mystery of the body, and that of a thought concerned (*soucieuse*) for the distinctions inherited from the Husserlian method of description." (*PV* 18) For in his analysis of Marcel's philosophy Ricoeur makes it plain that he considers Marcel's epistemology "imperfect," and hints that "Husserl's studies can be of great help in widening the somewhat narrow conception of the intellect which Gabriel Marcel criticizes forcefully" (MJ 369) and can "renew the existential epistemology" (*MJ* 386). Thus Ricoeur was clearly unprepared to go to the full length of Marcel's "mystic" anti-rationalism and tried to supplement it by the "rationality" of the Husserlian method.

Ricoeur's very first publication before the War consisted of a "Phenomenological Study of Attention and Its Philosophical Connections." But the War and several years of captivity in Germany diverted his interest for some time to an intensive study of Jaspers, to whose philosophy of existence he devoted, jointly with Mikel Dufrenne, his first book-size publication. In presenting Jaspers' thought against the background of other philosophies of existence the two authors did their best to conceal their respective shares in this impressive restatement, which has been sanctioned by Jaspers himself. Nevertheless, the critical questions raised in the last part, which is concerned with the possibility and the conditions of a philosophy of existence in the manner of Jaspers, show in some places Ricoeur's concern about the problem of reconciling the "broken unity," man: "Is a philosophy of radical rupture (*déchirure*) possible, or does not rather a philosophy of the paradox" (i.e., Jaspers' philosophy), "in order to be possible, have a presentiment of a deeper reconciliation than the paradox itself"?[1] In his answer to this question Jaspers is found to be wanting.

Even more important from Ricoeur's point of view is the subsequent separate confrontation of Marcel and Jaspers, in which Ricoeur's preference clearly goes to Marcel. Not much explicit criticism is offered in Ricoeur's highly illuminating cross sections through the works of the two co-called Christian existentialists. Nevertheless one can find even in this book indications of Ricoeur's reservations with regard to Marcel's existential philosophy: for instance, regarding the unresolved tension and rupture between Marcel's lyric attitude toward the cosmic, the personal, and the social mystery, and his dramatic

[1] Karl Jaspers et la philosophie de l'existence (1947), p 326.

despair and eschatological hope for a beyond (*MJ* 405 ff.).

Since then the center of Ricoeur's philosophical work has shifted back to phenomenology and especially to Husserl's phenomenology. By his masterful translation of Husserl's *Ideen*, supplemented by a critical introduction and a running commentary in the footnotes, he has made a unique contribution to the understanding of this classic text. After accepting a chair of philosophy at the University of Strasbourg he has added interpretative essays on the recent editions of Husserl's later writings and other phenomenological publications which go far beyond exposition and exegesis. It remains to be seen how far he will be able to continue this work in his new position at the Sorbonne.

But even more important than Ricoeur the critical interpreter is Ricoeur the original phenomenological explorer. As such he has produced chiefly the first volume of a *Philosophie de la volonté*, dealing with "*The Voluntary and the Involuntary*." It attempts an understanding (*compréhension*) of the interaction between these two spheres of human nature, based on a "pure description" which is also called phenomenological. Two more volumes, of which one is to deal with the "fault" in man, i.e., chiefly with his finiteness and his culpability, the other with "Transcendence," are announced. It remains to be seen how far and in what sense these will also contain phenomenological sections, since in Ricoeur's view these topics do not seem to lend themselves to "pure description." In the present context [1] two more succinct but amplified statements of Ricoeur's position, a presentation before the *Société Française de philosophie* and a paper read before the first International Phenomenological Colloquium in Brussels on "The Tasks and Methods of a Philosophy of the Will," deserve special mention. More recently Ricoeur has presented the outlines of a phenomenology of the second person, in which he attempts to show that personal respect in the Kantian sense is a more fundamental ethical phenomenon than sympathy in the sense of Scheler, but also expresses the conviction that such respect is not accessible to a purely phenomenological approach.

4. Ricoeur's Conception of Phenomenology

In addition to his concrete phenomenological studies, Ricoeur has formulated an original conception of phenomenology and also of its limits. Excluding some of the more fashionable misuses of the term, he recognizes three legitimate forms of phenomenology, Kant's, Hegel's, and Husserl's, and defines his own position in relation to them. As their common root he identifies the "autonomous" study of the manner in which things appear, while suspending temporarily or permanently the question of their being. To this extent it requires the phenomenological reduction, which implies a "special ascesis," to break the charm of the "natural attitude" in its preoccupation with the things which appear. Ricoeur sees an implicit critical phenomenology in Kant's study of the conditions for the possibility of knowledge, which however he does not consider successful, not only because of the absence of concrete descriptions but also because, in his investigation of the fundamental acts of the mind (*Gemüt*), Kant was sidetracked by his preoccupation with the problem of a priori knowledge. Hence his was merely a "captive phenomenology." Hegel's phenomenology studied the appearances understood as the logical order of manifestation of being itself, i.e., in close connection with an ontology, which Kant tried to avoid. Husserl's phenomenology represents a third possibility, in which the phenomenological reduction attempts to eliminate the ontological question for good.

Ricoeur's own conception is of course chiefly geared to Husserl's enterprise. But it does not form more than his point of departure. For Ricoeur is not prepared to abandon ontology (see *PE* 19. 10. 8). He also sees definite limitations to the phenomenological method when it approaches the range of the "mystery," and specifically the range of the involuntary phenomena. In fact Ricoeur has turned increasingly from Husserl to Kant as the philosopher who, while his work is not usable as a model for phenomenology, assigns it its proper place and its limited right:

The glory of phenomenology is to have elevated, by means of the reduction, the investigation of the appearance to the dignity of a science. But the glory of Kantianism is to have known how to coordinate the investigation of appearance with the limiting function of the Thing-in-itself and with the practical determination of the Thing-in-itself as freedom and as the community of persons. Husserl does (*fait*) phenomenology. But Kant limits it and gives it a foundation. (*KH* 67).

The "thing-in-itself," as Ricoeur accepts it, is to be sure hardly Kant's unknowable but simply a reality over and above the appearances through which it manifests itself. The reference to the "practical determination" of the thing-in-itself by Kant alludes to limits in our phenomenological knowledge of other people, of which Husserl gave an "admirable" but all the same unsuccessful account in his *Cartesian Meditations*. According to Ricoeur, the only way in which we can become sure of the existence of other people is by the act of respect, prior to all phenomenological reflection. In fact, even a phenomenology of sympathy in the spirit of Scheler presupposes an ethics of respect; otherwise it becomes a "deceptive" or "vain" phenomenology (*KH* 67).

But in addition to these Kantian limits Ricoeur sees specific ones in the concrete structure of certain phenomena. The "existential fault" and "transcendence" are the most momentous ones. In the field of the will itself it is the involuntary phenomena, including those of the body, which prove to be inaccessible to phenomenology proper.

As far as the phenomenological procedure itself is concerned, Ricoeur describes it felicitously in terms common to all phenomenologists as "going to the things themselves, respecting all the very complex aspects of consciousness, and not playing simply with the small number of concepts forged by Aristotelian analysis" (*U.V.I.* 26). Within this general framework he distinguishes three levels of investigation:

α. The level of descriptive analysis: its main function is to "spell out" (*épeler*) the phenomena, i.e., to spread out their aspects, particularly their intentional meanings and the act-content structure of the conscious phenomena. Ricoeur feels that this level of phenomenology has been unduly neglected by the later phenomenologists, and that it is anything but exhausted. Such description has to concentrate on essences, though Ricoeur protests, as Husserl did, against their hypostatization in the Platonic manner (*PV* 8). There is no way to by-pass eidetic phenomenology.

Phenomenology at this level begins with "pure" description, which is exemplified primarily by Husserl's studies but also by the earlier parts of Ricoeur's own analyses of the will. No explicit definition of this "purity" is given. But Ricoeur makes it plain that pure description applies only to the phenomena of lucid consciousness. It proves inadequate to grasp the relations between consciousness and the body, the chief "mystery" in human experience. Here Ricoeur suggests that what is required is a deepening of the descriptive attitude in the sense of Marcel's "participation in being," which takes account of our incarnation in the world. It does not become fully clear, however, how far this implies the existence of an "impure" description as a fundamentally new method. One gathers that the main difference lies less in the descriptive procedure itself than in the preceding attitude toward the phenomena. Existential description presupposes plunging into the experience rather than the "pure" and objective looking at it from the distance with all of one's practical commitments turned off.

β. "Transcendental constitution" makes up the second level in Ricoeur's phenomenology. But for him, determining the constitution of the phenomenon in consciousness does not mean what it meant for Husserl. Actually Ricoeur brings out the basic ambiguity in Husserl's conception of constitution: according to one version it means construction of the phenomena, according to the other it merely "gives" or delivers these phenomena (*EMC* 96 f.). While Ricoeur rejects the first version, he accepts the second one, although he seems to have failed to practice it, especially in his phenomenology of the will. It certainly does not take him as far as Husserl's transcendental idealism.

γ. Finally there is the level of ontological phenomenology or of an ontology of consciousness, which tries to determine the status of consciousness in the total framework of being. As to this level, Ricoeur gives thus far only a blueprint. One might expect further and clearer development from his future systematic volumes. In the meantime he makes it plain that his philosophy will not shrink away from ontology or even from metaphysics. The program of a third level of phenomenology implies clearly that he thinks phenomenology can serve as a gateway to metaphysics, even though it may not be able to develop and complete it.

In summation, Ricoeur's phenomenology is emphatically a descriptive phenomenology and even an eidetic phenomenology of essential structures in the sense of Husserl's early conception and of the Older German Movement. Of the "phenomenological reduction" he adopts only a rather toned-down version, with the main function of enabling us to focus on the appearances of the things as distinguished from the things appearing. Correspondingly, the "phenomenological constitution" consists merely in the determination of the way in which phenomena received from elsewhere establish themselves in our subjective consciousness. But phenomenological idealism in Husserl's "dogmatic" sense is thoroughly unacceptable to Ricoeur. Phenomenology is the beginning of philosophy. But it is not its end. In trying to go as far as possible toward such an end Ricoeur turns to Gabriel Marcel's "hyperphenomenology."

5. The Phenomenology of the Will

Ricoeur's most impressive demonstration of phenomenology thus far is in the area of the phenomena of the will. There are at least four reasons for his special interest in this field: (1) to him a study of the will offers a privileged avenue to the "mystery" of the body in Marcel's sense; (2) it provides a special opportunity for testing a phenomenology of essences; (3) it holds out a special chance to examine the validity of Husserl's idealism; (4) it prepares the way for a deepened and cautious interpretation of human freedom.

Ricoeur is not the first to explore the phenomenology of the will. Pfänder's descriptive study under this very title (1900), with which Ricoeur is familiar, preceded even Husserl's *Logische Untersuchungen*. Also several discussions of the will in Marcel's *Journal métaphysique* and in other writings of his seem to have attracted Ricoeur's special attention for their "phenomenological" content (MJ 209 ff., 215).

It would go beyond my powers of condensation to give an adequate idea of the richness of the first volume of Ricoeur's three-volume work, the only one that has appeared thus far. The general theme of this volume is to show in detail the "reciprocity" of the voluntary and the involuntary life, which in the case of man interpenetrate each other inextricably: no voluntary life without an involuntary counterpart and vice versa. The whole discussion in the first volume, however, is based on an abstraction, which Ricoeur also calls a "reduction," from two major factors which are reserved for the later volumes: the "existential fault" (*faute existentielle*), i.e., finiteness, culpability, and specifically the passions, which are responsible for the "brokenness" in human nature, and "transcendence," the factor from which Ricoeur expects the final reconciliation.

For the first volume Ricoeur sets himself a double task: "to describe the relations between the voluntary and the involuntary parts of human nature and to understand (*comprendre*) them" (*PV* 7). The second task, comprehension, presupposes description. But as Ricoeur conceives of description, namely as the description of subjective experience, it is not adequate to penetrate the realm of the involuntary phenomena in the same degree as it can elucidate the voluntary ones. "Pure" description therefore requires the complement of a study of our participation in existence beyond the range of consciousness.

Ricoeur distinguishes three stages in the development of voluntary action: that of decision, including choice and motivation, that of action (*agir*), which sets the body in voluntary motion (Ricoeur considers primarily action that requires bodily motion), and that of consent to necessities which are not dependent on us. In each of these stages there is a limited area of completely voluntary factors that can be approached by "pure description." But they are matched by an even wider group of phenomena which are not amenable to such treatment.

During the stage of decision the elaboration of the project, the determination of the self (*se décider* or *imputation*), and the motivation can be explored by pure description. But the involuntary range of the correlative phenomena of need (*besoin*), of pleasure and pain, as they enter such decisions, are so intimately related to the experience of the body and its history that they cannot be encompassed by a description of one's pure consciousness. It remains true that "subjectivity is the common measure of the voluntary and the involuntary" (*PV* 319). But the involuntary comprises more than the subjective. This holds true not only of the objective body as studied by science, which does not enter Ricoeur's philosophy of the will; it applies even to the experienced body, which forms an integral part of the experience of the will, as Ricoeur conceives of it.

At the stage of action, pure description can at least try to clarify the voluntary part of the executive phase of the will, the "pragma." But the role of the body as the instrument of action raises at once considerable difficulties, since action is inserted immediately into the thick of reality, in which it introduces the fulfilment of the empty intention of the preceding decision. Besides, the voluntary aspect of action interpenetrates with the much more voluminous range of the involuntary components, specifically in the form of what Ricoeur calls the "preformed know-how," i.e., primarily the instincts, the emotions, and the habits. The phenomenon of effort shows the final fusion of the voluntary and the involuntary at this stage.

As the last phase or cycle between the voluntary and the involuntary Ricoeur discusses the act of consent, which is characterized as "taking upon oneself, assuming, making one's own." It provides the "ultimate conciliation between freedom and nature," or freedom and necessity. Consenting too is the correlate of an involuntary factor, notably of necessity, not of an objective scientific necessity but of a lived necessity (*nécessité vécue*). This lived necessity takes the form of the human character, of the unconscious, and, in a larger sense, of "life," with its outstanding episodes of growth and, even more fundamental, of birth, a theme which is particularly important to Ricoeur.

All this leads to a final appraisal of human freedom, which Ricoeur characterizes as dependent independence or a conciliation of the voluntary and the involuntary elements in human nature, but not as absolute creation.

The total picture which emerges from this approach is one of remarkable freshness and comprehensiveness. It attempts with considerable success to incorporate the best insights of a behaviorism like Tolman's, of gestalt psychology, and of Freudian psychoanalysis properly reinterpreted. To be sure, these are used as guides rather than as binding authorities. But Ricoeur is anxious to stress the mutual compatibility and complementarity of phenomenology and true scientific psychology (PV 16).

Besides, the work contains an abundance of concrete phenomenological descriptions, particularly of the voluntary aspects
of the will, something quite unusual among French phenomenologists, whose primary concern is the existential significations
of the phenomena. This latter element is by no means absent
from Ricoeur's descriptions, nor could this be expected in the
case of a phenomenon which includes purposive meaning among
its primary features. Not all of these descriptions are completely
new. And few of them are comprehensive beyond the scope of
Ricoeur's limited concern. Thus there is little discussion of
modifications and varieties of the fundamental phenomena. All
the more impressive is the coherence of the scheme, in which the
interdependence of the voluntary and the involuntary in the
unity of human nature provides the dominating theme.

6. Concluding Observations

It seems safe to say that at the moment Ricoeur is the French
philosopher best qualified to bridge the remaining gap between
German and French phenomenology, and to preserve the continuity of the phenomenological tradition in a creative fashion.
But at the same time he is more than a phenomenologist in the
traditional sense. His discipleship to Gabriel Marcel and his
basically existential concern make him go beyond phenomenology
in a manner which he himself no longer seems to consider as
phenomenological. Phenomenology is the base but not the
pediment of his philosophy. It goes beyond "pure description"
in exploring the "mystery" of the body, the "existential fault,"
and transcendence, and ultimately in the quest for a reconciliation of a broken creation. But what is the real nature of the
method to which Ricoeur's ambitious enterprise appeals? Has
it nothing in common with the description which he invoked on
the properly phenomenological level? Or is it just an "impure"
form of it, a modification which does not transform it basically?
After all, description in the literal sense of the word is nothing
but a recording of what has been found by intuitive search and
observation. Could it be that the only legitimate difference
between "pure" and "impure" description is a matter of differences in the underlying intuition, one being of a more contemplative nature, the other presupposing the active com-

mitment of the explorer in order to actualize potentialities otherwise not accessible to him?

Ricoeur's practice of his supposedly transphenomenological method will be the measure of his commitment to phenomenology. But it cannot affect his achievement and his impressive contribution to the creative development of phenomenology in the sixth decade of this century.

SELECTIVE BIBLIOGRAPHY

"L'Attention. Étude phénoménologique de l'attention et de ses connections philosophiques," *Bulletin de la Société de Philosophie de l'Ouest.* Janvier-Mars 1940

Gabriel Marcel et Karl Jaspers. 1948 (MJ)

Philosophie de la volonté, vol. I. 1950 (PV)

Husserl, Idées directrices pour une phénoménologie. Traduction, introduction, commentaire. 1950

"Analyses et problèmes dans *Ideen II* de Husserl," *Revue de métaphysique et de morale* LVI (1951), 357–394; LVII (1952), 1–16

"Méthodes et tâches d'une phénoménologie de la volonté," *Problèmes actuels de la phénoménologie* (Desclée de Brouwer, 1952), 113–140 (PA)

"L'Unité du volontaire et de l'involontaire comme idée-limite," *Bulletin de la Société française de philosophie* 1951, 1–29 (UVI)

"Husserl et le sens de l'histoire," *Revue de métaphysique et de morale* LIV (1949), 280–316

Appendice to Bréhier, E., *Histoire de la philosophie allemande.* 3e édition (1954), pp. 181–258 (HPA)

"Sur la phénoménologie," *Esprit* XXI (1953) 821–838 (SLP)

"Études sur les *Méditations Cartésiennes* de Husserl," *Revue philosophiques de Louvain* LII (1954), 75–109 (EMC)

"Sympathie et respect: phénoménologie et éthique de la deuxième personne," *Revue de Métaphysique et de Morale* LIX (1954), 380–397

"Kant et Husserl," *Kantstudien*, XLVI (1954), 44–67 (KH)

"Phénoménologie existentielle," *Encyclopédie Française* XIX (1957), 19.10.6–12 (PE)

"Le Symbole donne à penser," *Esprit* XXVII (1959), 60–76   [1]

B. THE PHENOMENOLOGY OF ESTHETIC EXPERIENCE:
MIKEL DUFRENNE (1910–   )

Mikel Dufrenne's *Phénoménologie de l'expérience esthétique* (PEE) in two volumes (1953) is the second large work in French that goes under the title "phenomenology," being preceded in this respect only by Merleau-Ponty's *Phénoménologie de la perception.* It is not only the most voluminous but easily the most impressive achievement of the Phenomenological Movement in esthetics thus far. During its German phase Moritz

Geiger, with whose studies unfortunately Dufrenne does not seem to be familiar, had developed its program along the lines of The Older Phenomenological Movement and had supplied some outstanding specimens of it. Also Roman Ingarden, with whose study on the literary work of art Dufrenne is well acquainted, had given important systematic analyses of several types of works of art based on their logical and ontological structure. Sartre had paid passing attention to the work of art at the end of his psychological phenomenology of the imagination (*L'Imaginaire*). And Merleau-Ponty had devoted several essays to esthetic problems in connection with recent artistic developments. But both in scope and comprehensiveness there had been no comparable phenomenological study of the esthetic field prior to Dufrenne's work. While it is far from exhaustive, and advisedly so, it stands out by its systematic structure as well as by the richness of its concrete insights based on a thorough and ecumenic familiarity with and sensitiveness for most arts.

Before this monumental work appeared, Dufrenne was known chiefly for his cooperation with Ricoeur in a critical presentation of Jaspers' philosophy. A study of the sociological concept of the basic personality showed his acquaintance with American social research and particularly with G. H. Mead's work, acquired in part during a year's stay in the United States after the second World War. In view of this fact it is a little surprising that Dufrenne does not record the often striking parallels between his theory of esthetic experience and John Dewey's *Art as Experience*.

Thus far Dufrenne has shown little interest in discussing his conception of phenomenology and in defining his place in the Phenomenological Movement. From the very beginning of his work on esthetics, however, he makes it plain that he intends not to "follow Husserl literally" but "to understand phenomenology in the sense in which Sartre and Merleau-Ponty have acclimatized this term in France," i.e., as "description which focusses (*viser*) an essence defined in turn as a signification which is immanent in the phenomenon and given with it" (PEE 4 n.). In agreement with them he also attempts to "naturalize" the transcendental subject and to substitute for it the incarnated human consciousness. However, he wants to leave aside, at least at the start, the Hegelian conception of phenomenology.

What separates him from Husserl is chiefly his opposition to phenomenological idealism, which in his opinion does not do justice to the essential nature of perception and least of all to our perception of others. Specifically he objects to the "hypertrophy" of transcendental subjectivity in Husserl's phenomenology (*Bulletin de la Société Française de philosophie*, 1955, p. 98).

Dufrenne expresses much more appreciation for Scheler and particularly for his idea of a non-formal a priori, a conception which he tries to extend to esthetics and to the affective phenomena in general. But this does not mean that Dufrenne accepts Scheler's views indiscriminately. At times he even goes beyond Scheler, for instance in asserting the "solidarity" between eidetic intuition of essences and empirical intuition.

Dufrenne also shows more than usual sympathy for Heidegger's ideas in matters that have a bearing on esthetic topics, and especially in his final interpretation of the ontological significance of the esthetic experience as a revelation of being. But this does not mean that he embraces Heidegger's entire philosophical position. Without referring to Heidegger's hermeneutic phenomenology explicitly he tries to assimilate as much of it as fits into his own more descriptive framework.

This attitude confirms Dufrenne's general solidarity with the position of the Paris phenomenologists, particularly with Sartre and with Merleau-Ponty. But not only does he dissent from Sartre's general ontology, he also objects to his neglect of perception in favor of the imagination and the emotions, making this responsible for Sartre's misinterpretation of the esthetic experience. This primary emphasis on the key position of perception in esthetics moves him closer to Merleau-Ponty, to whose general position he usually subscribes. He also shares his interest in and utilization of gestalt theory and of Goldstein's philosophy of organism. Where he wants to go beyond Merleau-Ponty is in placing more emphasis on the objective "truth" of the perceived object, i.e., its autonomy in its relation to the perceiving act (*PEE* 285). Also he attempts to vindicate the rights of a "reflective" perception and of the conceptual element in knowledge as a substantial addition to a merely pre-reflective perception.

By thus weakening the primacy of perception, Dufrenne tries to broaden Merleau-Ponty's base. On the other hand, Dufrenne does not go so far as Merleau-Ponty in claiming the coincidence of phenomenology with philosophy. For, while he does not set definite limits to phenomenology, he clearly implies that critical epistemology, ontology, and metaphysics have to be distinguished from it.

A report that could take the place of intensive sampling of a work of close to 700 pages would obviously be out of place here. Let it suffice to indicate some of the pervading themes and the general structure of the book, with special emphasis on its phenomenological features.

Its leading motif is that of the reciprocity between esthetic object and esthetic experience. (One cannot help feeling reminded here of the parallel with the "reciprocity" between the voluntary and the involuntary in the *Philosophie de la volonté* of Dufrenne's friend Ricoeur.) Although Dufrenne reserves the first and actually larger volume of the work for the esthetic object and the second for the esthetic experience, he states emphatically that the two are complementary, that the esthetic object is inseparable from the esthetic experience, and that the esthetic experience does not make sense apart from the esthetic object. Nevertheless he decides to break into this circle from the side of the esthetic object, an approach which seems to him to make for more "rigor." A deeper reason would seem to be that the esthetic object shows enough autonomy to be normative for the esthetic experience. For the esthetic object is definitely more than mere appearance: it also has a being in itself. Dufrenne is far from subscribing to a cheap esthetic relativism. In this respect as in others he follows the lead of Max Scheler, who attempted to reconcile the historical variety of the cultural phenomena with the objective validity of guiding values in ethics.

Dufrenne makes the experience of the spectator, rather than that of the creator, his point of departure. His reason for this preference is not that he considers the spectator all-important, but that he finds his experience more significant for the understanding of the esthetic phenomenon and less likely to involve the esthetician in problems of the personal psychology of individual artists.

Of the four parts of the work only two are labelled explicitly as phenomenological, i.e., Part I, the phenomenology of the esthetic object, and Part III, the phenomenology of the esthetic experience, in which it is given. Part II contains an "analysis of the work of art," which, in its attempt to establish the structure of the work of art in general, clearly aspires to yield systematic conclusions in the sense of a traditional esthetics. Part IV, a "critique of esthetic experience," transcends phenomenology of esthetic experience for its own sake. It introduces itself as a "transcendental" study of the foundations of esthetic experience and, ultimately, of its existential, its "cosmological," and even its metaphysical meaning, which appears to consist in a revelation of being itself. These "non-phenomenological" parts, which are of course still phenomenological in a wider sense and would easily have been claimed as such by a less scrupulous phenomenologist, make it plain that Dufrenne's final interest transcends phenomenology as such. They reveal his final concern as "ontology."

Obviously the primary interest of the present account attaches to Parts I and III. In the former, Dufrenne bases his phenomenology of the esthetic object on the work of art, reserving the case of natural beauty as a less pure case for a separate investigation. However, the work of art is not automatically an esthetic object. It becomes so only when it is "present" as a phenomenon. One might speak of it as a potential esthetic object which becomes actualized only as it appears to spectators. This approach accounts for the inclusion of a highly original discussion of the role of the performance for the esthetic object, a discussion which considers separately the case of production by special performers and by the author himself, and a similar discussion of the meaning of reproductions in "presenting" the esthetic object. For the same reason the public becomes an integral part of the esthetic object and is studied both for what the esthetic object expects of its public and what the public can receive from it. Next, the place of the esthetic object among other constituents of our world, such as living objects, natural things, articles of use, is considered and its distinguishing characteristic found in its gestalt or inner unity, in contrast to the merely external unity that holds together non-esthetic objects; hence Dufrenne eventually characterizes the esthetic object, in its union of being "for itself" and "in itself," as a quasi-subject. The relation of the esthetic world to the surrounding world of time and space reveals a unique type of "ambiguity." Finally, the "being," the peculiar type of existence, of the esthetic object, is studied on the basis of a critical discussion of prior solutions by phenomenologically oriented philosophers like Sartre and Ingarden, who had tried to interpret its being as imaginary or as "ideal." Dufrenne's conclusion is that the esthetic object, being essentially perceived, shares the status of the perceived objects as described by Merleau-Ponty. However, this being has a double or "ambiguous" character: since they are essentially "presences," esthetic objects are only for us; but in their inexhaustible nature they reveal an autonomous "truth" which makes demands on the spectator. Thus they embody another instance of a coincidence between consciousness and being, of "for itself" and "in itself," which Sartre had declared to be self-contradictory.

The corresponding part on the phenomenology of the acts of esthetic experience is briefer than that on the esthetic object, and designedly so, since much of it was anticipated in the discussion of the esthetic object. Again, perception, as the means for seizing the significance of the object, is the central theme. In esthetic perception itself Dufrenne distinguishes three aspects, the presence as mediated by the bodily senses, representation, and reflection. According to Dufrenne, reflection or thought forms an integral part of the esthetic experience. Representation is invoked as the mediator between presence and reflection, chiefly in the form of the imagination; this imagination he puts in much closer contact with perception, from which Sartre had tried to separate it sharply; its function is to widen and to enliven the perceived presence. Yet it is characteristic of esthetic perception that here the understanding (*entendement*) has to discipline the imagination, much more than in ordinary perception. However, reflective understanding is not the last word of esthetic experience. It leads to a "response" of our being to the being of the perceived esthetic object for which Dufrenne, giving credit for the whole conception to Marcel, uses the expression "sentiment," and which he distinguishes from mere emotion. It reveals Being not only as reality but as "depth" (*profondeur*), by which Dufrenne understands chiefly its "measureless" content beyond our immediate grasp. Sentiment is the experience in which the depth of our own experience answers to this depth of the object. This we can achieve by disciplining our imagination as well as by opening ourselves to a being for which our own being thus becomes deeply sensitive. Dufrenne's account of these experiences is unusually suggestive. I only regret that he failed to make use of Moritz Geiger's earlier inquiries into the phenomenon of depth of experience and of its various meanings. A final, somewhat brief discussion of the esthetic attitude is perhaps more remarkable for its purist opposition to esthetic pleasure and enjoyment, as being essentially self-centered, than for its emphasis on respect and admiration as essential components of the esthetic approach.   [1]

SELECTIVE BIBLIOGRAPHY

Phénoménologie de l'expérience esthétique. 2 vols. (1953)
La Notion d'a priori (1959). *Jalons* (1966).

C. THE PHENOMENOLOGY OF VALUE: RAYMOND POLIN (1911–   )

Raymond Polin's three books on value problems contain the most ambitious attempt of a young French philosopher to apply phenomenological methods to axiology. Other French phenomenological authors had touched on it only in an incidental and marginal manner, which is not surprising in view of the fact that the theory of value had never received so much attention in French philosophy as it had in either the German or the Anglo-American tradition.[1] Marcel's occasional references to the subject do not aspire to be based on any phenomenological foundation. Sartre's startling subjectivistic thesis that man creates his own values, as advanced first in *L'Être et le néant* in 1943, one year before Polin's first book, but not yet in *L'Imaginaire*, does not produce any phenomenological credentials, but presents itself chiefly as the logical consequence of his atheism. Besides, one may wonder whether his extreme insistence on man's total responsibility and the implied ethics of his existential psychoanalysis do not contain an implicit moralism

---

[1] Polin, R., "The Philosophy of Values in France" in Farber, Marvin, ed., *Philosophical Thought in France and the United States*, p. 203.

which is ultimately incompatible with his professed radical subjectivism. Merleau-Ponty refers repeatedly to values in a manner which shows that he does not consider them merely a matter of choice, but again does not offer any explicit phenomenology of value perception. The same applies to Ricoeur and Dufrenne, who however make it plain that they consider objective values incomplete, if not meaningless, without the active commitment of human existence to them.

By contrast, Polin explicitly applies the phenomenological method to value phenomena. In so doing he not only includes the commonly accepted procedures of phenomenological description. He also applies the phenomenological reduction to axiology in general and to ethics in particular. Polin actually carries out Husserl's program in a field in which the master, whose interest in these fields was at best secondary, apparently never put it to the test. Scheler's phenomenological ethics, which was already completed at the time when Husserl's theory of reduction was first published, had never even considered this. While thus Polin's extension of the Husserlian systematic suspension of belief to ethics is original and thoroughly legitimate,[1] it is another question whether he has been wholly successful in carrying it out. Even more important: how far has he preserved other parts of the phenomenological method, such as the faithful description of the perceptually given, once the reduction has been carried to its conclusion?

Unfortunately Polin's approach to philosophy and to phenomenology in particular is by no means free from ulterior objectives: "Phenomenological research is vain and futile if it does not constitute the introduction to a philosophy of action" (CV 3). Polin's peculiar type of activism consists in a commitment to the "practical liberty" of the "isolated" individual which comes very close to Nietzsche's position. To the extreme autonomism of such an individual even the data of an objective ethics would mean an interference with his free creativity. How far is such an attitude compatible with the phenomenological ethos of "going to the things" and of accepting the verdict of the phenomena as final?

[1] For a comparable attempt see the writer's "Indubitables in Ethics," in *Ethics* LVIII (1947), 35–50.

Polin is one of the generation of students of the *École Normale* who were under the growing influence of the new German philosophers. Among these, Husserl and Scheler are the leading names in Polin's texts, but Heidegger occurs with almost equal frequency. Moreover, Kant and Hegel figure conspicuously, and Nietzsche runs not far behind. Also Max Weber's axiological views are mentioned repeatedly at important places in the discussion. This does not mean that Polin is uninformed about the Anglo-American tradition. Thus the names of G. E. Moore and Ralph B. Perry occur several times, as well as those of the gestaltists. But Polin's chief interest is centered in the subjectivistic ethics of Thomas Hobbes, to whom he devoted his latest book, *Philosophie et politique chez Hobbes* (1955).

Thus far Polin has published three volumes on the value problem. The first and largest, *La Création des valeurs* (1944) (*CV*), lays the foundations by a critique of the objectivistic theories of value and by developing the thesis that values are a matter of human "creation." The method invoked for the establishment of this thesis claims to be phenomenological. A second volume, *La Compréhension des Valeurs* (1945), is chiefly concerned with the understanding of the valuations of other people as it results from differences in their creative "attitudes." It thus contains the preparation for a "sociology" of values and norms. The major part of this work outlines twenty-four possible creative attitudes developed on the basis of the permutation of four basic values, Reality, "Value" (obviously in a narrower sense than the one that comprises the four values), Man, and Subject; there is no need to discuss here this puzzling collection of ingredients, for which no phenomenological derivation is given. – The third book, *Du Laid, du mal, du faux* (1948), attacks the problem of values from the angle of negative value, which is in line with the preoccupation of the phenomenological existentialists with the phenomena of the negative. It contains a very suggestive collection of dyslogistic value terms. But it does not make any explicit claims to being a specifically phenomenological contribution. – A constructive development of Polin's own ethics under the title "The Sense of Action," announced as in preparation in 1945, seems to have been delayed.

Polin's first book is thus clearly the most important for an understanding of his conception and use of the phenomenological approach. He begins by declaring at once that phenomenology offers "the most adequate method for the study of values." Hence references to this method are conspicuous throughout the book. He implies that he considers Husserl's version as sufficiently clear and authoritative for his own needs. But he departs from Husserl by distinguishing at the outset between two phenomenological reductions, a distinction which does not occur in this form in Husserl: a "first reduction" which allows us to go back to "pure axiological consciousness and to define the essence of values"; and a second one "which interrupts the pressure exerted by the values and the accepted axiological doctrines, and which gives us the chance to suspend our judgments in order to *detach* us (*dégager*) and to liberate us from all the traditional axiological dogmatisms; we shall find in (such) isolation freedom and neutrality in relation to the values" (*CV* 1). To be sure, there seems to be little trace of these two stages in Polin's actual application of the phenomenological reduction. It makes its first explicit appearance in the "temporary and methodical doubt of the objectivity of values," which, according to him, reveals the intrinsic contradiction in the objectivistic position. The second part, "Values and Man," begins with a section that purports to give a "phenomenological analysis of valuation," starting from the indubitable fact of epistemological opinions (CV 46). After a rather brief critical discussion of Piaget's findings and of Köhler's gestaltist account, Polin introduces the imagination as the real foundation of the acts of valuation in their creative function. The analysis of the axiological acts is followed by a "phenomenological analysis of values" as their intentional referents. Here, after a critical examination of the objectivistic treatment of values by Kantian formalism and Scheler's non-formal a priori theory, Polin develops his own "axiological irrealism," which admits the "objective uncertainty of all value" (*CV* 127). It also leads him to reject axiological scepticism, in which he sees nothing but an implicit realism of value. The third part, "Values and Action," also begins with "phenomenological analyses" of ends and of norms. But these contain on the whole nothing but rather conventional characterizations of the meanings of these terms. – In the concluding part, "Values and Truths," phenomenology appears to be replaced by ontology, which Polin seems to be distinguishing from phenomenology (*CV* 278).

The preceding survey makes it plain that Polin's phenomenological reduction does not stop with a temporary questioning of our beliefs in objective values. It results in their permanent rejection and substitution by a subjectivism of "created" values. What, in the first place, is the basis for this drastic challenge to an objectivist ethics, including the phenomenological ethics of Scheler and Hartmann? For one thing, Polin sees a self-contradiction in the whole conception of knowledge of values. Knowledge, as Polin defines it, is essentially restricted to what is immanent or non-objective; hence the transcendent would be essentially unknowable (*CV* 36). It is easy to see that, if valid, this argument would involve a general philosophy of immanence in line with Husserl's phenomenological idealism, which, however, strangely enough, is never mentioned in Polin's text. Moreover, Polin believes that Scheler's intuition of value essences and their hierarchical order presupposes belief in a harmonious universe and a guaranteeing Deity, a belief which Polin considers to be unwarranted. Such refutations seem to be highly debatable, in both their assumptions and their conclusiveness. But even more important in the present context is the fact that they are all dialectical in nature, and that only by implication do they deny the phenomenological data on which Scheler's thesis about the intuitive givenness of objective values is based.

In what sense and to what extent can Polin's own subjectivistic reconstruction of value theory be considered phenomenological? What, in particular, does he mean by "creation" of values, and what is his phenomenological evidence for describing evaluation as a creative act? Creation, as Polin interprets it, is a "transcending" act that goes beyond the given. It has a negative aspect (*contra aliquid*) and a positive aspect (*ex nihilo*). The negative aspect consists in the negation of a given, which creation is to transcend, thus making room for the arbitrary invention of future possibilities. The positive aspect means the affirmation of something not given; this is the properly imaginative aspect of creation. There is, however, this difference between the merely imaginative creation and the creation of values: the former is self-sufficient, and has no immediate implication for action, the latter is essentially a transition to action and effective creation in the real world. But this does not change the fact that value is merely the result of imaginative creation in which cognition has no part.

But what about the phenomenological evidence for this "creationist" theory of values? Polin's book does not undertake to show concretely and specifically that our experiences of value, admirableness, meanness, or beauty are the results of creative acts. In fact he rarely if ever seems to come down to cases and relate his theory to concrete phenomena. Nor does he show how creation takes place in the manner in which specific values constitute themselves in our consciousness, an enterprise which in the light of Husserl's idea of a constitutive phenomenology would certainly make good sense. But neither such "constitution" nor its creative variety is ever fully described.

It is hard to avoid the impression that Polin approached the field of value in the attitude which he himself labels as "cynical," but which may be more appropriately described as one of extreme autonomism. This may have enabled him to adopt a fearless radicalism which allows him to draw the conclusions of Husserl's reductionist phenomenology in the field of values. But it is also apt to interfere with the readiness for a phenomenological intuition which accepts the phenomena in the way in which they present themselves to anyone whose phenomenology is not restricted by blinkers.

SELECTIVE BIBLIOGRAPHY

La Création des valeurs (1944) (CV)
La Compréhension des valeurs (1945)
Du Laid, du mal, du faux (1948)
"Against Wisdom," PPR XVI (1955), 1–17

D. SOME AFFILIATED THINKERS

Finally I shall list at least the names of some prominent members of the young French generation whose work shows considerable phenomenological ingredients.

1. Best known among them is probably RAYMOND ARON

(1905–   ), now chiefly a political commentator, but also a social scientist of rank. In his important "Introduction to the Philosophy of History" [1] he subscribed explicitly to the "descriptive or phenomenological method."

2. MAURICE NÉDONCELLE (1905–   ) is a Catholic theologian who, among other things, developed ideas of Max Scheler in a more systematic fashion. Besides, his book on "The Reciprocity of Consciousness" develops a suggestive phenomenological theme in the direction of a philosophy of religion. However, he himself has not expressed any preference for, or allegiance to, phenomenology in his writings. [2] It is Jean Hering who considers him one of the more important hopes of phenomenology in France.

3. PIERRE THÉVENAZ (1913–1955) was a highly gifted Protestant Swiss, whose premature death destroyed hopes for an original philosophy of religion, of which his friend Paul Ricoeur has been able to publish samples posthumously. [3] His series of articles in the *Revue de Théologie et de Philosophie*   [1] under the title *"Qu'est-ce que la phénoménologie?"* is one of the best historical and critical introductions to both the German and French phases of the Phenomenological Movement. He was particularly critical of Husserl's transcendentalism, whose radicalism he tried to outdo by de-absolutizing even phenomenological reason.

4. HENRY DUMÉRY (1920–   ) is a Catholic theologian who, starting from Maurice Blondel's philosophy of action, developed an original philosophy of religion so unorthodox that his theological works have since incurred ecclesiastical censure. [4] His concern for an adequate method that would support his position led him to an intensive study of the problems of methodology and to the final conclusion that, although the phenomenological method conceived in the sense of Husserl's reductive phenomenology was insufficient for theology, it nevertheless was its proper foundation

---

[1] *Introduction à la philosophie de l'histoire* (1933)

[2] *La Réciprocité des consciences* (1942); *La Personne humaine et la nature* (1943); *Vers une Philosophie de l'amour* (1946); *De la Fidélité* (1953).

[3] *L'Homme et sa raison*. 2 vols., ed. by Paul Ricoeur (1958).

[4] *Le Problème de Dieu en philosophie de la religion* (1957); *Critique et religion. Problèmes de méthode en philosophie de la religion* (1957); *Philosophie de la religion*. 3 vols. (1957 ff.); *Phénoménologie et religion. Structures de l'institution chrétienne* (1958).

(see, e.g., *Critique et religion*, p. 177). He also applies phenomenology to the study of a concrete religion like Judaism and Christianity, with a view to determining the "sense" expressed in these
"institutions," i.e., the fundamental intention they embody.
However, such a phenomenology, which aligns itself with the
work of the Dutch phenomenologist of religion Van der Leeuw,
is not meant to prejudge the question of validity. This critical
question is reserved for a trans-phenomenological philosophy
[1]   and specifically for a philosophy of religion.

PART IV

PHENOMENOLOGY AT MIDCENTURY

XIII

THE WIDER SCENE

The preceding chapter has brought the history of the Phenomenological Movement down to the present in at least one part
of the world: France. In no other country is phenomenology as
much a thing of the present as it is there. But this does not mean
that phenomenology has become an exclusively French affair.
The present chapter must give at least a bird's-eye survey of the
state and place of phenomenology in other parts of the philosophical world, Old and New. In several cases this will involve
also a brief sketch of the antecedents of the present phenomenological situation in the preceding decades. This chapter
also includes an appraisal of the general condition of the Phenomenological Movement and its prospects. It ends with a statement of certain agenda which seem to me important if phenomenology is to make the kind of contribution to contemporary
philosophy for which it seems to be particularly qualified.

In this chapter I shall waive the customary excuses for not
talking about the present and the future of phenomenology because of the impossibility of doing justice to a history which is
still in the making. The obvious difficulty and riskiness of
"picking the winners" in the face of developments which will
put such estimates to an immediate and ruthless test is a poor
reason for not taking stock, though with all the reservation.
which the handicaps, personal and geographic, impose upon the
present assayer.

One reason for a certain restraint is based precisely on the first
diagnosis which I shall venture to advance even before producing
the evidence as far as the world outside France is concerned:

phenomenology is not a mere matter of the philosophical past nor is it likely to become so. It has survived the death of its founder and also the decline of Husserlian orthodoxy. More important: it has survived Heidegger's embrace, not without injury but also enriched by some of the many important motifs which he introduced into the philosophical discussion. But this is not enough of a diagnosis. And it is certainly not enough foundation for a prognosis.

My first task will therefore be to present the basis for a reasoned appraisal by surveying the status of phenomenology in the main philosophical areas of the world outside France. I shall begin with the country of origin of the movement and proceed from there in several directions in an order which is debatable. I shall postpone the presentation of the Anglo-American picture to the end, largely because of special problems and opportunities of phenomenology in this part of the philosophical world, problems which can be assessed much more profitably against the background of the picture in other parts of the world.

For this whole section I would like to make special reference to H. L. Van Breda's recent chronicle and bibliography "La Phéno-ménologie" in Klibansky, Raymond, ed., *Philosophy in the Mid-Century* (Firenze, La Nuova Italia Editrice, 1958), II, 53–70.

A. THE SCENE OUTSIDE FRANCE

1. Germany: Eclipse and New Stirrings

At first sight, and especially in comparing post-Nazi Germany with France, one may have the impression that phenomenology has died out in its country of origin. Certainly when Husserl died on April 26, 1938, in almost complete philosophical isolation, and when six months later his papers were removed to Louvain, without any one's attempting to keep them in Germany, it looked as if phenomenology had no future there. Nor did phenomenology revive at once when the blanket of the Nazi Welt-anschauung was lifted from the German philosophical scene. No attempt has been made thus far to revive Husserl's *Jahrbuch*, chiefly because Heidegger and presumably Oskar Becker, the two surviving coeditors, remained disinterested. Of Husserl's last collaborators, Ludwig Landgrebe and Eugen Fink, Landgrebe stated in 1948 that phenomenology had become practically an unknown quantity,[1] especially to the younger generation, and in 1951 Fink even went so far as to say, "The Phenomenological Movement belongs to public history. It had its day. The thinkers who once formed a league (*Bund*), a school united by the same fundamental convictions, have died or gone their own ways." [2]

Since then, there has been an undeniable reawakening at least of historical interest in Husserl's philosophy. There is now a new Husserl Archive at the University of Cologne, the seat of Scheler's main academic activities, an offspring of the Louvain Archives, where such Husserl scholars as Walter and Marly Biemel have now been joined by Ludwig Landgrebe. The German post-war generation also numbers such promising students of Husserl's work as Rudolf Boehm, Gerd Brand, Alwin Diemer, Gerhard Funke, and Wolfgang Hermann Müller.

It is another question whether this revival of interest in the founder of phenomenology has already led to a revival of phenomenology itself. Any attempt to answer this question has to take account first of what has become of Husserl's last two assistants and obvious heirs presumptive since the master's death, Ludwig Landgrebe and Eugen Fink. Actually the courses they have taken differ considerably. But they both share a much stronger concern for the metaphysical implications of phenomenology than Husserl had ever expressed.

Landgrebe, (born 1902, Husserl's research assistant from 1923–1930) has become known chiefly as the editor of Husserl's *Erfahrung und Urteil* (1938). Among his independent publications the one most important for his own conception of phenomenology is a collection of essays which appeared in 1949 under the significant title *Phänomenologie und Metaphysik*. In the preface [1] Landgrebe made it clear that Husserl's phenomenology is still the foundation of his own philosophizing, but that he does not feel committed to Husserl's particular formulations (p. 8). Besides, he announces as his main objective the refounding (*Neubegründung*) of metaphysics (p. 9). The climactic essay of his book, "Phenomenological Analysis of Consciousness and

---

[1] *Phänomenologie und Metaphysik* (Hamburg, 1948), p. 7.
[2] *Problèmes actuels de la phénoménologie* (PA). Paris, Desclée de Brouwer, 1951). p. 54.

Metaphysics," gives some idea of how Landgrebe intends to utilize Husserl's phenomenology as an approach to such a metaphysics. Strangely enough, it is precisely the phenomenological reduction, seemingly the death of all speculative metaphysics, which Landgrebe wants to use as a start for his phenomenological metaphysics. It leads him toward an "intersubjective reduction," a reduction which is to yield the self-evidence of the "thou" or the other as not affected by the attempted reduction to a transcendental "I". For the world when phenomenologically reduced can be understood only by reference to other egos. This takes Landgrebe beyond Descartes with his isolated self via Augustine's prerogative of the thou to the assertion of a transcendent Absolute within transcendental intersubjectivity. The final outlook is that of a divine Absolute very similar to the Hegelian conception, a God who is present in the very existence of man. Clearly this theological and even Christian climax of Landgrebe's phenomenological metaphysics calls for a much fuller and more compelling derivation than can be given here and than Landgrebe himself has given thus far.

While Landgrebe thus still maintains his place in the phenomenological tradition, Eugen Fink's relation to phenomenology is much more puzzling. Fink (born 1905), after having studied under both Husserl and Heidegger, became known as the author of a penetrating though incomplete phenomenological study on "Presentation and Image" (*Vergegenwärtigung und Bild*) in the last volume of Husserl's *Jahrbuch* (XI). As Landgrebe's successor in the role of Husserl's research assistant after the latter's retirement, Fink obtained the master's confidence even to the extent that Husserl made him his spokesman in a much noted article in the *Kantstudien*.[1] Actually this article, which announced a further radicalization of the phenomenological reduction, contained an extreme formulation of phenomenological idealism, an interpretation of the phenomenological constitution as productive and even creative, and the distinction of three kinds of egos which left even some of Husserl's closer followers bewildered. Fink also drafted an unpublished sixth Cartesian Meditation with the program of a "constructive phenomenology,"

---

[1] "Die phänomenologische Philosophie Edmund Husserls in der gegenwärtigen Kritik," *Kantstudien* XXXVIII (1933), 319–383.

which has remained unpublished, and worked jointly with Husserl on a vast manuscript about the phenomenology of time.

It was therefore particularly surprising that Fink, who had faithfully stood by Husserl during his last years under the darkening clouds of the Nazi period, did not resume the line of work and the studies in which he had been engaged with Husserl, when he was appointed to a chair of philosophy in Freiburg in 1945, but struck out in a very different direction. Only little of his new ideas, which he has presented chiefly in his lectures, has been published thus far. But now he speaks with an entirely new voice, to be observed especially in his first independent book. Gone is the extreme emphasis which Husserl placed on subjectivity during his last years. More important, Fink no longer seems to identify himself with phenomenology in any of its historical forms.[1] In his contribution to the first international phenomenological symposium in Brussels (1951) he argued that phenomenology was wrong in repudiating all metaphysics; for Husserl's own position had contained unacknowledged speculative elements, notably in his interpretation of the *Sachen*, i.e., the things themselves as phenomena, in his demand for a completely new start of philosophy, in his assertion of the secondary status of the conceptual world, in the failure to give a clear meaning to the concept of constitution, in the vagueness of the phenomenological conception of life, and in the whole analytical method used.[2] Fink repeated and expanded these criticisms at the colloquia of Krefeld (1956) and Royaumont (1957). And in his book on the "Ontological Early History of Space, Time, and Movement" he speaks of the "fateful error of phenomenology, the belief that an absolute new beginning can be achieved by looking at the things themselves without prejudice" (p. 5). More concretely, he asserts that the phenomenological method is essentially incapable of clarifying such fundamental categories as space, time, and movement, which are not "phenomena" but are presupposed by all "phenomena." Of course this does not mean that Fink has abandoned phenomenology altogether.

---

[1] See, e.g., the reference to "the prejudices of phenomenology" in "Zum Problem der ontologischen Erfahrung," *Actas del primer congreso de filosofia*, Mendoza 1949, p. 741.

[2] "L'Analyse intentionelle et le problème de la pensée spéculative," *PA*, p. 82.

But it does imply that he no longer considers it the only philosophical method or even the fundamental one. More basic is now
the "ontological method." Its main feature seems to be the
conceptual interpretation of the categories that underlie even
the phenomena (*seinsbegriffliche Auslegung*).

In its general plan Fink's new philosophy is much closer to
Heidegger's than to Husserl's enterprise. To Heidegger's *Being
and Time* he ascribes epochal significance (*"säkulare Bedeutung"*),
and its title appears to him as the "watchword of the century"
(*Losungswort des Jahrhunderts*) (p. 41 f.). Fink's ambition consists
in expanding the scope of the title of the book by adding to Heidegger's emphasis on time the dimensions of space and movement in a way that would make "Being and World" rather than
"Being and Time" the proper sphere of ontology. It would seem,
however, that Fink's "Being" does not mean Heidegger's
beingness (*Sein*) but rather "what is" (*Seiendes*) in the manner
of Hegelian philosophy, and that in this case "Being" and
"World" practically coincide. The "world" is then described
in terms of the familiar Scholastic "transcendentals": *ens*,
interpreted by Fink as *Dingheit* (thinghood), *unum*, as *Seiendes
im Ganzen* (the totality of what is), *bonum*, as *Mass des Seins* or
Gott (measure of being, or God), and *verum*, as *Wahrheit* (truth).

Perhaps the most arresting feature of Fink's philosophizing
is its characterization of the fundamental philosophical experience as the "shock of amazement at the fact of the world," a
stunned amazement (*fassungslos*) to which he assigned the
function of converting the trivial into what is worth questioning.
This motif can be traced as far back as his essay on the fundamental intentions of Husserl's phenomenology, where he compares phenomenology with the amazement of Plato's *Theaetetus*,
and the condition of the phenomenologist with that of the
prisoner in Plato's allegory of the cave – something which Husserl
himself never had done. It is even more pronounced in the
beginning section of an apparently unfinished book on "The
Problem of Edmund Husserl's Phenomenology" which he
published soon after the master's death. Here he described the
prime task of philosophy as combating the naive indifference
(*Naivität*) of our everyday consciousness in the face of the fact
of the world. Initially he seems to have thought that Husserl's

"intentional analysis" was the most effective means for achieving his end. It appears that now he has reached the conclusion that only a specific kind of "ontological experience" and its conceptual interpretation can do this, not mere phenomenological experience with its descriptive techniques.

One of Fink's publications, the opening volume of *Phaenomenologica*, continues this new line of thought. It deals with anterior questions (*Vor-Fragen*) to the problem of the concept "phenomenon," notably with Being, Truth, and World. The guiding purpose of this course of lectures is announced as "illuminating (*aufleuchten lassen*) the cosmological horizon for the question of Being in an encounter with the phenomenological motifs in Husserl's and Heidegger's philosophies." The concept of phenomenon itself enters only in connection with the appearance of Being as that of a peculiar movement (*Bewegung*). Husserl's phenomenology and the phenomenological approach, while mentioned in quotes as the proper foundation for all human thinking, are not yet considered philosophy (p. 51). Nevertheless, a phenomenology of the "phenomenon" may profit considerably from the development of some of Fink's suggestive distinctions, expressed in an often striking and poetically sensitive language.

Works by EUGEN FINK:

Vom Wesen des Enthusiasmus (1947)
Nachdenkliches zur ontologischen Frühgeschichte von Raum – Zeit – Bewegung (1957)
Oase des Glücks. Gedanken zur Ontologie des Spiels (1957)
Sein, Wahrheit, Welt. Vor-Fragen zum Problem des Phänomen-Begriffs (1958). *Alles und nichts. Ein Umweg zur Philosophie* (1959)
Studien zur Phänomenologie 1930–1939 (1966)   [1]

Thus Husserl's two most qualified interpreters have both moved beyond and away from the master's conception toward a more or less theological metaphysics. Phenomenology is to them now at best a stepping stone to such more ambitious tasks.

Another noteworthy case is that of Oskar Becker (born 1889), once even a co-editor of Husserl's Jahrbuch In his "Contributions toward a Phenomenological Foundation of Geometry and of Its Applications to Physics," [1] Becker had developed Husserl's

[1] *JPPF* VI (1923), 385–560.

transcendental idealism with a view to discussing such problems as the continuum and geometrical axiomatics, and had included a phenomenological appraisal of the theory of relativity. His even more ambitious study of "Mathematical Existence," which appeared as a companion to Heidegger's *Sein und Zeit*,[1] had also applied the method of hermeneutic phenomenology in an attempt to interpret the differences between mathematical intuitionism and formalism by relating them to different ways of human existence (*Dasein*); besides, he had outlined the idea of a "mantic" phenomenology destined to explore the range of the unconscious. Disregarding here Becker's aberration from his philosophical course during the Nazi period, the most striking thing about his publications since his re-emergence as a philosopher of mathematics is the absence of more than incidental references to his phenomenological past.

On the other hand, there are also cases of a return to the older phenomenology. An example is Hans Reiner at the University of Freiburg. Having started his studies under both Husserl and Heidegger in Freiburg, Reiner had turned increasingly from phenomenology to existential philosophy and metaphysics.[2] Now, in his latest book,[3] he not only mentions "certain fundamental objections" to Heidegger's philosophy which he had entertained for a long time and which had crystallized only gradually (p. 158, n. 26); he also takes specific exception to the fact that in Heidegger's philosophy, and even more in that of several of his students, the task of phenomenological description and analysis had been neglected, with the result that whole areas of phenomena, decisive especially for the constitution of morality, have been skipped (p. 108). He even states his purpose as "vigorously defending Husserl's legacy under the watchword 'hands-off-metaphysics' until the phenomena have been sufficiently exhibited and cleared up" (p. 110). Thus Reiner resumes the value ethics of Scheler and Nicolai Hartman in a manner which suggests that the older phenomenology of value [1] may yet recover some of its lost nomentum.

Similar indications of a revival of interest in the phenomeno-

---

[1] *JPPF* VIII (1927), 439–809.
[2] See, e.g., his *Das Phänomen des Glaubens* (Halle, Niemeyer, 1934).
[3] *Pflicht und Neigung* (Westkulturverlag, Meisenheim, 1951).

logical style of the early phase of Husserl's work can be found in the "phenomenological studies" which the Swiss Michael Landmann published under the title *Erkenntnis und Erlebnis* (Berlin, de Gruyter & Co, 1951).

A number of new phenomenological groups have sprung up around such older phenomenologists in Göttingen as Kurt Stavenhagen, after his escape from Riga, and around Hedwig Conrad-Martius and Theodor Conrad in Munich. From the former group the names of Harald Delius and Hermann Ulrich Asemissen,[1] from the latter that of Franz Georg Schmücker should be mentioned.[2] To be sure, in the new Munich Circle the ontological or metaphysical interests predominate to an extent that seems to neglect phenomenological demonstration. Adolf Reinach, rather than Husserl or Scheler, is seen as the model phenomenologist by this group, which conceives of phenomenology primarily as a "pure doctrine of essences" (*reine Wesenslehre*).[3] The Göttingen group is highly critical of Husserl and has recently taken a strong interest in Wittgensteinian analysis.

Phenomenology in Austria seems to be limited to such expressions as Amadeo Silva Tarouca's "*Ontophänomenologie.*"[4]

2. Belgium: Louvain, the New Center

The focus of Belgian phenomenology is at the Catholic University of Louvain, the home of a distinctive type of Neo-scholasticism that goes back to Cardinal Mercier. In order to understand this situation, one has to take account of the interest in phenomenology even on the part of other, especially German, Neo-scholastics, who saw in phenomenology not only a rival growth but a potential graft for the old tree. Josef Geyser seems to have wavered between these two reactions. Since then Jesuits like Erich Przywara and particularly August Brunner have made more sustained efforts to utilize phenomenology for their metaphysical and theological enterprises. But nowhere

[1] *Strukturanalytische Probleme der Wahrnehmung in der Phänomenologie Husserls* (Köln, Universitätsverlag, 1957).
[2] *Phänomenologie als Methode der Wesenserkenntnis*. Munich Dissertation. (München, 1956).
[3] See, e.g., Hedwig Conrad-Martius' preface to the new edition of Adolf Reinach's *Was ist Phänomenologie?* (München, Kösel, 1951), p. 7.
[4] *Philosophie im Mittelpunkt*. Entwurf einer Ontophänomenologie (Graz, Stiasny, 1957).

has this interest in phenomenology taken so definite and sustained a form as at Louvain. Since Mercier's days the school of Louvain has been distinguished by its special study and utilization of contemporary philosophy in the attempt to bring scholastic philosophy up to date. Originally, positivism and Kantianism offered the major challenge. Phenomenology presented itself as a constructive alternative in which Mercier's successor Monsignor L. Noel and later Joseph Maréchal took a particular interest. Louis de Raeymaeker, the present head of the Louvain *Institut Supérieur de Philosophie,* takes a similar course. To him a reflection on the basic structure of human consciousness (the *cogito*) constitutes the primary point of departure for metaphysics; for this approach he invokes both St. Augustine and Descartes, as Husserl had done in his *Cartesian Meditations,* without mentioning this work specifically.[1]

This approach also accounts for the remarkable support which the *Institut Supérieur* gave to the Franciscan Herman Leo Van Breda in the rescue of the Husserl papers from Freiburg and in the establishment of the Husserl Archives under the very roof of the Institute. The actual work of preserving, ordering, transcribing, and preparing critical editions of the Husserl papers was done chiefly by Germans under the auspices of the Archives. Among the Belgian colleagues of Van Breda Alphonse de Waelhens (1911–   ) and Albert Dondeyne (1901–   ) deserve particular mention. The former has devoted most of his efforts thus far to critical analyses of the work of major phenomenologists, especially Heidegger and his French successors such as Merleau-Ponty; the latter has chiefly explored the bearing of phenomenology on Catholic theology. On the whole the work of the Belgian friends of phenomenology has been largely one of critical assimilation. For original and direct phenomenological studies one must turn to the Louvain psychologist Albert Michotte and his school, who however have been inspired much more by Brentano and by the Würzburg school than by Husserl. In fact, Michotte's classical work on the perception of causation is to a large extent experimental.[2]

[1]

---

1 *Philosophie de l'être.* (Louvain, Nauwelaerts, 1947), p. 17 ff.
2 See Murchison, Carl, ed., *A History of Psychology in Autobiography* (Worcester, Clark University Press), IV (1952), 228–33.

Of a more independent nature is the work of Stephan Strasser, an Austrian by origin, now associated with the Dutch university of Nijmegen, who first became known as the able editor of the German version of the *Cartesian Meditations* in the first volume of the Louvain edition of Husserl's works. In his own phenomenological studies, mostly in the field of psychology, he has made it clear that he "rejects... phenomenology as a science." Nor is he prepared to accept the "metaphysics" of Husserl's transcendental idealism. Instead he sees in phenomenology a method in the service of a metaphysics of Being in the manner of de Raeymaeker.[1] Strasser's major interest thus far is in metaphysical psychology. His studies on the problem of the soul explore the self incarnated in the body as author of its acts and as inward consciousness with results which corroborate a Thomist anthropology. His phenomenological investigations of the emotional life[2] are even more concrete. He begins with an examination of the pertinent psychological and phenomenological literature and distinguishes in an original manner between moods (*Stimmungen*), intentional sentiments (*Gesinnungen*), fundamental attitudes (*Grundhaltungen*), passions (*Leidenschaften*), and other emotional experiences; he adds a fresh and illuminating phenomenology and typology of happiness and related experiences like the feeling of achievement, enjoyment, and joy, and offers original distinctions between various levels of the emotional life. This descriptive work does not keep him from adding hermeneutic interpretations concerning the sense of these experiences: thus he sees the experience of happiness as essentially one of transcending anticipation (*Vorgriff*); these interpretations seem to be much more debatable than Strasser's descriptive work.   [1]

3. The Netherlands: Extensions

The situation differs considerably in the Protestant Netherlands. Here the foundation for the interest in phenomenology goes back to the "phenomenology of religion" of Chantepie de la Saussaye (see Introduction, p. 10f.), which was developed further

[1] *Le Problème de l'âme* (Louvain, Publications universitaires, 1953), p. XII f.; English as *The Soul in Metaphysical and Empirical Psychology* (Pittsburgh, Duquesne, 1957).
[2] *Das Gemüt. Grundgedanken zu einer phänomenologischen Philosophie und Theorie des menschlichen Gefühlslebens* (Utrecht, Spectrum, 1956).

by his student Gerardus Van der Leeuw. It was only in the second edition of his *Phänomenologie der Religion* that Van der Leeuw (1890–1950) tried to establish a connection with the new philosophical phenomenology. Since then these two currents have fused and spread remarkably. Thus, there are now three chairs of the phenomenology of religion, in the universities of Groningen, Utrecht, and Leyden respectively.

A more philosophical approach to phenomenology was initiated by thinkers interested primarily in the phenomenology of language such as Hendrik J. Pos (1898–1955). Among the younger Dutch philosophers Husserl's transcendental phenomenology has an able interpreter in C. A. Van Peursen (Leyden), [1]   originally a student of Van der Leeuw.

But perhaps even more important and original is the work of the Dutch biologists, psychologists, psychopathologists, and psychiatrists. Best known among them is F. J. J. Buytendijk (1887–   ), who started out as an animal psychologist. To be sure, his major concern is apparently philosophical anthropology, as developed mainly in his book on human posture and movement.[1] But several of his publications go by explicitly phenomenological titles, the later ones also revealing the influence of French existential phenomenology.[2] Among the Dutch psychopathologists the studies of H. C. Rümke (1893–   ) on the phenomenology of happiness[3] and those of J. H. Van den Berg may serve as examples. The latter, also an "External Lecturer on Phenomenological Psychopathology" at the University of Utrecht, has written a vivid and instructive English introduction to this new psychopathology.[4] An international *Festschrift* for Buytendijk [5] and the first volume of a collection of contributions to phenomenological psychology and psychopathology edited by several Utrecht phenomenologists

---

[1] *Algemene theorie van de menselijke houding en beweging.* Utrecht-Antwerpen, 1948; German translation (*Allgemeine Theorie der menschlichen Haltung und Bewegung,* 1956); French translation (*Attitudes et mouvements,* 1957).

[2] "The Phenomenological Approach to the Problem of Feelings and Emotions" in Reymert, M. L., ed., *Feelings and Emotions* (*The Mooseheart Symposium,* New York, 1950), p. 127–41 – *Phénoménologie de la rencontre.* (Paris, Desclée de Brouwer, 1952).

[3] *Zur Phänomenologie und Klinik der Glücksgefühle* (Berlin, Springer, 1924).

[4] *A Phenomenological Approach to Psychiatry* (Springfield, Ill., Thomas, 1955).

[5] *Rencontre-Encounter-Begegnung* (Utrecht, Spectrum, 1957). – Contains a full bibliography.

afford a good picture of the concrete work spearheaded by this Dutch group.[1]

4. Switzerland: A New Phenomenological Anthropology

Switzerland, particularly in its German-speaking part, has always shared major developments within the German cultural orbit including philosophy. This is true of phenomenology too, which after 1931 had an able German spokesman in Hermann Schmalenbach (1885–1950), who had come from Göttingen. But the native Swiss who opened the way for phenomenological thinking on an original scale was the psychopathologist and psychiatrist Ludwig Binswanger (1881–   ), head of a mental sanatorium at Kreuzlingen near Constance, who originally had been a student of Eugen Bleuler and a friend of Sigmund Freud.[2] His attempt to develop a general psychology (verstehende Psychologie) led him first to Husserl: "The intensive study of Brentano, of Husserl's Logische Untersuchungen and his phenomenology freed my eyes once and for all from the naturalist cataract," as he himself puts it.[3] But while he credits Husserl with having developed a method which goes beyond mere factual knowledge to an unconditional respect for the phenomena according to their content as meant,[4] his underlying concern for a philosophical understanding of man as such soon led him to Heidegger's more comprehensive phenomenological ontology, in which he discovered the tools for developing a "phenomenological anthropology" based on a Daseinsanalyse (i.e., interpretation of existence) which tried to understand man from his living contact with the phenomenal world of his existence. Yet, different from Heidegger, Binswanger believes that love, understood as coexistence (Miteinandersein), is at least as

---

[1] Situation, edited by J. H. van den Berg, F. J. J. Buytendijk, M. J. Langeveld, J. Linschoten. Utrecht, Spectrum, 1954. – See especially Buytendijk's Avant-propos, pp. 7–14.

[2] About the influence of Husserl and Heidegger on Binswanger in his emancipation from Freud, see especially his Erinnerungen an Freud (Bern, Francke, 1956), pp. 87, 92.

[3] Ausgewählte Vorträge und Aufsätze. Vol. I: Zur phänomenologischen Anthropologie (Bern, Francke, 1947), p. 7; see also the Vorwort to volume II for a significant correction: "naturwissenschaftlich" has been replaced by "naturalistisch" in this quotation.

[4] Grundformen und Erkenntnis menschlichen Daseins. (Zürich, Niehans, 1942), p. 642. See also "On the Relation between Husserl's Phenomenology and Psychological Insight" in PPR II (1941), 199–210.

important to human existence as concern (*Sorge*). In fact, it provides a unique access to the knowledge of human existence (*Daseinserkenntnis*). Binswanger's concrete and practical development of this conception in his case studies is not the least important part of his work.[1]

Phenomenological anthropology of a similar type can be found in a number of Swiss writers inspired to a considerable extent by Paul Häberlin's anthropology, among whom Hans Kunz (1904–   ) deserves special attention. After a dissertation on the "Phenomenological Analysis of Expression" (1931) he published chiefly an impressive two-volume work on the anthropological significance of the imagination [2] based on a phenomenological description of phantasy as distinguished from related phenomena; it goes on from there, however, to an ambitious interpretation of its significance and its foundations.

Roland Kuhn (1912–   ), another Swiss psychiatrist, is known particularly for the application of the phenomenological approach to the Rorschach test.[3]

The share of French-speaking Switzerland in the Phenomenological Movement, represented chiefly in the person of Pierre [1] Thévenaz, has been mentioned in Chapter XII.

5. Italy: Scatterings

Up to very recently there has been no active interest in phenomenology in Italy. It never seems to have aroused the curiosity [2] of Italy's leading idealist philosophers such as Benedetto Croce and Giovanni Gentile. Antonio Banfi published a considerable number of books and articles on Husserl's phenomenology; but his ultimate Marxist commitment seems to have made him increasingly critical of Husserl. An impressive monograph by Sofia Vanni Rovighi [4] reflects the familiar Neo-Thomist interest. In 1955 this resulted in a special meeting of "Christian university professors of philosophy" at the Gallarete Center with a partially international panel, which concerned itself mainly with the

---

[1] See May, Rollo, Angel, Ernest, and Ellenberger, Henri F., *Existence. A New Dimension in Psychiatry and Psychology* (New York, Basic Book, 1958), esp. Chaps. VII–IX.

[2] *Die anthropologische Bedeutung der Phantasie* (Basel, 1946).

[3] French translation under the title *Phénoménologie du masque à travers le test de Rorschach* (1955). – See also May, Rollo, *op. cit.*, Ch. X.

[4] *La filosofia di Edmund Husserl* (Milano, Vita e Pensiero, 1930).

question of the metaphysical import of phenomenology.[1] But this interest in phenomenology appears relatively minor and theoretical compared with the extraordinary influence of existentialism, particularly in its Heideggerian form.[2] Yet even the most original Italian existentialist, Nicolo Abbagnano, shows little explicit interest in phenomenology as such. It is possible, however, that a recent special issue of the *Archivio di Filosofia* entitled "The Task of Phenomenology"[3] with an international roster of contributors, indicates a more active concern in the development of phenomenological studies, not only on the part of the editor, Enrico Castelli, who stresses chiefly Heideggerian *Daseinsanalyse*, but also on the part of such Italian contributors as Renato Lazzarini and Raffaele Pucci. [1]

6. Eastern Europe: First Response, Blackout, and Remnants

At this time phenomenology, like all the other non-Marxist philosophies, has obviously no recognized status in countries under Soviet philosophical control. This must not make us overlook the early influence of Husserl's thought on Russian philosophy, all the more since, paradoxically, this seems to have had an indirect effect on the spread of phenomenology to the west of Germany. There is to begin with the remarkable fact that Husserl's *Logische Untersuchungen* were translated into Russian as early as 1909, followed by "Philosophie als strenge Wissenschaft" in 1911 (the very year of its appearance). It seems that the philosopher chiefly responsible for this early interest in Husserl was Nicolay Lossky (1870–   ), whose intuitionistic realism found unexpected support in Husserl's logical studies, which Lossky acknowledged in one of his major works as early as 1906 (*The Foundations of Intuitivism*).[4] At least equally important was probably the fact that a number of young Russian philosophers studying in Germany came in contact with

---

[1] See *Atti del XI Convegno: La Fenomenologia* (Brescia, Morcelliana, 1956).

[2] See, e.g., the article by J(ean) L(ameere) in the *Revue internationale de philosophie* XIII (1949), 348–59, on "L'Existentialisme en Italie" with detailed bibliography, which includes some explicitly phenomenological titles under the names of A. Banfi, N. Bobbio, E. Grassi, A. Massolo, C. Mazzantini, E. Paci, A. Pastore, and S. Vanni-Rovighi.

[3] *Il compito della fenomenologia* (Padova, Cedam, 1957).

[4] See Jakowenko, Boris "Edmund Husserl und die russische Philosophie," *Der russische Gedanke* I (1929), 210–12.

Husserl's thought and possibly even with Husserl personally, among them in 1904 David Victorovic Victorov, a lecturer at the University of Moscow at the time, followed by Georges Gurvitsch, later one of the chief transmitters of phenomenology to France, Henry (Henrich Ernestovich) Lanz (later at Stanford) and Gustav Gustavovich Shpet (1879–   ). Alexandre Koyré (see p. 225), who studied with Husserl intensively, was a younger and particularly influential member of this group of Russian philosophers passing through Germany on their way to France; so was Alexandre Kojève (see p. 402, 414).

Shpet seems to have been the one who knew and supported Husserl's developed phenomenology most fully. A. E. Losev (1892–   ) was one of the more original "Russian Husserlians"[1] who tried to combine phenomenology with dialectics and was able to publish his studies in Russia as late as 1927. Leo Shestov (1866–1938), a follower of the mystic Russian philosophy of Vladimir Soloview, saw in Husserl chiefly the arch-rationalist; so, after his emigration to France in 1920, he singled him out for attack as the chief antagonist of his own anti-rational metaphysics of wisdom in a conspicuous article, *"Memento Mori. À propos de la théorie de la connaissance d'Edmund Husserl,"* *Revue philosophique* CI (1926), 5–62.

Naturally the influences were much stronger in the western parts of the Slavic world. The Baltic states with their considerable German element were most directly involved. In Latvia the leading and original minds were Kurt Stavenhagen and Theodor Celms, one of the keenest critics of Husserl's idealism. But both had to go into exile. Poland is still represented by one of the outstanding members of the older phenomenological generation, Roman Ingarden, who, in spite of the preponderance of positivism in Poland, had a considerable following at the universities of Lwów and Cracow.

But all this came to a temporary end soon after the Russian Revolution, especially after 1922, when some of the leading non-Marxist philosophers were sent into exile, and perhaps even more definitely when all philosophical relations with the western world were broken off. Phenomenology, in the eyes of the official

---

[1] See V. V. Zenkovsky, *A History of Russian Philosophy*. Translated by George L. Kline. (New York, Columbia University, 1953) II, 829–39.

Russian philosophy as set forth by M. Rosenthal and P. Ioudine
in a recent Dictionary of Philosophy, constitutes nothing but

an idealist subjective reactionary theory, founded by the German philosopher Edmund Husserl, current in bourgeois philosophy during the
period of imperialism. ... The main goal of this decadent philosophy
is to confuse human reason, to turn it away from the burning problems of
life and science, from the judicious and fruitful methods of theoretical
thought. ... The seat of the International Phenomenological Society is
New York (sic). It organizes the adepts of this theory for the struggle
against the growing influence of the advanced ideas of philosophical
materialism.[1]

It remains to be seen how far the weird clichés of this official
line – weird particularly in view of some of the leftist sympathies
of the French phenomenologists – will stand in the way of future
relaxations and exchanges. At least the Polish example makes it
not altogether phantastic to hope for a less rigid control of
philosophical thought in some of the satellite countries, and for
a revival of some of the earlier phenomenological traditions.

Czechoslovakia, actually the native country of Edmund
Husserl, whose first President Thomas G. Masaryk was one of
his early fellow students, has been more under the Brentano
tradition than under the influence of phenomenology in the
narrower sense. But quite a few Czechoslovakian philosophers,
both Czech, like Jan Patocka, and German, like Emil Utitz,
used to display a more than sympathetic interest in phenomenological thought, for which the *Cercle philosophique de Prague*
provided a hospitable forum. Here Husserl gave his last public
lectures in 1935. Plans to find a final refuge for him there,
however, failed to materialize.

7. Spain: Ortega's Part and Its Significance

The situation is very different and rather unique in Spain and
the Ibero-American countries. For here phenomenology itself,
not only its existentialist modification, has become one of the
dominant philosophies. This happened independently of, and
almost simultaneously with, the phenomenological invasion
of France. But, very differently from France, the medium for
this transmission was one single philosopher, José Ortega y
Gasset, in the final analysis not even a phenomenologist himself.

[1] *Petit Dictionnaire Philosophique* (Editions en langues étrangères. Moscou, 1955).

The effect upon Spanish letters and philosophy of Franco's victory in the Civil War was that the center of Spanish phenomenology has now moved to the American hemisphere, where its position is in striking contrast to that of phenomenology in the United States and in Canada.

The story behind this amazing naturalization has still to be told in detail by someone more closely familiar with Spanish philosophical literature than the writer. But at least the beginnings can be traced in Ortega's intellectual biography as it can be gathered from his published works.

Actually, the interest in phenomenology was only a phase in Ortega's own development. But it had consequences far beyond his own philosophizing. José Ferrater Mora in his introduction to Ortega's philosophy [1] divides Ortega's search for a new philosophy into three phases: objectivism (1902–1914), perspectivism (1914–1923), and ratio-vitalism (1924–1955). During the first period he spent two momentous years of study in Germany. In Leipzig (1904) Wilhelm Wundt with his psychologism apparently failed to meet his objectivist needs. In Berlin he remained equally unimpressed; besides, he missed Dilthey, whom he did not "discover" until 1933, when his personal stake in phenomenology was on the decline. It was in Marburg (1906) that he found in Hermann Cohen and Paul Natorp the philosophers whom he called in retrospect "my teachers" (maestros).[2] But although he credited Cohen with having given him some inspiration toward his philosophy of "existence," he certainly became anything but a Neo-Kantian. It is not altogether unlikely that Natorp was the first to bring Husserl to Ortega's attention, as he had done before in the case of W. E. Hocking. But there is no evidence of such interest before 1913, when Ortega wrote an extended review (Obras I, 245–261) of a Göttingen dissertation by Heinrich Hofmann on the concept of sensation ("Über den Empfindungsbegriff"), a dissertation which had appeared in the Archiv für die gesamte Psychologie XXVI (1913), 1–136. The fact that this rather specialized study in descriptive psychology by one of the less known members of the

---

[1] Ortega y Gasset. An Outline of His Philosophy (New Haven, Yale University Press, 1957).

[2] Obras completas (Madrid, Revista de Occidente, 1946), VI, 383, note.

Göttingen Circle, which referred to Husserl only in passing, should have been singled out for such special attention is still in need of an explanation. Ortega's unusually long review also included three intermediate sections on Husserl's *"fenomeno-logía,"* characterized as a pure description of essences; here he used Husserl's *Ideen,* just published, as his main reference. Ortega's discussion of this work was one of the earliest and most detailed at the time. It was also a very sympathetic one, expressing great hopes for the future of phenomenology. It stands to reason that for Ortega Husserl's new approach promised important help in the elaboration of the philosophy of his second period, perspectivism, and, more specifically, of his new conception of "human life." In fact, after 1914 Ortega presented Husserl's Phenomenology in his courses at the University of Madrid in the light of his own theory, but found it wanting in several respects. To be sure, Ortega's criticisms were not published during his lifetime for several reasons, of which he stated only one in retrospect: "plainly and simply ... timidity." For Ortega's own doctrine of life as fundamentally different from consciousness seemed to him too much out of tune with the climate of the first quarter of the century. His "liminal objection" to Husserl's transcendental phenomenology was that suspending our positing belief extirpates the most constitutive character of direct consciousness, i.e., its "executive" character, granting absolute being, without adequate reason, only to reflective consciousness. Instead, according to Ortega, positing consciousness and posited object should enjoy equal rights. This led him to the formulation of his concept of the "real human life" as coexistence of the ego and its circumstances.[1]

However, Ortega became quite outspoken in his criticisms of Husserl during his third period, that of the philosophy of the *razón vital.* Thus, in the appendix to his "Notes on Thinking," [2] while still calling Husserl "the most influential figure for nearly a century" (p. 521), he characterizes Husserl's phenomenology as "no different from the philosophies preceding it, ... as one of the naive and unjustified philosophies, i.e., philosophies which

---

[1] *La idea de principio en Leibniz y la evolución de la teoria deductiva* (Buenos Aires, Emece, 1958), p. 332, note 2.

[2] "Apuntos sobre el pensamiento, sa teurgía y su demiurgía," (1941) *Obras,* V, 517 ff.

do not include their own motives." Perhaps more serious, Husserl is to Ortega "an extreme rationalist, in fact the last great rationalist," whose thought represents "the quintessence of rationalism." He is also "the last representative of idealistic philosophy." In fact "the phenomenological attitude is radically opposed to the attitude that I call 'living reason' " (V, 545). Nevertheless, Ortega always thought of Husserl as having initiated "the most gigantic innovation between the time of positivist emptiness and ours" (IV, 509). As late as 1934 he even went to Freiburg to see him.[1]

But to Ortega "the first man of genius in the new land of phenomenology ... the Adam in the new paradise" was Max Scheler. To Scheler Ortega also refers as "my great friend." No information about the extent of this friendship is available thus far, but Scheler acknowledged Ortega's "following" in the 1926 Preface to his *Formalismus in der Ethik*.[2] Not only do the references to Scheler in Ortega's works outstrip by far those to Husserl or to any other of the phenomenologists, but Ortega also devoted to Scheler two separate texts, a long critical review of his controversial book *The Genius of War and the German War* in the second volume of *El Espectador* (1917) (II, 192–209), and a shorter obituary article in the *Revista de Occidente* under the title "Max Scheler, An Intoxicate of Essences" (IV, 507–511). To him Scheler was the "thinker par excellence, whose death in 1928 has deprived Europe of its best mind."

But while the philosopher of "vital reason" was thus fascinated by Scheler's philosophy of life and value, he was by no means uncritical of him, as shown by his first review of Scheler's book on the genius of war. Ortega introduces him here as "one of the most illustrious German thinkers of the new generation, "curious, subtle, gifted with intellectual ubiquity," but he adds that thus far his writings are distinguished more by keenness (*acuidad*) and subtlety than by rigorous argumentation (II, 194). In particular, Scheler's phenomenology of war incurs Ortega's

[1] *El Hombre y la gente*, (Madrid, Revista de Occidente, 1957) p. 154. – According to the very revealing footnote quoted on page 613, note 1 the conversation does not seem to have amounted to much, since "the age and the frailty" of the "admirable Husserl," (who seems to have referred him for a discussion of his objection to his assistant Eugen Fink) "did not permit him to enter into difficult topics concerning his own production."
[2] *Gesammelte Werke* II, 25.

repeated critical censure, quite apart from the fact that Ortega, politically an Anglophile, confesses to conclusions "radically opposed" to those of Scheler. However, Scheler's *Formalismus in der Ethik*, a work whose translation Ortega initiated, ranks for him as "one of the most formidable books produced by the twentieth century" (VI, 328 note). The final verdict remains ambivalent: as "Dionysus-Platon" Scheler appears to be the genuine embodiment of vital reason, but as an "intoxicate of essences" (*embriagado de esencias*) he seems to offend Ortega's sense of measure and to neglect the existences, in which Ortega remains equally interested. In conclusion, "his work is characterized by the strangest pair of qualities: clarity and disorder. In all his books – in their lack of architecture – there is talk of almost everything. ... Now it is necessary to complete his effort by adding what it lacked: architecture, order, system."

Ortega was also familiar with the studies of other phenomenologists and with the preparatory work of Brentano. Apparently he was particularly impressed by Alexander Pfänder, whose definition of love is included in his own *Estudios sobre el amor* (V, 553 ff.) [1] and by such less known phenomenologists as Aurel Kolnai. However, it is strange, especially in view of Ortega's objection to Scheler's lack of system, that Nicolai Hartmann's name is conspicuous by almost complete absence from his writings.

Ortega's strained relationship to Heidegger is a case by itself. Except for one major footnote in his Goethe essay of 1932 (IV, 403) he hardly ever referred to Heidegger explicitly during his own lifetime. This footnote revealed the understandable bitterness of the man who had formulated ideas strikingly similar to Heidegger's some twenty years before *Sein und Zeit*, who, two years before its appearance, had announced the program of a restatement (*replanteamiento*) of the problem of Being with a view to opening a series of publications by his students to explore it, and who had even formulated the so-called ontological difference between Being and things-in-being, without receiving any credit for it. To be sure, Ortega paid tribute to the "admirable excellence of Heidegger's major work," in which he acknowl-

---

[1] Translated under the title "Features of Love" by Toby Talbot in *On Love* (New York, Meridian, 1959). – See also the account of Pfänder's description on p. 186.

edged "fine" truths along with fine errors, though he thought the truths had been anticipated by Dilthey's ideas (IV, 341).[1] Only in his posthumous book on Leibniz does Ortega state his objections to Heidegger's philosophizing and to his role as the inspirer of Paris existentialism more fully and openly (see, e.g., pp. 330 ff., 369 ff.). However, in all these respects Heidegger is for Ortega chiefly the philosopher of existence and the ontologist, not the phenomenologist.

What is Ortega's attitude toward phenomenology in his own work? Until recently no explicit statement answering this question was available. However, in the posthumous Leibniz book Ortega quotes literally a formulation which he apparently presented to his Madrid students and which reads as follows:

"1.   It is necessary to renew the traditional problem of Being from its roots;

2.   this must be done with the phenomenological method insofar and only insofar as it means *synthetic* or *intuitive thinking*, not merely conceptually abstract thinking like the traditional logical thinking;

3.   but it is necessary to integrate the phenomenological method by adding to it a dimension of *systematic thinking*, which, as is known, it does not possess;

4.   and finally, in order for systematic phenomenological thinking to be possible, it is necessary to start from a phenomenon which is *by itself* (*el por sí*) a system. This systematic phenomenon is human life, and it is necessary to start with its intuition and analysis."

Ortega adds: "In this manner I abandoned Phenomenology at the very moment of adopting it" (p. 332 f.). What this paradox seems to say is that from the very start Ortega bent the intuitive method of phenomenology in the direction of a systematic analysis guided by his conception of human life, hence that he [1] adopted it only in a very conditional manner.

But what about his practice of the phenomenological method? In a few of his essays, especially in his "Introduction to a Theory of Values" of 1923 (VI, 315–23) one can see a definite attempt

---

[1] For an even more sympathetic appraisal of Heidegger's merits as a philosophical writer see Ortega's German essay "Martin Heidegger und die Sprache der Philosophen" (*Universitas* VII (1952), 897–903), although in the end he refers to him as "Hölderlin's ventriloquist."

to make use of its new powers. His famous essay of 1925 on "The Dehumanization of Art" contains a whole section, entitled "A Few Drops of Phenomenology," (III, 360–3), which offers a good illustration of perspectivism, showing how the same event is "split up" in the minds of several observers, and leading to the development of the conception of a scale of emotional distance from an event.

But with all of this conditional and partial acceptance of phenomenological techniques, it must be realized that the German philosopher whom Ortega found ultimately most congenial to his own thinking was not Husserl or Scheler but Wilhelm Dilthey. This is made clear particularly in Ortega's Dilthey essay of 1933, (*"Guillermo Dilthey y la idea de la vida"*) which tells the story of how he finally discovered the man whom he had missed in Berlin during his student days because of an accident which, as he states it, had cost him ten years (VI, 165–214). Thus to Ortega phenomenology was a stage rather than a goal on the way toward the formulation of his metaphysics of vital reason; but it was certainly not his only method.

Yet, regardless of where Ortega's own final sympathies lay, the influence of his plea for phenomenology kept spreading, especially among his many followers and students. At least from this point of view, just as important as Ortega's own writings were the various activities which emanated from his initiative, not only from his academic teaching at the University of Madrid, but also, after 1923, from his editorship of the new quarterly *Revista de Occidente*, of which some fifty volumes appeared. It included among many other things translations of lesser phenomenological essays. Finally it branched out into a vast translation project, whose main part consisted of works of German philosophers.

For an understanding of the perspective of phenomenology in Spain and Spanish America it is not without interest to list some of the major translations in Ortega's series as well as those in other Spanish American publications:

1926 Scheler, "La idea del hombre y la historia" (*Revista* XIV)
1927 Brentano, *El origen del conocimiento moral* (Madrid)
    Scheler, *El resentimiento en la moral* (Madrid)
1928 Pfänder, *Lógica* (Madrid; second edition, Buenos Aires, 1940)

1929 Husserl, *Investigaciones lógicas* (M. G. Morente y J. Gaos) (Madrid)
     Scheler, *Il puesto del hombre en el cosmos* (*Revista* XXV) (Madrid)
1931 Pfänder, *Fenomenología de la voluntad* (Madrid)
     Gurvitch, *Las tendencias actuales de la filosofía alemana* (from the
     French) (Madrid)
     Scheler, *Muerte y supervivencia. Ordo amoris* (from *Nachlass I*)
     (Madrid)
1933 Heidegger, *¿Qué es metafísica?* (Zubiri) (Madrid)
1934 Scheler, *El saber y la cultura* (from *Philosophische Weltanschauung*)
1935 Brentano, *Psicología* (with Ortega's Preface; see *Obras* VI, 37)
     (Madrid)
     Scheler, *Sociología del saber* ("*Die Typen des Wissens und die
     Bildung*") (Madrid)
1939 Husserl, *Meditaciones cartesianas* (J. Gaos) (Mexico)
1940 Scheler, *De lo eterno en el hombre* (Mexico)
1941 Scheler, *Ética* I (Mexico)
1942 Scheler, *Ética* II (Mexico)
1943 Scheler, *Esencia y formas de la simpatía* (Buenos Aires)
1949 Husserl, *Idéas relativas a une fenomenología pura y una filosofía
     fenomenológica* (Mexico)
1950 Husserl, *La filosofía como ciencia estricta* (Mexico)
1951 Heidegger, *Ser y tiempo* (J. Gaos) (Mexico)
1954 Heidegger, *Kant y el problema de la metafísica* (Gaos) (Mexico)

Clearly the Spanish-American world commands a fund of
translations of the original texts comparable only to that
available in French, but with a characteristically different
emphasis. For the selections favor realistic phenomenology
rather than Husserl's idealism. Translations of Heidegger's
texts follow relatively late and apart from Ortega's translation
project, apparently on the initiative of some of his more independent students, who experienced Heidegger's personal influence, not without disappointing their original master.

Of these students Xavier Zubiri (born 1898) wrote a doctoral
dissertation largely on Husserlian lines in 1923 ("*Attempt at a
Phenomenological Theory of Judgment*"), then studied under
Heidegger, produced a Spanish translation of his "What is
Metaphysics?" in 1933, and seems to reflect in his independent
writings Heidegger rather than Husserl. José Gaos (born 1902)
started out with a doctoral dissertation on Husserl's critique of
psychologism and translated, in collaboration with Manuel
García Morente, Husserl's *Logische Untersuchungen*, the *Cartesian
Meditations*, and, in 1950, the *Ideen*. But he too later turned to
Heidegger to the extent of preparing the first complete translation of Heidegger's *Sein und Zeit*, together with a separate

Introduction, both published in Mexico. Joaquín Xirau (1895–1946) brought out a competent book on Husserl's philosophy in 1941.

A position very similar to that of Ortega can also be found in one of his younger students, Julián Marías (1914–   ). Thus in his latest work, *Reason and Life*, he subscribes to the need of a descriptive method that goes beyond positivism and states that "we must accept everything that phenomenology has to say by way of response to a concrete demand ... but reserve complete liberty with respect to the concrete forms in which it has been clothed, as a philosophical doctrine." [1] Next to Ortega, Husserl is the contemporary author most frequently invoked in this significant work. Nevertheless, Marías rejects with Ortega Husserl's phenomenological reduction, and finally declares his phenomenology to be inadequate for the needs of a philosophy of vital reason.

8. The Ibero-American World: Double Wave

The Spanish Civil War and, perhaps even more, the subsequent emigration, temporary and permanent, of Spanish intellectuals under the Franco regime seem to have put an end to most phenomenological philosophy in Spain. This has spread all the more in the Ibero-American world with Mexico and Argentina as philosophical centers.

As far as Mexico is concerned, Patrick Romanell has supplied a most helpful background for such an account[2] in a way which makes it possible even for the outsider to understand the recent amazing spread of German philosophies and especially of phenomenology and existentialism. It appears from his account that in Mexico, as in other Latin American countries, the decline of nineteenth century positivism in its French form, discredited as it was by its political associations with dictators like Porfirio Díaz, had set the stage for a new beginning. Bergsonism, the French alternative, had considerable success for a while with such exponents as Antonio Caso, but had too much the appearance of "philosophic Romanticism." What the situation

---

[1] *Reason and Life. The Introduction to Philosophy*. Translated by Kenneth S. Reid and Edward Sarmiento. (New Haven, Yale University Press, 1956), p. 152.

[2] *Making of the Mexican Mind*. A Study in Recent Mexican Thought. (Lincoln, University of Nebraska Press, 1952).

called for was a philosophy which combined intuition and reason. Ortega held out hope for such a combination. Yet his own philosophy was no perfect answer to the needs of the Mexican Neo-Orteguans; especially his "play theory of life" as expressed in *The Modern Theme* seemed to them too flippant (*op. cit.*, p. 157). In fact, Ortega never set foot in Mexico, as he did twice in Argentina, although he had been invited by the University of Mexico in 1945.[1] More successful than Ortega himself were, however, the German thinkers for whom he made such a persuasive plea, first the Neo-Kantians and then, even more effectively, the phenomenologists and the "existentialists." Among the latter it was Heidegger more than Husserl who had a particular appeal for the Mexican philosophers, despite, and perhaps even because, of Ortega's conspicuous reserve (*op. cit.*, p. 144).

The first introduction of German phenomenology was actually the work of native Mexican thinkers, the so-called *Contemporáneos* (1928), notably Adalberto García de Mendoza, Samuel Ramos, and José Romano Muñoz. García de Mendoza was the first to study phenomenology in Germany in the twenties and offered courses and seminars on phenomenology, apparently based on Husserl, at the University of Mexico between 1927 and 1933. Ramos (1897–1959) had studied under Georges Gurvitch at the Sorbonne in 1928–29 and subsequently translated his French book on German contemporary philosophy, thus introducing not only Husserl but Scheler, Hartmann, and Heidegger into the Mexican world. Even the Bergsonian Antonio Caso expressed his interest in these new philosophies by giving courses on Scheler and Husserl, and by publishing the first Spanish book on Husserl in 1934: in fact he made a strong plea for phenomenology against positivism and neo-positivism in 1941.[2]

So the soil was not unprepared when the aftermath of the Spanish Civil War brought to Mexico a number of distinguished philosophical refugees, who soon became fully established in the New World, in whose language and tradition they were al-

---

[1] Personal communication from Professor Eduardo García Máynez of the Universidad Nacional Autónoma de Mexico.
[2] *Positivismo, Neopositivismo y Fenomenología* (Mexico, 1941).

ready at home. Among these *"transterrados"* were José Gaos, Eduardo Nicol, and Joaquín Xirau, all more or less familiar with phenomenology and existentialism. Gaos, the most influential among them, seems to have been particularly successful in focussing the spotlight on Heidegger rather than on Husserl. But there was now also a genuine interest in Scheler and Nicolai Hartmann, promoted particularly by the Mexican-born Eduardo García Máynez (1908–   ), who had studied under Nicolai Hartmann at Berlin in 1932–33. His *Ética* [1] culminates in a value ethics which is characterized as "objectivist phenomenology." Also, in his original and incisive studies in the theory of law he makes extensive and original use of Pfänder's as well as of Husserl's logic. [2] Even more recently interest has turned to the French phenomenological existentialists, especially to Sartre. Merleau-Ponty actually lectured in Mexico in 1947.

Argentina, the philosophically leading country in South America, also shows remarkable influence from European phenomenology and existentialism. Francisco Romero (1891–1962) was here the central figure. His sustained efforts to introduce German philosophy by means of his own publications, and his sponsorship of translations of texts by Scheler in his *Biblioteca Filosófica* were important factors in this development. But Husserl, Nicolai Hartmann, Dilthey, and the gestaltists are equally important to his thought, whose main concern is a philosophic theory of man as a self-transcending being. Ortega's influence in Argentina, especially as a result of his lectures in Buenos Aires during his exile from Spain, gave added momentum to these European philosophies. On the other hand, Argentina, as a result of Perón's dictatorship, lost to the U.S. the philosopher Risieri Frondizi, who has undergone particularly Husserl's influence. Carlos Astrada, interested especially in Heidegger's ontology, was his personal student.

But there are also traces of phenomenological influences in most other South American countries. Without any claim to completeness I shall merely mention *Peru's* Miró Quesada, who published an introduction to the Phenomenological Movement, Walter Blumenfeld, who wrote, e.g., on the phenomenology of

[1] Fifth Edition (Mexico, Editorial Porrúa, 1957).
[2] *Lógica del juicio jurídico* (Mexico, Fondo de Cultura Económica, 1956.)

play (*PPR* I, (1942), 470–78)) and Alberto Wagner de Reyna, a Neo-Thomist, who discussed Heidegger's ontology, after having studied under him as well as under Nicolai Hartmann; Venezuela's, Juan García Bacca, who as a refugee from Franco Spain brought the Spanish version of phenomenology, and Ernesto Mayz Valenilla, who produced a remarkably conscientious thesis on Husserl's transcendental phenomenology[1]; and Colombia's Julio Enrique Blanco. [2]

Obviously, this survey of phenomenological activity in the Latin-American countries had to remain on the surface. I do not feel qualified to judge how far the lively interest in phenomenological philosophy in this vast area has gone beyond interpretative studies of the classical phenomenologists. Indications are that the phenomenological interest is still in the receptive stage. Original achievement, if any, seems to take mostly the line of existentialist philosophizing.

9. *Oriental Countries: Sprinklings*

Like other international movements in philosophy, phenomenology has reached even more distant shores. In most instances the evidence is only worth mentioning for the sake of the record. Thus there are signs of interest in phenomenology in India, where its intuitionism and even more Husserl's transcendental idealism could have been expected to elicit some resonance.[3] At one time even Scheler had quite a following in China.[4] Viet Minh's Tran-Duc-Thao, while turning eventually to dialectical materialism, showed remarkable penetration of Husserlian phenomenology, which he seems to have acquired in Paris and Louvain (see also p. 418).

Perhaps the liveliest interest in phenomenology appeared in Japan. There were, especially in the twenties, a number of Japanese visitors in Freiburg who studied under both Husserl

---

[1] *Fenomenología del Conocimiento* (Caracas, 1954).

[2] "Tres lecciones sobre Husserl" in *Universidad Católica Bolivariana* (Medellín, Colombia), V–VII; see the review by Patrick Romanell in *PPR* IV (1944), 119 f.

[3] J. N. Mohanty, "Phenomenology in Indian Philosophy" in *Proceedings of the XIth International Congress* (Brussels, 1953), XIII, 255–62. "Husserl's Phenomenology and Indian Idealism" in *Philosophical Quarterly, India* XXIV (1954) no. 3. – Also, P. J. Chaudhury, "Knowledge and Truth: A Phenomenological Inquiry" in *PPR* XV (1955), 535–40.

[4] Oral information from Professor Y. P. Mei (now at the State University of Iowa).

and Heidegger. Probably the most original among them was Kitaro Nishida. Tomoo Otaka, later Dean of the Law School at Tokyo University, showed Husserl's influence particularly in his penetrating German book on social philosophy, *Die Lehre vom sozialen Verband* (Wien, 1932). Later these Freiburg students imported phenomenology into their native country. In fact, Husserl contributed two original semi-popular articles, which have not yet appeared in Europe, to two Japanese magazines. There is however no evidence of a permanent effect of these infiltrations. Apparently they have been overtaken by the wider appeal of existentialism.[1]

10. *Great Britain: Low Ebb*

An appraisal of the place of phenomenology in the Anglo-American countries might suitably begin with the British scene. There can be little doubt that at the present moment phenomenology, along with existentialism, has less philosophical status in Britain than in any other country outside Soviet Russia. It has no spokesmen in either Oxford or Cambridge, and but few sympathizers elsewhere, e.g., at the Universities of London (J. N. Findlay), and Bristol,[2] and at the Scotch universities. Some of the more explicit statements about phenomenology express an animus which reveals that there is more than sheer indifference behind the present low ebb of its affairs. The following verdict of Professor Gilbert Ryle, published in 1946, represents perhaps a climax of this anti-phenomenological mood:

I do not expect that even the corporate zeal of the International Phenomenological Institute (sic!) will succeed in winning for Husserl's ideas much of a vogue in the English-speaking world. ... In short, Phenomenology was, from its birth, a bore. Its oversolemnity of manner more than its equivocal lineage will secure that its lofty claims are ignored.

Yet even Ryle foresaw that "an off-shoot of Phenomenology known as Existentialism ... may well be smuggled overseas in

---

[1] See Matuo Noda, "Modern Japanese Philosophy and the Philosophy of K. Nishida" in *Proceedings of the XIth International Congress of Philosophy* (Brussels, 1953), XIII, 263–67.

[2] See, e.g., Stephan Körner (born and educated at first in Prague), "Some Types of Philosophical Thinking" in A. C. Mace, ed., *British Philosophy at Midcentury* (London, Allen, 1957), p. 116 ff. and *Conceptual Thinking* (Cambridge University Press, 1955), p. 289 ff.

[1]

someone's warming pan," and that Martin Heidegger's "graft
upon his master's former stock is not unlikely before long to be
[1]   adorning Anglo-Saxon gardens.[1]

An even more recent attempt "to explode phenomenology" by
one of the best advocates of linguistic analysis in ethics, P. H.
Nowell-Smith, expresses at least a more sympathetic interest
in possible parallels between the two movements.[2] So do more
recent attempts to examine the relationships between phenomenology and linguistic analysis.[3]

But what may give even more pause is the fact that time was
when phenomenology found a much more sympathetic hearing
among British philosophers. Without attempting to tell the full
story, I shall mention at least some of its highlights.

Apparently the first major British philosopher to give serious
and sustained attention to phenomenology was Bernard Bosanquet. Not only did he devote an eleven-page close-printed
review to the first volume of Husserl's Jahrbuch,[4] but in his
last two works, *Implication and Linear Inference* (1920) and
The Meeting of the Extremes in Contemporary Philosophy (1921),
he tried to assimilate some of Husserl's ideas for the support of
his own generally idealistic and "speculative" position. Even
his correspondence with his friend R. A. F. Hoernlé shows
traces of his deep involvement,[5] which was shared by the latter.[6]
There is also definite evidence of a correspondence between
Husserl and Bosanquet after the first World War in a letter
from Bertrand Russell to Husserl in the Louvain Archives
(see p. 93 n.). – But not only idealists like Bosanquet and Hoernlé,
even an anti-idealist like G. Dawes Hicks, though as a
"critical realist" still more interested in Meinong, gave to
Husserl's first *yearbook* a very sympathetic long review in
1913.[7] In fact, he was the one and only British philosopher to

[1] *Philosophy XXI* (1946), p. 268.
[2] *Philosophy XXXII* (1957), 170 ff.
[3] Thus the papers read at the symposium on "Phenomenology and Linguistic
Analysis" at St. Andrews in July 1959 (*The Aristotelian Society*, Supplementary
Volume XXXIII, 93–124) by Charles Taylor and A. J. Ayer discuss phenomenology
appreciatively, though critically, and bring out the contacts with J. L. Austin's
[2]   "linguistic phenomenology."
[4] *Mind* XXIII (1914), 587–597.
[5] *B. Bosanquet and His Friends*, Letters edited by J. H. Muirhead (London, 1935).
[6] See, e.g., "A Plea for a Phenomenology of Meaning" in *Proceedings of the
Aristotelian Society* XXI (1921), 71–89.
[7] *Hibbert Journal* XII (1913), 198–202.

appear on the advisory board of the newly founded International Phenomenological Society until his death in 1941. Shortly before Bosanquet's death in November 1923, Husserl, apparently as the first and only German philosopher since the war to be so honored, was invited to deliver four lectures at the University of London. They were given under the title "Phenomenological Method and Phenomenological Philosophy" under the chairmanships of G. Dawes Hicks, James Ward, H. Wildon Carr, and G. E. Moore. These lectures presented phenomenology chiefly as the science of transcendental subjectivity in the Cartesian and Platonic spirit. The article on "Phenomenology" in the *Encyclopaedia Britannica* of 1928, freely translated by C. V. Salmon, the only British student in Freiburg during the early twenties, further underlined the idealistic implications of Husserl's transcendentalism, as did his outspoken Preface to the translation of his *Ideen* by W. R. Boyce Gibson, which appeared in Muirhead's Library of Philosophy in 1931.

Yet there was interest in phenomenology even on the part of non-idealists. Thus a symposium of the Aristotelian Society in 1932, conducted by Gilbert Ryle, H. A. Hodges, and H. B. Acton, showed at least considerable curiosity and a serious attempt to understand. Apart from Husserl, only Nicolai Hartmann attracted enough attention to have his *Ethics* translated (see p. 360). Scheler, perhaps understandably in view of his anti-British bias, did not find a translator of his *Nature of Sympathy* until 1953. Until recently only a few of Heidegger's essays were translated, and these had little if any connection with his phenomenology. Franz Brentano and Alexius Meinong had a much greater impact, Brentano chiefly because of G. E. Moore's plea for his ethics, which was translated, and because of G. F. Stout's strong interest in his psychology.

It would not be difficult to account for the small initial response and the subsequent decline in the British interest in phenomenology on the basis of definite mistakes in the way it was first presented. It was particularly unfortunate that little attempt was made to show the connections between Husserl's new enterprise and British empiricism, from which it had derived so much inspiration, and that the parallels with neo-realists like G. E. Moore, Bertrand Russell, and C. D. Broad were not discovered in time. However, it is not wholly a matter of tactical errors on the phenomenological side. Much more significant was the "revolution" which overtook British philosophy in the thirties under the banner of philosophical analysis, first in Cambridge and then, perhaps even more sweepingly, in Oxford, a revolution whose central figure was another Austrian, Ludwig Wittgenstein. The very fact that Wittgenstein himself, in his preoccupation with linguistic analysis, seems to have ignored phenomenology was probably enough to divert any potential attention from phenomenology to his much more dynamic, direct, and unencumbered style of philosophizing. The future of phenomenology in Britain may well depend on how far the unconscious rapprochement between Wittgenstein's later philosophy (see Chapter XIV, p. 670) and a genuine descriptive phenomenology will be discovered in time.

Brief mention should be made of the somewhat different situation in the British Dominions. In Canada phenomenology has achieved some status not only among philosophers, both Catholic and non-Catholic, exemplified by John A. Irving, but particularly among certain psychologists. The University of Toronto and McGill University are the centers of this interest.

But even more important is Australia, the main sphere of action for the British-born W. R. Boyce Gibson (1869–1935) at the University of Melbourne, who after a visit to Freiburg in 1928 not only published his important translation of Husserl's *Ideen*, but also gave considerable attention to Scheler and Nicolai Hartmann in the *Australasian Journal of Philosophy*. To this Australian source may be traced the phenomenological element in the thought of A. C. Garnett, now at the University of Wisconsin.

South Africa is noteworthy chiefly in connection with Scheler's influence on H. G. Stoker at the University of Potchefstrand in the Transvaal.

11. United States: Spurts and New Outlets

Phenomenology is hardly one of the leading philosophical movements in the United States, any more than it is in Britain. Judging from some recent surveys of philosophical trends it even seems to have lost ground after 1950. In contrast to other philosophical movements recently imported from continental Europe, it has not secured a major place in the leading universities of the country. Its most outspoken representatives are [1] to be found in Buffalo, at the New School of Social Research (formerly the University in Exile) and at some of the private Liberal Arts colleges without graduate schools. This seems the more surprising since in many ways conditions for a full hearing were by no means unfavorable. The philosophical climate in the United States in the first half century was probably more hospitable and open to foreign ideas than that of any other country in the world, although it may be said that the influence of British philosophy, including its idiosyncrasies, dominated the scene increasingly. There were remarkable affinities, anticipations, and parallels to phenomenological ideas around the turn of the century, which were perhaps even more pronounced in the psychology of William James than in C. S. Peirce's phaneroscopy, which went temporarily by the name of "phenomenology" but remained largely unknown until the middle thirties.[1] Yet the first response to Husserl's yearbook, a review by Albert Chandler, took a little longer in coming than in England and was distinctly unfavorable.[2] An article by Henry Lanz, himself a Russian in exile, in the *Monist* of 1924 ("The New Phenomenology") was more sympathetic but still reserved.   [2]

To be sure, there had also been a number of native American students with Husserl, both in Göttingen[3] and in Freiburg.[4] The one who has the historic merit of having put phenomenology on the philosophical map of the States was unquestionably Marvin Farber (1901–   ). His Buffalo disser-   [3] tation of 1928 on "Phenomenology as a Method and as a Philosophical Discipline," remained at first an isolated attempt. But when after 1933 a number of German and Austrian phenomenologists appeared as refugees on American soil (among them Moritz Geiger, who until his death in 1937 taught at Vassar

[1] See my article on "Husserl's and Peirce's Phenomenologies" in *PPR* XVII (1956), 164, note 1.

[2] "Professor Husserl's Program of Philosophic Reform" in *Philosophical Review* XXVI (1917), 634–48.

[3] W. E. Hocking (1902), Walter Pitkin (1904 f.), and the Canadian Winthrop Bell (1911–1914; Göttingen Ph. D. 1914).

[4] Marvin Farber (1923–24). Dorion Cairns (1924–26 and 1931–32), Charles Hartshorne (1924–1925).

College), Farber took the initiative in 1939 in organizing an International Phenomenological Society, which was international at least in the original intent, but has for all practical purposes remained restricted to the United States. Since 1940 its main function has been the publication of a philosophical quarterly, *Philosophy and Phenomenological Research* under the auspices of the University of Buffalo. Its title resumes in part that of Husserl's *Jahrbuch für Philosophie und phänomenologische Forschung*, which had ceased to appear after 1930. But as a quarterly journal it differs considerably in character, not only by the inclusion of much more non-phenomenological material but also by the absence of extensive studies that might later have appeared as independent books. Soon the circle of collaborators and the scope of its interests expanded far beyond phenomenology. Only very few of its contributions now make any explicit claim to embody the phenomenological approach. The Phenomenological Society also held a number of smaller meetings until 1947, but has been inactive since then. A symposium on phenomenology arranged by the Eastern Division of the American Philosophical Association in 1940 probably set the high watermark of this enterprise. But the attempt to formulate a common platform for the new society on this occasion came to nothing. In 1940 Farber also edited a volume of *Philosophical Essays in Memory of Edmund Husserl*, which preceded the new journal and brought together a number of short expository, critical, and independent studies by phenomenologists and sympathizers. In his numerous editorial enterprises since then, phenomenology has had only a subordinate role.

Farber himself followed up his organizational work with a monograph on Husserl's early philosophy under the title of *The Foundation of Phenomenology*, consisting largely of a condensed paraphrase of Husserl's writings up to the beginning of his phenomenology proper, but also raising some rather basic objections to Husserl's fully developed position. Farber has been anything but a mere reporter. Even in his expository work he has expressed increasing dissents from the master Husserl and still more vehement ones from such members of the Movement as Scheler. Thus, he suspects both Husserl and Scheler of being basically opposed to science, which he considers the foundation of all philosophy. He also considers it essential to free phenomenology from all idealist entanglements, and has made it plain that he, along with other "naturalists," sees the future of philosophy in a "new materialism." [1] To him, Phenomenology is simply a reflective method, which as "pure reflection" is merely "a stage in the complete process of reflection ... sufficient for one dimension of problems – the clarification of basic concepts in terms of direct experience – and thus an important auxiliary method. But it should not be used exclusively, beyond its proper range of application." [2] Its proper function is to serve as an aid to the "scientific method." In his systematic studies, e.g., "Types of Unity and the Problem of Monism" (*PPR* IV (1944), 37 ff.), "On Unity and Diversity" (*PPR* VI (1946), 547 ff.), and "Modes of Reflection" (*PPR* VIII (1948), 588 ff.) Farber makes no explicit claim to exemplify the phenomenological method.   [1]

A cursory survey of the inner circle of the native American phenomenologists ought to mention at least the following names, if only by way of example:

Dorion Cairns (1901–   ), now teaching at the New School of Social Research, one of the most competent and faithful interpreters especially of the later philosophy of Husserl, with whom he was in close contact in Freiburg for several years; Husserl put particularly high trust in him. His introductory essays on phenomenology are perhaps the most concise accounts of phenomenology in English thus far.[3] Some of his translations of Husserl's works should be available soon.   [2]

Among the European phenomenologists resettled in the States those who have been able to prepare the most extensive original work are Aron Gurwitsch and Alfred Schuetz. Fritz Kaufmann and Felix Kaufmann – no relations – should be mentioned chiefly for having attracted wider attention to the Phenomenological Movement.

---

[1] *Philosophy for the Future: The Quest of Modern Materialism.* Edited by R. W. Sellars, V. J. McGill, Marvin Farber (New York, Macmillan, 1949).

[2] "Modes of Reflection" in *PPR* VIII (1948), 600.

[3] The following can be particularly recommended:

1. "An Approach to Phenomenology" in Farber, M., ed., *Philos. Essays.*, pp. 1–18.
2. Article "Phenonenology" in Runes, D., ed., *Dictionary of Philosophy* (New York, Philosophical Library 1942); about other contributions to this dictionary, see the preface to the Index of Subjects.
3. "Phenomenology," in Ferm, Virgilius, ed., *A History of Philosophical Systems* (New York, Philosophical Library, 1950), Ch. 28.

Aron Gurwitsch, Russian – born (1901), but educated in Germany, is engaged chiefly in developing the phenomenological foundations of gestalt psychology and the organismic biology of Kurt Goldstein. While he did not study directly under Husserl, he was in regular touch with him after about 1920. In the thirties he also became an important link in the transmission of German phenomenology to Paris. Since coming to the United States in 1939, his academic positions were at Johns Hopkins, at Brandeis University, and at the New School in New York. His recent [1] *Theory of the Field of Consciousness*, published only in French,[1] constitutes the most substantial original work produced by a European phenomenologist in the United States.

Next to Cairns, Gurwitsch is probably the American phenomenologist closest to Husserl's later philosophy. Not only does he insist on the essential connection between phenomenology and Husserl's phenomenological reduction, he also subscribes to the idea of a constitutive phenomenology and to Husserl's transcendental idealism, although not in its most extreme form; for he does not accept Fink's Husserl–approved interpretation of the constitution in the sense of a productive or creative construction. Even more outspokenly does he reject Husserl's last distinction between several types of ego. In fact, with Sartre and Husserl before the *Ideen*, he objects to the entire conception of the ego and the ensuing "egology" of consciousness. This interpretation of Husserl's phenomenology takes him much closer to the Neo-Kantianism of Cassirer, for whom Husserl himself had shown increasing sympathy.

Gurwitsch's recent book on the field of consciousness incorporates and develops phenomenologically some of the insights of William James, Jean Piaget, the analytical psychologists such as James Ward and G. F. Stout, the gestaltists, and Kurt Goldstein's organismic biology. But the organization in a phenomenological framework is new and illuminating. The field of consciousness is shown to be divided into three zones: the thematic object, the thematic field (controlled by the gestalt principle of relevance), and the marginal field (where such relevance is absent).[2]

---

[1] *Théorie du champ de la conscience* (Paris, Desclée de Brouwer, 1957).

[2] Articles in English which include some of the ideas incorporated in Gurwitsch's book are:

1. "On the Intentionality of Consciousness" (Farber, M., ed., *op. cit.*, pp. 65–83.

Alfred Schuetz (1899–1959), who taught at the New School of Social Research, Vienna-born and first trained as a sociologist interested chiefly in the thought of Max Weber, was also not a student of Husserl in the academic sense. Yet, partly as a result of later contacts, he became not only one of his most perceptive students, but also one of his most acute critics, especially as far as Husserl's social philosophy of intersubjectivity was concerned. The focus of his own phenomenological work was a "mundane" or non-transcendental phenomenology of the social world. Schuetz's American articles developed several ideas from a German work on the subjective meanings which constitute the social world.[1] Starting from Max Weber's basic concepts, Schuetz investigates in this book by means of Bergsonian and especially Husserlian categories the temporal constitution of the meaning of actions in individual experiences, utilizes the insights so obtained for a searching theory of our understanding of other persons, and makes some highly original contributions to a structural analysis of the social world, in which he distinguishes the social ambiance (*Umwelt*) consisting of our close associates, the social environment (*Mitwelt*) consisting of our more distant and indefinitely known contemporaries, the social background world (*Vorwelt*) of our ancestors (*Vorfahren*), and the world of tomorrow (*Folgewelt*) of our successors (*Nachfahren*). Later, Schuetz utilized some ideas of William James, of whom he had made a close study, in exploring the "multiple realities" or "worlds" in which we find ourselves involved, from the world of our daily life to the world of dreams, showing concretely how, for instance, the scientific interpretation of human action has its base in the world of common sense, the *Lebenswelt* of Husserl. Other phenomenological analyses concerned the act of choosing,

2. "A Non-egological Conception of Consciousness." *PPR* I (1941), 325–38.
3. "William James' Theory of the 'Transitive Parts' of the Stream of Consciousness." *PPR* III (1943), 449–77.
4. "On the Object of Thought" *PPR* VII (1947), 347–56.
5. "Gelb-Goldstein's Concept of the 'Concrete' and 'Categorial' Attitude and the Phenomenology of Ideation" *PPR* X (1949), 172–96.
6. "Phenomenological and Psychological Approach to Consciousness" *PPR* XV (1955), 303–19.

[1]

[1] *Der sinnhafte Aufbau der sozialen Welt* (Wien, Springer, 1932); for an extended English abstract of this application of phenomenology to the social sciences, whose German version will soon be available again, see Stonier, Alfred and Bode, Karl, "A New Approach to the Methodology of the Social Sciences," *Economica* IV (1937), 406–24.

so often appealed to, but so little analyzed by the existentialists. Schuetz also explored concrete experiences like "making music together," as models of social communication. On the theoretical level he gave particular attention to the phenomenological theory of intersubjectivity, based on a critical examination of the theories of the *alter ego* in Husserl, Scheler, and Sartre. In this context he has also made use of some of the new insights of G. H. Mead. All these studies converged on a systematic phenomenology of the social world and on a book dealing with the structure of the *Lebenswelt*, for which he was poised at the time of his untimely death.[1]

Felix Kaufmann (1895–1949), another native Austrian with an unusual range of interests and achievements, including mathematics, physics, the social studies, and jurisprudence, wrote several books on law in which he tried to give Hans Kelsen's theory of pure law a less Kantian and more phenomenological turn. His greatest concern was the development of scientific method in its relation to a deductive logic of procedural rules. Hence he was particularly interested in Husserl's early logical work. Being close to, but never a member of, Moritz Schlick's and Rudolf Carnap's Vienna Circle, but feeling even closer to Husserl, he made a sustained effort to strengthen the relations, sometimes rather strained and hostile, between phenomenology and logical empiricism,[2] as well as to establish contacts with

---

[1] American articles and studies related to phenomenology:
  1. "Phenomenology and the Social Sciences" in Farber, M., ed., *Philosophical Essays in Memory of Edmund Husserl*. Cambridge, Harvard University Press, 1940, p. 164–86.
  2. "William James' Concept of the Stream of Thought Phenomenologically Interpreted" *PPR* I (1941), 442–52.
  3. "Scheler's Theory of Intersubjectivity," *PPR* II (1942), 323–47.
  4. "On Multiple Realities," *PPR* V (1945), 533–76.
  5. "Some Leading Concepts of Phenomenology," *Social Research XII* (1945), 77–97.
  6. "Sartre's Theory of the Alter Ego," *PPR* IX, (1948), 181–99.
  7. "Language, Language Disturbances, and the Texture of Consciousness," *Social Research* XVII (1950), 365–94.
  8. "Making Music Together," *Social Research* XVIII, (1951), 76–97.
  9. "Choosing Among Projects of Action," *PPR* XII, (1951), 161–184.
  10. "Common Sense and Scientific Enterprise," *PPR* XIV (1953), 1–38.
  11. "Tiresias, or Our Knowledge of Future Events," *Social Research* XXVI (1959), 71–89.

A comprehensive edition of Schuetz's philosophical and sociological essays is in preparation.

[2] "Phenomenology and Logical Empiricism" in Farber, M., ed., *op. cit.*, pp. 124–42.

[1]

operationalism and with John Dewey's logic of inquiry. Yet he was never willing to sacrifice Husserl's best insights to the cause of positivistic purity. His main American publication, a methodological discussion of the social sciences, consisting of an entirely rewritten version of an earlier German work,[1] is actually the only full-scale book brought out in English by a member of the older European group; yet it is not particularly phenomenological in character. Kaufmann's main phenomenological publication since coming to the States was a paper originally read at the first meeting of the Phenomenological Society, in which he outlined a program for distinguishing several strata of experience, beginning with those of sensation and leading to the "intentional strata" in Husserl's sense.[2]

Fritz Kaufmann (1891–1958), one of Husserl's later Göttingen and early Freiburg students, taught between 1938 and 1958 at Northwestern University, the University of Buffalo and Ohio State University. His particular interests were in philosophy of history, esthetics, and philosophy of religion. Though a loyal defender of Husserl he has followed a course of his own, adopting features not only from Husserl's earlier and later thought, but also from Dilthey and Heidegger. The spirit of phenomenology shows in his writings chiefly in the sensitivity of his approach to a vast variety of topics including literary criticism. He also made interesting suggestions for a special type of eidetic reduction from fact to essence as an aid in the discovery of such individual historical essences as Romanticism.[3] Besides, Kaufmann had related Husserl's reductive phenomenology to the approach of the artist and had started a metaphysical interpretation of this phenomenology to the effect that Husserl's absolute consciousness can serve as an approach to the Absolute,[4] and anthropologically as a way to an interpretation of man as an imaginative being.[5] These studies, in combination with a number of earlier

---

[1] *Methodology of the Social Sciences* (New York, Oxford University Press, 1944).
[2] "Strata of Experience," *PPR* I (1941), 313–24.
[3] "The Phenomenological Approach to History," *PPR* II (1941), 159–72 – "Phenomenology of the Historical Present," *Proc. of the Xth International Philosophical Congress* at Amsterdam, 1949, pp. 967–70. For a discussion of more ontological problems in the philosophy of history, see also "Truth and Reality in History" in *Perspectives in Philosophy* (Ohio State University, 1953), pp. 43–54.
[4] "Art and Phenomenology" in Farber, M., ed., *op. cit.*, pp. 187–202.
[5] "On Imagination," *PPR* VII (1947), 369–75.

German publications, were to lay the ground for a book on the phenomenology of art, which, at the time of his premature death, was scheduled to appear in German.[1]

Fortunately, American phenomenology has not remained limited to an esoteric group. Even in native American philosophy signs of a promising osmosis of some of its more universal motifs have appeared. A typical example of this occurs in C. I. Lewis's Carus lectures. For instance, on one occasion he refers to the task of tracing the "phenomenological constitution of reality" as "the logical upbuilding of meanings" starting from the merely passively given of our sensuous data,[2] a task, to be sure, which he himself did not want to undertake at the time; clearly, it would have paralleled Husserl's constitutive phenomenology. Also, the later discussions in the book which describe "the nature and the conditions of the esthetic in experience" prior to esthetic judgment are called in retrospect "phenomenology of the aesthetic" (*op. cit.*, p. 457); actually, this phenomenology exemplifies Husserl's pre-predicative approach to experience, which merely studies its phenomenal content and does not prejudge its inherence in an "object."

However, the mere mapping out of such a phenomenology and the incidental development of one of its chapters would not justify the claim that C. I. Lewis identifies himself consciously with Phenomenology as a philosophical movement. In fact, in a personal letter to me for which I am in his debt he summed up his relation to "the phenomenologists" in the sentence: "I am aware of but not acquainted with them." He added that during the early twenties he had read some of Husserl's *Ideen* and later on had "had a go" at Heidegger. But as far as influences on Lewis are concerned, the much more likely source is C. S. Peirce, of whose manuscripts Lewis was the first custodian. Thus, the concept of the given as a "quale" is definitely reminiscent of Peirce's description of "Firstness." Lewis himself puts it in the following way:

> When on occasion I have used the word "phenomenology," it has been uncritically, as a report of findings in experience and generalization

[1]

---

[1] For a fuller bibliography of his writings, see Landgrebe, Ludwig, "*In memoriam*," *Zeitschrift für philosophische Forschung* XII (1958), 613–15.

[2] *An Analysis of Knowledge and Valuation* (La Salle, Open Court, 1946), p. 21.

about them as such. One wants a word for the directly observable which frees it from the connotation of psychologizing – either old-fashioned or behavioristic. As such, phenomenology is any philosopher's first business; as physiological psychology is not.

It would not be hard to point out other examples in the elder statesmen among living American philosophers. An outstanding instance is William Ernest Hocking, actually for part of a semester one of Husserl's earliest students. However his metaphysics, while never leaving the basis of a phenomenologically broadened experience, has gone far beyond mere phenomenology.[1]

There are, besides, also promising beginnings among younger indigenous American philosophers. There is in fact a whole group within the "Association of Realistic Philosophy," founded by John Wild (1902–   ) of Harvard, which has expressed a strong interest in phenomenology. To be sure, its platform and most of the "Essays in Realistic Philosophy" [2] do not refer explicitly to phenomenology. But the two leading contributions carry the word in their very titles. The author of the first, "Realism and Phenomenology," Harmon M. Chapman of New York University, who had studied in Freiburg in 1931 after Husserl's retirement, credits Husserl for having taught him how to look and see; but he also states that he has broken away from his lead and turned to that of Aristotle and St. Thomas. John Wild, who is represented by an essay on "Phenomenology and Metaphysics," had been in Freiburg likewise in 1931, studying under Heidegger, for whom he entertains considerable admiration. Yet in his earlier publications and particularly in the elaboration of his peculiar Platonic and Aristotelian Realism he does not refer to phenomenology explicitly. Also, his contribution to the Memorial Essays for Husserl is comparatively non-committal as to the extent of his stake in phenomenology and sharply critical of Husserl's version of it as another lapse into psychologism.[3] Nor does Wild commit himself in his earlier contributions to *Philosophy and Phenomenological Research*. However, in his recent publications he makes a strong bid for enlisting phe-

[1] See, e.g., "Outline-Sketch of a System of Metaphysics," in Farber, M., ed., *op. cit.*, pp. 251–56.

[2] Wild, John, ed., *The Return to Reason* (Chicago, Regnery, 1953).

[3] "Husserl's Critique of Psychologism" in Farber, M., ed., *op. cit.*, pp. 19 ff. – A more positive estimate of Husserl's significance for a philosophical anthropology was given by Wild at Royaumont (1957).

nomenology as epistemological support for a realistic meta-physics.[1] This non-Husserlian phenomenology, defined as a descriptive discipline, is to assimilate what Wild considers to be the phenomenological elements of existentialism. The outcome is a "direct realism" designed to buttress a renewed Aristotelian metaphysics and an ethics of natural law. This direct realism is based on the affirmation of the "pervasive and indubitable" phenomenon of existence, an affirmation that clearly goes far beyond the traditional phenomenological position, which recommends at least an initial neutralism with regard to reality, rather than an outright commitment to realism. Also Wild's phenomenology is concerned primarily with the contents of the things given, not with their ways of appearing. His discussion of the various senses of givenness and some specific studies in the phenomenology of signs deserve special mention.[2] More lately he has taken a strong interest in Husserl's conception of the *Lebenswelt* as a key concept for a new philosophy and as a possible meeting ground with the analytic philosophers.[3]

[1]

Very different in spirit is the phenomenological ethics of Maurice Mandelbaum (1908–   ) of Johns Hopkins University.[4] While Mandelbaum declines any specific commitment to the Phenomenological Movement as such, he acknowledges debts to Scheler and Dietrich von Hildebrand. What makes his approach even more congenial to that of the more orthodox phenomenologists is his confinement to the task of examining man's moral consciousness without any attempt to derive valid standards from such a "generic" or neutral approach; for he suspends the question of validity or invalidity. Another significant feature of Mandelbaum's phenomenology is the connection he establishes with the phenomenological elements of gestalt theory for which Swarthmore College provided a particularly hospitable climate after Wolfgang Köhler's arrival in 1933. Furthermore, Mandelbaum's phenomenology establishes a long

---

[1] *The Challenge of Existentialism.* Mahlon Powell Lectures (University of Indiana Press, 1955).

[2] "The Concept of the Given in Contemporary Philosophy," *PPR* I (1940), 70–82. "An Introduction to the Phenomenology of Signs," *PPR* VIII (1947), 217 ff.

[3] "Is there a World of Ordinary Language?" *Philosophical Review* LXVII (1958), 460–76.

[4] *The Phenomenology of Moral Experience* (Glencoe, Free Press, 1955). – For a discussion of its phenomenological aspects see *Social Research* XXIII (1956), 117 ff.

overdue contact between phenomenology and the British intuitionist moral philosophy of W. D. Ross.

Closer to the European approach is William Earle, (1919–   ) of Northwestern University, who had studied in France under Gaston Berger.[1] Among the other young Americans who have displayed a vigorous interest in phenomenology I shall mention only Maurice Natanson (1924–   ) of the University of North Carolina, who in his critical studies of the philosophies of Jean-Paul Sartre and G. H. Mead has stressed phenomenological considerations, and who is also working in the field of phenomenological esthetics.   [1]

Nevertheless, the importance of such beginnings of an indigenous American phenomenology must not be overestimated. Compared with other currents in contemporary American philosophy, they are relatively tenuous. Actually in the United States phenomenology has had a much bigger impact on extra-philosophical studies such as psychology and theology, though to be sure in forms which differ considerably from those stressed by the philosophical phenomenologists. Of particular importance in this connection is the fact that two leading European scholars, who in their home countries maintained a much more reserved and critical attitude toward phenomenology, now have come forward with a strong plea for the phenomenological approach: Wolfgang Köhler and Paul Tillich.

Gestalt psychology in its European days had at first few if any direct contacts with phenomenological philosophy. Its principal originators expressed hardly any interest in Husserl's work, although there had been some remarkable parallels (e.g., the gestalt factor and Husserl's *"figurales Einheitsmoment"*). It was only after its transplantation to the United States, beginning with Kurt Koffka's appointment at Smith College in 1928, that in widening and deepening their approach the gestaltists began to discuss phenomenology explicitly. One memorable climax of this phenomenological restatement of gestalt theory was the

---

[1] See especially his thesis on *Objectivity* (New York, Noonday Press, 1955), a study of knowledge based on an analysis of consciousness; also his article "Memory" in *Review of Metaphysics* X (1956), 28–34. – But his allegiance to phenomenology is limited by his even stronger commitment to existentialism; see his paper on "Phenomenology and Existentialism" read at the annual meeting of the American Philosophical Division in Madison, April 1959, *Journal of Philosophy* LVII (1960), 75–84.

delivery of Wolfgang Köhler's William James lectures at Harvard in 1934–35.[1] Here Köhler appealed to a realistic phenomenology on non-Husserlian lines as a foundation for both philosophy and non-behaviorist psychology, while making it clear that he did not consider phenomenology sufficient for their development. The central axiological phenomenon investigated in these lectures as underlying our value experience was requiredness, a phenomenon also stressed by Max Wertheimer.[2] – Other members of the gestalt group like the late Karl Duncker went even further in an attempt to strengthen the connections between psychology and phenomenology.[3]

It would require at least a chapter by itself to trace the spread of phenomenological ideas in American psychology. In the present context it will suffice to point out some more or less independent nuclei of an indigenous American phenomenological psychology. There is a group around Robert B. MacLeod, formerly of MacGill and Swarthmore, now at Cornell University, whose interest in phenomenology goes back to David Katz and thus indirectly to the Göttingen Circle of Husserl's earlier period. However, American psychologists usually reject the Husserlian version of phenomenology, as they interpret it.[4]

A remarkably independent new type of phenomenological psychology has been launched by Donald Snygg (Oswego) and Arthur W. Combs (University of Florida).[5] Their attempt to understand human behavior by starting from the phenomenal field of the subject is of course not without antecedents. According to information for which I am indebted to him, Snygg, who had started as a behaviorist, came to develop his phenomenology after having been in contact with Kurt Lewin and Wolfgang Köhler. Combs came from the client-centered or non-directive psychology and psychotherapy of Carl Rogers. Rogers' own ·

---

[1] *The Place of Value in a World of Facts* (New York, Liveright, 1938).

[2] "Some Problems in the Theory of Ethics" in *Social Research* II (1935), 353–67.

[3] See, e.g., "Phenomenology and Epistemology of Consciousness of Objects," *PPR* VII (1947), 505–42.

[4] "The Phenomenological Approach to Social Psychology" in *Psychological Review*, LIV (1947), 193–210. "The Place of Phenomenological Analysis in Social Psychological Theory" in Rohrer, J. H. and Sherif, M., ed., *Social Psychology at the Crossroads*. (New York, Harper, 1951) pp. 215–41.

[5] *Individual Behavior*. A New Frame of Reference for Psychology (New York, Harper, 1949).

approach also shows phenomenological ingredients without any commitment to its philosophical phenomenology.

Phenomenological elements can also be traced in other developments of psychology. Gordon Allport has expressed considerable sympathy with the phenomenological approach in several of his works. Floyd H. Allport in his studies on perception shows a remarkable shift from a merely behaviorist to a deliberately, though modified, phenomenological approach,[1] and so do a number of other recent students of perception. Also, without using the label, much of the Group Dynamics movement, based as it is on Kurt Lewin's topological psychology, shows elements of the phenomenological outlook in its conception of the field; it can be traced ultimately to Lewin's German beginnings, in which, to be sure, Carl Stumpf's phenomenology figures much more prominently than Husserl's. Finally "psychiatric phenomenology," capably introduced by Henri F. Ellenberger on the basis of European sources, now seems to be spreading, in combination with "existential analysis," in psychiatry.[2]   [1]

In American theology, phenomenology has received important support from Paul Tillich's recent recourse to the phenomenological method. This step is all the more remarkable since during his German career Tillich rejected the phenomenological method along with that of pragmatism in favor of a "critical-dialectical" approach.[3] His major objection at the time was its unhistorical and anti-existential character. Indications are that it was largely the advent of Heidegger's version of phenomenology which changed Tillich's attitude. In fact he seems to consider phenomenology the primary method of existential philosophy. More important, in his *Systematic Theology* he now asserts the need of a phenomenological method based on Husserl's conception in the *Ideen* as essential to theology:

Theology must apply the phenomenological approach to all its basic concepts, forcing its critics first of all to see what the criticized concepts mean and also forcing itself to make careful descriptions of its concepts and to use them with logical consistency, thus avoiding the danger of trying to fill in logical gaps with devotional material. (I, 106)

---

[1] *Theories of Perception and the Concept of Structure* (New York, Wiley, 1955).
[2] See May, Rollo, ed., *op. cit.*, pp. 92–126.
[3] "Religionsphilosophie" in Dessoir Max, ed., *Philosophie in ihren Einzelgebieten* (Berlin, 1925), pp. 780–83.

The method itself is characterized as an attempt "to describe 'meanings,' disregarding for the time being the question of the reality to which they refer." To be sure, Tillich finds a "pure phenomenology" unable to decide the question of what determines typical examples in "the realm of spiritual realities like religion" and points to Scheler as a warning example. But to him the cure seems to be merely the introduction of a "critical element" into Husserl's "pure phenomenology," resulting in a "critical phenomenology," which is to "unite an intuitive-descriptive element with an existential-critical element." However, as to the nature of this "existential-critical element" we learn merely that it is a matter of a decision which is "critical in form and existential in matter" and actually "dependent on a revelation which has been received and which is considered final," and which is "critical with respect to other revelations." Obviously this use of the word "critical," related as it is to the theology of crisis, has little to do with what is usually called critical in philosophy. It also threatens a phenomenology of revelation with a petitio principii. It remains to be seen how far the remarkable impact of Tillich's theology will also give to its phenomenological methodology further outlets and development.[1]

B. THE OUTLOOK

What, we may ask, is the outlook for the future of the Phenomenological Movement as a whole? Predictions are never better than the evidence that supports them. Any attempt to extrapolate from the present to the future has to be based on the tendencies of the recent past, their vigor and their spread. Some of this evidence is contained in the preceding survey according to geographical areas. But there are some additional facts which are relevant to a more comprehensive prognosis.

Among these is the record of three international colloquia on phenomenology held in 1950, 1956, and 1957, in Brussels, Krefeld (Germany), and Royaumont near Paris respective-

---

[1] For another application of phenomenology to the study of religion, see the program of the late Joachim Wach, once a student of Husserl and Scheler, in his *Types of Religious Experience* (University of Chicago Press, 1951). His phenomenology of religion was meant to go considerably beyond Van der Leeuw's mere exposition of the manifestations of religion (see p. 10 f.).

ly, of which the first two were arranged under the auspices of the Husserl Archives at Louvain. The one at Brussels was devoted to a consideration of present problems of phenomenology. It included on its panel some, though not all, of the major figures of French and German phenomenology such as Merleau-Ponty, Ricoeur, and Fink. While Husserl's phenomenology was clearly the common point of departure for all participants, the attitude toward his work was anything but uncritical. Actually the French phenomenologists were even more sympathetic to Husserl than the Germans, notably Fink. The general trend was in the direction of a definitely metaphysical and even speculative development and use of phenomenology. Besides, some concrete phenomenological contributions in the field of phenomenology of language (Merleau-Ponty) and the will (Ricoeur) were presented.

The Krefeld Colloquy held six years later, with a different but similar panel, revealed an equally critical attitude, particularly toward Husserl's transcendental idealism. Apparently the phenomenological reduction found its main defender in the able French interpreter of Hegel's phenomenology, Jean Hyppolite. Otherwise the emphasis in the viewing of Husserl's phenomenology seems to be shifting more and more toward his relatively late conception of the *Lebenswelt* as the matrix of all philosophical and scientific thought.[1]

Perhaps even more significant was the symposium on "The Work and Thought of Edmund Husserl" held half a year later in the setting of the French colloquies at the abbey of Royaumont near Paris. Here some of the leading experts probed deeply into such fundamental concepts of Husserlian phenomenology as constitution (Ingarden) and intersubjectivity (Schuetz). The apparent result is that, unless some basic clarifications can be achieved soon, transcendental phenomenology with its doctrines of reduction and constitution has a dubious future. But in the light of the new materials which the Louvain editions have made and will continue to make accessible the discussion of these problems will have to go on for some time to come.

In any case, there is ample reason for expecting that phenomenology as a whole will survive the difficulties encountered by transcendental phenomenology, perhaps by elimination of

[1] See the report by Alexandre Lowit in *Études philosophiques* XII (1957), 64 f.

its most controversial concepts and by an increasing return to an unencumbered phenomenology of the *Lebenswelt* and its [1] phenomena. In the next phase of the Phenomenological Movement there will be no room for orthodoxy. The chief basis for such subdued optimism is the fact that behind the present emphasis on criticism stand the productive energies, achievements, and announced projects of some of the best minds of the older and younger phenomenological generation.

It would however be misleading to take such evidence as conclusive. Phenomenological meetings, actually a novelty of the post-Husserlian and international phase of phenomenology, are not more likely to be high points of the philosophical life than are general philosophical meetings. The opposite may be closer to the truth. Husserl, Scheler, Heidegger, and Sartre seem to have made it almost a point never to attend group meetings. Nevertheless, adding to this evidence other known facts, I shall venture the following general estimate:

The Phenomenological Movement as a whole has not yet lost its momentum. It is very much in the center of the philosophical stage in Western Europe, the only part of the world where it has continued to be productive. To a lesser extent this seems to hold true for the Spanish-American world. It would be much more risky to express any such expectations for the Anglo-American world. But it seems not altogether unlikely that phenomenology will obtain a better hearing and an improved chance as a result of the widespread dissatisfaction with the sterility of a merely "analytic" philosophy.

Breaking up this estimate for the main branches of the Phenomenological Movement as of today, one might add:

Transcendental phenomenology is at the moment its most controversial branch. While it will continue to keep and attract considerable attention – and rightly so in view of the unfinished task of studying Husserl's still unknown work – it will require a great deal of critical and reconstructive effort to bring his ideas to life and make them reproductive.

Existential phenomenology, i.e., a phenomenology which is based on the perspective of incarnated man and his projects, seems to be at the moment its most flourishing branch. While much of it appears to be due for severe critical questioning, it has a good chance of surviving, though in a chastened and less spectacular form.

In general, phenomenology is likely to shed increasingly its traditional neutrality toward metaphysics. Specifically, the "brackets" of the phenomenological reduction, put in by Husserl seemingly as a preliminary measure, will have to be removed definitively and openly. It may well be that a conscientious phenomenology cannot answer ultimate questions: for such an assignment its resources may be necessary but they are hardly sufficient. Yet this is no excuse for evading the bracketed questions for good. But this prospect calls for a sober warning: indulgence in metaphysics may add to the prestige of phenomenology among those who, with Hegel, regard a philosophy without metaphysics as a temple without a holy of holies. But it will also make it more vulnerable to those who are equally or more concerned about the scientific rigor which was Husserl's first and pervading concern. There is unfortunately considerable reason to fear that the coming flood of "phenomenological" metaphysics will be anything but critical, and will discredit a method which is in danger of being stretched beyond its natural limits.

There remains the much humbler task of descriptive phenomenology, often called "eidetic," since its major task is the elucidation of the general essence of the phenomena under investigation. For some time this task seemed to have fallen in disrepute, outshone by the more spectacular revelations of existential phenomenology. Of late there is an increasing realization that descriptive phenomenology holds a vast amount of unfinished business. This business comprises not only the phenomena in the sense of the "things themselves," but it includes the modes of their givenness and the acts in which they are given. Recent descriptive work is usually supplemented by existential or metaphysical interpretations. But it seems likely that concrete descriptive analysis will enter even into non-phenomenological philosophies as an essential procedure. This applies even more to fields outside philosophy proper, such as psychology. Here the reaction against behaviorism takes more and more the form of developing a wider phenomenological approach, which tries to give introspection as objective and

critical a refinement as possible. In fact, there seems to be a
considerable future for phenomenological procedures in other
specialized fields of human knowledge, and particularly in all
the sciences of man, the being whose behavior cannot be understood except in terms of his reaction to his phenomenal
world. But much of this return to the descriptive study of
the phenomenal matrix of scientific knowledge may remain
independent of developments in philosophical phenomenology.

> "The people who talk most about research are not those
> who have done any."
>> John Burnet (according to Lucian Price, *The
>> Dialogues of A. N. Whitehead*. Boston, 1954, p. 127.

C. DESIDERATA

Instead of closing this survey with questionable prognoses,
it may make more sense to say something about the lessons
which will have to be learned by those who believe that phenomenology has something to offer to the future, even to the
future of Anglo-American thought. It is in this spirit that I shall
try to formulate some of the agenda which seem to me particularly important at the present juncture. I shall first try to state
some of the needs on the international level, and then enumerate
some of the special problems that phenomenology faces in the
Anglo-American world.

I. General Needs

The first need which confronts a phenomenological movement
that wants to hold its own and to win new friends is to *do* phenomenology and not merely to talk about it (even the present
work is an exhibit of this unfortunate preoccupation). There is a
serious temptation to substitute the blessed name for the thing,
the *Sache*. True, there is reason to explore the historical background of phenomenology, and there is a need to make more of
the original work of the past accessible and more understandable. But the first and final need is still the actual application
of the method to concrete tasks, new and old. Phenomenology
has to show its fruitfulness by widening and deepening the range

of philosophic insights in a setting which at the moment shows more and more the results of the impoverishment that has resulted from the misuse of Occam's razor. But phenomenology can and must also show its ability to tackle some of the time-honored problems which other schools have been analysing, sometimes with rather distressing results. One might safely assert that most of the key concepts used in contemporary ethical and esthetic discussion are still waiting for phenomenological dredging and deepening.

'This may easily sound as if the phenomenologist intends to enter the scene like another one of those philosophical quacks who discount and discard all previous work in the field. Actually most concrete phenomenological studies reveal that some of the best work had been done long before phenomenology arrived, though without the pompous label. There is no reason for fanfare and plenty of reason for humility. Phenomenology can show its mettle only by doing the actual job, not by making fanciful claims, but by offering its services on approval. Too much good will has been lost by bombastic advertising.

Phenomenology, more than other methods, is at the moment on trial, if not under suspicion. In order to prove and to clear itself, it must proceed with the greatest care. For the phenomenological method is anything but foolproof. And plenty of fools have rushed in where neither angels nor conscientious phenomenologists have set foot. More fools will follow – and no railing will protect them or their more gullible listeners. There is no substitute for constant checking and re-checking, not even a professional license. It will not do to simply claim intuitive self-evidence. The fact that phenomenological statements cannot be proved in the same manner as the assertions of a deductive or even an inductive science offers no excuse for giving no substantiation whatsoever. Obviously, phenomenology cannot produce the same type of records as an observational or experimental science, particularly in this photographic and audio-visual age. But the phenomenologist can and must not only test and retest his personal intuiting but also lead others to the same experience. Phenomenology must also consider carefully diverging descriptions of its phenomena, and, even more, diverging interpretations. Phenomenological insights are not simple assertions but assertions whose foundations in the phenomena have been critically double-checked and triple-checked. It is not always easy to give proof of such phenomenological verification, and it would be pedantic and ineffective to reaffirm it in each single case. The best that can be done is to make the fullest possible use of illustrative examples selected in such a way that they can be reenacted by a reasonably sympathetic reader. No doubt the phenomenologist has to make unusual demands on the cooperative effort of his readers; all the more do the latter deserve as much aid as they can possibly receive in duplicating the writer's intuitions. There is danger that unsupported claims by the phenomenologist will be taken as illegitimate attempts at persuasion, which are more apt to discredit phenomenology than to help it. It should give the phenomenologist pause that Husserl himself claimed less and less finality for his own insights.

The problem of making phenomenological insights as reliable and verifiable as possible raises the whole problem of phenomenological communication. Actually the Phenomenological Movement, especially since the dispersal of the original Circles, has been less organized and gregarious than many other philosophical groups. Husserl himself philosophized finally in almost deliberate solipsistic isolation. Only since his death have there been attempts to form phenomenological organizations with meetings and exchanges. Much of the dispersal of the original phenomenology after the first World War may have been due to its surprising absence of personal and group exchange. The danger of merely subjective introspection can best be countered by constant comparing of notes and by challenging one's non-matching "intuitions."

It is another question how such a "socialization" can best be achieved. Organization alone, and even the arrangement of meetings and the printing of symposia, with the mere juxta-position of participants, is hardly the cure. On the other hand, the institution of more intimate colloquia now initiated in Western Europe would seem to be a move in the right direction. Intensive workshops, especially for those new to the practice of phenomenology, would seem to be worth exploring and developing. The whole problem of phenomenological education and training will have to be considered. This includes the need of providing systematic introductions and particularly of source books which would incorporate some of the best phenomenological case studies.[1]

2. Anglo-American Needs

If the preceding considerations apply to the position of phenomenology in the philosophical world in general, they apply in an even higher degree to the situation of phenomenology in the Anglo-American world. But here additional points have to be stressed:

α. The need of more (and more adequate) translations of the pioneer works and, no less important, of case studies in the phenomenological method. As the preceding chapters and sections with their bibliographies have shown, the Anglo-American countries, compared with the French and the Spanish-American world, are handicapped in this regard.

β. No paraphrases, however detailed, will do, if they report only in indirect discourse, as is done for Husserl's *Logische Untersuchungen* in the central chapters of Farber's otherwise helpful book on *The Foundation of Phenomenology*. This does not mean that translations would have to be complete, particularly where the texts deal with outdated problems. Even so there can be no doubt that translations will tax the combined efforts of two or more persons, as is indicated by the fact that W. R. Boyce Gibson's translation of Husserl's *Ideen* is far from adequate although per se a creditable achievement. I would consider the present book a failure if it should reduce, rather than strengthen, the desire for more and better translations of the texts.

The following list contains the titles which the present writer feels to be particularly needed. The most important items are indicated by asterisks. [1]

FRANZ BRENTANO, *Psychologie vom empirischen Standpunkt* (in preparation)
— **Vom Ursprung der sittlichen Erkenntnis* (translated by Cecil Hague in 1902 but now out of print; new translation in preparation).
CARL STUMPF, **Zur Einteilung der Wissenschaften – Erscheinungen und Funktionen*
EDMUND HUSSERL, **Logische Untersuchungen*
— **Cartesianische Meditationen*

---

[1] See also Roman Ingarden, "Über die gegenwärtigen Aufgaben der Phänomenologie." *Il compito della fenomenologia* (Padova, 1957), p. 236.

— *Die Krisis der europäischen Wissenschaften und die transzendentale Phänomenologie (Husserliana VI).
— *Erfahrung und Urteil
ALEXANDER PFÄNDER, *Logik
— Zur Psychologie der Gesinnungen
— Motive und Motivation
ADOLF REINACH, *Was ist Phänomenologie?
— Die apriorischen Grundlagen des bürgerlichen Rechts (earlier sections)
MORITZ GEIGER, *Beiträge zur Phänomenologie des Genusses
— Zugänge zur Aesthetik
MAX SCHELER, *Der Formalismus in der Ethik (earlier sections)
— *Vom Umsturz der Werte (Selections)
— Vom Ewigen im Menschen (Selections)
— Nachlass I (Selections)
— *Die Stellung des Menschen im Kosmos (announced by Beacon Press)
EDITH STEIN, Zum Problem der Einfühlung
HEDWIG CONRAD-MARTIUS, Zur Ontologie und Erscheinungslehre der realen Aussenwelt
DIETRICH VON HILDEBRAND, *Die Idee der sittlichen Handlung
— *Sittlichkeit und ethische Werterkenntnis
ROMAN INGARDEN, *Das litterarische Kunstwerk
JEAN HERING, Bemerkungen über das Wesen, die Wesenheit und die Idee
— Phénoménologie et philosophie religieuse
OSKAR BECKER, Beiträge zur phänomenologischen Begründung der Geometrie und ihrer physikalischen Anwendungen
EUGEN FINK, Vergegenwärtigung und Bild
ALFRED SCHUETZ, Der sinnhafte Aufbau der sozialen Welt
MARTIN HEIDEGGER, *Sein und Zeit (announced by Blackwell's)
— "Brief über den Humanismus"
— *Was heisst Denken?
NICOLAI HARTMANN, *Grundlagen der Metaphysik der Erkenntnis
— Systematische Philosophie
— Zur Grundlegung der Ontologie
JEAN-PAUL SARTRE, "Une idée fondamentale de la phénoménologie de Husserl: l'intentionalité"
— Visages
MAURICE MERLEAU-PONTY, *Structure du comportement
— *Phénoménologie de la perception
— Sens et non-sens
PAUL RICOEUR, *Philosophie de la volonté I
— "Méthodes et tâches d'une phénoménologie de la volonté"
MIKEL DUFRENNE, Phénoménologie de l'expérience esthétique
PIERRE THÉVENAZ, "Qu'est-ce que la phénoménologie?"

Obviously, at the present moment such an optimum list will look phantastic, and the only excuse for offering it is that it can guide the interested reader to take a good look at the original texts. But it may also provide the background for a "Reader in Phenomenology." True, a sourcebook, which should also include shorter essays from periodicals, can never take the place of the translations of entire books. But aside from serving the needs of introductory study, it may have independent and permanent value even after its preliminary function has ceased to exist.

γ. Thus far in the world outside Germany phenomenology has been presented chiefly as a revival and continuation of the Cartesian tradition. Husserl's *Ideen*, the first and only phenomenological work available in English, stressed this connection, and so did Husserl himself in his London lectures of 1922; his *Cartesian Meditations*, first published in French, presented phenomenology actually as "Neo-Cartesianism." This was certainly a proper and effective appeal in France. But in the Anglo-American countries the reliance on such an ancestry was a much more dubious affair, especially in the United States, where Descartes' stock has fallen rather low, particularly among the "classic" thinkers, whose first "major theme," according to Max Fisch, [1] was the "damnation of Descartes." But this is by no means the only possible avenue to phenomenology. It is even historically misleading. Husserl's *Logische Untersuchungen* show that his primary interest was in the British empiricists from Locke to Mill, and that it was largely out of his intensive study of the British tradition that his early phenomenology had developed. Moreover, we know now that no other thinker made such a deep impression on Husserl as William James with his *Principles of Psychology*. Under these circumstances it would seem that the proper approach to phenomenology for most Anglo-American readers should lead through the empiricist tradition and possibly through Kant, who may offer the best introduction to Husserl's later work.

δ. Very often the seemingly esoteric character of present phenomenology is not the result of a boycott from the outside or a deliberate retreat into a more or less splendid isolation, but rather an inadvertent loss of contact with the contemporary trends in the philosophic environment. There is a conspicuous lack of communication between inside and outside. Movements like logical positivism, philosophical analysis, and pragmatism have enough in common with phenomenology to make an exchange not only possible but profitable. In their latest development these other movements have even taken up a number of

---

[1] *Classic American Philosophers* (New York, Appleton-Century-Crofts 1951), pp. 19–20.

phenomenological motifs.[1] Such trends should not only be recognized but utilized for increased exchanges.

To be sure, at the present moment all such considerations may seem impractical and impracticable. But there are indications that before long phenomenology will have a chance for a re-hearing of its case even beyond the one of which the present enterprise is a symptom. It would be premature to make concrete suggestions for the next steps. But if and when such new op-portunities should arise, it would be well for phenomenologists to be ready to state their case in terms suited to the needs of the hour.

ε. This is not all. In addition to stating their case, phenomeno-logists must be able to back it up by practicing what too often they have only preached, and do it in a manner which is in-telligible and suggestive to an uninitiated but open-minded audience. Any attempt to introduce phenomenology as a living form of philosophizing must begin with concrete demonstrations of phenomenological research. Telling the story is not enough: Without original and sustained phenomenological case studies, it will not carry. Ultimately phenomenology can be transmitted only by the example of phenomenological seeing and showing.

---

[1] See, e.g., Gustav Bergmann, *Meaning and Existence* (University of Wisconsin Press, 1960), pp 3–38; Wilfrid Sellars, "Empiricism and the Philosophy of Mind" in Feigl H. and Scriven, M., ed., *The Foundations of Science and the Concepts of Psychology and Psychoanalysis*. University of Minnesota Press, I (1956), p. 311.

PART FIVE:

PRINCIPLES AND APPRAISALS

XIV

THE ESSENTIALS OF THE PHENOMENOLOGICAL METHOD

The preceding account of the Phenomenological Movement could easily have given the impression that all there is to phenomenology is its history as expressed in the multifarious and fluid ideas of sundry phenomenologists. Such an impression even contains a considerable amount of truth. Phenomenology not only shows vast differences in its manifestations, but it has served as a tool for extremely divergent enterprises. Besides, this impression may be highly salutary in counteracting the widespread tendency to treat phenomenology as a close-knit school and to judge it by the deeds, or more frequently misdeeds, of some one of its more peripheral figures. But this situation offers no excuse for dodging the persistent question of the more systematically-minded reader: What, after all this, *is* phenomenology? While our long story contains plenty of reasons why a meaningful answer cannot be given in one brief sentence, it calls all the more for a determined effort to satisfy a legitimate and even welcome demand for enlightenment and clarification. Even if there were as many phenomenologies as phenomenologists, there should be at least a common core in all of them to justify the use of the common label.

The most obvious way for discovering such a core would seem to consist in searching for the invariants of the different versions, ignoring the variables. The main disadvantage of such a procedure is that what could thus be distilled from the variety of concrete phenomena must appear rather thin and trivial. An example is the frequent characterization of phenomenology as descriptive philosophy. That would not even set it apart suf-

ficiently from several decidedly non-phenomenological philosophies. A more meaningful account of the essentials should
include at least those variables which have given phenomenology
its distinctive appearance and inspiring momentum. Between
the triviality of a mere common denominator and the abstruse-
ness of a merely esoteric formula there is need for a concise
statement of the main ingredients of a concrete phenomenology
in action. No satisfactory statement of this type offers itself
ready-made. The subsequent attempt to find it will therefore
have to be largely a personal venture with no better authority
than the evidence of the phenomena which it tries to cover. It
seems only fair to be frank about this unorthodox approach
in view of some of the heresies which the subsequent presentation
will reveal. This unorthodoxy will show up particularly in the
treatment of the later steps of the phenomenological method.
But its most debatable feature will be the treatment of Husserl's
phenomenological reduction, so basic to his fully developed
conception of phenomenology.

Any attempt to formulate the essentials of phenomenology
must make clear from the very start the extent of the field of
"phenomenologies" to be covered. Had I gone as far as most of
the French interpreters, who want to include even Kant and Hegel
as genuine representatives of phenomenology, I would have a
very different assignment from the one which I propose to
tackle; in some respects it would be easier, but the result would
also remain much less specific and substantial. The present
undertaking will be restricted to those phenomenologists who
have been included in the historical parts on the basis of my
conception of the Phenomenological Movement in its broad sense,
as stated in the Introduction (p. 6). I should like to widen this
range only by the inclusion of the collateral currents which have
appeared since Husserl's adoption of the term "phenomenology"
in such adjacent fields as psychology and psychopathology.
The most important of these may be the phenomenological
component in gestalt psychology. However, the concrete
demonstration of the connection of this component with Carl
Stumpf's phenomenology – rather than with that of Husserl –
must be left for another occasion.

A. PHENOMENOLOGY AND PHENOMENOLOGICAL METHOD

One might first consider the possibility of determining the essentials of phenomenology by a summary of its results. But these do not constitute a coherent system shared by all phenomenologists. Even some of the more specific and undisputed insights, such as the doctrine of the intentional structure of consciousness, are interpreted differently by Brentano, Husserl, Heidegger, Sartre, and Merleau-Ponty. And the agreements are more than counter-balanced by such basic disagreements as those between idealistic, realistic, and neutralistic phenomenologies. As to other findings reported by individual phenomenologists, such as those in the field of value, it would not be safe to infer from the silence of fellow phenomenologists that they either accept or reject such additions to the common stock. It would therefore be highly problematical if not impossible to define the essentials of phenomenology from its results.

At least at the present stage its most characteristic core is its method. There is little disagreement among phenomenologists about this point. The following attempt to present the essentials of phenomenology will therefore refer to its method only. It will present this method as a series of steps, of which the later will usually presuppose the earlier ones, yet not be necessarily entailed by them. Such a procedure will at the same time allow us to determine the systematic relation of the various types of phenomenology to each other. More important, it will make it possible for the critical reader to consider and appraise the main elements of phenomenology step by step, without committing himself to a wholesale adoption or rejection.

Each of these steps will be explained first in general terms and then applied to a single example. The one I have chosen is that of the phenomenology of force (in a sense to be explained presently). To be sure, this example has not been discussed much in the technical phenomenological literature.[1] All the more does

[1] Max Scheler's posthumous papers include a suggestive phenomenological study on effecting (*wirken*) in his fragment on "*Phänomenologie und Kausalerkenntnis*"; *Gesammelte Schriften* X, 475–92.
Considerable groundwork for a phenomenological approach is available in works that do not use the label, such as
C. D. Broad, *Scientific Thought* (London, Kegan Paul, 1927), pp. 162–6.
G. F. Stout, *Mind and Matter* (N. Y., Macmillan, 1931), pp. 15–20 and *Aristotelian Society*, Supplementary Volume XIV (1935), 54–58.

it offer a good opportunity for testing the fruitfulness of the phenomenological approach in a field which has been the battle-ground of opposing camps of philosophers and scientists. A more valid ground for this choice is that it makes it possible to introduce the various steps of the phenomenological method one by one. Clearly, no exhaustive treatment is possible and the results must be considered as tentative.

However, before considering the specific steps of the phenomenological method I must make some general remarks about its final objectives and its chief oppositions.

B. THE PHENOMENOLOGICAL METHOD AS A PROTEST AGAINST REDUCTIONISM

The first objective of the phenomenological approach is the enlarging and deepening of the range of our immediate experience. Ever since Husserl's phenomenological manifesto, "Philosophy as a Rigorous Science," the reclamation of the immediate phenomena under the watchword "To the things themselves" (*Zu den Sachen*) has been the leitmotif of phenomenological research. Its interpretation may vary. But the common concern is that of giving the phenomena a fuller and fairer hearing than traditional empiricism has accorded them. In this sense the phenomenological goal is closely related to that of William James in his essay "Against a Certain Blindness in Human Beings."

This program has a negative and a positive aspect, a turning away from something and a turning toward something else. Negatively, it expresses a revolt against an approach to philosophy that takes its point of departure from crystallized beliefs and theories handed down by a tradition which only too often perpetuates preconceptions and prejudgments. This negative part, the identification and deliberate elimination of theoretical constructs and symbolisms in favor of the return to the unadulterated phenomena, is by no means a simple and easy affair; it takes a determined effort to undo the effect of habitual patterns of thought and to return to the pristine innocence of

A. C. Benjamin, *An Introduction to the Philosophy of Science* (N.Y., Macmillan, 1937), pp. 323–331.

Wolfgang Köhler, whose *The Place of Value in a World of Facts* (N.Y., Liveright, 1938) is based upon a partial phenomenology, gives elements of a "phenomenology of force" under this very name (pp. 341 ff.).

first seeing. Nevertheless this negative aspect, the emancipation from preconceptions, is perhaps the most teachable part of the phenomenological method. It can be one of its chief tangible contributions to an enriched philosophy.

Among these preconceptions one of the most baneful is the principle of simplicity, or economy of thought. This principle has been espoused particularly by the positivists. As such it has actually vitiated their basic program of a return to the positive data of experience, which is so congenial to the phenomenological approach. Now the principles of simplicity and economy have their definite uses in life and even in certain areas of science, where, in Whitehead's words, simplicity should be sought but distrusted. Nevertheless it remains true that, if we want to explore the finer structures of the phenomena for their own sakes, simplicity and economy are instruments that are both blunt and blunting. The genuine will to know calls for the spirit of generosity rather than for that of economy, for reverence rather than for subjugation, for the lens rather than for the hammer. Positivists in Anglo-American countries are fond of Occam's proverbial razor: the principle that entities ought not to be multiplied beyond necessity.[1] Literally interpreted, even this injunction does not call for any drastic simplification of the data but only opposes unnecessary complication in introducing explanatory concepts and hypotheses. It does not ask us to strip the phenomena to the bare bones or to scrape off their skins along with the stubbles. Such a principle had better be called the positivist's bulldozer. Against the genuine principle of Occam's razor phenomenology would only urge the additional clause: "nor are the phenomena to be diminished below what is intuitively given." If one likes to stick to barber shop language, one might thus contrast Occam's razor with Husserl's phenomelogical brush: its function would be both to remove foreign bodies and to refurbish the genuine phenomena without pulling them from their roots. The positivists are right in refusing to honor the checks of a high-sounding metaphysical terminology unless they can be paid off, at least in principle, in the specie of concrete data. But the question is whether there is any good reason to

---

[1] On the historical misunderstandings of this principle see W. M. Thorburn, "The Myth of Occam's Razor" in *Mind* XXVII (1918), 345–353.

restrict these data to *sense* data, thus refusing access to any other possible data without even looking at their credentials.

The phenomenological protest against this narrowing down of experience in the name of Occam's razor is not a mere difference in emphasis. In this respect phenomenology stands for a kind of rebellion against the trend in modern science which begins with simplifying abstractions and ends with a minimum vocabulary of scientific concepts. Since the advent of Whitehead and other critics of that trend of science, phenomenology no longer stands alone in its battle against uncritical simplification. But it might well be claimed that it constitutes the most concerted and most concrete manifestation of this counter-movement. As such it need not deny the right and usefulness of simplification for limited objectives. But it has the right and the duty to protest against a simplification which claims to supply the only legitimate and the full picture of reality.[1]

Another obstruction to an open-eyed approach to the phenomena might be called the sense-organ bias. It could be formulated as a principle: nothing is to be recognized as a datum unless it can be assigned to a specific sense organ (in the biological organism) as its receptor. A good many positivistic rejections of phenomenological data, such as the denial of distance perception, may well be ascribed to some such negativistic prejudice.

C. THE STEPS OF THE PHENOMENOLOGICAL METHOD

The chief meaning of phenomenology, however, is not that of a revolt but of a fertilizing and reconstructive effort. The watchword "To the things themselves" has primarily a positive objective, bids us to turn toward phenomena which had been blocked from sight by the theoretical patterns in front of them. But what does this positive turn imply? That question will have to be answered by a more detailed discussion of the positive steps

---

[1] It was significant that Husserl, even before stating the program of his phenomenology, challenged in the first volume of his *Logische Untersuchungen* Mach's principle of the economy of thought as inadequate to do justice to the peculiar nature of logical thoughts and laws. Mach's puzzled but generous acknowledgment of Husserl's criticism in a later edition of his *Science of Mechanics* (in the climactic chapter IV, 4 on the economy of science), shows that he was aware of the deeper implications of Husserl's attack on psychologism as constituting the beginning of a new approach to philosophical problems.

of the phenomenological method, which we shall take up in the
following order:

1. investigating particular phenomena;
2. investigating general essences;
3. apprehending essential relationships among essences;
4. watching modes of appearing;
5. watching the constitution of phenomena in consciousness;
6. suspending belief in the existence of the phenomena;
7. interpreting the meaning of phenomena.

The first three steps have been accepted, at least implicitly,
and practiced by all those who have aligned themselves with the
Phenomenological Movement; the later ones only by a smaller
group. There is, in fact, no reason why even the very first step
should not be adopted by itself, regardless of the later ones.
Thus the gestaltists, in declaring their partial solidarity with
phenomenology, usually accept only the principle of descriptive
research without subscribing to the investigation of essences and
essential relations, at least not under these ambitious names.

I. Investigating Particular Phenomena

Under this heading I include three operations which are
usually not clearly distinguished, since they are intimately
related: the intuitive grasp of the phenomena, their analytic
examination, and their description. The customary label for these
operations is "phenomenological description." The following
account is meant as an attempt to show that there is a definite
need for distinguishing between the intuitive, the analytic, and
the descriptive phase of this step, even though they belong
closely together.

a. PHENOMENOLOGICAL INTUITING – To intuit the phenomena seems at first blush a fairly elementary affair, if one
approaches this task without preconceptions. This may be so
in theory, but it is certainly not so in practice. It is one of the
most demanding operations, which requires utter concentration
on the object intuited without becoming absorbed in it to the
point of no longer looking critically. Nevertheless there is little
that the beginning phenomenologist can be given by way of
precise instructions beyond such metaphoric phrases as "opening

his eyes," "keeping them open," "not getting blinded," "looking and listening," etc. Some help in the attempt to grasp the uniqueness of specific phenomena can be obtained by comparing them with related phenomena, giving special attention to similarities and differences. Watching trained practitioners in their approach to the phenomena, usually by studying their subsequent accounts, may further sensitize one's own intuiting.

Unfortunately, there is reason for insisting that there is nothing "mystical" about such an approach. For the use of the term "intuition," and especially that of its German equivalent *"Schau,"* has given rise to some particularly odd misinterpretations. Actually, it has been applied to such a variety of procedures, from a highly rational mathematical intuition to the metaphysical intuition of Bergson and the ecstasy of the Neoplatonists, that there is no need for such an irrationalist interpretation of the term and of phenomenology. However, in order to avoid these connotations, I intend to utilize the less abused noun form of the verb intuit, "intuiting."

It is even more important to realize that such intuiting of particular phenomena has its characteristic pitfalls. Insensitivity to the finer shades of the phenomena is only one of these. But there is also such a thing as hypersensitivity, extending to shades which, if distinguishable at all, are irrelevant to the context. The Older Phenomenological Movement was not always immune to this danger.

EXAMPLE: How can such intuiting be applied to the phenomenon of force? Before we attack this example it will be necessary to clarify what is meant by "force" in the present context. In the case of a concept with such a long and confused philosophical and scientific history any attempt to intuit and to exhibit the corresponding phenomenon presupposes a previous clarification of the meaning of the major terms that point to it.

By "force" I shall understand here the referent of such phrases as "using force," e.g., in forcing a door, or in sentences such as "a stone hit me with considerable force" or "the car struck the tree with great force." In the latter two cases we may also use the word "impact" (*Wucht*). In focussing upon this referent of the term it is particularly important to keep out some adjacent meanings introduced partly in connection with physics and especially with dynamics. Thus "force" as used here must not be confused with "power," in so far as "power" stands for something merely potential, a capacity or ability to do something. By the same token it must be distinguished from "energy" in the sense in which physics defines it, namely as a capacity or ability to do work. (This does not apply to the ordinary use of the word "energy.") Also, "force" must not be understood in the sense of "cause." For "cause" is a relational concept based upon a causal relation of something to its effect. Whether or not a force in our sense is also the cause of an event, is a question which a phenomenology of force has to postpone. The phenomenon of cause raises a much more complex and controversial question: whether cause and causation are observable phenomena. Force in the sense involved here is a non-relational concept. It probably coincides with some of the original meanings of the term "live force" (*vis viva*) as used by Leibniz, but not if it is defined as the ability to do work measured by the product of half the mass times the square of the velocity.

Whether or not "force" as used here is what has been understood by force in the past discussions of this concept, the idea of force has been under increasing fire from various schools of empiricists. David Hume was the first to announce its meaninglessness, since no impression of power, force, energy, or necessary connection (all of which he seems to identify) occurs among our "sensible qualities." Positivists like Ernst Mach and Karl Pearson seem to share Hume's denial but chiefly stress the uselessness and expendability of the concept of force in the interest of economy of thought. Bertrand Russell called it a "mathematical fiction, not a physical entity" (*The Principles of Mathematics*, no. 455), and even in his *Human Knowledge* he simply states that "it turned out to be superfluous and was eliminated from classical dynamics during the nineteenth century" (p. 16).

To a phenomenological approach, the question of whether or not physics can get along without the concept of force is irrelevant. The only question is whether it is a phenomenon in our actual experience. This is what Hume seems to be denying when, for understandable reasons, he questions the experience of necessary connection. When at the same time, however, he denies the experience of force it may well be that, in addition to rashly identifying the two, he was also subject to what I called the sense-organ prejudice: since there is no separate sense organ for forces as there is for touch qualities, he concluded that forces could not possibly be perceived, and discredited in his reflection whatever the word force may have previously meant to him.

Removing the sense-organ prejudice is therefore of particular importance in the case of the phenomenology of force. Whether or not sense-organs for forces can be identified and sense data belonging to them can be traced, the decisive question is whether or not we perceive forces. It may of course be the case that such forces appear only in combination with or are founded upon the perception of pressures, strains, etc. But this circumstance does not prove that they are *nothing but* such pressures.

However, in order to determine definitely whether there can be such a thing as a genuine intuitive perception of forces as here understood, I shall have to point out specific situations in which they are clearly given.

Two situations seem to me to reveal forces with particular clarity: one is the active use of our own force, the second the undergoing of the impact of a foreign force. Both situations occur in the context of the experience of our own body. However, it is important to realize that the body here involved is not that of biological science with its bones, muscles, sinews, joints, and nerves; for of these, of their number and locations, we have no direct awareness. The body in which the experience of force is localized is the subject of a special phenomenology, which describes merely the body as it is given to our direct awareness and in the way it is given. True, this experienced body and the "scientific" body overlap. But it is in the non-overlapping sphere that the phenomenon of force makes its appearance.

In the active experience of bodily force we encounter two characteristic phases. The first may be called the "mobilization" of force, the second its release. What is it that we perceive in the first phase, for instance, when in response to an alarm we "get set" for an effort? Not only does our attention become alerted to an expected signal. We also experience a unique transformation in our lived body and specifically in those parts of it which are being readied for action. They become in a peculiar sense "charged" with a dynamic "agent," the very agent which the word "force" is meant to designate.

What happens in the second phase when this mobilized agent is "released" on the occasion of a signal like a starting gun or in response to some spontaneous initiative? There is of course the change in the position of the body, at least in the case of un-obstructed motion, and in the inner sensations, summarily labelled "kinesthetic," that go with it. But we also experience a more specific change with respect to the force which had been dammed up by the preceding mobilization. It involves such a thing as a "discharge" of the mobilized "charge." As force is "expended," the charge drops more or less suddenly. Moreover, we seem to have "passed on" this force to the object acted upon. This is more than the mere relaxing of our body, an experience which would go just as well with a mere "demobilization." Something has been given off, lost from the reservoir of mobilized force, even though we may be keeping some on reserve or may be able to replenish it with more or less effort by further "mobi-lization," ultimately from the supply that goes by the name of "second wind."

Force is perceived from a different angle in the passive experi-ence of suffering an impact. Here our body is attacked or in-vaded suddenly by an outside force. Such an experience may be contrasted with one in which we are merely touched, without receiving any dynamic influx. A clear case is that of suffering a blow which imparts its force to a particular part of our body. The experience of force reaches an even deeper level when our whole body is carried away by it. What is most characteristic about such dynamic invasions is that, after a perfectly relaxed and non-dynamic condition, our body undergoes a sudden burst or shock which transforms the part so invaded into a force-charged zone. This experience differs characteristically from that of a sudden internal spasm or cramp. In being hit by a foreign force and in becoming, however temporarily, the carrier of this force, our body is, as it were, alienated from ourselves. Such an alienating force may of course simply "spend itself," as it is "absorbed" by our resettled body. But we may also be flung against another object in such a way that the foreign force is transmitted to it in very much the same manner as our active mobilized force was given off to an object to which we applied it.

Compared with these two cases, the perception of force in objects other than our own body is much more indirect. Nevertheless, there is something almost irresistible about the way in which we perceive force when we see a not too rapidly moving object like Hume's celebrated billiard ball "hit" (not only "meet") another billiard ball and hear the sharp click of their brusque encounter. But this may well be an illusion, and we would certainly do well at this stage to keep out all implications of a causal or necessary relation. All we assert is that the hitting ball presents itself as carrying a force, and that the hit ball appears to be carrying a similar charge immediately after the collision.

It seems appropriate, however, to refer in this connection to the brilliant studies by which the Belgian psychologist Albert Michotte has demonstrated, even by the use of experimental techniques, the inescapableness of the impression of a causal connection, not only in the case of Hume's billiard balls but also in artificially devised new situations.[1] He himself is careful to avoid making any epistemological claims beyond the phenomenological evidence, which is striking enough. In the present context I assert even less, since I disregard the whole question of causal relationship and confine myself to the mere phenomenon of a dynamic factor, whether causal or not.

It is customary to brush aside such examples as flagrant cases of anthropomorphism. To meet this charge fully a detailed discussion of the meaning and the rights and wrongs of that dreadful heresy would be required. In the meantime it might help to make at least the following two points:

α. Whatever may be the explanation for our impression that an external object displays force, the decisive phenomenological consideration is whether or not we perceive now and here in the impelling and impelled objects a factor which distinguishes them from moving objects, engaged in a mere change of position.

β. The charge of "anthropomorphism" seems to imply that

---

[1] See, e.g., his account in Carl Murchison, ed., *History of Psychology in Autobiography* IV (Clark University Press, 1940), pp. 228 ff. and *La Perception de la causalité* (Louvain, 1946).

man (*anthropos*) has nothing in common with non-human nature and that any common shape (*morphe*) which we may find in nature must have been illegitimately projected upon it from the observation of the human original. While it would obviously be a prejudice to ascribe to inanimate nature such reactions as malice, stubbornness, pleasure, and the like, it would seem just as prejudiced to deny it features which are not even psychological. Anthropomorphism is not animism. We should deprive ourselves of our privileged access to nature if we discredited offhand all experiences about our own body which are not reducible to merely psychological data. The non-psychological phenomenon of force is a case in point.

The hue and cry about anthropomorphism is a stereotype which dogmatically denies the continuity between man and nature. It remains true, however, that the perception of forces in objects outside our body is far from infallible, and that it should not be accepted at face value. There is certainly a strong temptation to imaginatively project such forces into all kinds of objects. Conscientious examination reveals only too often that we have merely attributed forces habitually on the basis of past associations.

This is not the place for an epistemological justification of the belief in forces in nature. Nevertheless it may be suggested that there are times when we have good reasons for extrapolating from the experience of forces within our own body to such forces in foreign bodies beyond its range. Such an extrapolation may be buttressed by the consideration of cases where forces are transmitted from one part of our body to another part, and where we experience the forces in both these parts, for instance when one member exerts and the other undergoes such force, or vice versa. Such cases would seem to justify an inference by analogy to the effect that forces are present even where the other member of such a relationship is no longer our own body but some foreign or inanimate object. Moreover, insofar as this first extrapolation can be justified, there would seem to be no basic objection to a final extrapolation to cases where our body and its forces are no longer involved, i.e., to the interaction between inanimate bodies. The epistemological value of such extrapolations may not exceed that of hypotheses. But these hypotheses can at least be derived from, and connected with, our direct phenomenological experience of force.

Excursus: Does Phenomenology Explore only Subjective Phenomena?

There is a widespread belief that phenomenology consists essentially in a study of merely subjective or private phenomena, and that it constitutes nothing but a return to a subjective psychology, if not a relapse into introspectionism. How legitimate is this belief?

It is certainly true that in his later years Husserl described his phenomenology as a study of transcendental subjectivity, in which he saw the source or "origin" for the whole world of our everyday experience and even of science. But even here the word "transcendental" suggests that more is involved than a mere reflecting upon one's private and personal phenomena. For Husserl's phenomenology of subjectivity involves the attempt to discover the essential – i.e., the objective or absolute – structures in what otherwise would be merely subjective phenomena. Even more important is the fact that phenomenology in this sense is disinterested in the whole question of whether or not the reports of such "introspection" are faithful accounts of one individual's actual experience at the time, whether, for instance, the particular introspectionist is or was really in doubt or in love or merely believed that he was. All that matters is that his experience presented him with the phenomenon of doubt or of love, which is to be studied for its own sake, regardless of the specific case and the subjectivity or objectivity of the concrete observation that brought the phenomenon before him. What is most important for our present inquiry is the fact that Husserl's conception of phenomenology as the attempt to find objective essences in the very heart of subjectivity is by no means common ground for all phenomenologists. Thus particularly the Older Phenomenological Movement in its deliberate "turn to the object" was definitely anti-subjectivistic. More recently, Merleau-Ponty has questioned the whole distinction between subjective and objective phenomena, seeing in phenomenology a deliberate attempt to overcome it.

This entire interpretation and criticism suffers, of course, from a nearly hopeless confusion as to the meaning of the terms "subjective" and "objective." Without expecting to disentangle it completely in this context, I shall try to distinguish at least some of the relevant meanings and consider in the light of these distinctions in what senses phenomenology is or is not "subjective."

α. If by "subjective" we mean what is accessible only to reflective introspection, then phenomenology is certainly not completely subjective. For its descriptions deal not only with the subject's side of experience, with his acts and dispositions which can become thematic only in a reflective return upon himself, but at least as much with those contents of his acts which confront him as the objects of his experience and which do not require any reflective turn. Thus colors, melodies, and specifically those "forces" which we experience in our own lived body appear, as it were, in front of us. No particular direction, inward or outward, is prescribed by the essential nature of phenomenological intuiting.

β. If, however, by "subjective" we mean the "merely subjective" observations which characterize the reports of uncritical and untrained observers chosen at random, then phenomenology is definitely opposed to "subjectivity." It is fully aware that careful intuiting and faithful description are not to be taken for granted and that they require a considerable degree of aptitude, training, and conscientious self-criticism. Insofar as "introspection" is at all admitted as a source of phenomenological insight, it has certainly to undergo careful screening.

γ. The "subjectivity" of the phenomena of phenomenology may also be understood in the sense of their essential privacy. Now, it should be realized that originally all phenomena are essentially "private." Whether or not in addition to that they are also public, i.e., shared by others, is something which at best the subsequent "comparing of (private) notes" can reveal. There is no reason to doubt a priori that the private phenomena of phenomenological intuition are shareable. In fact there is sufficient evidence that in most cases such sharing does take place, even though there is no guarantee that this will always be the case. But it would be preposterous and self-defeating not to admit any phenomenon before it has proved to be public. No such proof can even be started before we have taken stock of our private phenomena. In fact, not even the exclusive privacy of any phenomenon can be asserted legitimately before it has been established that this phenomenon is not shared by others.

This seems to be the proper place to make a more general point: Even merely private phenomena are facts which we have no business to ignore. A science which refuses to take account of them as such is guilty of suppressing evidence and will end with a truncated universe. Besides, recent developments in clinical psychology and therapy have made it plain that even prediction of "public" behavior is impossible without taking account of the private phenomena in the "phenomenal field" of the "client." And while it is true that there is no direct access to the private phenomena, e.g., of the psychopathic and especially of the psychotic personality, the sensitive observer has enough clues for indirect and hypothetical reconstruction of these phenomena, and for the verification of his hypotheses.

δ. If, finally, the "subjectivity" charged against phenomenology refers to its dependence upon the verdict of immediate experience, then it is of course no more and no less subjective than any approach based on "pure" uncensored experience. For all experience is basically "subjective" in the sense that it is our own experience. Even a mere protocol of objective behavior or a report about measurements is a "first-person experience," to use W. H. Werkmeister's telling expression. No empirical knowledge, however purged and "objectified," can get away from this subjective matrix of all experience. Phenomenology deals with objective phenomena no more and no less than any genuinely empirical knowledge does. If it differs from it, this is due only to the open-minded generosity with which it accepts phenomena before asking them at once whether they are "subjective" or "objective." If they are "merely subjective" this will show up in due time. But this is no good reason for outlawing them on mere suspicion.[1]

---

[1] For a discussion of the epistemological problems connected with the "subjectivity" of phenomenology, see my paper "How Subjective is Phenomenology?" *Proceedings of the American Catholic Philosophical Association* XXXIII (1959), 28–36.

b. Phenomenological analyzing – *"Phenomeno-
logical analysis"* is a step rarely if ever distinguished from phenomenological intuition or especially from phenomenological
description. Yet it is one which deserves separate consideration.
This is particularly important in the interest of clarifying the
relation between phenomenology and the various enterprises
that go by the name of logical or philosophical analysis. No
attempt will be made here to give an "analysis," though one is
badly needed, of the whole range of procedures for which this
term is now being used. However, it may be safe to state that the
subject matter of all these analyses consists of certain linguistic
expressions, and that their general objective is the discovery
of certain equivalent expressions preferably consisting of a
smaller number of terms with a simpler structure to take the
place of the original expressions.[1] Thus the new analysis amounts
actually to a construction of new expressions rather than a
study of the component parts of the original ones.

By contrast, phenomenological analysis is not primarily
concerned with linguistic expressions. It is true that even phenomenologists often take their point of departure from certain
characteristic phrases and try to determine their meanings and
their equivocations. Some of them, including the Husserl of the
Logische Untersuchungen, engage in the exploration of subtle
shades of meaning to such an extent that phenomenology was
suspected of a revival of "scholasticism" (Wilhelm Wundt).
But this misinterpretation overlooked the fact that such analyses
of terms were merely preparatory to the study of the referents,
i.e., of the phenomena meant by the expressions. Phenomenological analysis, then, is analysis of the phenomena themselves,
not of the expressions that refer to them.

But what, exactly, does analysis undertake to do in this case?
Primarily nothing but to trace the elements and the structure
of the phenomena obtained by intuiting. It does not in any sense
demand dissecting them into separate parts. It comprises the
distinguishing of the constituents of the phenomena as well as

---

[1] "By analysis they (the analytic philosophers) meant something which, whatever
precise description of it they chose, at least involved the attempt to rewrite in different and in some way more appropriate terms those statements which they found
philosophically puzzling." (J. O. Urmson, *Philosophical Analysis*, Oxford, Clarendon,
1956, p. vii).

the exploration of their relations to and connections with adjacent phenomena.

At this place it seems worth pointing out that recent developments in British analytic philosophy, beginning with the realization of "the impossibility of reductive analysis" (Urmson) and culminating in Ludwig Wittgenstein's "new philosophy" and related developments (Gilbert Ryle, John Wisdom), have led to a remarkable rapprochement, thus far apparently hardly noticed, with phenomenology in the wider sense. Wittgenstein's posthumous *Philosophische Untersuchungen* (the parallel of this title to Husserl's classic *Logische Untersuchungen* could be more than a coincidence) inculcate with remarkable insistence the watchword: "Don't think but look" (*schau*) (section 66). This kind of "intuiting" consists in the methodical inspection of entire series of phenomena with a view to discovering the "manifold structural similarities" between them. But it also pays careful attention to their subtler differences (sec. 172). Everywhere Wittgenstein tries to explore "what goes on" in our experience (*Erlebnis*), not merely to study the grammatical structure of the expressions we use in talking about it. All this sounds surprisingly like the attempts of the earlier phenomenologists to catch the phenomena themselves in their common essences and in their full variety, free from interpretation and without any attempt to reduce them to one another.

On the other hand, it must not be overlooked that, in his rather evocative aphorisms, Wittgenstein rarely goes beyond calling our attention to family resemblances and differences in experience which are not sufficiently expressed in ordinary language, ending mostly with a question which seems to be addressed more to himself than to his reader. No attempt at analysis follows, if analysis is understood as a taking apart of the phenomena into their component parts or of their painstaking description. Wittgenstein considers this either impossible or undesirable. Besides, even this "new philosophy" does not seem to be interested in the intuiting of phenomena for its own sake. Its ultimate objective remains the cure of metaphysical puzzles as forms of a peculiar disease (sec. 255) or "to show the fly the way out of the fly-bottle" (sec. 309). Yet the relation between this incipient philosophy of "seeing" and phenomenology is close

enough to deserve more careful and detailed examination than
I can give it here. [1]

In his later writings Husserl often uses the expression "intentional analysis" (*intentionale Analyse*) as an equivalent for
phenomenological analysis. Actually, this substitution is merely
a reflection of the fact that intentional reference is the basic
structure in the phenomena on which Husserl concentrated his
attention. By itself the expression suggests nothing but an
analysis which pays systematic attention to the parallel aspects
of intending act (*noesis*) and intended content (*noema*). More
specifically, it focusses on the way in which intentional act and
intentional referent correspond to one another. However, as
interpreted by Eugen Fink, it also implies the attempt to
uncover the constituting functions of the intentional acts. I shall
leave this more ambitious kind of intentional analysis for later
consideration. In the present section phenomenological analysis,
including intentional analysis, stands simply for the general
examination of the structure of the phenomena according to
their ingredients and their configuration.

EXAMPLE: How could such phenomenological analysis be
applied to the experience of a force as given in its mobilization
and its use, or in undergoing its impact? As force permeates our
mobilized body and is then released from it, or as it suddenly
invades it from the outside, it constitutes a continuous phenomenon which does not allow for the analytic distinction of parts
and their configuration. Rather does it permeate a certain area
of the phenomenal body – for instance our "poised" arms or
legs – in its entirety. Thus force fills the arms all over, by no
means appearing only in their frontal parts, where the anatomist
localizes a variety of distinct nerves and muscles ready to
contract. Also, our phenomenal force is not always polarized
in the direction of a definite goal with a definite vector. This
does not preclude the possibility of giving special attention to
definite zones in the force-charged area with a view to determining the distribution of that force. One might also observe the
relation of the affected area to other parts of the phenomenal
body, which will be more or less affected by such an alarm.
And one might discover that such adjacent areas are either

depleted of force or are no longer represented in the profile of our general body awareness. But such analysis would soon merge with that of our total inner body consciousness, a field which has been opened up, but by no means adequately explored, by the pioneer studies of Paul Schilder. – Another dimension for analysis of the bodily force-phenomena is that of their intensity, a characteristic which they all display in varying degrees.

c. PHENOMENOLOGICAL DESCRIBING – *"Phenomenological description"* of the phenomena thus intuited and analyzed goes usually and – according to some phenomenologists, essentially – hand in hand with the preceding steps. Yet it seems to me that the distinctive nature of this procedure has as a rule not been sufficiently considered. At the same time its importance has been overemphasized, as for instance when phenomenology has been characterized simply as descriptive science. Thus there is definite danger in beginning a description of the phenomena before we have explored them intuitively and analytically. Phenomenology begins in silence. Only he who has experienced genuine perplexity and frustration in the face of the phenomena when trying to find the proper description for them knows what phenomenological seeing really means. Rushing into descriptions before having made sure of the thing to be described may even be called one of the main pitfalls of phenomenology. Description is primarily predication. But predication, as phenomenology has brought out increasingly, presupposes pre-predicative experience. And this pre-predicative experience deserves first attention, even if, for purposes of communication, we cannot very well dispense with descriptions.

What, then, is this culminating description? To give an adequate account of phenomenological description, its nature, its problems, and its limitations, we would have to fall back on a general theory of description, of which there are promising though not completely satisfying beginnings.[1] Let it suffice here to stress a few features which are of particular significance for phenomenological description. As Mill pointed out long ago, "to

---

[1] Of particular interest is J. S. Mill's chapter in his *System of Logic* Book IV Ch. 1 (Of Observation and Description). See also W. H. Werkmeister, "On 'Describing a World' " in *PPR* XI (1950), 303–25.

describe is to affirm a connexion between it (an individual thing) and every other thing which is either denoted or connoted by any of the terms used" (§ 3). Describing is based on a classification of the phenomena. A description, therefore, presupposes a framework of class names, and all it can do is to determine the location of the phenomenon with regard to an already developed system of classes. This may be adequate for the more familiar phenomena. But as soon as we want to describe new phenomena or new aspects of old phenomena, we can do little more than assign them places within the wider framework of classes with whose other members they show at least some similarity or structural resemblance, being unable to indicate their distinguishing features. Of course it is possible and necessary to refine the system of coordinates for these phenomena by stipulating new class names; but these will be of little help before full acquaintance with the new phenomena has been established and communicated. In the meantime description by negation is usually the simplest way to at least indicate the uniqueness and irreducibility of such phenomena. The only other way is by metaphor and analogy, which are often suggestive, but not without dangers, particularly if presented without the necessary cautions. What must be borne in mind is that the main function of a phenomenological description is to serve as a reliable guide to the listener's own actual or potential experience of the phenomena. It is in this sense never more than ostensive, or better, directive. Its essential function is to provide unmistakable guideposts to the phenomena themselves.

Another feature of description which deserves mentioning in this context is that description, and phenomenological description in particular, can never be more than selective: it is impossible to exhaust all the properties, especially the relational properties, of any object or phenomenon. But selection may be a virtue as well as a necessity. It forces us to concentrate on the central or decisive characteristics of the phenomenon and to abstract from its accidentals. To this extent description already involves a consideration of essences, the next step to be considered in our scale of the phenomenological method.

EXAMPLE: An attempt to describe a particular "force" – as identified above – will have to consider first the possibility of finding an appropriate genus or class for it. Apart from the most general classes, like "something which," no more specific ontological category would seem to apply. It is certainly not a thing or a substance in the sense of an independent entity or continuant, since it clearly cannot subsist by itself in the way in which an organism or even a limb can. Force mobilized, expended, or inflicted always appears in close conjunction with the body in which it occurs; it is thus a dependent being in the sense that it is always the force of something which "carries" it. On the other hand, it is not simply a property or state of such an object, like shape, change, or motion, whether permanent or transient. For it permeates its carrier about as a certain dye or a dynamic charge permeates it. Yet it would be just as misleading to describe it as a "stuff." It is obviously an entity *sui generis*, a dynamic, unstable quasi-stuff attached to a thing, i.e., specifically to our body as we experience it.

How is it related to comparable entities? Perhaps the most successful attempt to rescue the phenomenon of "force" from the attack of Hume and his followers has been that of C. D. Broad, who defines it in terms of "strain." [1] But it would seem that there can be strain without the accompanying phenomenon of force. Strain as experienced, for instance, in the tensions of our body is a much more static affair; it is also one which is not always accompanied by the experience of a dynamic charge which tends to seek release. Nor is force as we experience it always combined with the feeling of tension as we undergo it in a "tense" moment or "under stress." This does not preclude an essential affinity and frequent association of the two phenomena.

Another defender of the phenomenon of force, G. F. Stout, has tried to describe it in terms of activity. But he also uses equivalents like "active tendency," without any definite attempt to distinguish between the various expressions used. [2] However, the most important aspect of Stout's conception is that he sees in force essentially a cause of effects. It would seem extremely important not to burden the phenomenology of force immediately

---

[1] *Scientific Thought*, p. 163 f.
[2] *Mind and Matter*, Chapter II.

with the load of the problem of causation and its possible perception. Force, as we have tried to present it, is not a relation or even a relational concept based on such a relation. We experience it as an unrelated entity perceived in our body. Whether or not a force can be causal and support the conception of causation, is a secondary matter. Before this question can be discussed, it must be established that force exists as a distinct and unrelated phenomenon. It is this telescoping of the phenomenology of force with the phenomenology of the causal relationship which has strengthened the hand of the followers of Hume, who lump together "necessary connection, power, energy, and force."[1]

Force, then, would seem to differ from the state of strain as well as from the process of activity, and certainly from the experience of being the cause of some effect beyond. At first sight such a description will appear as merely negative. But it has at least the positive value of showing that force is closely related to the phenomena from which it is distinguished. Otherwise all we can do is to resort to metaphors. But metaphoric description has at best limited value and is often more misleading than helpful. Thus one might think of comparing force with a kind of bodily secretion. But force is clearly not secreted by its carrier like a biochemical substance. The model of an electric charge may seem more appropriate. But how far can our understanding of electricity shed light on the phenomena of our direct experience? Probably Leibniz' characterization of "active force" as "a mean between the faculty of acting and action itself," is still the best approximation to a positive description.[2]

* * *

Intuiting, analyzing, and describing particulars in their full concreteness may be considered a common program for all those who think of themselves as members of the Phenomenological Movement. This does not mean that they practice these steps equally, and equally well. In fact, in the recent development of

---

[1] *Inquiry into Human Understanding*, Part VII, Section II.

[2] "De primae philosophiae emendatione" (*Opera*, ed. Gerhardt IV, 649). – His continuation, however ("It includes effort and thus passes into operation of itself, requiring no aids, but only the removal of hindrance") is phenomenologically much more dubious.

phenomenology they have been taken too much for granted, and the existentialist emphasis on hermeneutic interpretation has seriously interfered with it. On the other hand this program is by no means restricted to phenomenologists in the self-declared sense. Thus, the gestaltists and other psychological groups are in substantial agreement with this part of the phenomenological method and have practiced it extensively and impressively. But this is not the place to give proper credit to such allies of phenomenology. Let it suffice to point out the common concern.

2. Investigating General Essences (Eidetic Intuiting)

What has aroused much more suspicion and antagonism than the intuiting, analyzing, and describing of particular phenomena is the phenomenology of general essences, usually called *Wesens-schau* or eidetic intuition. Not only outsiders and antagonists of the Phenomenological Movement but some of its forerunners, like Brentano and Stumpf, and sympathizers, like the gestaltists, betray a certain irritated irony whenever this procedure is mentioned. Not only was it suspected as a new type of mysticism. Equally serious was the misinterpretation according to which it implied a commitment to a Platonic "realism."

It is of course true that Husserl's battle against nominalism entailed the recognition of "universals" as irreducible entities in addition to the particulars. It is also true that Husserl always acknowledged his debt to Plato as the discoverer of the "one" in the "many." Yet he insisted with equal vigor that the general essence or eidos has no reality superior or even equal to that of particular entities, but merely "ideal" being. In fact, in his later writings Husserl characterized this ideal mode of being as another constituted achievement of transcendental sub-jectivity, hence as dependent upon it. Still, no other pheno-menologist has made higher claims for the general essences. Besides, "eidetic intuition" constitutes a common element of the phenomenological method as interpreted by the Move-ment, even though it is played down or reinterpreted by the existentialist phenomenologists. There is no use dodging the obnoxious name in favor of possible substitutions, as long as the procedure itself can and must be maintained. Yet it should not be forgotten that even phenomenologists often use less burdened terms such as "experience of essences" (*Wesenserfahrung*), "insight into essences" (*Wesenseinsicht*), and even "cognition of essences" (*Wesenserkenntnis*). These synonyms may in the long run be preferable to "essential intuiting" (*Wesensschau*). For there is no good reason for distinguishing the intuiting of essences from experiencing or grasping them cognitively.

But what is the operation itself which is meant by these more or less misleading terms? While no explicit and generally agreed formula can be offered, the following may be considered as implied in the eidetic method especially as practiced by Husserl himself: There is no adequate intuiting of essences without the antecedent or simultaneous intuiting of exemplifying particulars. Such particulars may be given either in perception or in imagination or in a combination of both. But while this is the necessary condition of genuine intuiting, it is certainly not its entire content. In order to apprehend the general essence we have to look at the particulars *as examples*, i.e., as instances which stand for the general essence. Thus, using the particular red of an individual rose as a point of departure we can see it as an instance of a certain shade of red in general. But we can also see it as exemplifying redness and, finally, color as such. Thus the intuiting of particulars provides stepping stones, as it were, for the apprehension of the general essences.

What does the apprehending of essences add to the intuiting of particulars and to their interpretation as examples? Certainly general essences or universals are different from particulars. And while no full discussion of the phenomenological theory of universals can be given here, it must at least be mentioned that general essences are conceived of as phenomena *sui generis* that differ from particulars. There is ultimately nothing that can be done to demonstrate this point except to refer to situations in which we are engaged in exploring, for instance, the nature of heat, the cell, consciousness, or goodness *in general*. Only reflection on what is going on in such explorations can supply the foundation for further clarification. In referring to the operation by which we proceed from the particular to the universal (the so-called "ideating abstraction" or "ideation"), Husserl makes use of the German verb *"herausschauen,"* giving it a new but literally defensible transitive connotation which could be rendered as "ejective intuiting." This neologistic interpretation could well be utilized to describe the way in which we project the general type, starting with particular examples and looking through them, as it were.

Going beyond Husserl, I would like to suggest an additional way by which we can proceed from particular to general essences. It consists in lining up particular phenomena in a continuous series based on the order of their similarities. This may be illustrated by the way in which we arrange the chromatic colors in a circle. The elements for each such collection actually come from perception and imagination. The next stage is the observation that in some of these series, especially the qualitative ones, certain groups of phenomena cluster around cores that stand out as nodal points or vertices in the sequence of phenomena. Such are, for instance, the pure colors. The surrounding shades of color "belong together" in distinct groups according to their affinity to the pure colors. There is nothing arbitrary about this belongingness, for it is based on "natural" affinities. Arbitrary incisions have their place only in the transition areas between several such clusters, where indeed any boundary is essentially artificial. I submit that the configuration of phenomena thus belonging together in a "natural" group is comparable to that of a genuine good gestalt.

Now whenever particular phenomena show this kind of affinity, when, for instance, all the reds cluster together in this way, we can hardly overlook the fact that underlying it is some common pattern or essence in which they all share in varying degrees, and which they all in a sense embody. Seeing reds as red we also see redness, the general essence which is exemplified in all of them. Now it is certainly possible to see these particulars without seeing the general essence. But it is not possible to see them *as particulars* without seeing the general essence which they particularize. Thus what happens is that on the basis of seeing particulars in their structural affinities we also become aware of the ground of their affinities, the pattern or essence.

EXAMPLE: Any attempt to apprehend intuitively the general essence "force" would have to take its departure from particular cases in which we experience bodily force. We might find it helpful to line up a series of such cases in a sequence of typical dynamic experiences, such as hurling, flinging, throwing, pushing, attacking, tackling, probing; or, going in the opposite direction, dragging, pulling, jerking. By way of contrast we may add to these series such experiences as tending-toward, feeling attracted, being inclined, in short, processes which do not yet show the phenomenon of force fully developed. On the basis of the first two series we can apprehend a structural similarity and a pervading essence which is reflected in all of them. To be sure, in order to apprehend the essence "force," we must focus not on these processes as such but on the factor which permeates them and is expressed through them. This pervasive dynamic factor is either totally missing or not yet fully shaped out in the last-mentioned series, which contains only various degrees of tendencies but not yet distinct force phenomena.

The intuitive apprehension of these general essences is obviously to be followed by the same operations of analysis and description as those we distinguished from intuiting in the case of particular phenomena. In fact, here too the three are usually lumped together, as they were on the level of the phenomenological investigation of particulars. And yet, in principle we should detach from intuiting and study apart the task of analytic distinguishing of the elements that go into general essences, which is what the geometrician, for instance, does in the case of the general essence "triangle." And we should keep apart from this second operation the task of description, which involves determining the place of such a general essence in the framework of our descriptive concepts. But these two additional operations do not differ in principle from the procedures which we examined in the case of particulars. All that is needed in this context is therefore a reminder of our previous discussion. Likewise I shall dispense with a detailed analysis and description of the general essence "force." A complete development of our example would of course have to include the entire range of phenomena which embody the common essence.

3. Apprehending Essential Relationships

Analyzing an entity in itself acquaints us only with its components. But a phenomenological study of essences claims to achieve more. It also includes the discovery of certain essential relationships or connections (*Wesenszusammenhänge*) pertaining to such essences. It is this kind of relationship which is involved when we use such phrases as "it is of the essence (or: in the nature) of," or "it belongs to the essence (or: is part of the essence) of"; also, the adverb "essentially" usually points to such relationships.

Now, these essential relationships are actually of two types: relationships within a single essence or relationships between several essences. I shall begin with the former.

α. In the case of internal relations within one essence, we are concerned with the question whether its components are or are not essential to it. Thus, in the case of the triangle we shall have to determine whether three sides, three angles, and certain shapes and sizes of these sides and angles are necessary to them or required by the essence "triangle," or whether they are merely compatible with it. Questions like the following would arise: Can a triangle without these elements still be a triangle rather than another figure? Or would a figure without them be an essential impossibility, since it would include incompatible ingredients?

The way to settle such questions is chiefly by an operation which Husserl called "free imaginative variation" (*freie Variation in der Phantasie*), but which is still in need of fuller analysis and description. It may involve two things: the attempt either (1) to leave off certain components completely or (2) to replace them by others. Such experiments in the imagination can lead to three possible results: Either the essence in the sense described, i.e., the fundamental structure designated by the general name, will remain unaffected by such an omission or substitution, which proves the omitted or replaced component to be unessential (e.g., alphabetical symbols or specific sizes or angles or sides); or such an omission or substitution, while conceivable, will change the character or gestalt of the entity fundamentally (e.g., increasing the sum of the angles in a triangle beyond two straight angles will convert it from a two-dimensional into a spherical triangle) ; or it will not only affect the total configuration but "explode" the whole essence, since its components are completely incompatible among themselves (e.g., a triangle without angles or a plane triangle in Euclidean space with the sum of its angles equal to three straight angles). In the first case the component in question is admitted by the essence, and stands in essentially possible connection with it (essential possibility). In the second it is relatively necessary to it, i.e., as long as the specific essence is to be maintained (relative essential necessity). The third case, where the components are completely incompatible among themselves, is one of absolute essential necessity.

Insights based on the results of the method of imaginative variation are often called essential insights (*Wesenseinsicht*). One might suspect that such essential insights into connections within general essences are simply cases of analytic knowledge, not worth bothering about. If one means by analytic knowledge propositions that are true by definition of the concepts analyzed, then essential insights are certainly not analytic. For they do not refer to terms but to "things" meant by the terms. But even if one substitutes the analysis of essences for the analysis of concepts, essential insights involve more than separating an essence into its component parts. For what we try to explore is the nexus among them in its necessity, possibility, or impossibility as revealed by the free imaginative variation. This is clearly a case of "synthetic" knowledge.

EXAMPLE: Essential insights into the structure of the general essence "force" would have to be based on a previous distinction of constituent elements within it as attempted in the earlier analysis of particular force phenomena. Having distinguished spatial zones in the profiles of such forces as they appear in our phenomenal body, we have to vary the relation of these zones imaginatively or even to omit them. This might lead to such insights as: essentially force is extended over an area; essentially it has intensity; essentially it can increase and decrease; essentially, it can never reach an absolute maximum.

β. Essential relations between several essences are established by the procedure of imaginative variation too. Keeping one essence constant we try to combine it with various other essences, leaving off some of its associates, substituting others for them, or adding essences not hitherto encountered together with them. Wherever the omission or substitution of associated essences proves impossible, we diagnose an essential necessity; where they prove at least compatible with one another, an essential possibility; where they repel each other, an essential impossibility. The stock example of such a relationship is that between the essences color and extension. Color in this case proves to be inseparable from extension, which goes to show that color is essentially linked up with extension. What is as a rule not sufficiently realized is that the converse does not hold: Extension can very well be imagined without color, for instance in the case of a transparent medium. Hence extension is essentially possible without color, and color is not required by it. This example also brings out that essential connections are by no means always symmetrical. Yet in any case it is always the essential nature of the essences in relation to each other which determines their essential relationships.

While the essential relationships within one essence remind one of analytical knowledge, those among several essences suggest the idea of synthetic knowledge. However, here again it should be remembered that we are not concerned with propositions or with knowledge, but with their ontic referents. Consequently, what is involved is not what is or is not "included" in a concept, but in its referent. Thus, the whole distinction as applied to essential relationships is at best misleading. The question at issue is whether or not several essences stand in relationships not contained in either of them alone, but entailed by them jointly. Again, these relationships are discovered best by the attempt to vary in imagination the components of the relationship. The fact that the relation between several essences is determined by their joint essences shows at the same time that they are nothing isolated, but that they belong essentially to contexts from which they can only be cut out artificially. Color and extension are not separate essences but are inserted into a wider pattern of encompassing essential relationships of essences.

* * *

What is the logical and epistemological foundation for such insights into essential relations, whether internal or external? How are they possible? The fact that even essential insights are based on the intuiting of particulars may suggest that this is simply a case of empirical induction. However, induction from private or shared experiences, which is essentially limited and particularly so in the case of the few sample cases on which essential insights are based, could never yield the generality and necessity which are the earmarks of the insights under consideration. This fact makes it plain that essential insight is related to the much vaunted and taunted a priori knowledge, and particularly to its synthetic variety. While the expression "a priori" has been openly, and perhaps a little too freely, used to label insights into essential relationships, at least two features should be noted which are usually not ascribed to a priori knowledge:

α. Phenomenological a priori insight refers to phenomena which are known to us only from experience, taking this term not only in the traditional but in the phenomenologically enlarged sense. Had not experience already acquainted us with both color and extension, we could not arrive at any a priori insight into their essential relationships. A priori insight in this sense is therefore a type of experience, but an experience which gives us structural understanding of the linkage between the phenomena to such a degree that we can read off one phenomenon from the other without waiting for an indefinite number of repetitions.

β. Such insight cannot be obtained by mere "thinking" or reasoning in the sense of non-intuitive operations. It requires the type of non-sensuous intuition which Husserl called "categorial intuition." [1] Furthermore, in order to achieve such insights, we have to resort to our "free imagination," an imagination which, to be sure, has to proceed in a highly systematic fashion. Nevertheless, a priori insights into essential relationships are anything but merely logical operations. They have to utilize experience and intuitive procedures in conjunction. Yet they are not mere a priori intuitions in Kant's sense either, since they also have to appeal to the imagination. Thus insight into essential

---

[1] W. E. Johnson's substantially identical conception of "intuitive induction" (*Logic*, Part II, Chapter VIII) was not made public until 1922.

relationships is clearly an operation *sui generis*. It is also an operation which has its characteristic pitfalls. Hasty generalization occurs even in the area of essential insights. Phenomenologists like Scheler and Sartre may well have failed to carry out the imaginative variation of essences as systematically and patiently as Husserl had prescribed before making their often all too sweeping assertions about essential connections among phenomena.

EXAMPLE: The case of the force phenomenon allows for a number of essential insights into its relation to other essences. For one thing, force, like color, cannot·subsist by itself. It inheres essentially in a "carrier," which is filled or animated by it, as it were. For instance, in the case of bodily force such a carrier is an arm poised for action or launching into motion or hit by a foreign force. Hence force differs fundamentally from what is technically called a substance, i.e., an entity that can be conceived in and by itself. However, this does not mean that force is a mere stationary property like color. One of its essential characteristics is that it is not self-contained. It reaches in a peculiar sense beyond itself; it is essentially "transitive" or aggressive. Hence it is oriented toward other objects which it encounters. It would not be safe, however, to assert that every force acts essentially as a cause of effects beyond itself, or to identify a force with a cause. Premature assertions to this effect have actually interfered with the proper intuitive apprehension of force in itself. All that can be safely asserted is that forces tend to "spill over" and to radiate into their vicinity, and even that they *tend* to become causal in relation to objects against which they are exerted.

4. Watching Modes of Appearing

Phenomenology is the systematic exploration of the phenomena not only in the sense of *what* appears, whether particulars or general essences, but also of the *way* in which things appear. To be sure, not all phenomenologists have paid equal attention to this aspect of phenomenological research. But it has been prominent in Husserl's phenomenological work, beginning with the *Logische Untersuchungen*. Here the studies of intentional acts laid particular emphasis on the ways of appearance (*Erscheinungsweisen*) of the intentional objects. Obviously the contrast between the appearance and what appears, as implied in this connection, is not that between appearance and a reality which may actually be an unknowable thing-in-itself. What is involved is merely the way in which an object which is by no means beyond our range of knowledge presents itself to us. These ways of appearing are usually overlooked in our preoccupation with what appears.

One may wonder about the significance of such a special study of the modes of givenness. The most obvious answer is that genuine philosophy, and not only phenomenology, has no reason and no right to ignore any authentic phenomenon, whatever actual or potential use its knowledge may have. But there is also definite reason to believe that a conscientious study of the ways of givenness can throw light on certain problems of epistemology. Thus the distinction between different types and layers of givenness can be of considerable help in clarifying questions of direct or indirect verification.

There are actually at least three different senses of appearance which a careful study of the modes of givenness must distinguish, and which even phenomenologists have not always kept apart sufficiently:

α. The side or aspect of the given object from which we know the object as a whole. Thus what we are given of a solid and opaque cube is only its front (or top) and possibly one or two of its other sides, while its back and a minimum of two and a maximum of four sides of it are hidden from us. And this is so, not merely as a matter of empirical fact and generalization, but for essential reasons. Nevertheless, it is not only the sides that are given. For they are given as sides of a single cube with "empty lots" for the missing sides. Consequently the cube cannot be reduced to a mere series of lateral phenomena, as phenomenalism seems to think. *In* them and *through* them the cube appears as an encompassing structure, in which they have their definite places. In other words, the sides of the cube are transparent to the extent of presenting us with an identical solid object in which they are embedded, as it were.

β. The appearance of the object may be the perspectively

"deformed" or slanted view which the sides offer to the perceiver – something for which Husserl used the expression "*Abschattung*," perhaps best rendered as "perspective shading-off." Thus, any one of the appearing sides of the cube, except the one facing us head-on, is shaded off into a trapezoid, which nevertheless is transparent, as it were, toward the square shape of the side of which it constitutes the perspective aspect. Hence, far from being misleading as to the real size and shape of the object represented, such perspective deformations are the very means by which the identical size and shape of the object are maintained.

Spatial shadings-off are by no means the only kind of such perspective modifications of the "appearance" of the object. As the very name "shading" suggests, the primary modifications occur in the realm of lighting and color. The identical color of an object presents itself with different color in different lighting. As David Katz has shown, the same color appears differently under direct and indirect or artificial light, in the bright sun and in the shade. Yet these different "perspectives" are appearances of the same color. And the same shape can present itself through very different perspectives, such as sight and touch. It requires a special kind of reflection, practiced for instance by the draftsman or painter in perspective art, which focusses particularly on these appearances.

γ. Different from this type of appearance are what may be called modes of clarity. The same object, appearing with the same sides and in the same perspective, may still be given with very different degrees of clarity and distinctness. This applies particularly to the peripheral areas of our phenomenal field, where fringes and halos surround the focal section of our perception. Here something comparable to a haze or a veil intervenes between what appears and the perceiver. It quite clearly does not attach to the appearing object itself, but is connected with our own perception of it. Usually, at least, we know very well how to distinguish between an indistinct object like a smudge and a distinct object given through a haze. We may at times be uncertain where the indistinctness resides. But precisely such cases of doubt bring out the difference in principle. Appearances in this sense have been of particular interest to impressionist painters. By contrast, styles like post-impressionism and "magic realism" seem to have made a special point of suppressing this whole dimension of appearance in favor of the absolute transparency and lucidity of the medium between appearing object and perceiver.

EXAMPLE: Force, too, can be given in several such modes of appearance. It can even display different sides, as it were. Thus when we meet a force "head-on" or have a "narrow brush" with it, force appears from a different side than when we are "behind it," for instance in releasing it or watching it laterally. Not all these sides give us an equally good idea of the whole. But through all of them the pervading core of the dynamic directional agency "force" is manifested.

Besides, force can appear through various perspective shadings, dependent on the position of the perceiver. It appears different from the side of the agent and from that of the patient. It can be perceived not only through visual but also through acoustic, through tactile and kinesthetic aspects. Seeing an accelerated motion suggests it perhaps most strikingly. So do trails left by a moving body in its wake. Similarly, vibrations or increasing and decreasing noises and sounds create particularly vivid impressions of force. Pressures and felt strains, while not coinciding with the experience of force, can nevertheless convey it, particularly if they are increasing or decreasing. But the sensation of pressure alone leaves it still undecided on which side of it the force resides. In the case of the experience of force in one's own body, the most telling experiences are those tactile ones usually lumped together under the label "kinaesthetic." Yet they too are by no means identical with force phenomena. Only under specific conditions, which need further determination, do such sensations of spatial dislocation also have dynamic character.

Finally, force phenomena appear with various indexes of clarity. Very slow movements like those in the starry sky carry hardly any clear suggestions of force, as the motions of rockets do. The uncertainty of relative motions, even of the accelerated motion of two railroad cars with regard to each other, leaves also the phenomenon of force in a strange twilight of indistinctness or reversibility. And there are the usual threshold problems, where the lack of clarity is due either to the indistinctness of the objective boundary or to that of our perception.

5. Exploring the Constitution of Phenomena in Consciousness

"Constitution" is one of the key terms in Husserl's phenomenology, particularly in its developed phase. But as we have seen, its meaning has remained fluid. It became a basic concept for his transcendental idealism with its idea that the objects of our consciousness were the "achievements" of constituting acts. For the present purpose I shall interpret the term in a less demanding sense and confine myself to the reflexive use of the verb according to which objects "constitute themselves" in our consciousness. Such a conception does not involve an epistemological commitment. Thus constitutional exploration consists for us merely in determining the way in which a phenomenon establishes itself and takes shape in our consciousness. Tracing the stages of such a "crystallization" does not mean, however, a psychological, and especially not a factual, case study of what actually happens to concrete individuals. The purpose of such a study is the determination of the typical structure of a constitution in consciousness by means of an analysis of the essential sequence of its steps.

A first illustration of such a constitution can be the experience of getting oriented in a new city, whose "picture" gradually takes shape in our mind. Having arrived at night and having lost all our bearings in retiring to our quarters, with only a very confused idea as to how we got there, we may find ourselves awaking in a strange bed with the task of building up a new space pattern, thus far quite unrelated to our previous life spaces. This is not the place to pursue the way in which this space is gradually constituted and developed, until finally it is reintegrated somehow into the pattern of the world we had left behind, and which we still carry with us. Perhaps the most important process here is how the "empty lots" of our new spatial pattern are more and more "built up" by corridors, stairs, streets, and houses that establish themselves more or less firmly until the pattern gets sedimented, usually after a good many upsets, which break up the first outlines as a result of disorientations, "getting lost," and similar adventures.

Comparable cases of "self-constitution" of the world occur, for instance, in the way in which the personality of someone we meet takes shape in our mind, beginning with our first impressions, with the observations of his movements, followed by the hearing of his voice, etc. More complex and significant examples could be given from our perception of social phenomena.

The fact that this constitution is normally "spontaneous" and "passive" does not preclude the possibility of an active constitution in the wake of explicit reflections and attempts to integrate unrelated phenomena. The case when, after complete disorientation, we reorient ourselves with considerable effort so that our present space pattern is reincorporated into our previous world, may give a first indication of what such a deliberate constructive constitution of a phenomenal field may mean.

But regardless of whether or not such a constitution is under our conscious control, there is a definite pattern in its development. Its building stones are perceptions of the more elementary kind. These fall into larger patterns, as our perceptions enlarge and enter into relationships with other perceptions and with our acquired fund of perceptual patterns. This is not merely a matter of chance associations. For this integration follows structural "laws." There is a definite affinity between them and the laws of "good gestalt." Also they show the characteristic features of essential relationships as these were characterized above.

EXAMPLE: "Phenomenological constitution" in the case of force phenomena means primarily watching the way in which our perceptions of non-dynamic objects acquire the additional character of force. Thus, watching experiences in parts of our body that can be activated, we find the latter normally without any dynamic "charge." We are simply aware of them as "locations" in our body in which we happen to be present. This character changes as soon as we get ready for action. A certain tenseness, an "alert" spreads over this area, as it moves into the focus of our body consciousness. But even then there need not be any dynamic "charge." It is mostly in connection with the feeling of the "swelling" of a specific limb and with slight trial movements that the phenomenon of force begins to crystallize as something more than tension and "alert." Force becomes actualized as we initiate a movement thus prepared for. In the experience of meeting and overcoming resistances of various degrees the phenomenon of exerted force establishes itself with even more clarity and distinctness.

Force as undergone from the outside constitutes itself a little differently. Regardless of whether it hits us by surprise or upon preceding expectation, we usually notice a sudden pressure sensation, possibly painful, combined with a displacement or deformation, or a tendency thereto, in the part of our body under attack. Soon our entire body is invaded and, as it were, sucked into the current of the invading force. As it is carried along, it even tends to impart this foreign force to other parts, unless the force is so weak that it is absorbed. What is characteristic of the experience of this particular manifestation of force is that it does not involve any experience of tension. The experience may be just as pronounced when we put up some feeble surprised resistance as when we are simply carried away by a force which "lifts us off the ground."

6. Suspending Belief in Existence

To mention the phenomenological reduction almost at the end rather than at the very start of my account of the phenomeno-logical method must appear to be a flagrant violation of Husserl's unequivocal instructions, for whom the reduction had become increasingly the master key to phenomenology. One defence for this manifest "heresy" can be taken from the fact that the phenomenological reduction has never been common ground for all those who have otherwise aligned themselves with the Pheno-menological Movement. Besides, even those who pay lip service to the reduction do not always practice it, at least not explicitly. Furthermore, it can be argued that Husserl himself was able to carry out some of his best phenomenological analyses in the later parts of the *Logische Untersuchungen* without appealing to this method, which he did not announce until much later. Finally, Husserl himself never succeeded in formulating the meaning and the function of the phenomenological reduction in an unambiguous and definitive fashion, not even in a way that satisfied him personally. Under these circumstances the safest course would seem to consist in stating the mimimum meaning of the reduction, followed by a brief hint about its development and a final consideration of its significance for other phases of the phenomenological method.

Husserl himself associated the original and basic meaning of the reduction with the mathematical operation of bracketing (*Einklammerung*). The underlying idea of this metaphor is that we are to detach the phenomena of our every day experience from the context of our naive or natural living, while preserving their content as fully and as purely as possible. The actual procedure of this detachment consists in suspending judgment as to the existence or non-existence of this content. This by no means implies that we deny or even doubt its existence to the extent of writing it off, as Descartes had done. Eventually we could, and, I might even add, we should, return to the question of existence, although Husserl himself never did so explicitly after developing his transcendental idealism. To this negative or "bracketing" aspect of the reduction corresponds as its positive complement the possibility of concentrating exclusively on the non-existential or essential content, the "what," of the phenomena. It is in connection with its positive aspect that Husserl expected the phenomenological reduction to open up entirely new dimensions for phenomenological research.

If suspension of belief in this sense were all that is meant by the phenomenological reduction, Husserl's amazing claims for this part of his method would hardly be comprehensible. In Chapter III, where I dealt with the development of Husserl's philosophy, I have tried to determine at least some additional features of this step which are not described explicitly in his initial interpretation. They include the systematic cancellation of all those acts by which consciousness supposedly constitutes the phenomena. Quite apart from the implied assumption that there are such acts, which can hardly be taken for granted, any further consideration of this extension of the phenomenological reduction would be inadvisable in the present context.[1]

Considering these circumstances, what can be the function and the possible value of the phenomenological reduction, understood

---

[1] For a condensed and suggestive formulation of these additional aspects see Van Breda, H. L., "Notes sur réduction et authenticité d'après Husserl" in *Phénoménologie-Existence* (Paris, Colin, 1953), pp. 7–9.

in the sense of a mere suspension of existential beliefs? Its most obvious use would seem to be that it facilitates genuine intuiting, analyzing, and describing of the given. For it frees us from our usual preoccupation with "solid reality," which makes us brush aside what is "merely in our imagination" or "by convention only" as unworthy of our attention. This does not mean that suspension of existential beliefs is indispensable for an unbiased stock-taking of our phenomena. What is all-important in phenomenology is that we consider all the data, real or unreal or doubtful, as having equal rights, and investigate them without fear or favor. The reduction will help us to do justice to all of them, especially to those which are under the handicap of initial suspicion as to their existential claims.

The same plea can be made for the reduction in the case of the general essences, endangered as they are by the suspicions which the nominalists and positivists have directed against such Platonic "hypostatizations." Here too the suspension of the whole question of being, including that of a possible ideal being of these entities, is certainly the best preparation for an unprejudiced exploration of their structures and essential relationships. However, this does not mean that the explicit performance of the reduction is a necessary condition for the practice of essential intuition. Thus mathematics as the main "eidetic" science seems to have flourished without it. In fact, Husserl himself thought that the "eidetic reduction" or idealising abstraction provides an adequate foundation for it without the added step of the phenomenological reduction, the latter being needed only for a final "transcendental" appraisal of the eidetic sciences.

Watching modes of appearance is again a step in which the suspension of existential beliefs can aid the phenomenologist by diverting his attention from his usual preoccupation with what appears to the consideration of how it appears. Treating cases of "real" and "unreal" objects on the same level can restore the balance by giving to all these cases equal attention. On the other hand, perspective drawing shows that an unbiased study of the appearances is possible without explicit performance of the reduction, in fact that it can coincide with the interest in coming as close as possible to, and giving the semblance of reality to, the perspectively rendered object.

Constitutional studies may also benefit from not being diverted immediately by the question of whether the object that constitutes itself in our consciousness does or does not enjoy autonomous existence. In fact, only if we study our constituting acts without any such preoccupation can we prepare an answer to the question of how much our consciousness may have contributed toward the constitution of the phenomena. Here Husserl's insistence on the necessity of prior reduction may be singularly pertinent.

·The result of this brief survey would seem to be that the phenomenological reduction, while a distinct aid to all the steps which I have distinguished, is still not indispensable for the investigator who is already immune to the possible distractions of the existential bias. The fact that even in Husserl's own concrete phenomenological analyses, other than those in the first volume of his *Ideen*, the performance of the reduction is implied or presupposed rather than explicitly described would seem to confirm this verdict.

Besides, it must not be overlooked that in certain contexts the suspension of the question of existence has its definite dangers. Reductive phenomenology has often been taken to task for its preoccupation with essences to the detriment of questions of existence. Consequently it has been declared unfit to carry out an ontological exploration of "being," and especially unfit to analyze "existence" taken in the sense of the "being" of man, the thing-in-being whose whole enterprise is "concerned about Being." To me this charge seems to be exaggerated. For even after the suspension of belief in the existence of the world, which forms the content of our "intentional" life, we do not cease to study the acts of believing or the character of existence as believed by these acts. Even then there is no reason against, and in fact every reason for, a phenomenology of our beliefs in reality, and, as part of it, the study of the meaning of reality as such. Likewise, there is nothing in the phenomenological reduction as such which forbids it to take account of man's concern about being as central to his essence.

However, the performance of the suspension becomes hazardous and can indeed falsify the approach to the phenomena when this temporary suspension of belief hardens into a cancellation and unnoticeably leads to the permanent neglect of the suspended question. Carrying out the reduction may supply us with all the evidence needed to answer this question. But the reduction cannot dispense us from returning to it. Reductive phenomenology is no substitute for epistemology. Nor can it ultimately become a substitute for metaphysics. There is no escape from the seriousness and persistence of the questions of reality and of being.

EXAMPLE: The case of the force phenomenon may show the merits of a limited phenomenological suspension more vividly than many other examples. For in this case the suspicion that the whole conception is a mere "fiction," a sheer anthropomorphism, has worked havoc with the phenomena and has done serious damage even to the cause of an unprejudiced empiricism. To methodically keep out the question of the existential status of this phenomenon may be the only way in which we can clarify the meaning of such terms and prepare the ground for their intuitive verification. Otherwise the phenomenon of force does not call for any specific handling of the existential suspension. But we should perhaps realize that phrases like "mobilizing our forces" are particularly apt to bring on the charge of "mythology." What, after all, can we find when we dissect a part of our body readied for action? But suppose it to be a myth. What the suspension permits and asks us to do is to turn our full sympathetic attention to this "myth" and let us watch and describe it, i.e., give a faithful account of what we experience in our lived body, and what place the phenomenon of force has in its context. The reduction frees us for a job that has to be done, without our being hamstrung by epistemological doubts or subjected to the sneers at the "scientific" impossibility of force phenomena.

7. Interpreting Concealed Meanings

It is only with considerable hesitation that I introduce the possibility of a final step in the phenomenological procedure. This hesitation is due not only to the fact that Husserl never encouraged it, although he does not seem to have rejected it explicitly, but that very little has been done to elucidate the nature of the method employed.[1] Its fullest and most explicit demonstration is still to be found in Heidegger's *Sein und Zeit*.

Nevertheless, the influence of Heidegger's hermeneutic phenomenology and its modified application by Sartre and Merleau-Ponty make it desirable to spell out as far as possible what a hermeneutic phenomenology may mean and what it might add to the preceding steps. Needless to say, Heidegger himself does not conceive of it as such an additional step, especially since he does not even mention the preceding steps explicitly; he implies that they are dispensable, if not downright misleading, as is, in his eyes, Husserl's phenomenological reduction.

Hermeneutics is an attempt to interpret the "sense" of certain phenomena. To be sure, even pre-hermeneutic or "descriptive" phenomenology has not been unconcerned about meanings. In fact, the whole study of intentional structures consisted largely in an interpretative analysis and description of the meanings of our conscious acts. For not only our purposive behavior but our whole cognitive and emotional life, as phenomenology sees it, is shot through with meaning and meaningful intentions. No description can leave them out, even though it may refrain from accepting them at face value. Thus hermeneutic phenomenology must aim at something different and more ambitious: its goal is the discovery of meanings which are not immediately manifest to our intuiting, analyzing, and describing. Hence the interpreter has to go beyond what is directly given. In attempting this, he has to use the given as a clue for meanings which are not given, or at least not explicitly given. One might suspect that such an enterprise amounts to the kind of explanatory hypotheses which descriptive phenomenology had set out to abolish, and that it therefore implies a complete abandonment of phenomenological principles. In order to defend its phenomenological right one would have to maintain that hermeneutic interpretation is a matter not of mere constructive inference but of an unveiling of hidden meanings, or at most of an intuitive verification of anticipations about the less accessible layers of the phenomena, layers which can be uncovered, although they are not immediately manifest.

[1] For a lucid critical discussion see Harald Delius, "Descriptive Interpretation," *PPR* XIII (1953), 305–323.

Heidegger's "analytics" of human being (*Dasein*) and Sartre's existential psychoanalysis provide the main examples of such interpretations. Heidegger takes certain structures of human being, such as the fundamental moods, as indications (*Anzeichen*) for a certain meaning which is clearly not immediately manifest, namely "concern" (*Sorge*) about being and ultimately being-toward-death (*Sein-zum-Tode*). This interpretation is not advanced in the spirit of hypothesis with the possibility of subsequent confirmation or infirmation. What is so frustrating about Heidegger's interpretations is their apodictic tone, which does not seem to allow for any alternatives or for critical verification. The only meaningful explanation for this fact would seem to be that Heidegger merely reports what, as a result of his own unveiling interpretations, has revealed itself to him as the unquestionable verdict of the phenomena themselves, once they had been subjected to his interpretative scrutiny. – A similar claim would have to be made for Sartre's analysis of man's existential projects. For Sartre too, in referring to the fundamental choices of human beings, can appeal only to whatever intuitive self-evidence such interpretations may ultimately display as the result of the intensification and deepening of intuition which his "deciphering" of the phenomena demands.

How far can such phenomenological interpretation expect to go? Clearly only as far as there are meanings and, to be sure, meanings capable and in need of such deciphering interpretation. To Heidegger, the primary field for such interpretation seemed to be human existence. However, Sartre's "psychoanalysis of matter" suggests that, at least to as intrepid a pioneer as he is, even "matter" reveals its more or less insidious meanings. And I gather that even Heidegger now seems to be in touch with "openings" of being which reveal to him a cosmic sense about which at this stage we are still kept in suspense, especially since it seems to be no longer in our power to make "Being" reveal it, as the initiative for such revelation has shifted to "Being" itself.

What can an uncommitted phenomenologist say at this stage in favor of a hermeneutic addition to phenomenology? There is certainly reason to admit that not all meanings of human experience and behavior are immediately accessible. Phenomenology has always been aware of this and has even emphasized the fact that the focal areas of clarity in our picture of the world are surrounded by halos of vagueness and indefiniteness. And some of these halos are not only temporary and accidental but essential, founded on the very structure of such knowledge. The question is whether apart from explanatory hypotheses we have means of extending our access to hidden meanings, and in particular whether phenomenology can put at our disposal a new tool for widening our access to phenomena which are normally beyond our immediate reach, without our abandoning all standards of phenomenological discipline and rigor. Thus far the examples of such extensions are not very encouraging. In any case, not until the anticipations of hermeneutics can be followed up by an elucidation which will turn the full light of intuitive clarity upon them is there much hope for a genuine expansion of the scope of "descriptive" phenomenology. Short of this we will have to fall back on the standard method for the indirect verification of hypotheses as practiced in the inductive sciences. In any event, a major effort will have to be made to make the penetrating and often startling interpretations of the hermeneutic phenomenologists more accessible to the verifying counter-checks of sympathetic but critical fellow phenomenologists.

In this sense and to this extent we should keep the doors open for a possible enrichment of descriptive phenomenology. There is, besides, good reason to wish its hermeneutic extension every possible success. There has been understandable disillusionment and impatience with the older phenomenology on the score that, in its descriptive purism, it had turned its back on the problems of human existence and man's situation in an enigmatic cosmos. Any meanings which such an existence and such a cosmos may contain are hardly on the surface. Our best though dubious hope would seem to lie in a method which uses our available resources to their limit. One cannot forbid man, phenomenologist or not, to search for the best available answer to inescapable questions, be it only the answer that there is none. Only he should be aware that what he may gain in depth, he is likely to lose in compelling clarity. Hermeneutic phenomenology has at least the right to try. But such a try, if unsupported by further credentials, should hardly sail under the flag of phenomenological "science." Perhaps it should not even sail under the flag of philosophy. Actually, this seems to be Heidegger's own conclusion, although for rather different reasons.

EXAMPLE: What could a hermeneutic interpretation contribute to a phenomenology of force? Any such attempt would clearly depend on the assumption that force as we experience it contains meanings which allow for and demand interpretative reading. This would certainly be a highly speculative assumption, which only a metaphysics on the scale of Leibniz or Schopenhauer could encourage. Nevertheless it might be legitimate to engage in considerations on a more limited scale in connection with the phenomena of force as experienced in our own body. Could there be any underlying sense in the possession and use of such forces by an "incarnated" human existence? Certainly such a being as man makes use of the forces which are at his disposal. To him, force is more than a brute fact. It gives him some measure of control over an area of the world, however limited. On the biological plane at least, force has a definite function. This may give an indication of the possibility that even in the framework of bodily existence force plays a certain role and has a meaning to which we have no immediate access. But I would hesitate to make any more concrete suggestions as to the way in which force, and particularly our use of it, can have specific meanings which only a hermeneutic interpretation can reveal. Let it suffice to have suggested that there is scope and reason to look for deeper and hidden meanings wherever the conscious meanings do not adequately account for a phenomenon in our experience and for the total pattern in which it occurs. But such a suggestion does not mean that we can regard the rights of hermeneutics as established. For it rests on assumptions which can be justified phenomenologically only by the ultimate intuitive verification of our hermeneutic anticipations of "sense."

D. IN CONCLUSION

At this stage the reader is entitled to an answer to the obvious question: What , if anything, is original about the phenomenological method, as it has been presented above? What contributions, if any, can it make that are not made equally well or better by other methods?

I shall attempt to answer these questions by way of a quick review of the main steps of the phenomenological method as set forth above.

Investigating particular phenomena by intuitive, analytic, and descriptive means is something which has been undertaken with considerable success by other approaches, philosophical, scientific, and even artistic. If there is anything distinctive about the phenomenological approach to this task, it has to be found in its deliberateness and in its conscious challenge to the reductionism of Occam's razor.

Investigating general essences can likewise be found in retrospect in any number of philosophic methods, even though the name "essence" does not always occur in this connection. Actually phenomenologists take a good many examples of supposed insights into essences from the pre-phenomenological literature. Here again phenomenology has done little but to make this search more conscious and more determined. The same may be said about apprehending essential relationships.

It is at the stage of the methodical investigating of the modes of appearance that we reach one of the more original steps in the phenomenological procedure. Prior to the advent of phenomenology, little if any explicit attention had been paid to the variety of modes in which phenomena are given us and the greater or lesser adequacy with which we perceive them.

There is also something essentially new about the study of the stages by which phenomena establish themselves in our consciousness and gradually crystallize before our inner eye. Psychology may have paved the way for such studies, and there is plenty of material on which we can draw, for instance in imaginative literature. But work of a more systematic kind needs to be done by an approach like the phenomenological.

There are precedents for the phenomenological suspension of belief in existence, and they are even suggested by Husserl's terminological allusion to the *epoché* of the Sceptics. This is another case in which the claim to originality would have to rest on the new interpretation and the methical utilization of this step.

As far as the hermeneutic interpretation of concealed meanings can be considered a genuine element of the phenomenological method, it has probably less claim to originality than most of the preceding steps. Quite apart from the methods of psychoanalysis, to which the advocates of this method often appeal, it has antecedents among many of the "divining" methods of the intuitive types of metaphysics.

Thus phenomenology, taken piecemeal, has certainly no claim to be considered as a completely original approach. Some of its steps, notably the watching of modes of appearance and the exploration of the constitution of the phenomena in our consciousness, may qualify as quite new, but it is by no means sure that phenomenology has made its most notable contributions on these particular levels. It is much easier to identify definite contributions in areas where phenomenology shares at least some of its tools with other approaches.

However, the decisive question is whether the phenomenological method considered as a whole constitutes a new and original approach. But this question presupposes that the several steps of this method which I distinguished above still make up a whole based on a unifying idea. Can this be defended? Eventually this question will have to be faced.

The affirmative answer can point first of all to certain negative characteristics: On all levels the phenomenological approach is opposed to explanatory hypotheses; it confines itself to the direct evidence of intuitive seeing. A more positive character of the phenomenological approach is that it constitutes a determined attempt to enrich the world of our experience by bringing out hitherto neglected aspects of this experience. Besides, there may be an even deeper motive behind such an omnivorous desire for variety. It might be called: reverence for the phenomena. William James once characterized metaphysics as "an unusually obstinate attempt to think clearly and consistently." Exploiting and expanding this definition, one might describe the underlying unity of the phenomenological procedures as the unusually obstinate attempt to look at the phenomena and to remain faithful to them before even thinking about them.

Ultimately the originality of the phenomenological approach as a whole is based on the dominating influence of this motive.

What distinguishes phenomenology from other methods is not so much any particular step it develops or adds to them but the spirit of philosophical reverence as the first and foremost norm of the philosophical enterprise. The violation of this norm in an age of reductionism constituted the *raison d'être* for phenomenology at the time of its birth. Its continued importance will depend on the extent to which this spirit permeates other philosophies.

SURVEY OF THE DEVELOPMENT OF THE PHENOMENOLOGICAL MOVEMENT IN GERMANY

CHART I

	Husserl	Pfänder	Scheler	Heidegger	Nic. Hartmann	Others	Important Events
1900	*Logische Untersuchungen* I	*Phänomenologie des Wollens*	Habilitation in JENA				
1901	*Log. Unt.* II Professor in GÖTTINGEN	Habilitation in MUNICH	Meets Husserl				
1902							Daubert visits Husserl
1903							
1904		*Einführung in die Psychologie*					Husserl in Munich
1905							Seefeld meeting
1906			Transfers to MUNICH				
1907	Lectures on "Die Idee der Phänomenologie"					Geiger's habil. in MUNICH	
1908							
1909					Habil. in MARBURG	Reinach's habil. in GÖTTINGEN	
1910			Leaves MUNICH				
1911	"Philosophie als strenge Wissenschaft"		"Über Ressentiment"				

CHART I (con't)

Year							Jahrbuch
1912							
1913	*Ideen I*	*Psychologie der Gesin-nungen*	*Formalismus Phänomenologie der Sympathie-gefühle*			Geiger's *Phäno-menologie des ästhetischen Genusses* Reinach's *Apriorische Grundlagen* .... Jaspers' *Allgemeine Psychopathologie*	*Jahrbuch für Philos. und phän. Forschung I*
1914							
1915				Habil. in FREIBURG			
1916	FREIBURG				*Duns Scotus*		
1917						† Reinach	*Jahrbuch II, III*
1918							
1919			Professor in COLOGNE				
1920							
1922		*Logik*	*Vom Ewigen im Menschen*	*Metaphysik der Erkenntnis*			*Jahrbuch IV*
1922							*Jahrbuch V*
1923	London Lectures			Professor in MARBURG		Geiger in GÖTTINGEN	*Jahrbuch VI*
1924		Visits France	*Ethik*				
1925			Transfers to COLOGNE				*Jahrbuch VII*

CHART I (con't)

Year	Husserl	Pfänder	Scheler	Heidegger	N. Hartmann	Others	Important Events
1926			*Die Wissensformen*				
1927			*Die Stellung des Menschen*	*Sein und Zeit*			*Jahrbuch VIII*
1928	Retirement		Transfers to FRANKFURT † May 19	Transfers to FREIBURG			*Jahrbuch IX*
1929	Paris lectures *Formale und transzendentale Logik*			*Kant und das Problem der Metaphysik*			*Jahrbuch X* *Festschrift Husserl*
1930	*Nachwort zu Ideen I*			*Was ist Metaphysik?*			*Jahrbuch XI*
1931	*Méditations cartésiennes*				Transfers to BERLIN		
1932							
1933	Fink-Husserl article in *Kantstudien*	*Die Seele des Menschen*	*Nachlass I*		*Das Problem des geistigen Seins*		
1934						Geiger at Vassar	
1935					*Grundlegung der Ontologie*		
1936	*Die Krisis der europäischen Wissenschaften*			*Hölderlin u.d. Wesen d. Dichtung*			
1937						† Geiger	

CHART I (con't)

Year				
1938	† April 26		*Möglichkeit und Wirklichkeit*	Husserl's papers transferred to Louvain by Van Breda
1939		*Erfahrung und Urteil*		
1940	† March 20		*Aufbau der realen Welt*	
1941				
1943		*Wesen der Wahrheit*		
1945			Transfers to GÖTTINGEN	
1947		"Brief über den Humanismus"		
1950	*Husserliana I–III*	*Holzwege*	*Philosophie der Natur* † October 9	
1951				Husserl Archives in Cologne
1952	*Husserliana IV, V*			
1953		*Einführung in die Metaphysik*	*Ästhetik*	
1954	*Husserliana VI*	*Was heisst Denken?*		
1955				
1956	*Husserliana VII*	*Der Satz vom Grund*	Colloquy at Krefeld	
1957				
1958	*Husserliana VIII*			

CHART II

SURVEY OF THE DEVELOPMENT OF THE PHENOMENOLOGICAL MOVEMENT IN FRANCE

	BOOKS AND ARTICLES	TRANSLATIONS	IMPORTANT EVENTS
1910	Noël, "Les Frontières de la logique"		
1911	Delbos, "Husserl: Sa critique du psychologisme"		
1912–18			
1919			Nouvelle École (de théologie protestante) de Strasbourg
1920			Koyré settles in Paris
1924			Scheler in Pontigny and Paris
1925			
1926	Hering, *Phénoménologie et philosophie religieuse*; Groethuysen, *Introduction à la philosophie allemande*; Shestov, "Memento mori"		Scheler in Paris
1927	Marcel, *Journal Métaphysique*		
1928	Gurvitch, "La philosophie phénoméno-logique"	Scheler, *La Nature de la sympathie*	Levinas in Freiburg
1929	Levinas, "Sur les Ideen de Husserl"		Husserl's lectures at the Sorbonne and in Strasbourg
1930	Gurvitch, *Les Tendances actuelles de la philosophie allemande*; Levinas, *La Théorie de l'intuition dans la phénoménologie de Husserl*		

CHART II (con't)

Year	Publications	Events
1931	Husserl, *Méditations cartésiennes* Heidegger, "De la Nature de la cause" —— "Qu'est ce que la métaphysique?"	Husserl Foreign Member of the Académie de France Beginning of the *Recherches Philosophiques*
1932		Société Thomiste discusses "La Phénoménologie" at Juvisy
1933	Minkowski, *Le Temps vécu*	Kojève begins lectures on Hegel's Phenomenology of the Spirit Sartre in Berlin
1934	Minkowski, "Esquisses phénoménologiques" Marcel, "Phénoménologie de l'avoir"	Gurwitsch and Landsberg in Paris
1935	Marcel, *Être et avoir*	
1936	Minkowski, *Vers une Cosmologie* Sartre, *L'Imagination* Sartre, "La Transcendance de l'égo" Scheler, *Le Sens de la souffrance*	
1937		
1938	Sartre, *La Nausée* Sartre, "La Structure intentionelle de l'image" Heidegger, *Essais*	Husserl Archives established at Louvain
1939	Sartre, *Esquisse d'une théorie des émotions* Hegel, *La Phénoménologie de l'esprit I*	
1940	Marcel, *Du Refus à l'invocation*	
1941	Berger, *Le Cogito dans la philosophie de Husserl* Hegel, *La Phénoménologie de l'esprit II*	
1942	Merleau-Ponty, *La Structure du comportement*	
1943	Sartre, *L'Être et le néant*	
1944	Polin, *La Création des valeurs*	

CHART II (con't)

	BOOKS AND ARTICLES	TRANSLATIONS	IMPORTANT EVENTS
1945	Merleau-Ponty, La Phénoménologie de la perception; Marcel, Homo viator		Beginning of Sartre's Les Temps modernes
1946	Sartre, L'Existentialisme est un humanisme		
1947	de Beauvoir, Pour une Morale de l'ambiguité		Beginning of Berger's Études philosophiques
1948	Merleau-Ponty, Sens et non-sens	Heidegger, De l'Essence de la vérité	
1949			Marcel's Gifford Lectures
1950	Ricoeur, Philosophie de la volonté I; Marcel, Le Mystère de l'être		Merleau-Ponty at the Sorbonne
1951		Husserl, Idées directrices pour une phénoménologie; Scheler, La Situation de l'homme	Colloque de Bruxelles
1952	Sartre, Saint Genet		Merleau-Ponty at the Collège de France
1953	Dufrenne, Phénoménologie de l'expérience esthétique	Heidegger, Kant et le problème de la métaphysique	
1954			
1955	Merleau-Ponty, Les Aventures de la dialectique	Husserl, La philosophie comme science rigoureuse; Scheler, Le formalisme en éthique	
1956			
1957		Husserl, Logique formelle et logique transcendentale	Ricoeur at the Sorbonne; Colloque de Royaumont

INDEX OF SUBJECTS

COMBINED WITH

A SELECTIVE GLOSSARY OF
PHENOMENOLOGICAL TERMS

Terms peculiar to the phenomenological literature or given special meanings in it are marked by asterisks and are followed by brief definitions. In view of the fact that most of the terms in need of such explanation are foreign and that there are few recognized English equivalents, they are mostly given in the original languages (except where they can be easily anglicized); in such cases the closest English literal synonym is also added. Cross references are given for some of the better known English equivalents.

In the case of Husserl's terminology several items have been included that do not occur in the text of this book. From Heidegger's and Sartre's technical vocabulary only a few key terms could be considered.

It should be understood that the definitions offered in the glossary are not meant to be technically accurate. Rarely if ever are they based on specific passages in the texts, although they were checked against them. My main purpose is to help the reader who approaches the subject for the first time. Hence I have tried as far as possible to use non-phenomenological terms in the definitions and to avoid chasing the user from definition to definition before he can obtain a sufficient grasp of the basic meanings. In the case of Husserl's usage the advanced reader, anxious about accuracy and finding out the full variety of the meanings of phenomenological terms, should consult Dorion Cairns's contributions to the *Dictionary of Philosophy* edited by Dagobert Runes (New York, Philosophical Library, 1942), where however only the following items have been printed:

Act-character, Actuality, Adequation, Analysis (Intentional), Apophantic, Appresentation, Attitude, Categorial, Cogito, Concept, Confused, Consciousness, Consequence-logic, Constitution, Distinctness, Doxa, Egological, Eidetic, Evidence, Explication, Expression, Formalization, Founded, Fulfilment, Intentionality, Positionality.

Cairns's *Guide for Translating Husserl* (also to be published in *Phaenomenologica*), while not containing technical definitions, should be a unique tool for finding the best English equivalents of difficult terms.

Maurice Natanson, who suggested the addition of a glossary, also recommended the inclusion of several items. Dorion Cairns, who gave me a detailed critical commentary after my first draft, should be credited with having prevented several misdirections and suggested many improvements, but should not be blamed for my final formulations.

* apodictic (HUSSERL): synonym for necessary, indubitable, and even infallible; applied not only to knowledge but also to objects known and to methods, 140, 302

* apophantics: the part of formal logic which deals with propositions, 96

aporetics (NICOLAI HARTMANN): the systematic study of the apories or impasses that result from the phenomenological exploration of the phenomena, 369, 376

appearance, see *Erscheinung*

* apriori: based on insight into essences and essential structures: at times applied to phenomena and their properties which are accessible to such insight, e.g., values, 199 ff., 202 ff., 209
— formal: based on merely structural characteristics of an object, disregarding material content such as color, 252 f.
— material: based on the specific content of an object, which has first to be given in experience, 253 ff.

* *Appräsentation*, appresentation: the indirect perceptual presentation of an object mediated through the direct presentation of another, e.g., of the rear through the frontal aspect, or of other minds through their bodies, 158 f.

* archaeology: HUSSERL's favorite name for phenomenology, 82

atheism, 34, 173, 309, 367, 471, 474, 525

attitude, see *Einstellung*

* *ausweisen*, show forth: act of exhibiting in which signitive (or empty) intentions are filled by the presentation of intuitive content; in the reflexive form also used for an object exhibiting itself to intuition

authenticity, see *Eigentlichkeit*

* Bad faith (*mauvaise foi*), see faith

behaviorism, 540 f.

* *Bewusstsein*, consciousness:
    (1) intentional act or state referring to objects
    (2) the stream of acts and states made up of such acts

body, see *Leib*

* bracketing, see *Einklammerung* and reduction, phenomenological

* Categorial intuition, see *Anschauung, kategoriale*
causality, 62f., 661f., 675, 684
coefficient of adversity (*coefficient d'adversité*): term introduced by GASTON BACHELARD and taken over by SARTRE to indicate the degree of resistance put up by the phenomena, 452, 490

* *cogito:* the Cartesian "I think," functioning in HUSSERL's phenomenology for the conscious acts of the ego which remain unaffected by the phenomenological reduction, 140ff., 407f., 479, 549ff.

* —, new or true (MERLEAU-PONTY): "there is consciousness", 549

* —, pre-reflective (SARTRE:) the consciousness (*conscience*) of which we are aware prior to thematic reflection without explicit knowledge (*connaissance*) about it, 483f.
concrete (Philosophy of the Concrete), 405, 427, 526

* *conscience,* as opposed to *connaissance* (SARTRE), see cogito, pre-reflective
consciousness, see *Bewusstsein*
conspective method (NICOLAI HARTMANN): the final stage in the ontological method, which synthesizes the findings of the descriptive-phenomenological and dialectical stages, 378f.

* constitution, phenomenological: the act by which an object is built up in consciousness; also what is so constituted 75, 109f., 146ff., 641, 688ff.
—, active and passive, 147
—, transcendental: constitution originating in transcendental consciousness, 146ff.
See also *Urkonstitution*

* *Dasein,* being there
   (a) EARLY PHENOMENOLOGY: opposed to *Sosein* (essence), equivalent to factual existence; see the contrast between thatness and whatness, 102f., 134
   (b) HEIDEGGER: man as the being which comprehends Being (*Seinsverständnis*), equivalent to SARTRE's *réalité humaine,* 285, 300

* *Daseinsanalyse* (BINSWANGER): analysis of man's being in the world, which, although inspired by HEIDEGGER's ontological analytics of *Dasein*, differs from it in its objective and in some results; used primarily in existential psychotherapy, 607

* *Deckung*, c o v e r i n g: relation of coincidence between several acts in which the objects meant by several intending acts fuse; example: an expectation and a subsequent fulfilling perception

* d e c i p h e r i n g (*déchiffrer*) (SARTRE): a method used in his existential psychoanalysis for the purpose of interpreting manifestations of existence from their underlying pre-reflective choices, 495 f.
d e s c r i p t i o n, 37 ff., 672 ff.

* d e s t r u c t i o n, p h e n o m e n o l o g i c a l (HEIDEGGER): method for breaking down the philosophical tradition in order to provide free access to the original phenomena, 300 f., 319 ff., 346

* d i f f e r e n c e, o n t o l o g i c a l (HEIDEGGER): distinction between *Sein* (Being) and *Seiendes* (t h i n g-i n-b e i n g), the former being the subject matter of ontology, the latter of metaphysics, 286, 322

* d i s c o n n e c t i o n, see r e d u c t i o n, p h e n o m e n o l o g i c a l

* *doxa:* belief or belief factor in such modifications of belief as doubt, surmise, or question, which modify the basic doxa (*Urdoxa*), 141

e g o (*ich*): the identical subject pole of several acts
— * t r a n s c e n d e n t a l: the ego which remains as an irreducible residue after having been subjected to the phenomenological reduction, 87, 140 f., 189, 465 f., 557 f., 630

* e g o l o g y (HUSSERL): the study of the ego and its types, especially the transcendental ego and its role in transcendental constitution, 140 f., 505, 630

* *eidos* (adjective: e i d e t i c): Plato's alternate term for Idea (Form), utilized by HUSSERL for designating universal essences, 134

* *epoché*, abstention: Greek term used by the ancient Sceptics for suspension of beliefs, by HUSSERL for the phenomenological reduction, 134, 182, 452

* *Erfüllung*, fulfillment: the filling out of the empty predelineations or signitive intentions of certain acts or symbolic expressions by intuitive content, 105, 109

  Erlebnis, lived experience: an intensified form of experience with pronounced ego-involvement, a term vitalized particularly by Dilthey, 242

* *Erscheinung*, appearance: the way in which an object given in experience appears; in the phenomenological literature *not* a correlate to an unknowable thing-in-itself (*Ding an sich*), nor to be identified with apparition or semblance (*Schein*), 8, 14, 39n., 59, 131f.

* essence: the whatness of things, as opposed to their thatness, i.e., their existence, 242
  — a priori, 202
  — basic, 188f.
  — empirical, 188f.
  — general (universal), 105f.
  — individual, 223

* *être-au-monde*, being-within-the-world (MARCEL and MERLEAU-PONTY): phrase used to indicate man's insertion into the world and the world's presence to man, 522, 549ff.

* *Evidenz*, self-evidence (HUSSERL): the outstanding meaning (among many peculiar ones to him) is that of an act of insight in which the presence of the object is ascertained as the result of the cumulative fulfillment of all anticipatory intentions, 44ff., 131ff., 243f.

* existence
  (1) the thatness of things, as opposed to their whatness
  (2) HEIDEGGER: the possibility invested in man (*Dasein*) to be or not to be authentically (*eigentlich*); see also *Ek-sistenz*, 327
  (3) SARTRE: synonym for *Dasein* (*réalité humaine*), more specifically for the freedom which precedes man's essence or character, 481 f., 546

* *Existenzial* (HEIDEGGER): adjective used for an analytics of *Dasein;* see *Analytik, existenziale,* 301 f.

existentialism, 289, 369, 418 ff., 433 f., 473 ff., 521, 527, 557 f., 609, 621, 636, 637 n.

* *existentiell* (HEIDEGGER): adjective used for an analysis of *Dasein* as to its ontic characteristics, as pursued in Jaspers' philosophy of existence and BINSWANGER's *Daseinsanalyse* 301 f., 481

experience, 117, 241

* *Extase* (adjective: ecstatic) (HEIDEGGER and SARTRE): the three dimensions of temporality as forms in which *Dasein* reaches beyond itself in time, 335 f.

* Facticity (HEIDEGGER and SARTRE): the factual being of *Dasein*, 330 f., 490 f.

* faith, bad (*mauvaise foi*) (SARTRE): the self-deception practiced by consciousness pre-reflectively, 487

freedom, 250, 305, 455 f., 485 f., 553 f.

fringe, see horizon

* *Fülle*, fullness: intuitive concreteness with which an object is given

* fulfillment, see *Erfüllung*

* *Fundamentalontologie* (HEIDEGGER): the ontology of *Dasein* as the privileged access to a general ontology of Being, 290, 307

* *Fundierung*, founding: the relation among acts or their referents where one is the necessary basis (*fundierend*) for the other as founded upon it, as, e.g., enjoyment is founded on intuitive presentation of the enjoyed

* *fungieren*, functioning (HUSSERL): a verb used to indicate the productive or achieving functions of intentionality, 161

Geisteswissenschaften, 20, 123, 315, 372

* *Generalthese*, general thesis (HUSSERL): the continuous habitual affirmation of existence implied in the natural attitude and the acts based on it, 134

gestalt psychology, 54, 151, 529 ff., 541 ff., 546, 621, 630, 676

glance (*Blick*), 505 f.

* immanent (also *reell*, but not real) (HUSSERL): what forms an intrinsic component of an act, as opposed to what is intended as lying beyond the act (transcendent or intentional object), e.g., the *hyle*, 39, 40n., 108, 490f.

incarnation (MARCEL and MERLEAU-PONTY): imbeddedness of consciousness in a (phenomenal) body, 439, 442, 530, 550

* intention: property of an act (*Aktcharacter*) which points to a referent; in phenomenology strictly to be distinguished from the practical intention in the sense of purpose; also the property of a meaningful symbol to point to an object meant

* intentional: adjective applied to both the act which intends (intentional act) and the object intended (intentional object), 40n., 107ff.

* intentionality
  (1) BRENTANO: the property of all psychical phenomena to contain an object as inexistent, combined with the property of referring to an object, 39ff., 107f., 650
  (2) HUSSERL: the property of consciousness of being consciousness *of*, i.e., of referring to something, 107ff., 655
  (3) SARTRE: the property of consciousness to be directed toward being which is more than merely phenomenal, i.e., transphenomenal, 488ff., 535ff.

* intersubjectivity: a plurality of subjectivities making up a community sharing a common world, 157, 261ff., 440, 505ff., 517n., 556f., 598

introspection, 38f., 149, 244, 641, 666ff.

intuition, see *Anschauung*

* irreal (HUSSERL): the property which pure phenomena of transcendental phenomenology have of not being part of a real world, 138

* *Jemeinigkeit*, each-his-own-ness (HEIDEGGER): the property of *Dasein* to be personalized in relation to specific individuals, 326ff.

* *néantisation*, "naughting" (SARTRE): the operation which establishes a negative entity (*négatité*), 472, 504

* *négatité* (SARTRE): the ontological correlate of a negation, e.g. ,an absence, 485, 503f.

* neutralization: modification of consciousness in which all belief is deactivated so that it is no longer belief, and that what is believed is left in abeyance (its relation to the phenomenological reduction is hard to determine)

* *noema* (adjective: noematic): the object-referent of a noetic act or *noesis*, 103, 141

* *noesis* (adjective: noetic) any act directed to an intentional object (*noema*)
  nominalism, 105, 210

* nominalization or substantivization: conversion of a propositional or complex thought into a noun thought

  Objectivism, 150f., 210, 539
  "Occam's razor" 9, 377, 480, 657f.

* ontic (HEIDEGGER): descriptive of a structure inherent in Being itself

* ontological (HEIDEGGER): descriptive of a structure in the understanding of Being

* ontology
  (1) HUSSERL: study of the essential or a priori structure of possible beings (*apriorische Gegenstandslehre*), 96, 99
  (2) HEIDEGGER: the study of Being (*Sein*) as opposed to that of the things-in-being (*Seiendes*) in metaphysics, 290
  (3) SARTRE: the study of Being and Nothing in all their aspects
  — critical (NICOLAI HARTMANN): the systematic study of the basic structures of all beings, 360ff.
  — formal (HUSSERL): general theory of objects and their properties as a part of pure logic, e.g., theory of the whole and its parts, 96, 322f.
  — material (HUSSERL): theory of the concrete essences for specific regions of knowledge, e.g., the region "life"; opposed

to the empirical study of its merely factual, contingent properties, 322f.

* *originär* (*originär gebende Anschauung*) (HUSSERL): characteristic of an *Anschauung* which supplies first-hand contact with the phenomena, 128

* *Paarung*, pairing (HUSSERL): associative combination of two objects of consciousness, e.g., of an ego with its directly perceived body, 159

perception, 38, 131 ff., 183 ff., 189 f., 219, 498, 544 ff.

phenomenalism, 143, 451, 489

phenomenon

  (1) BRENTANO: any item for scientific exploration, notably physical and psychological phenomena; see Newton and Comte, 39

  (2) Hegel: whatever appears in the history of the Spirit; manifestation of the Spirit, 14

  (3) HEIDEGGER: what shows itself directly (*das Sich-an-ihm-selbst-zeigende*); the apparent (*das Offenbare*)

  — *vulgär*: what is given in experience

  — "phenomenological": what is hidden to the extent that it needs uncovering, 321 f.

  (4) HUSSERL: pure phenomenon; the phenomenon which, having been subjected to the phenomenological reduction, is purified from the reality attributed to it by naive consciousness, 126

  (5) STUMPF: the correlate of a "physical function" or act on the side of the object, 59

* phenomenology, see Introduction

  — eidetic (HUSSERL): phenomenology of universal essences, their structure and relations, based on the eidetic reduction, 170, 246, 643

  — genetic (HUSSERL): phenomenology which studies the "genesis" of the phenomena, i.e., their constitution in consciousness in its essential sequence; opposed to static phenomenology, 147

  — hermeneutic (HEIDEGGER): interpretative phenomenology of the phenomena of *Dasein*, 297, 318 ff., 344 ff., 477 ff., 695

— mundane (HUSSERL): phenomenology which studies the phenomena of the world prior to subjecting them to the transcendental reduction, 160, 631

— static (HUSSERL): opposite of genetic phenomenology, 147

— transcendental (HUSSERL): phenomenology based on the phenomenological or transcendental reduction, 124ff., 640ff.

* phenomenological method, 653ff.

* polythetic: the property of acts which constitute an object synthetically by several distinct intentions

* positional, see thesis, thetic
positivism, 9f., 20, 56, 120, 128ff., 220, 241, 632, 649

* *pour-autrui*, for others (SARTRE): being related to others; social existence, 469, 472f., 508f.

* *pour-soi*, (for itself) (SARTRE): being related to itself as the basic structure of consciousness; individual existence, 469, 472
pragmatism, 67, 248, 649

* pre-predicative (HUSSERL): term designating the structures of immediate experience which precede logical predications, 132
presuppositions, and freedom from presuppositions, see *Voraussetzungslosigkeit*

* primordinal (better: primordial): term designating the world of first order, i.e., the world of the private self or monad in abstraction from the world of the other or the intersubjective world
problem (MARCEL), 426

* protention: the immediate forward reach of consciousness toward the future, corresponding to its retentive reach toward the past; immediate expectation, 148
psychoanalysis and phenomenology, 216ff., 492ff., 501, 607f.

* psychologism
(1) narrow sense (HUSSERL in Logische Untersuchungen): the attempt to derive logical laws from psychological laws, 93f.
(2) wider sense (HUSSERL after Log. Unt.: any attempt to

reduce non-psychological entities to psychological phenomena, 20, 49 ff., 56, 93 ff., 171, 282, 293
   (3) transcendental: confusion of pure immanent psychology with transcendental philosophy, based on a misinterpretation of the transcendental reduction
psychology, phenomenological, 149 ff., 179 ff., 185 ff., 213 ff., 259 ff., 462 ff., 498 ff., 528 ff., 540 ff., 575 ff., 605 ff., 637

Rationalism and irrationalism, 83 f., 178, 257, 502 f.
razón, vital (vital reason), 612 f.

* realism, phenomenological, 183, 194, 210, 226, 245, 382 ff., 489, 553, 655

* reduction
— eidetic (also ideation, ideating abstraction): the act which leads from particulars to universal "pure" essences
— phenomenological or transcendental: the act by which the general thesis of belief in factual existence characteristic of the natural attitude is inhibited, suspended, bracketed (*eingeklammert*), or turned off (*ausgeschaltet*), and which uncovers in transcendental subjectivity the acts which constitute pure phenomena, 120, 153 ff., 182 f., 245 f., 534, 586, 690 f.
— philosophical: adoption of a neutral position toward past philosophy, 133 n.
reell, see immanent

* reflection: the act by which consciousness turns inward, reversing its usual forward (*geradeaus*) orientation
   (1) HUSSERL: phenomenological reflection: reflection on the immanent elements of consciousness
   (2) MARCEL: first reflection: scientific analysis; second reflection: a method that attacks the rigid division between object and subject, 435 ff.
   (3) SARTRE: purifying reflection: a reflection which purges consciousness of its futile ambition to become absolute (God); impure reflection: a reflection in which consciousness remains immersed in its futile aspirations, 482 ff.

* stream of consciousness, 112, 141, 148
  Stück, piece: essentially self-sufficient part of a thing which can
    be conceived of without the other parts, although it may not
    be able to exist without them; opposed to moment, 62
  subjectivism, 284, 310, 314f.

* subjectivity (HUSSERL): the sphere of the subject and his
    consciousness, 87f., 666

* symbolic, see *signitiv*
  syncategorematic, 48, 117f.
* synthesis of identification, see *Identifikationssynthese*

* Teleology (of consciousness) (HUSSERL): the purposive
    structure of consciousness, 86f., 156, 552f.

* temporality (*Zeitlichkeit*): the time-structure of *Dasein*, 305,
    334ff., 552f.

* thatness, see *Dasein* (1)
  theism, 30, 86, 178, 262ff., 342

* theme (adjective: thematic): the focus of the field of conscious-
    ness, 630

* *thematischer Kern*, thematic core

* thesis (adjective: thetic): the positing of existence implied in
    beliefs and other acts, absent only from neutral modifications
    of consciousness. See also * *Generalthese*

  time, 44, 119, 146ff., 288, 296f.
  time consciousness, 148f.

* transcendent
    (1) HUSSERL: status of an intentional object constituted by
        intentional acts and lying beyond their immanent
        constituents, 108, 479f.
    (2) HUSSERL: absolute being, as implied in the phrase
        immanent transcendence, attributed to transcen-
        dental consciousness
    (3) HEIDEGGER and others: act of transcending, stepping
        beyond, 305, 381f., 409, 491f.
    (4) NICOLAI HARTMANN: the separation between knower and
        known

INDEX OF NAMES

SUPPLEMENT

The first numbers refer to the pages of the main text, the numbers in brackets to the corresponding marginal numbers in the main text.

XXIX [1] Karl Löwith's "Grundzüge der Entwicklung der Phänomenologie zur Philosophie und ihr Verhältnis zur protestantischen Theologie" (*Theologische Rundschau* II, 1930, 26–64) outlines and interprets the development from Husserl's descriptive phenomenology in the *Logische Untersuchungen* to the hermeneutics of Heidegger's *Sein und Zeit*.

4 [1] I would like to withdraw the characterization of Traugott Konstantin Oesterreich as a "self-styled phenomenologist." His book, published in 1910 before Husserl had staked out his claim, was a scholarly study in the area of descriptive psychology.

9 [1] Professor Johannes Linschoten has drawn my attention to a discussion in Jakob Friedrich Fries, *Die mathematische Naturphilosophie* (1822), which shows a very similar meaning of the term.

11 [1] Recently the term "phenomenology" has reappeared independently in the works of Pierre Teilhard de Chardin. The purpose of his main work, *The Phenomenon of Man*, is the study of man as a "phenomenon." By this Teilhard means to indicate his program of exploring man not metaphysically or theologically but scientifically, in an attempt "to see and to show what happens to man." The term "phenomenology" occurs at the beginning of the second chapter of Part I, where it is the name for a "generalized physics in which the internal aspect of things as well as the external aspect of the world will be taken into account." Also, in several texts prepared for the journal *Les Études philosophiques* Teilhard stated that his thought was "a kind of phenomenology," in contrast to metaphysics, or a "phenomenological perspective of the world" (*Teilhard de Chardin. Présentation par l'abbé Paul Grenet*, Éditions Seghers, 1961, pp. 191, 216). Such a phenomenology could easily be related to the positivistic

uses of the term. However, when Teilhard began to write *The Phenomenon of Man* in 1940, the term had clearly acquired new connotations in France. Nevertheless, in a passage reported by Grenet (p. 45), Teilhard remarks about existentialist phenomenology: "I do not understand how one can call oneself a 'phenomenologist' and write whole books without mentioning cosmogenesis and evolution." In any case, Teilhard's adoption of a phenomenological terminology for his grand vision may well have attracted further attention to phenomenology – and again deflected its meaning from its merely philosophical connotations.

13 [1] Two revealing references occur also in the supplements to *Husserliana*, VII, 310 and 312, footnote 2.

19 [1] The following additional occurrences seem to me worth recording:
1. Hermann Lotze in his *Microcosmus* (1856 ff.) calls the soul a "phenomenological term" for different entities. But this usage, presumably still related to Hegel's, occurs only in the table of contents preceding Book V (*Der Geist*) Ch. I.
2. One of Lotze's followers, Gustav Class, published in 1896 *Untersuchungen zur Phänomenologie und Ontologie des menschlichen Geistes*.
3. A rather original development of nineteenth century phenomenology can be found in Henri-Frédéric Amiel's journals. See my forthcoming article on "Amiel's 'New Phenomenology' " in *Archiv für Geschichte der Philosophie*.

51 [1] Three such sections can now be found on pp. 39–75 of the book, which appeared in 1960. Their quality is promising.
51 [2] *Grundzüge der Ästhetik* (1959)
Geschichte der griechischen Philosophie (1963)

52 [1] BARCLAY, JAMES, "Themes of Brentano's Thought and Philosophical Overtones," *New Scholasticism*, XXXIII (1959); 300–18.
GROSSMAN, REINHART B., "Acts and Relations in Brentano," *Analysis*, III (1960), 1–5.
MERLAN, PHILIP, "Brentano and Freud," *Journal of the History of Ideas*, VI (1945), 375–77 and X (1949), 451.
SRZEDNICKI, JAN T. J., "Remarks Concerning the Interpretation of the Philosophy of Franz Brentano," *PPR*. XXII (1962), 308–16.
MAYER-HILLEBRAND, FRANZISKA, "A Reply to Dr. Srzednicki," *PPR*, XXIII (1963), 438–44.
SRZEDNICKI, JAN, "A Reply to Professor Mayer-Hillebrand," *Ibid.*, 445–46.

52 [2] For the latest list of writings about Brentano published since his death see: MAYER-HILLEBRAND, FRANZISKA, *Zeitschrift für philosophische Forschung* XVII (1963), 162–69.

Thanks to Dr. J. C. M. Brentano's labor and generosity, microfilm sets of the Brentano papers are now available in major European, American, and other centers such as Frankfurt (Goethe House), Innsbruck, Munich (Bayerische Staatsbibliothek), Berkeley, Harvard, Minnesota, the Library of Congress, the University of Mexico, and Melbourne.

77 [1] Since discussion about the meaning of the much-quoted passage from Beilage XXVIII has not subsided (see Landgrebe, Ludwig, in *Philosophische Rundschau* IX, 1962, 157 and Gadamer, Hans-Georg, *Ibid.* XI, 1963, 25), I should like to add two corroborative references for my interpretation:

1. Husserl's letter to Roman Ingarden of July 7, 1935, which contains the following passage (in translation):

"In Germany all these themes are no longer topical (*aktuell*). Philosophy as a 'rigorous science' belongs to the finished past, just like the scholasticism of the thirteenth century. Even in the rest of Europe irrationalist scepticism is spreading."

2. Postscript to the *Ideen* (1930) in *Husserliana* V, 162, lines 22 ff., about "the scepticism of our time ... against admitting any validity of the goal of a philosophy as rigorous science."

85 [1] See also the testimony of Eugen Fink in *Edmund Husserl 1958–1959*, p. 115, about one of Husserl's last words: "I have lived as a philosopher and I want to die as a philosopher."

86 [1] See the judicious article by Stephan Strasser, "Das Gottesproblem in der Spätphilosophie Husserls," *Philosophisches Jahrbuch der Görresgesellschaft* LXVII (1959), 130–42.

86 [2] In the meantime a most interesting letter by Husserl to Rudolf Otto of March 5, 1919, discussing the latter's book on *The Holy*, has come to the surface. Here Husserl refers to himself as "a free Christian and an undogmatic Protestant."

91 [1] For further evidence see Husserl's letter to Dorion Cairns of March 31, 1933, in *Edmund Husserl 1859–1959*, p. 283, and additional items in my article "Concerning 'The Phenomenological Tendency,' " *Journal of Philosophy* LX (1963), 587.

93 [1] This review appeared in *Zeitschrift für Philosophie und philosophische Kritik* CIII (1894), 313–32.

111 [1] See also Johannes Linschoten, *Auf dem Wege zu einer phänomenologischen Psychologie. Die Psychologie von William James*, Berlin, 1962, esp. pp. 2 ff.

112 [1] The interesting fact that Husserl's collection of reprints contains one of James's essay "A World of Pure Experience" from the *Journal of Philosophy, Psychology, and Scientific Method* of September 29, 1904, with the inscription "*Vom Verf(asser)*" (from the author) hardly proves much.

113 [1] See also Husserl's remark to Arnold Metzger in "William James and the Crisis of Philosophy," in *In Commemoration of William James* (Columbia University Press, 1942), p. 209.

123 [1] See also Husserl's lectures on *Phänomenologische Psychologie* in *Husserliana* IX, 3–21.

125 [1] There is evidence that Husserl's feelings about the *Jahrbuch* remained ambivalent. Sometimes he pointed to it with pride. At other times he declared that hardly any of the later contributions were phenomenological in his sense. Finally, in a letter to Hans L. Stoltenberg of June 6, 1934, he went so far as to declare that the yearbook had become an institution aimed at annihilating the fundamental meaning of his own life work (*Zeitschrift für philosophische Forschung* XIII (1958), 179).

136 [1] See also the particularly revealing information by Rudolf Boehm in the *Cahiers de Royaumont* III (Husserl), 1959, p. 166, mentioning among other things eight reductions distinguished by some of Husserl's students, which the master himself, however, rejected.

142 [1] About Husserl's initial aversion to German idealism see the testimony of Helmut Plessner in *Edmund Husserl 1859–1959*, p. 35.

144 [1] The statement about the lack of mutual references in Royce's and Husserl's writings has to be amended in the case of Royce. As early as January, 1902, in a presidential address to the American Psychological Association in Chicago on "Recent Logical Inquiries and Their Psychological Bearings" (*Psychological Review* IX (1902), 113–33; republished in Robinson, D. S., ed., *Royce's Logical Essays* (1951), Royce mentions specifically the *Logische Untersuchungen*, in the following sentences:

Husserl has vigorously protested against all *psychologisierende Logik*. Logic, he insists, must go its own way, yet Husserl, in his still unfinished and very attractive researches, yet lingers over the problems of what he now calls the "phenomenological analysis" of the thinking process, and his farewell, as a logician, to psychology proves to be a very long one, wherein the parting is such sweet sorrow that the logician's escape from the presence of psychology is sure to lead to further psychological complications. (p. 111)

How Royce, to be sure a former Göttingen student under Lotze, came to know about Husserl so much earlier than most German philosophers has still to be explained. But these remarkably keen comments may well throw a light on Peirce's acquaintance with Husserl, mentioned on p. 18.

146 [1] The phrase "for the first time" needs modification. The term "constitution" occurs as early as the *Logische Untersuchungen*, and the phrase *sich konstituieren* was used by Husserl in his lectures on "Die Idee der Phänomenologie" of 1907 (*Husserliana* II, 12). – About the ambiguity of Husserl's use of the term and the underlying conception see Eugen Fink in the *Cahiers de Royaumont* III, p. 228 and Roman Ingarden, "Le Problème de la constitution et le sens de la réflexion constitutive chez Edmund Husserl," *Ibid.*, pp. 242–63. Ingarden distinguishes four senses of the term in Husserl's development.

148 [1] Some indications may be found in Eugen Fink's "Die Spätphilosophie Husserls in der Freiburger Zeit," *Edmund Husserl 1889–1959*, pp. 111 ff.

153 [1] On the problems of her collaboration with Husserl, see the revealing letters to Roman Ingarden published by him with an introduction in *PPR* XXIII (1962), 155–75.

155 [1] The lectures on phenomenological psychology which Husserl gave in Amsterdam in 1926 have now been published in *Husserliana* IX, 302–49.

156 [1] See the authoritative account of Eugen Fink in *Edmund Husserl 1859–1959*, pp. 99–115.

158 [1] See the paper by Alfred Schütz, "Le Problème de l'intersubjectivité transcendentale chez Husserl" and the subsequent discussion in *Cahiers de Royaumont* III, pp. 334–65.

159 [1] The term "Lebenswelt" can be found as early as 1924, in the article "Kant und die Idee der Transzendentalphilosophie" (see *Husserliana* VII, 232, 2. 6), and October, 1925, in a research manuscript (Beilage XXVII) of *Husserliana* IX, 496, 1. 40, as something shared by several people in the same community of life; see also

Walter Biemel's editorial Introduction, p. XXV f. The idea itself came to the surface in a subsection of Husserl's discussion of Galileo's "mathematization of nature," which uses the term in its title ("The Lebenswelt as forgotten foundation of meaning for natural science," *Husserliana* VI, 48); this section was published in 1936 in *Philosophia*. Landgrebe's elaboration of the conception in Husserl's *Erfahrung und Urteil* (Sec. 10, p. 38) appeared posthumously in 1939.

160 [1] The merely preliminary purpose of this study was stressed by Husserl in letters such as the one to Karl Löwith (*Edmund Husserl 1859–1959*, p. 50 of February 22, 1937 and, even more explicitly, in a letter to Helmut Kuhn of February 4, 1937.

164 [1] A comparison of the article with the original of the German versions now published in *Husserliana* IX, 237–99 reveals that it can no longer be considered as a translation, but at best as a telescoped paraphrase. A new complete translation is urgently needed.

164 [2] Translation: English (1964) by William Alston and George Nakhnikian – careful and readable.

164 [3] *Phänomenologische Psychologie. Vorlesungen Sommersemester 1925, Husserliana* IX.

164 [4] *Husserl:* Cahiers de Royaumont. Philosophie No. III, Paris, Editions de Minuit, 1959. Papers and discussions of the most extensive international colloquy about Husserl's work and thought, important for their critical analyses.

Edmund Husserl, 1859–1959 (Phaemenologica 4)

A centennial collection of memoirs of Husserl and of independent essays.

164 [5] ROTH, ALOIS, *Edmund Husserls ethische Untersuchungen* (Phaenomenologica 7), 1960. A report on Husserl's early ethical lecture manuscripts. The interesting ideas of these texts parallel the antipsychologistic stage of the Prolegomena of *Logische Untersuchungen.*

SZILASI, WILHELM, *Einführung in die Phänomenologie Edmund Husserls*, Tübingen, 1959. Freiburg lectures, concentrating on some of the major ideas; for a fuller characterization see *Philosophical Review* LXX (1961), 266–68.

165 [1] BIEMEL, WALTER, "Die entscheidenden Phasen der Entfaltung von Husserls Philosophie," *Zeitschrift für philosophische Forschung* XIII (1959), 187–213.

166 [1] FARBER, MARVIN, "First Philosophy and the Problem of the World," *PPR* XXIII (1963), 315–34.

166 [2] MULLER, GUSTAV E., "On the Historical Significance of Husserl's Phenomenology" *Sophia*, XXI (1953), 54–62.

166 [3] SCHMITT, RICHARD, "Husserl's Transcendental-Phenomenological Reduction," *PPR* XX (1959), 361–72.

SHESTOV, LEON, "In Memory of a Great Philosopher: Edmund Husserl." Translated from the Russian by George L. Kline, *PPR* XXII (1962), 449–71.

Sinha, Debabrata, "The Phenomenology of Edmund Husserl," *The Calcutta Review* (1960), 241–50.

167 [1] FISCHER, GILBERT, "A Study in the Philosophy of Husserl," University of Chicago, 1962.

PIETERSMA, HENRY, "Edmund Husserl's Concept of Philosophical Clarification. Its Development from 1887–1913," University of Toronto, 1962.

167 [2] Most complete bibliography of Husserl's publications by H. L. Van Breda (119 items) in *Edmund Husserl, 1859–1959, Phaenomenologica* 4, pp. 289–306.

169 [1] The name of Wilhelm Schapp has to be removed from this group, since he did not come to Göttingen until 1906, having studied under Dilthey and Stumpf in Berlin (see *Edmund Husserl 1859–1959*, p. 13; also written communication). He was preceded by Heinrich Hofmann (1904–12), whose thesis on the concept of sensation, published in *Archiv für die gesamte Psychologie*, XVI (1913), 1–136, aroused the interest of Ortega y Gasset, and by Karl Neuhaus (1903); the latter wrote a dissertation on Hume's ethics.

169 [2] See also W. E. Hocking's "From the Early Days of the 'Logische Untersuchungen' " in *Edmund Husserl 1859–1959*, pp. 1–11.

170 [1] Replace the name "Th. Conrad" by "Alfred v. Sybel" as the author of the "Phänomenologenlied."

171 [1] This is an error. At least in the early twenties there was, according to Gerda Walther (*Zum anderen Ufer*. Remagen, Otto Reichl Verlag, 1960, p. 213), a "*Freiburger phänomenologische Gesellschaft*").

172 [1] Hans Cornelius was not a student of Lipps nor did he consider himself a real positivist; he even thought the expression "pure phenomenology" the proper designation for his a priori psychology ("Selbstdarstellung" in Raymund Schmidt, ed., *Die deutsche Philosophie*, vol. II, p. 86). – Because of their later significance for the development of phenomenological psychiatry the names of two other

students of Lipps should be added: Viktor E. von Gebsattel and Alfred Schwenninger.

177 [1] *Pfänderiana* 1; some of these drafts can now be found in my *Alexander Pfänders Phänomenologie* (The Hague, Martinus Nijhoff, 1963), pp. 51 ff.

192 [1] The *Phänomenologie des Wollens* and the *Logik* have now been reprinted by Johannes Ambrosius Barth and Max Niemeyer in a joint edition of Pfänders *Gesammelte Schriften* (1963), the former with an editorial preface by the present writer and an enlarged bibliography of Pfänder's writings.

Translation: Spanish (1931) by Manuel G. Morente.

192 [2] The above section has now been published in a slightly expanded German version under the title *Alexander Pfänders Phänomenologie* (The Hague, Martinus Nijhoff, 1963), and supplemented by original texts from the posthumous papers and further bibliographical references.

194 [1] *Zum anderen Ufer* (1960)

An autobiography, in which the sections on Freiburg and Munich phenomenology are of particular interest.

218 [1] ZELTNER, HERMANN, "Moritz Geiger zum Gedächtnis," *Zeitschrift für philosophische Forschung*, XII (1960), 452–66.

221 [1] "Die transzendentale und die ontologische Phänomenologie," in *Edmund Husserl, 1859–1959*, pp. 175–84. – An important clarification.

Schriften zur Philosophie, ed. by E. Avé-Lallemant (Munich, Kösel, 1961).

The first of three projected volumes covers the period from 1927–1935, the second (1964), containing mostly studies in philosophy of nature and cosmology, comprises the period between 1936 and 1948.

223 [1] SCHWARZ, BALDWIN, ed., *The Human Person and the World of Values*. A Tribute to Dietrich von Hildebrand (1960).

Contains a comprehensive bibliography (pp. 195–210).

223 [2] "Quelques Thèmes d'une phénoménologie du rêve," in *For Roman Ingarden*, The Hague, Martinus Nijhoff, 1959), pp. 75–87.

Complete bibliography in *Revue d'histoire et de philosophie religieuse*, XXXVII (1957), 3–4 and XLVI (1966), 113–115.

227 [1] *Untersuchungen zur Ontologie der Kunst* (1962).

227 [2] *Translation* of a chapter on "Aesthetic Experience and Aesthetic Object" in *PPR* XXI (1961), 289–313.

227 [3] Translation of part of the first volume under the title

Time and Modes of Being by Helen Michejda (Springfield, Charles C. Thomas, 1964).

227 [4] ———, The Second Phenomenology," in *For Roman Ingarden. Nine Essays* pp. 1–5.

231 [1] A particularly explicit formulation of Scheler's general objectives can be found in a letter which he sent to the Munich philosopher Georg v. Hertling on April 17, 1906, published in Finke, Heinrich, *Internationale Beziehungen der Görresgesellschaft*, Köln, J. P. Bachem, 1932, p. 48 f. It contains such statements as: "I subordinate the specific problems to the questions of Weltanschauung." I am indebted to Professor J. Nota, S.J., author of an important Dutch work on Scheler (Utrecht, *Spectrum*, 1947), for this reference.

237 [1] "Eleven" as Scheler's age at the time of his baptism seems to be wrong; apparently it was later. In view of contradictory information I have received since writing my chapter, I shall leave it to future biographers to establish the precise date. In 1923 Scheler himself wrote (*Gesammelte Schriften* VI, 224) that "at no time of his life and his development could the author call himself a 'believing Catholic' according to the strict standards of theology of the Roman Church."

239 [1] Helmut Plessner reports that in a conversation he had with Scheler toward the end of his years in Cologne he stated: "One really should no longer use the word 'phenomenology.' After all, it does nothing but what philosophy has always done." (*Edmund Husserl 1859–1959*, p. 38.)

245 [1] About the phenomenological reduction see also *Gesammelte Schriften* VIII, 138 f., 282, 362.

253 [1] In this connection Scheler's awareness and appreciation of G. E. Moore's "similar conception of the problem of value" (II, 13) deserves special mention.

258 [1] The essay on "Das Ressentiment im Aufbau der modernen Moral" (*Vom Umsturz der Werte*) is now available as a book in the free but usually reliable translation by William W. Holdheim, preceded by an introductory essay by Lewis A. Coser (Free Press, 1961).

268 [1] *Translation:* English (1960) by Bernard Wall – adequate, but not free from serious mistakes.

268 [2] *Translation:* English (1961) by Hans Meyerhoff – deliberately free, but good, with helpful introduction.

269 [1] Since 1959 volumes 6 and 8 have been added.

269 [2] LAUER, QUENTIN, S.J., "The Phenomenological Ethics of Max Scheler," *International Philosophical Quarterly* I (1961).

270 [1] SWEENEY, ROBERT DANIEL, *Material Value in Max Scheler's Ethics. An Exposition and Critique.* Fordham University, 1962.

271 [1] In view of the rapidly growing number of Heidegger's publications since this chapter was written, the statement about the paucity of his literary production may seem outdated. However, it remains true that his initial fame preceded the bulk of his printed work. Also, his most recent publications consist either of lectures from the period after 1930 or of short pieces based on recent lectures.

272 [1] See also Sidney Hook's account in the *New York Times Book Review* of November 11, 1962, p. 6.

278 [1] About the temporary omission of this dedication in the book edition of 1942 as the price Heidegger paid to avoid the suppression of the book, while leaving the tribute to Husserl in footnote form, see *Unterwegs zur Sprache*, p. 269.

279 [1] This draft has now been published in *Husserliana* IX, 256–263.

281 [1] This letter can now be found in *Husserliana* IX, 600 ff.

282 [1] A few translated specimens can also be found in Farber, Marvin, *Naturalism and Subjectivism*, pp. 356 ff.

283 [1]*The information I gave about Heidegger's part in the notorious letter forbidding all Jewish members of the staff to enter the premises of the University of Freiburg seems to be incorrect. But I have not seen the letter which supposedly shows Heidegger's signature.

283 [2] A translation of this text by Richard Schmitt can now be found in Chisholm, R., ed., *Realism and the Background of phenomenology*, pp. 129–42.

285 [1] In a separate little study, *Zur Seinsfrage* (1956; English translation by W. Kluback and J. T. Wilde, 1959), on pp. 30 ff. the

* For 283 [1a] see page 763.

word *Sein* is put behind crossed diagonal bars, which are meant negatively to counteract the habit of treating *Sein* as something set apart from man, and to point positively toward the four regions of human dwelling (*Geviert*), earth and heaven, the divine beings and the mortals – a puzzling conception adumbrated in *Vorträge und Aufsätze*, p. 149 f. – and toward their unity at the intersection.

291 [1] In *Unterwegs zur Sprache* (p. 121) Heidegger says, about the elimination of such terms:

"This was not done, as many believe, in order to deny the significance of phenomenology, but in order to leave my path of thinking in the nameless (*im Namenlosen*)."

291 [2] Further important information can now be found in "Aus einem Gespräch über die Sprache," in *Unterwegs zur Sprache*, pp. 92 ff.

292 [1] According to *Unterwegs zur Sprache* (p. 92) the place of this incident was the Gymnasium in Konstanz, and the teacher was Conrad Gröber, later Archbishop of Freiburg.

309 [1] This is intimated in such passages as p. 152 of *Einführung in die Metaphysik*.

309 [2] One of the oddest mixtures of worship of the Führer and of the Will to Being can be found in his appeal to the German teachers of November 10, 1933, republished in Schneeberger, Guido, *Nachlese zu Heidegger*, Bern, 1962, pp. 148–50.

309 [3] In view of the new information in the supplement to p. 462, that Sartre did not visit Freiburg during his year in Germany, this sentence is to be dropped.

310 [1] In *Unterwegs zur Sprache* (p. 93) Heidegger says, in discussing the significance of the relation of language and Being for his path of thinking: "Perhaps the basic defect of the book *Sein und Zeit* is the fact that I ventured too early too far." An even more important hint is given in the Nietzsche lectures (II, 194 f.), where, in trying to explain the utter misunderstanding of *Sein und Zeit*, Heidegger speaks about the breaking off (*Abbruch*) of the path at a "decisive place": "This breaking off had its ground in the fact that unintentionally the chosen path and attempt runs the risk of becoming once more a consolidation of subjectivity, and that it precisely blocks the decisive steps, i.e., its adequate presentation in its essential performance" (*Wesensvollzug*).

311 [1] Most important among these lecture courses are those on *Nietzsche* in the longest of Heidegger's publications (two volumes),

meant also as a perspective of his own path of thinking between 1930 and 1947.

311 [2] A still unpublished lecture which Heidegger gave in Freiburg in January, 1962, under the title "Zeit und Sein," apparently made no explicit claim that the decisive turn had now been achieved.

311 [3] In *Unterwegs zur Sprache* Heidegger states that this interest in poetry dates back to a much earlier period and particularly to that "earthquake" when in 1910 he became acquainted with the original Hölderlin (*op. cit.*, p. 182).

317 [1] For a preliminary sketch of such a history of Being see the "drafts" of 1941 in *Nietzsche*, II, 458–80.

317 [2] For a list of polar opposites describing Being, dating back to 1940, see *Nietzsche*, II, 250–53 ("the emptiest and the richest, the most general and the most unique, the most intelligible and the most refractory to conceptualization, the most in use and still arriving, the most reliable and most treacherous (*Ab-gründigste*), the most forgotten, and the most reminding, the most mentioned and the most passed over in silence").

320 [1] In retrospect Heidegger has this to say about his new "hermeneutic phenomenology": "I was not interested in a new *Richtung* within phenomenology and even less in its novelty. On the contrary, I tried to think the essence of phenomenology in a more basic fashion (*ursprünglicher*), in order to reinsert it in this manner specifically into the proper context (*Zugehörigkeit*) of occidental philosophy." ("*Unterwegs zur Sprache*, p. 95")

342 [1] This motif has been further developed in *Unterwegs zur Sprache*, an attempt to "have an experience with language," where experience (*Er-fahrung*) is interpreted as obtaining something on the way" (p. 177).

348 [1] See *Unterwegs zur Sprache:* "Phenomenology presented possibilities of a path" (p. 92) and the reference to "my experiment (*Versuch*) with phenomenology" (p. 127).

353 [1] While, in accordance with my announcement in the second Preface, I do not intend to bring my account of post-Heideggerian philosophy up to date, I should like to add at least a brief account of some developments in this area which seem to me to have significance for the future. Thus among Heidegger's more independent followers, particularly those who also studied under Husserl, there seems to be now a definite effort to achieve a synthesis between the phenomenologies of their two masters. As outstanding examples of such

attempts I shall single out the work of Wilhelm Szilasi and Hans-Georg Gadamer.

The major objective of SZILASI (1889–   ) has been to strengthen the weakened bond between philosophy and natural science in a way which would allow us once more to think of "science as a philosophy." However, such a reunification is conceived not in the sense of a merger but of a dovetailing cooperation. In this spirit Szilasi assigns to science the task of exploring the *what* of nature, to philosophy the task of understanding the Being of what this nature is in its different modifications from physics through biology to psychology. In this, Schelling is his great model. Methodologically he tries to combine Husserl's transcendental phenomenology, putting particular weight on the doctrine of constitution, with Heidegger's fundamental ontology, making *Dasein* the foundation of such a constitution. Experience is stressed as the basis of all science. In fact, Husserl's position is called "transcendental positivism." Also, the receptive aspect of phenomenological constitution is played up so much that Szilasi labels his own position a priori or transcendental realism, rather than idealism. Szilasi's conception, not yet developed in detail in his own writings, has had particular influence on psychiatrists such as Ludwig Binswanger.

Major Works
Macht und Ohnmacht des Geistes (1946)
Wissenschaft als Philosophie (1945)
Philosophie und Naturwissenschaft (1961)

GADAMER (1900–   ), who had come to Husserl and Heidegger from Paul Natorp, has made his main contributions to the history of philosophy. But his latest work, *Wahrheit und Methode* (1961), containing "outlines of a philosophical hermeneutics," [1] offers probably the most solid achievement of systematic German philosophy since World War II. Husserl's phenomenological description and Dilthey's historical perspective are combined with Heidegger's hermeneutics in an attempt to provide a new philosophical foundation for the cultural sciences (*Geisteswissenschaften*). Since the present context calls only for its evaluation as a piece of phenomenology, the substantive thesis of this work will be disregarded here. Suffice it to point out that it attempts to vindicate their "truth" and even their scientific status without making them dependent on "method," a term which for Gadamer characterizes the methods of the natural sciences. This is

[1] The main ideas of this work are also developed in the Louvain lectures on *Le problème de la conscience historique* (1963).

achieved by a concrete and thorough consideration of the phenomenon of understanding (hermeneutics), which starts from understanding in the aesthetic field, then turns to the humanities in general, and finally discovers in language the basic phenomenon from which the problem of truth in the humanities has to be approached. Much of the material discussed on the way deserves consideration even apart from the context and the overarching thesis.

354 [1] English (1962) by J. Macquarrie and E. Robinson – conscientious, but overly literal and in places even misleading. See John Wild and James Millikan in *Review of Metaphysics*, XVI (1963), 296–315 and 780–85.

354 [2] English (1962) by James S. Churchill – good, but not free from minor inaccuracies.

354 [3] Translations: Barrett, W. and Aiken, H., ed., *Philosophy in the Twentieth Century* (1962) contains a translation of the first (II, 251–70) by John Barlow and of the second (II, 270–302) by Edgar Lohner – both adequate.

354 [4] *Translation:* English (1960) by Kurt F. Leidecker – fair, but freer than necessary.
Unterwegs zur Sprache (1959)
Gelassenheit (1959)
Nietzsche. 2 vol. (1961)
Die Frage nach dem Ding (1962)
A very helpful *Index zu Heideggers Sein und Zeit*, with cross references to his later works, by Hildegard Feick, appeared in 1961.

355 [1] Pöggeler, Otto, *Der Denkweg Martin Heideggers*, Pfullingen, 1963. Very helpful.

355 [2] Vycinas, Vincent, *Earth and Gods*. An Introduction to the Philosophy of Heidegger, Martinus Nijhoff, 1961. An ambitious attempt to condense Heidegger's thought, dealing especially with his last phase in his own phraseology – hardly of much help to the novice.

355 [3] Allers, Rudolf, "Heidegger on the Principle of Sufficient Reason," *PPR* XX (1959) 365–73.

Ballard, Edward G., "A Brief Introduction to the Philosophy of Martin Heidegger," *Tulane Studies in Philosophy* XII (1963), 106–51.

356 [1] Farber, Marvin, "What is Philosophy?" *PPR* XXI (1960), 255–59.

356 [2] Munson, Thomas N., S.J., "Heidegger's Recent Thought on Language," *PPR* XXI (1961), 361–72.

356 [3] Wild, John, "The Philosophy of Martin Heidegger," *Journal of Philosophy* LX (1963), 664–77.

357 [1] SCHNEEBERGER, GUIDO, *Ergänzungen zu einer Heidegger-Bibliographie*, Bern, 1960.

398 [1] About the use of the term by H.-F. Amiel see the supplement to p. 19.

404 [1] The historical importance of Levinas' *Théorie de l'intuition dans la phénoménologie de Husserl* (1950, republished in 1963) as an informative and critical study of considerable influence on Sartre, seeing in Heidegger Husserl's legitimate heir, needs underscoring. Its *Avant-propos* gives a good survey of proto-phenomenology in France, showing, among other things, the role of Jean Hering.

405 [1] The story of the salvage and transfer of the Husserl papers has now been described in detail by H. L. Van Breda in *Phaenomenologica* 2 (1959), 1–42 and 4 (1959), 116–22.

406 [1] Republished in *Critique de la raison dialectique* (1960), p. 23.

408 [1] *Monographs:*
"Gaston Berger: In Memoriam" and other essays in *Les Études philosophiques* XVI (1961), 307–78.

409 [1] Jaspers himself, in an interview he gave me in April 1962, did not support this hypothesis. Husserl had friends invite Jaspers, when he happened to pass through Göttingen.

415 [1] See also Hyppolite's attempt to show the closeness between Husserl's and Hegel's phenomenologies in *Genèse et structure de la Phénoménologie de l'Esprit de Hegel* (Paris, 1946), pp. 15, 16.

418 [1] About the role of Thao in the early history of the Husserl Archives, see Van Breda, H. L., "Merleau-Ponty et Louvain," *Revue de métaphysique et de morale* LVII (1962), 422 f.

424 [1] References to "phenomenology" are also quite frequent in *Présence et immortalité* (1959) and particularly in the continuations to the *Journal métaphysique* from 1938–1943, which the book contains. – In *The Existential Background of Human Dignity* (1963), while refusing to "endorse existentialism as defined by Sartre," Marcel asserts "the rights of phenomenology, in the light of which the primacy of experience over what could be called pure thought must be rigorously preserved" (p. 96).

430 [1] In a restatement of his "fundamental project of 1937" (*Présence et Immortalité*, p. 23), Marcel even goes so far as to say that no other philosophical text had impressed him more strongly than Hocking's demonstration of the close connection between our grasp of

others and of ourselves in *The Meaning of God in Human Experience*.

443 [1] Translation by Robert Rosthal (1964) as *Creative Fidelity* – not always reliable.

443 [2] *Présence et Immortalité* (1959).

The Existential Background of Human Dignity (1963). William James Lectures.

443 [3] *Books in English*

GALLAGHER, KENNETH T., *The Philosophy of Gabriel Marcel* (1962). Stresses Marcel's metaphysics, particularly the idea of participation.

444 [1] MICELI, VINCENT P., S.J., *The Life of Communion and Community in the Philosophy of Gabriel Marcel*. Fordham University, 1961.

STEARNS, J. BRENTON, *Gabriel Marcel's Repudiation of Idealism*. Emory University, 1961.

444 [2] For a more complete and up-to-date bibliography of Gabriel Marcel in English see *Review of Existential Psychology and Psychiatry* II (1962), 117–19.

458 [1] Much new light on Sartre's childhood experience is now available in an autobiographical essay, *Les Mots* (1964).

462 [1] It now appears that nearly all the hypotheses of the following paragraph are erroneous. I owe to Mme. Simone de Beauvoir the following information in reply to an inquiry, based on her *La Force de l'Âge* (1960); I quote in translation:

Sartre was in Berlin from November 1933 to July 1934 and has never set foot in Freiburg. Aron was the one who talked to Sartre for the first time, as I report, and, as I also report, (Sartre) bought immediately the book by Levinas: this is to what he alludes in "Merleau-Ponty vivant" (*Les Temps Modernes* XVII (1961), p. 306). Groethuysen has played no part in Sartre's thought.

Raymond Aron's account of German phenomenology after his return from a year in Berlin and its effects on Sartre is reflected vividly in *La Force de l'Âge*, pp. 141 f. Professor Aron, in a letter for which I am in his debt, confirmed Mme. de Beauvoir's information, adding that his own recollections were, however, less precise: "I can well believe that I presented to Sartre Husserl as the philosopher who could give him the possibility of formulating his realism and who gave us the means to philosophize on anything we please."

468 [1] According to Simone de Beauvoir (*La Force de l'Âge*, pp. 84 and 363) Sartre did not study Heidegger intensively and profitably until 1939.

476 [1] A discussion of Sartre's *Critique de la raison dialectique* from the phenomenological angle in the present context would seem premature, particularly until the announced second part has been published. Thus far explicit references to phenomenology are conspicuous by their absence. Of course, Sartre's major interest is now a substantive one, i.e., prolegomena for anthropology and history, not one in general methodology including phenomenology. However, his new attempt to insert existentialism into the larger frame of Marxism involves a critical justification of the dialectical method in terms of existential experience. This could at least be reconciled with his earlier phenomenological objectives.

513 [1] Translation: English (1962) by Forest Williams – sometimes rather free; the subtitle and the table of contents are additions.

513 [2] Translation: English (1963) by Frechtman.

513 [3] *Critique de la raison dialectique (précédé de Question de méthode)*. Tome I: *Théorie des ensembles pratiques* (1960).

Translation of "Questions de méthode" as Search for a Method (1963) by Hazel Barnes.

514 [1] DILMAN, I., "An Examination of Sartre's Theory of Emotion," *Ratio* V (1963), 190–212.

514 [2] LEVI, ALBERT WILLIAM, "The Meaning of Existentialism for Contemporary International Relations," *Ethics* LXXII (1962), 13–22.

514 [3] MOROT-SIR, EDOUARD, "Sartre's Critique of Dialectical Reason," *Journal of the History of Ideas* XXII (1961), 573–81.

514 [4] PLANTINGA, ALVIN, "Existentialist Ethics," *Review of Metaphysics* XII (1958), 108–32.

516 [1] That this whole chapter needs considerable rewriting in the light of the most untimely death of Merleau-Ponty has been pointed out in the preface. It would, however, seem wise to delay a more drastic revision until all the pertinent posthumous materials are accessible.

516 [2] This sentence in particular is now outdated by Sartre's contribution to the special issue of *Les Temps Modernes* on Merleau-Ponty, in which Sartre's article "Merleau-Ponty vivant" (pp. 304–76) gives a full and even moving account of their troubled friendship and of the role which phenomenology played in it (esp. pp. 306–308).

517 [1] The following passage from a preface Merleau-Ponty wrote for a book by Dr. Hesnard (*L'Oeuvre de Freud*) seems worth quoting:

"The more one practices phenomenological thinking, the better one enters into Husserl's enterprise via the publication of his unedited materials, and the better one distinguishes it from the new philosophy of consciousness which it is at first believed to be" (*Les Temps Modernes* XVII (1963), 255.

520 [1] About a last more conciliatory phase in their relations see Sartre's "Merleau-Ponty vivant," pp. 370–72.

522 [1] The final paragraph of Merleau-Ponty's preface to *Signes*, his last publication, puts it, with a clear allusion to Camus' *L'homme révolté*, as follows: "The final word is not rebellion but *virtù* without any resignation. A deception for the one who has believed in salvation, and in only one means of salvation, on all levels." (p. 47).

525 [1] According to Sartre and a few other sources, during his last years Merleau-Ponty refused to let himself be listed as an atheist (*Les Temps Modernes*, XVII, 360).

528 [1] Sartre, however, distinguishes at least two stages in his development: that of the phenomenology of perception, remaining on a static level in the interpretation of existence, and that of "Humanism and Terror," ten years later, opening a more dynamic phase (*Les Temps Modernes* XVII, 308).

530 [1] For the full story of this visit (differing slightly from the one in my first edition) see H. L. Van Breda, "Maurice Merleau-Ponty et les Archives-Husserl à Louvain," *Revue de métaphysique et de morale* LVII (1962), 410–30.

531 [1] In fact, according to Sartre (*Les Temps Modernes* XVII, 316, 319), for several years Merleau-Ponty was the actual editor of the review and "saved" it.

531 [1] Fragments of Merleau-Ponty's projected major book to be entitled *Le Visible et l'invisible* have been put together ably by Claude Lefort and followed by work notes from 1958–61. While these fragments do not go beyond often brilliant introductory observations, the plans and the work notes give a revealing picture of Merleau-Ponty's attempt to move beyond the phenomenology of perception toward a new ontology, leading from the visible through nature to the logos of culture.

562 [1] Translation: English (1963) by Alden Fisher, conscientious and readable.

562 [2] Translation: English (1962) by Colin Smith – readable, but

not always reliable; the helpful addition of an index does not make up for the abridgment of the table of contents.

562 [3] Translation announced by Northwestern University Press.

562 [4] The three preceding essays will be included in the translation of *Signes* announced by Northwestern University Press.

562 [5] Translation: English (1963) by John Wild and James M. Edie – good.

562 [6]
Signes (1960).
L'Oeuil et l'esprit (1961),
Le Visible et l'invisible (1964).

562 [7] KWANT, REMY C., *The Phenomenological Philosophy of Merleau-Ponty* (1963) – the best monograph, but by no means comprehensive. Translated from the Dutch.

"Maurice Merleau-Ponty," *Les Temps Modernes*, Numéro spécial 1963. One last essay and 7 articles about M.-P.

562 [8] BALLARD, E. G., "The Philosophy of Merleau-Ponty," *Tulane Studies in Philosophy* IX (1960), 165–87.

——, "On Cognition of the Pre-cognitive," *Philosophical Quarterly* XI (1961), 238–44.

562 [9] KOCKELMANS, JOSEPH A., "Merleau-Ponty's Phenomenology of Language," *Review of Existential Psychology and Psychiatry* III (1963), 39–82.

— —, "Merleau-Ponty's View on Space-Perception and Space," *Ibid.* IV (1964), 69–105.

KULLMAN, MICHAEL and TAYLOR, CHARLES, "The Pre-objective World," *Review of Metaphysics* XII (1958), 108–32.

LANGAN, THOMAS, "Maurice Merleau-Ponty: In Memoriam," *PPR* XXIII (1962), 205–16.

562 [10] KWANT, REMY C., *op. cit.*, pp. 245–52.

Robinet, André, *Merleau-Ponty* (Collection "Philosophes") 1963, pp. 67–74, 119–20.

571 [1] Part II of the *Philosophy of the Will* entitled "Finitude and Culpability," appeared in 1960, subdivided into two volumes. The first, under the subtitle "Fallible Man," dealing with the possibility of a fall as based in man's broken nature, still uses largely the phenomenological method in the form of "pure reflection" upon his finitude. But the second, under the subtitle *La Symbolique du mal*, starts out from the "symbolism of evil" in the form of impurity, sin, and guilt, which are approached subsequently through the symbols of the myths. Even this part is based on an explicit phenomenology of confession (*aveu*). However, in interpreting the symbols Ricoeur calls for a "philosophi-

cal hermeneutics" which goes beyond descriptive phenomeñology. Yet the last word seems to belong to a philosophical thought (*pensée*) for which even symbolism serves only as a propedeutics. It remains to be seen what the final criteria for this "thought" will be, how far it can dispense with phenomenological intuition or will ultimately have to fall back upon it as the ultimate justification of the mythical symbols.

579 [1] "Le Sentiment," *Edmund Husserl 1859–1959* (1959), 260–74. *Philosophie de la Volonté*, vol. II, 1 and 2 (1960)

585 [1] Of particular interest to Anglo-Americans readers are Dufrenne's Mahlon Powell lectures on *Language and Philosophy* (1963), translated by Henry Veatch, as an attempt to establish closer contact between Anglo-American analytic philosophy and continental phenomenology by the introduction of the phenomenology of speech into linguistic analysis. Obviously these brief lectures could not do much more than outline the idea of such a phenomenology. Its development could do much toward narrowing the notorious rift in western philosophy.

Claude Piguet's *De l'esthétique à la métaphysique* (1959) (*Phaenomenologica 3*) pursues a similar objective.

591 [1] A partial translation of these essays, augmented by other characteristic texts, by James M. Edie came out in 1962 (Quadrangle Club Paperbacks).

592 [1] The latest and most ambitious work by Emmanuel Levinas, *Totalité et Infini* (1961), presents a good occasion to draw attention to one of the most original French thinkers, who not only played an important role in the transmission of phenomenology to France, but used Husserlian and even more Heideggerian inspirations for the development of his own independent philosophy.

Already his little studies *De l'Existence à l'existant* (1945) showed his originality. His latest work is an impressive attempt to use phenomenology in an effort to develop a metaphysics of being in general based on the study of social phenomena. Its main assertion is that the world forms not a totality, with nothing external to it, but a self-transcending infinite.

597 [1] With one exception these essays are included in a new collection under the title *Der Weg in die Phänomenologie. Das Problem einer ursprünglichen Erfahrung* (1963), which adds four later essays.

At this point it should be mentioned that the earlier title had been used in 1933 by Arnold Metzger (1892–   ), whose main concern was, however, the problem of the conquest of relativism, and whose main conclusion at the time was that phenomenology was unable to overcome it. Metzger should also be mentioned as one of the more active members of the Freiburg group in the early twenties, who spent some twenty years in the States, but then resumed teaching in Germany and published a metaphysical work on death and freedom (*Freiheit und Tod*, 1955).

Even more important is the posthumous influence of one of Husserl's Göttingen students, Hans Lipps (1889–1941), whose later work, under the influence of Heidegger, turned to such fields as anthropology and to hermeneutic logic, dealing also with the phenomenology of language.

601 [1] *Spiel als Weltsymbol* (1960).

602 [1] For further clarifications of Reiner's conception of phenomenology see "Sinn und Recht der phänomenologischen Methode," *Edmund Husserl 1859–1959*, 134–47 (discussion of Fink's position) and "Der Ursprung der Sittlichkeit dargestellt auf Grund der phänomenologischen Methode," *Zeitschrift für philosophische Forschung* XIII (1959), 263–87. His earlier "phenomenological investigations toward the problem of free will," *Freiheit, Wollen und Aktivität* (1927) must not go unmentioned.

604 [1] His recent systematic study, *La Philosophie et les expériences naturelles* (*Phaenomenologica* 9, 1961), contains an examination of the relation between philosophical reflection and non-philosophical experience, beginning with the experience of the self through that of the body, a field of particular interest to de Waelhens, and ending with the comprehension of Being.

605 [1] Strasser's most recent book on *Phenomenology and the Human Sciences. A contribution to a New Scientific Ideal* (1961; English translation by John R. Kanda, 1963) is an important step in the attempt to introduce the new phenomenology of the life-world as a third alternative to the objectivistic approach of behavioral science and the subjectivism of existentialist psychology. Of particular interest is the discussion of the rise of objectivity in three stages out of the "everyday" or life world. His final self-critical evaluation of phenomenology calls for a dialectical development of phenomenology beyond its merely intuitionistic approach as the basis for an empirical science of man.

606 [1] A characteristic work in this line is William A. Luijpen's *Existential Phenomenology* (1960· English translation, 1960), which attempts a fusion of phenomenology and an existential philosophy in Heidegger's style in an effort to achieve a metaphysical solution.

608 [1] Mention should be made, however, of the painstaking examination of the idea of phenomenology by André de Muralt (1958), which deals particularly with the problem of Husserl's exemplarism, but goes beyond a merely philological study. *L'Idée de la phénoménologie. L'Exemplarisme husserlien* (1958).

608 [2] Sofia Vanni Rovighi, in her contribution to *Edmund Husserl 1859–1959* (pp. 185–94), quotes from a letter by Croce of 1941, in which he questions the legitimacy of Husserl's attempt to suspend the movement of human thought by his reduction, comparing this attempt with the action of the monastic saint who, forbidden by his superior to perform miracles, suspended a falling stone mason in midair until he could obtain permission to save him.

609 [1] The interest in phenomenology, perhaps already much stronger at the time when I wrote this section than I realized, has grown since then. One of the most impressive signs was the publication of the only national memorial volume on the occation of the centennial of Husserl's birthday under the title *Omaggio a Husserl*, under the editorship of Enzo Paci, apparently now the leading Italian phenomenologist, trained by Banfi. Paci's latest work is called *Funzione delle scienze e significato dell' uomine* (1963).

610 [1] See, however, Shestov's much more appreciative article, "In Memoriam," added to the Husserl bibliography.

616 [1] See Julián Marías, "Cosciencia y realidad ejecutive – La primera superación orteguiana de la fenomenología," *Obras* (Madrid, 1960), V, 411–18.

622 [1] D. Sinha, "Phenomenology and Positivism," *PPR* XXII (1963), 562–77.

623 [1] Yamamoto, Manjiro, "Why I am interested in Phenomenology," *Edmund Husserl, 1859–1959*, pp. 123–33.

624 [1] In 1960, on the occasion of the Colloque de Royaumont on analytic philosophy, in his paper on "La Phénoménologie contre *The Concept of Mind*," Ryle tried to humor his French audience by allowing them to call his book "a sustained essay of phenomenology, if this label sets you at ease" (*La philosophie analytique*, Cahiers de Royaumont IV, pp. 75 and 82).

624 [2] About the meaning of Austin's coinage and its relation to developments in Continental phenomenology see my paper read at the XIIIth International Congress of Philosophy 1963 in Mexico City, "Linguistic Phenomenology: John L. Austin and Alexander Pfänder."

627 [1] Since 1963 the situation has changed considerably. Farber transferred from the University of Buffalo to the University of Pennsylvania, taking along the still inaccessible set of transcripts from the Louvain Archives. At the New School there will soon be the "Husserl Archives, Established in Memory of Alfred Schütz" with a set of xerox copies of the Louvain transcripts for general use. Northwestern University, since John Wild's two years as head of the Department, has developed a strong interest in phenomenological existentialism. Now Yale University bids fair to follow this example, and a number of large universities, including Harvard, offer at least some courses on phenomenology and existentialism, on a more or less permanent basis. – See also Edie, James M., "Recent Work in Phenomenology," *American Philosophical Quarterly* I (1964), 115–28.

627 [2] In this context several articles by J. S. Bixler, especially one on "German Phenomenology and Its Implications for Religion," in *Journal of Religion* IX (1929), should also be mentioned.

627 [3] Farber's book, originally a Harvard dissertation (1925), was published in 1928 as a monograph in the University of Buffalo studies.

629 [1] Farber's latest work, *Naturalism and Subjectivism* (1959), immediately takes the side of naturalism and rejects subjectivism, here identified with idealism, as its disjunct; phenomenology is introduced as "the last stronghold of idealism." The treatment of phenomenology consists largely in a running series of criticisms of Husserl's *Ideen*, charging him with the "error of illicit ignorance," i.e., with "disregarding what we know as a matter of fact" (71), with "sophistical reasoning" (114), with "prating at frequent intervals" (about the dependence of nature on experience), with "wearing idealistic blinkers" (142), with "shaking his fist at nature for all time" (187), with a "shabby argument in the well-worn tradition of idealism" (213), with "verbal play" (240), with "retreating from the really important thought-movements of the twentieth century." His final verdict is that Husserl "should have known how to draw the line for an ancillary, subordinate discipline" (260). Husserl's later and posthumous works are discussed much more summarily. Here Farber suggests that a "more complete reflective view" would have shown Husserl "to be the true son of the first Reich, as one who accepted its privileges and class distinctions" (277). The remaining two chapters are summary condemnations of Scheler, Heidegger, and their French successors as rank subjectivists, based on very little evidence and on some of Husserl's handwritten marginal comments in his copy of Heidegger's *Sein und Zeit*.

629 [2] In the meantime Cairns's translation of the *Cartesian Meditations* has been published by Martinus Nijhoff, The Hague.

630 [1] An English version of Gurwitsch's book appeared under the title *The Field of Consciousness* in 1964 (Duquesne University Press).

631 [1] 7. "The Problem of Existence in Constitutive Phenomenology," *Journal of Philosophy* LVIII (1961), 625–32.

632 [1] In the meantime the first of three volumes of Schütz's *Collected Papers*, edited with an introduction by Maurice Natanson, has appeared in *Phaenomenologica* 11; it contains the numbers 1, 3, 4, 5, 6, 7, 9, and 10. See also Aron Gurwitsch, "The Common-Sense World as Social Reality, A Discussion of Alfred Schütz," *Social Research* XXIX (1962), 30–72.

634 [1] The "building stones" for this work have since been published under the title *Das Reich des Schönen. Bausteine zu einer Philosophie der Kunst*, with an interesting postcript by Hans-Georg Gadamer (Stuttgart, 1960).

636 [1] Since 1960 John Wild has developed this conception of the *Lebenswelt* with considerable additions from Merleau-Ponty in a large number of papers and addresses. Most of these have been published in *Human Freedom and Social Order* (1959) and *Existence and the World of Freedom* (1963).

This would also seem to be the place to mention the foundation, largely at John Wild's initiative, of a *Society for Phenomenology and Existential Philosophy*, whose first two meetings at Northwestern University (1962 and 1963) promise further growth. A series of *Studies in Phenomenology and Existential Philosophy*, just started by Northwestern University Press, is to publish original contributions along with translations of important texts from French and German phenomenology.

637 [1] Natanson's "Essays in Existentialism and Phenomenology," under the title *Literature, Philosophy, and the Social Sciences* (1963), and other more recent pronouncements show him widening his range. On the one hand he stresses the "sense of reality" as something of a "magical" power, on the other he intensifies Husserl's transcendental phenomenology with its idealistic implications as basic even for his conception of the *Lebenswelt*.

639 [1] Of two new periodicals, *The Journal of Existential Psychiatry*, started in 1960, and the *Review of Existential Psychology and*

Psychiatry (1961), the latter stresses more specifically the "phenomenology of man" as one of its concerns. The proceedings of a first meeting on "Phenomenology: Pure and Applied" at the Veterans Hospital in Lexington, Kentucky in April 1963 are to be published in the near future.

642 [1] Discussions of the *Lebenswelt* have continued on the national and international level. Most conspicuous in this respect was the symposium between José Gaos, Ludwig Landgrebe, Enzo Paci, and John Wild at the ·XIIIth International Congress of Philosophy in Mexico City (1963) on the Husserlian concept of the *Lebenswelt*. Some of these discussions are merely historical, concerning the origin and significance of this conception in Husserl's own thinking. Others try to develop the new theme independently as the basis for a new phenomenology and foundation for philosophy and the sciences, particularly the sciences of man.

647 [1] As this Supplement shows, quite a few of these translation needs have since been filled: Husserl's *Cartesianische Meditationen*, Scheler's *Vom Ewigen im Menschen* and *Die Stellung des Menschen im Kosmos*, Edith Stein's *Zum Problem der Einfühlung*, Martin Heidegger's *Sein und Zeit* and *Brief über den Humanismus*, Merleau-Ponty's *Phénoménologie de la perception* and *La Structure du comportement* and Thévénaz' "Qu'est-ce que la phénoménologie?" are out in translations, Husserl's *Erfahrung und Urteil, Die Idee der Phänomenologie, Pariser Vorträge* and *Vorlesungen zur Phänomenologie des inneren Zeitbewusstseins*, Schütz's *Der sinnhafte Aufbau der sozialen Welt* and Merleau-Ponty's *Sens et nonsens* are now in preparation.

671 [1] In the meantime, Thomas N. Munson, S.J., in an article entitled "Wittgenstein's Phenomenology" (*PPR* XXIII (1962), 37–50), has presented a much more elaborate argument for calling Wittgenstein's philosophy "phenomenology" because of "his espousal of description divorced from explanation" (47). But this alone would hardly justify foisting such a label posthumously on Wittgenstein or, for that matter, on any positivist. – C. A. Van Peursen's "Edmund Husserl and Ludwig Wittgenstein" (*PPR* XX (1959), 181–97) merely compares the two philosophies and stresses parallels.

There is now, however, concrete evidence of a historical connection which calls for a fresh investigation of Wittgenstein's relation to Husserl's phenomenology. It consists mainly of the following passages from an article by Rush Rhees [1] and some related circumstantial

---

[1] "The Tractatus: Seeds of Some Misunderstandings," *Philosophical Review* LXII (1963), 213–20.

evidence:

1) "In 1929 Wittgenstein discussed the idea of a 'phenomenological language" (213).

2) "When he was discussing the incompatibilities of color statements, Wittgenstein wanted 'a purely phenomenological theory of colours' which would include nothing 'hypothetical' like references to light waves or the physiology of the retina: colors as they are given in 'immediate experience.' And he suggested that we might have a 'phenomenological language' which would take in also the phenomena of visual space, of sounds, and so on: 'an account free of everything hypothetical' ...." (217).

3) "Wittgenstein gave up the idea of a phenomenological language (a few months after he had suggested it), but for a time he spoke of 'phenomenology' as concerned with the grammars or the possibilities of the various sensory fields.'" (218).[2]

I am indebted to Mr. Rhees for the following additional information about the background of his references to Wittgenstein's phenomenology: "I know of only one reference which he made to Husserl. Schlick had asked Wittgenstein what he thought of the view that the statements of phenomenology are synthetic propositions *a priori*, and Wittgenstein gave a brief discussion of this."

Now it seems to me more than likely that Schlick's inquiry was related to his controversy with Husserl, beginning with his criticisms of Husserl in the first edition of his *Allgemeine Erkenntnislehre* of 1918, followed by Husserl's reply in the preface of the second edition of his *Logische Untersuchungen*, vol. II, 2, p. VI f., and Schlick's slight modification of his strictures in his own second edition of 1925. Besides, in the *Wissenschaftlicher Jahresbericht der Philosophischen Gesellschaft an der Universität Wien für das Vereinsjahr 1930–31* Schlick published an article, now reprinted in translation in Feigl, H. and Sellars, W., ed., *Readings in Philosophical Analysis* (1949), pp. 277–85, under the title ' Is There a Factual *A Priori?*'', which severely criticized Husserl's views and ended with a tribute to Wittgenstein as the one who had solved the problem. It would seem strange if this occasion had not drawn Wittgenstein's attention to Husserl even more explicitly. However, any speculation about the significance of this evidence will have to wait for the publication of Wittgenstein's papers from the

---

[2] In the light of this information Wittgenstein's paper: Some Remarks on Logical Form," in the *Proceedings of the Aristotelian Society* of 1929 (IX, 162–71), is of particular interest, especially such passages as "we can only arrive at a correct analysis by, what might be called, the logical investigation of the phenomena themselves" (163) and "definite rules of syntax ... cannot be laid down until we have actually reached the ultimate analysis of the phenomena in question" (171).

transition period between the *Tractatus* and the *Blue Book*. But it may be pertinent to point out that this was also the time when Wittgenstein's interest in philosophy was reawakened by Brouwers' Vienna lecture (Von Wright, G. H., in Malcolm, Norman, *Ludwig Wittgenstein. A Memoir* (1958), p. 12 f.). For there is a definite affinity between Brouwer's intuitionism and phenomenology. – Wittgenstein's name occurs in Husserl's writings apparently only once, when Oskar Becker, in his appendix to the *Formale und transzendentale Logik* (1929) refers on p. 297 to Wittgenstein's treatment of tautology in the *Tractatus*.

283 [1a] The momentous book by William J. Richardson, S.J., *Heidegger: Through Phenomenology to Thought* (Phaenomenologica 13) did not come into my hands until this Supplement was already in the galley stage. But Heidegger's latest and most explicit statements about his own conception of phenomenology and his relation to Husserl as expressed in his prefatory letter of April 1962 to the author are so important that they must not go unmentioned here.

Heidegger's point of departure is a new formula for phenomenology as based on the principle "To the Things themselves" (*Zu den Sachen selbst*) according to which phenomenology means "letting the thing itself show itself" (*das Sichzeigenlassen der Sache selbst*) and, a little later, "letting the most proper topic of thought" (*die eigenste Sache des Denkens*)," i.e., Being, "show itself" (pp. XV, XVII). Seen in this light

"phenomenology" ("*die Phänomenologie*") in Husserl's sense was elaborated into a distinctive philosophical position predelineated from the direction of Descartes, Kant, and Fichte. The historicity of thought remained thoroughly foreign to such a position. (Husserl's article on "Philosophy as a Rigorous Science" is specifically referred to as evidence).

The question of Being as unfolded in *Being and Time* set itself apart from this philosophical position, and that on the basis of what I believe even today to be an adherence to the principle of phenomenology more in accordance with the matter at hand (*sachgerechter.*)

Hence Heidegger approved of Father Richardson's first subtitle ("From Phenomenology to Thought"), provided phenomenology was to be understood in Husserl's sense. But taking it in his own sense Heidegger suggested the title "A Way *through* Phenomenology into the Thought of Being"). This would seem to imply that even such a phenomenology would be only one, but not the only possible, way to the thought of Being.

INDEX OF NAMES TO THE SUPPLEMENT